Unpublished Fragments

(Spring 1885–Spring 1886)

Based on the edition by

Giorgio Colli & Mazzino Montinari

First organized in English by Ernst Behler

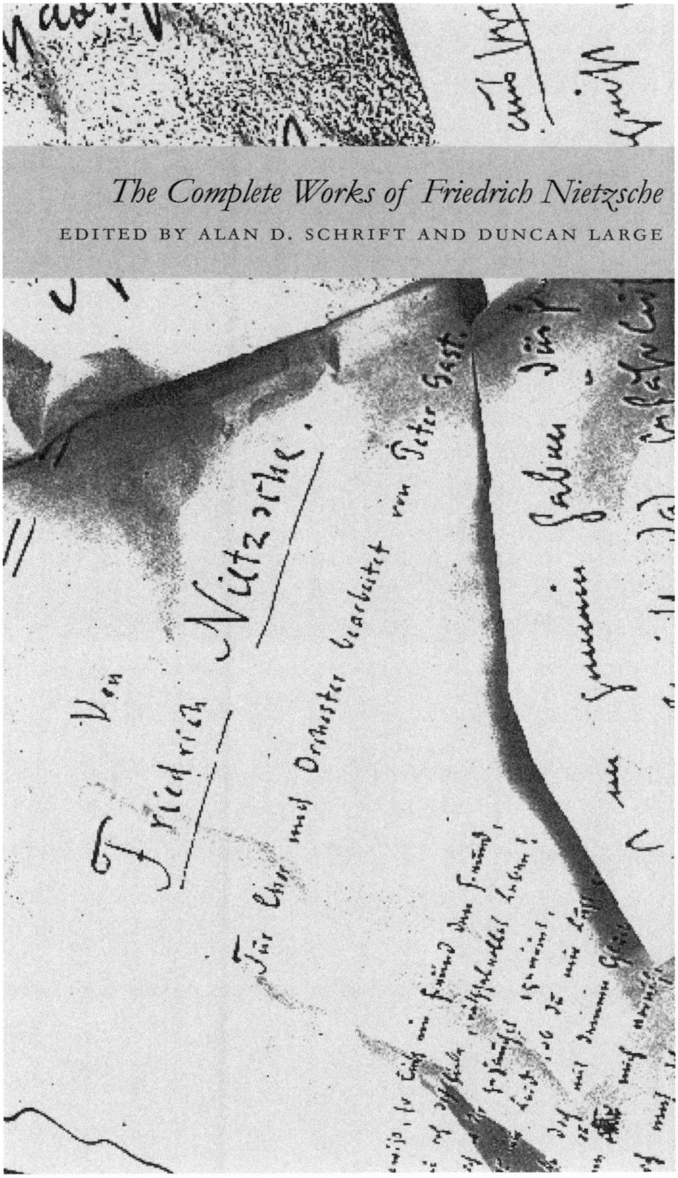

The Complete Works of Friedrich Nietzsche

EDITED BY ALAN D. SCHRIFT AND DUNCAN LARGE

Friedrich Nietzsche

Unpublished Fragments

(Spring 1885–Spring 1886)

Translated, with an Afterword,
by Adrian Del Caro

STANFORD UNIVERSITY PRESS
STANFORD, CALIFORNIA

Stanford University Press
Stanford, California

Translated from Friedrich Nietzsche, *Sämtliche Werke: Kritische Studienausgabe*, ed. Giorgio Colli and Mazzino Montinari, in 15 vols. This book corresponds to Vol. 11, pp. 423–710, and Vol. 12, pp. 9–184.

Critical edition of Friedrich Nietzsche's *Sämtliche Werke* and unpublished writings based on the original manuscripts.

Printed in the United States of America on acid-free, archival-quality paper

CIP data appears at the end of the book.

Contents

A Note on This Edition

This is the first English translation of all of Nietzsche's writings, including his unpublished fragments, with annotation, afterwords concerning the individual texts, and indexes, in nineteen volumes. The aim of this collaborative work is to produce a critical edition for scholarly use. Volume 1 also includes an introduction to the entire edition, and Volume 19 will include a detailed chronology of Nietzsche's life. While the goal is to establish a readable text in contemporary English, the translation follows the original as closely as possible. All texts have been translated anew by a group of scholars, and particular attention has been given to maintaining a consistent terminology throughout the volumes. The translation is based on *Friedrich Nietzsche: Sämtliche Werke. Kritische Studienausgabe in 15 Bänden* (1980), edited by Giorgio Colli and Mazzino Montinari. The still-progressing *Nietzsche Werke: Kritische Gesamtausgabe*, which Colli and Montinari began in 1963, has also been consulted. The Colli-Montinari edition is of particular importance for the unpublished fragments, comprising more than half of Nietzsche's writings and published there for the first time in their entirety. Besides listing textual variants, the annotation to this English edition provides succinct information on the text and identifies events, names (except those in the Index of Persons), titles, quotes, and biographical facts of Nietzsche's own life. The notes are numbered in the text and are keyed by phrase. The Afterword presents the main facts about the origin of the text, the stages of its composition, and the main events of its reception. The Index of Persons includes mythological figures and lists the dates of birth and death as well as prominent personal characteristics. Since the first three volumes appeared, important corrections to the 1980 edition of the *Kritische Studienausgabe* have been noted, and these corrections have been incorporated into the translation that appears here.

ERNST BEHLER AND ALAN D. SCHRIFT

Unpublished Fragments

(Spring 1885–Spring 1886)

[34 = N VII 1. April–June 1885]

34[1][1]

Gai saber.[2]
Self-Confessions.
By
Friedrich Nietzsche.

S⟨elf-confessions⟩: At bottom for me the word is too solemn: for myself I believe neither in confessing nor in the self.

At bottom the word is too solemn for me: but if I wanted to name the book as I would prefer, "500,000 Opinions," it would sound too buffoonish to my readers. Thus in consideration of my readers — — —

Higher Education.

The Highest Education.

Thoughts on the Philosophers of the Future.[3]

Conjectures on the Ph⟨ilosophers⟩ of the Future.

34[2]

Year after year I become more candid, to the extent that my eye for this nineteenth century, for this century of great mor⟨al⟩ tartuffery, becomes deeper and deeper: I find fewer and fewer reasons today — to beat around the bush. What opinions could be dangerous today! when nothing falls "into deep wells" anymore! And if they were dangerous and destructive: it is desirable that much collapses so that much has to be built

34[3][4]

I had a mishap in my youth: a very questionable p⟨erson⟩ crossed my path: when I recognized him for what he is, namely a great actor who has a genuine relationship to nothing (not even to music): I was so disgusted and sick that I believed all famous p⟨eople⟩ were actors otherwise they would not have become famous, and in that which I called "artist" the main thing was merely the *acting* force.

34[4][5]

How disguised was my presentation of what I perceived as "Dionysian"! How scholarly and monotonous, how not scholarly enough by far to produce even the effect of opening a new field of work to several generations of philologists! For this **ac***cess* to antiquity is what has been buried best; and whoever fancied himself to be especially wise about the Greeks, Goethe for example, and Winckelmann, has not smelled anything from that direction. It seems the Greek world is a hundred times more hidden and foreign than the obtrusive manner of today's scholars would wish. If there is ever to be any recognizing here, then certainly only the same by the same. And for that matter — only experiences from leaping fountains — they provide that new great eye for recognizing the same in the world of the past.

34[5]

NB. The greatest events are the hardest for people to feel: e.g., the fact that the Christian God "is dead," that in our experiences *no* longer a heavenly goodness and instruction are expressed, *no* longer a divine justice, not any immanent morality at all. This is a terrible novelty that still needs a couple of centuries to get to the *feeling* of Europeans: and then it will appear for a long time as if all the gravity of things was gone. —

34[6]

I did not let myself be deceived by the lustrous appearance of the German empire. When I wrote my *Zarathustra*, I took as a background a European condition in which the same horrible and filthy partisan activity we already find in France today also rules in Germany.

34[7]

Has anyone ever conceded "profundity" to a female? So far I have not had respect for any female. D'Epinay compared with Galiani!

And justice — has this ever — — —

34[8]

The Italians genuine and original *only* in the bloody satire. From Buratti on, who provided the decisive turn to the genius of Byron.[6] Even in Carducci there is nothing that Germans or French would not have done better.

34[9][7]

I do not know myself: the demand for self-knowledge seems to me a divine joke or a *Greek* childishness (*niaiserie*[8]): they have a wealth of it! — But if someone has given his opinion on 500 things, then it is possible that others will "know" him. Well then!

34[10]

Affectation of "scientism" e.g., "*femininisme*,"[9] but also German periodicals' "reviews-style."

34[11]

Our time consumes and lives on the morality of earlier times.

34[12]

Pascal offended by the idea that the weather, that bright and cheerful skies influence him.[10] Now — the theory of *milieu*[11] is most convenient! *everything* exerts an influence, the result is the human being itself.

34[13]

Things which my stomach digests poorly or not at all: potatoes, ham, mustard, onions, pepper, anything baked in fat, puff pastry, cauliflower, cabbage, lettuce, all oily vegetables, wine, sausage, butter sauce on meat, chives, fresh breadcrumb, all sourdough bread.

Anything roasted, any meat served rare, veal, roast beef, leg of lamb, egg yolk a⟨nd⟩ milk also whipped cream, rice, semolina, cooked warm apples green peas beans carrots roots fish, fresh butter brown white bread crust.

34[14]

The kind of open and hearty familiarity that is needed today in a democratic age in order to be beloved and respected — in sum that for which someone today is treated as an "upright human being": this gives a moralist much to laugh about. All profound people enjoy their kind of relief here; it is such a pleasure to play at comedy and — — —

34[15][12]

The ancients read *aloud*.

34[16]

Among immoderate people, e.g., English rabble, naturally the doctrine of abstinence acquires *tremendous* power. Among the moderate it is a laughable matter.

34[17]

Dionysian. What unfortunate shyness to speak as a scholar on a subject of which I should have been able to speak as an "experienced one." And what does someone who has to write poetry care about "aesthetics"! One should practice one's trade, and send curiosity to the devil!

34[18][13]

The XXth Century.

Abbé Galiani once said — — — now since I do not in the least share the unwarlike views of my departed friend Galiani,

I am not afraid to prophesy a few things and therefore, possibly, bring about the cause of wars.

34[19][14]

A tremendous *coming to one's senses* after the most terrible earthquake: with new questions.

34[20]

NB. The centuries just prior to the last rejected the Gothic as barbarism (the Goth back then was synonymous with the barbarian): the next to last century rejected Homer. Therein lies a *taste*: a strong will to *one's* Yes and *one's* No. — The capacity to enjoy Homer again is perhaps the greatest achievement of European people — but it has been paid for dearly enough.

34[21]

Baudelaire, already entirely German, except for a certain hyper-erotic ailment that smells of Paris

34[22][15]

Taine, who had the boldness of invention to find the typical between Hegel and Henri Beyle,[16] *his method*, which essentially means: history can be comprehended only through concepts; but the concepts must be created by the historical human being: and the history in which there are only 4, 5 factors is the most comprehensible.

34[23][17]

the masquerade of the *bourgeois*, e.g., as Salambô and as Saint Anthony

34[24]

Some who are at bottom shallow and light beings — peoples as well as individuals — have their most estimable and supreme moments when all of a sudden, to their astonishment, they become heavy and melancholy. In the same way, perhaps for the cattle-rabble that formerly started grunting morally in English Puritanism or today as English Salvation Army — the penitential spasm is their highest achievement of "humanity"; we should simply acknowledge this. —

But others become superior when they become lighter! There is no doubt: when a kind of human being has lived out entire generations as teachers physicians pastors and models, and without constantly looking out for money or honor or positions: then ultimately a higher and subtler and more spiritual type arises. In this manner the priest, providing that he reproduces through strong women, is a kind of preparation for the future emergence of superior human beings.

34[25]

Such dogmatic people as Dante and Plato are the *most distant* and perhaps for that reason the most alluring: who live in a house of knowledge that is carpentered and held together by faith. The first in his own, the other in the Christian-patristic.

There is an entirely different strength and mobility to maintaining oneself in an incomplete system, with free, open vistas, than in a *dogmatic* world. Leonardo da Vinci stands higher than Michelangelo, Michelangelo higher than Raphael.

34[26]

Praised among the educated of today (who all *pro pudor*![18] read newspapers) are the profound people. But what do those who are in a position to praise profound people know about profundity themselves! — They are dangerous people: of this there is no doubt at all. We otherwise do not tend to praise the abysses!

34[27][19]

Letters
To a Philosophical Friend.
On the Occasion
of Thus Spoke Zarathustra.
By
Friedrich Nietzsche.

34[28]

Superstition: to believe in the being,[20] in the absolute, in pure spirit, in absolute knowledge, in absolute value, in the thing in itself! These approaches are riddled with a *contradictio* everywhere.

34[29]

Skeptical Objections.

34[30]

Perception on the part of our senses happens to us unconsciously: everything that becomes conscious to us is already processed perceptions

34[31]

He makes the great detachment for *himself* — not because he demands it of others or even sees it as his duty to communicate it to and force it on others.

34[32]

The great millennia-long *ebb* in the invention of values

34[33][21]

The Lawgivers of the Future.

1. Descent.
2. The Most Bound Spirit.
3. The Great Detachment.
4. Suffering from Human Beings.
5. The New Will.
6. The Hammer.

34[34]

My version of *acedia*[22] — the opposite of that of the monks. I am perturbed about my overly large compassion: I am pleased when my ego is alert and in good spirits.[23]

34[35]

1. Abelard wanted to bring reason to ecclesiastical authority: ultimately *Descartes* found that *all* authority resides in reason only.[24]

2. *The self-overcoming of reason* inner problem of Pascal — for the sake of Christian "faith."

34[36]

The problem of "faith" is actually: *whether instinct has more value than reasoning, and why*!

Beneath the many disputes over "knowledge and faith," util⟨itarianism⟩ and intuitionism *this* question of *value estimation* is concealed.

Socrates naïvely sided with reason, against instinct. (At bottom though he had indeed followed all moral instincts, only with a *false* motivation: *as if* the motives came from reason. Likewise Plato etc.)

Involuntarily Plato sought to demonstrate that reason and instinct *want* the same. Likewise up till today Kant, Schopenhauer, the English.

In "faith" the instinct of *obedience toward the highest authority* is uppermost, therefore *a single* instinct. The categorical imperative is a *desired* instinct, where *this* instinct and reason are one.

34[37]

Kant, a subtle mind, a pedantic soul

34[38]

NB. I should be forgiven this presumptuous assertion: precisely because I have a higher and deeper, also more scientific conception of woman than the emancipators and emancipatresses have of her, I resist emancipation: I know *better* where their strength is and say to them: "they know not what they do."[25] They are dissolving their instincts! with their strivings of today.

34[39]

Bentham and utilitarianism depend on *Helvétius* — he is the last great *event in morality*. In German philosophy (Kant Schopenhauer) it is still "duty" or "instinct of compassion"— the **old** problems since Socrates (i.e., stoicism *or* Christianity, aristocracy of the individual *or* goodness of the herd)

34[40]

I need

a) someone to watch over my stomach
b) someone who can laugh with me and has a boisterous spirit.
c) someone who is proud of my company a⟨nd⟩ "the other" also maintains the proper *façon*[26] of respect toward me
d) someone who reads to me without dumbing down a book

34[41]

Plaire[27] — the great secret of the French will, and at bottom of *herd morality*. "To have compassion," altruism, are the *hypocritical* expressions for it.[28]

34[42]

NB. So far most artists (including the historians), even some of the greatest, belonged among the servants (whether of classes or princes or women or "masses"), not to mention their dependency on the Church and moral law. Thus *Rubens* produced portraits of the noble world of his time, but according to the taste *it* had in mind, not according to *his* standard of beauty — on the whole therefore *against* his taste. In this *van Dyck* was nobler: who added to all those whom he painted something of that which he valued most highly in himself: he did not step *down*, rather up to himself when he "reproduced" something.

The slavish *subservience* of the artist before his public (as Sebastian Bach himself expresses it in immortally offensive words in the dedication to his High Mass[29]) is perhaps harder to recognize in music, but it is lodged all the deeper and more thoroughly in it. If I were to communicate my observations on this, one would not be able to tolerate listening to me.

34[43][30]
NB. The slow emergence and rise of the middle and *lower* classes (including the lower kind of spirit and body), which preluded abundantly already before the French Revolution and in any case would have moved forward without revolution, on the whole then the preponderance of the herd over all shepherds and bellwethers brings with it

1) A dimming of the spirit: The coexistence of a stoic and frivolous *appearance* of happiness as it belongs to noble cultures decreases: much suffering is allowed to be *seen* and *heard* which earlier was tolerated and concealed.

2) *moral* hypocrisy, a manner of wanting to *distinguish* oneself morally, but through herd virtues compassion welfare good deeds, which tend not be acknowledged and respected outside the herd capacity

3) the *real* great quantity of compassion and shared joy, enjoyment of large-scale socializing as all herds have it — "common purpose," "fatherland," everything in which the individual does not come into consideration

34[44]
In Goethe's judgment *Diderot* showed himself to be truly German (Saint Ogan, p. 248)[31] in everything that the French reproached. But the Neapolitans according to Galiani[32] also accepted his taste completely.

34[45]
Baudelaire, of German taste if ever a Parisian could have it, perceives things like a German when he does not tolerate Victor Hugo and calls him an "ass of a genius." [33]

34[46]

If *I* have something of a unity in me then it certainly does not lie in the conscious ego and in feeling, willing, thinking, but somewhere else: in the preserving, appropriating, distinguishing, surveilling prudence of my entire organism, of which my conscious ego is only a tool. — Feeling willing thinking everywhere reveal only end phenomena whose causes are entirely unknown to us: the succession of these end phenomena as if one resulted *from* the other is probably *only* an illusion: in truth the causes might possibly be bound to one another in such a way that the end-causes give me only the *impression* of logical or psychological binding. *I deny* that a spiritual or psychic phenomenon is the direct *cause* of another spiritual or psychic phenomenon: even though it appears so. *The true world of causes is hidden from us*: it is unspeakably more complicated. The intellect and the senses are above all a *simplifying* apparatus. But our *false*, miniaturized, *logicized* world of causes is the world in which we are able to live. We are "knowing" to the extent that we can satisfy our needs.

The study of the body offers a sense of the unspeakable complications.

If our intellect did not have a few *firm* forms, then it would be impossible to live. But this proves nothing for the truth of all logical facts.

34[47]

The underhanded self-deprecation of Socrates, used to render his opponent unsuspecting and safe, so that he lets himself go and *blurts straight out* what he thinks: a trick of the rabble man! Logic was not at home in Athens.

34[48]

NB. A bit more brightness of mind and a bit of good will: and one no longer tolerates, for reasons of taste, interpreting his experiences to suit the "glory of God," I mean seeing everywhere the traces of God's solicitude, warning, punishment, instruction. Just as a good philologist (and generally any philologically trained scholar) has an aversion to false textual interpretations (e.g., those of Protestant preachers in their pulpits — which is why the educated classes no longer go to ch⟨urch⟩ —), likewise and not as a result of great "virtue," "honesty" etc., the counterfeiting of religiously interpreting all experiences offends one's taste. —

34[49]

Our pleasure in simplicity, surveyability, regularity, brightness, from which ultimately a German "philosopher" could extract something like a categorical imperative of logic and the beautiful — for this I confess that a strong *instinct* must be present. It is so strong that it reigns in all our sensual activities and reduces, regulates, assimilates etc. the abundance of real perceptions (the unconscious ones —) and first *displays them to our consciousness* in this contrived form. This "logical," this "artistic" something is our continuous activity. *What* made this force so sovereign? Obvious that without it no living being could live on account of the chaos of impressions.

34[50]

(I do not see why the organic even had to *originate* at any point in time — —)

34[51]

In chemistry is revealed that every substance pushes its force as far as it can, then a third something emerges.

The qualities of a child cannot be *deduced* from the most accurate knowledge of the father and the mother. For they are the *effects* of the third thing on us, these qualities: but the effects of the first and the effects of the second, i.e., *their* qualities are impossible to add as "effects of the third"

34[52]

The chain of causation is concealed from us: and the relationship and the sequence of effects only yields a succession: however regular this may be, *we do not comprehend it as necessary.* — Yet we can consecutively determine different series of such successions: e.g., in piano playing the succession of struck keys, the succession of struck strings, the succession of sounding notes.

34[53]

Critique of the instinct of causality.

The *belief* that an action happens on the basis of a motive was instinctively, gradually generalized at the time when everything that happened was imagined in the manner of conscious living beings. "Every occurrence happens on the basis of a motive: the *causa finalis* is the *causa efficiens*"[34] —

This belief is *erroneous*: purpose, motive are means to make the occurrence palpably practicable to us. — The generalization was likewise erroneous and illogical.

No purpose.
No will.

34[54]

The inverted order of time.

The "external world" acts upon us: the effect is telegraphed to the brain, where it is arranged, shaped and traced back to its cause: then the cause is *projected* and *only now does the fact enter our consciousness. I.e.*, "the world of appearance" first *appears* like a cause after "it" has acted and the effect has been processed. I.e., *we constantly invert* the *order of what is happening.* — Whereas "*I*" see, *it* already sees something else. The situation is like that of pain.

34[55]

The belief in the senses. Is a fundamental fact of our intellect, which receives from them the raw material that it *interprets.* This relationship to the raw material offered by the senses is, *morally* speaking, *not* accompanied by the intention to truth, but instead purely by a will to overpowering, assimilation, nourishment. Our constant functions are absolutely egoistical,

Machiavellian, unscrupulous, subtle. Commanding and obeying driven to the highest extreme, and in order that there can be complete "obedience," the individual organ has much freedom.

The error of believing in purposes.

Will — a superfluous assumption.

The inverted order of time.

Critique of the belief in causality.

The belief in the senses, as the fundamental fact of our being.

The central-force — must not be essentially different from that which it rules.

The history of emergence does not explain qualities. The latter must already be known. *Historical* explanation is reduction to a succession to which we are *accustomed*: by analogy.

34[56]

The mechanistic explanation of the world is an *ideal*: to explain as much as possible with as little as possible, i.e., to put it in formulas. Still needed: the denial of empty space; to think space as defined and limited; just like the world as eternally repeating itself.

34[57]

How a people's character, a "people's soul" emerges provides information about the emergence of the individual soul. First a *series* of *activities* is forced upon a people, as conditions of existence, it grows accustomed to them, they become firmer and establish themselves more deeply. Peoples who experience great transformations and end up under new conditions show a new grouping of their strengths: this and that emerges and gets the upper hand because it is now *more necessary* for existence, e.g., the practical, sober sense of today's Germans. All character is first *role*. The "personality" of philosophers — at bottom *persona*.

34[58]

Numbers are our major means for making the world manageable. We comprehend as far as we can count, i.e., as far as a constancy can be perceived.

34[59][35]

The course of philos⟨ophy⟩ has so far been impeded most by moral ulterior motives.

34[60]

Even within our world of the senses, if only we sharpen or think of it sharpened, a world arises that has a quite different effect on our *feeling*

34[61]

The prejudice of causality
the prejudice of will
the prejudice of purpose
the prejudice of personality

Knowledge: a false concept i.e., a concept we have no *right* to propose.

Abolition 1) of *will*
2) of *purposes* as "why" and "by what means"
3) *consequently* also of *causality*
(which derives from both)

34[62][36]

"How are synthetic judgments a priori possible?" — "*by means of a faculty for them*" was the famous Kantian answer, which gave such satisfaction to many.

34[63]

The *most useful* concepts have survived: however falsely they may have originated.

34[64]

In the first book shatter the *belief in the truth*: truthfulness is useful, but only in a small quantity, above all for those who do not have to answer for anything. Likewise respect for philosophers.

34[65]

The general *coarsening* of the European spirit, a certain clumsy straight-forwardness that likes to hear itself praised as straightness, honesty or good science:[37] this belongs to the dominance of thinking of the democratic zeitgeist and its humid air: more specifically — it is the effect of reading newspapers. People want convenience or intoxication when they read: by far the majority of what is read is newspaper or newspaper-like. Just look at our revues, our scholarly journals: everyone who writes there speaks as if before "informal company" and lets himself go, or rather sit, in his armchair. — Someone has it rough there if he places the most value on ulterior motives and loves the dashes in his books more than everything that is articulated. — Freedom of the press will drive style to ruin and ultimately the spirit too: Galiani knew this already a hundred years ago. — "Freedom of thought" drives *thinkers* to ruin.[38] — Between hell and heaven, and in the danger of persecution, exile, eternal damnation and the disapproving glances of kings and ladies the spirit had grown supple and daring: alas, what is the "spirit" *becoming* these days!

34[66]

Always *ironice*:[39] it is a precious sensation to watch such a truthful thinker. But it is even more pleasant to discover that this is all foreground, and that at bottom he wants something else and wants it in a very daring manner. I believe this was the magic of Socrates: he had a soul and behind it another and behind it another. In the first Xenophon slumbered, in the second Plato and in the third Plato once more, but Plato with his own second soul. Plato himself is a man of many back parts and foregrounds.[40]

34[67][41]

NB. Our age is in its most essential instincts skeptical: nearly all subtler scholars and artists are, even if they do not like to admit it to themselves. Pessimism, of *No-saying*⟨,⟩ is only *easier* for the convenience of the spirit: our humid age with its democratic air is above all convenient. Where the spirit is more delicate it says: "I do not know"; and "I no longer trust myself or anyone" and "I no longer know which way to turn," and "hoping — that is a phrase for the mendacious or for demagogic orators and artists." Skepticism — is the expression of a certain *physiological* condition as it necessarily arises in a major interbreeding of many races: the many inherited valuations are at war with each other, disrupt each other in their growth. The force that is lost most here is the *will*: therefore great fear of responsibility, because no one can vouch for himself. Hiding under communities, "one hand *covers* the other" they say there. Thus a *herd-species* gets developed: and whoever has a strong commanding and daring will definitely achieves supremacy in such times.

34[68][42]

There are complaints about how bad philosophers have had it so far: the truth is that at all times the conditions for the education of a powerful crafty daring implacable spirit were more favorable than today. Today the demagogue spirit and also the scholar spirit have favorable conditions. But just look at our artists: whether nearly all of them are not perishing from lack of discipline. They are no longer tyrannized, so they no longer learn to tyrannize themselves either. When was woman as insignificant as today! Everyone is getting weaker because everyone wants to have it convenient. — I have gone through the harshest school of physical pain: and the consciousness of having kept myself intact despite it, and silently — —

34[69]

The subtlest minds of the previous century, Hume and Galiani, all entrusted with service to the state: likewise Stendhal Tocqueville.

34[70]

Hume challenges (to use Kant's words[43]) reason to account for and answer with what right it thinks to itself: that something could be constituted in such a way that, when it is posited, something different therefore must necessarily also be posited, for that is what the concept of *cause* says. He proved irrefutably that it is entirely impossible for reason to think such a connection a priori and from concepts etc. — But the folly was in asking for reasons for the right to the justification. He did the very deed that he wanted to test.[44]

34[71]

The *lie* of the educator e.g., in Kant's categorical imperative. "Could God be a deceiver after all, despite Descartes?"

34[72]

NB. Truthful, morally rigorous and *ugly* belong together: Christianity sensed this well. A beautiful human being can be neither truthful, nor kind, only as an exception.

34[73]

What separates us from Kant just as from Plato and Leibniz: we believe only in becoming, also in matters of spirit, we are *historical* through and through. This is the great reversal. Lamarck and Hegel — Darwin is only an aftereffect. The manner of thinking of *Heraclitus* and *Empedocles* has risen again. Even Kant did not overcome the *contradictio in adjecto*[45] "pure spirit": but we did.

34[74][46]

The human horizon. Philosophers can be perceived as those who make the most extreme effort to *test* how far humanity can *elevate* itself, Plato especially: how *far* its force reaches. But they do it as individuals; perhaps the instinct of the Caesar⟨s⟩, the founders of states etc. was greater, those who think about how far humanity can be driven in terms of *development* and under "favorable conditions." But they did not sufficiently understand what "favorable conditions" are. Big question: where so far the plant "human being"[47] has grown most magnificently. For this the comparative study of history is necessary.

34[75]

It is remarkable how the Stoics and almost all philosophers have no gaze for the distance. And then once more the stupidity of the socialists who always represent only the needs of the *herd*.

34[76]

To put the mechanistic idea first as the regulative principle of method. Not as the *best proven* worldview, but as the one which makes necessary the greatest severity and rigor and does the most to set aside all sentimentality. Simultaneously a test of physical and psychic prosperity: failed weak-willed races are destroyed by it, through sensuality or through melancholy or, like the Indians, through both.

34[77]

Great praise of Christianity as the genuine *herd* religion.

34[78][48]

Noon and Eternity.

1. Free for "true" and "untrue"
2. free for "good" and "evil"
3. free for "beautiful" and "ugly"
4. the superior human being as the mightier, and the attempts so far: "it is the right time."
5. the *hammer* — a danger on which human beings can be smashed

34[79][49]

Kant believed, with his table of categories in hand, "this is the most difficult task that could ever be undertaken for the benefit of metaphysics."[50] — we had better not misunderstand where he placed his pride.

34[80]

Crudeness and delicatesse[51] at the same time in Petronius, in Horace too: what I like best. It belongs to *Greek* taste. Homer was too crude for the people around La Rochefoucauld, they could not enjoy the trivial. They held on to a certain high perception among themselves, as now many Germans, and despise⟨d⟩ *themselves* if perhaps a pleasure in the lower spheres stir⟨red⟩ in them. Aristophanes is the opposite: *nihil humani*[52] — is ancient.

34[81]

To place at the top: the *instincts* also have *become*, they prove not⟨hing⟩ for the supersensual, not even for what is animal, not even for what is typically human.

That the spirit has become and is still becoming, that among countless kinds of concluding and judging somehow the one most familiar to us now is most useful to us and has been inherited because the individuals who think in this manner had better chances: that nothing about "true" and "untrue" is proven by this, — — —

34[82][53]

— *Anti-Kant.*

"Faculty, instinct, heredity, habit" today whoever seeks to explain something using such words must be modest and moreover poorly trained. But it raged at the end of the previous century. Galiani explained everything on the basis of habits and instincts.[54] Hume explained the sense of causality on the basis of habit; Kant said with great calm: "it is a faculty."[55] Everyone was happy, especially as he had also discovered a moral faculty. Here lay the magic of his philosophy: the young theologians of the Tübingen Seminary[56] went into the bushes — they all searched for "faculties." And what didn't they find! Schelling christened it "intellectual intuition," a faculty for the "supersensual." Schopenhauer believed he had found the same thing and more, namely "the thing in itself," in an already sufficiently respected faculty, in the will. In England there arose the instinctivists and intuitionists of morality. It was the old subject of faith and knowledge, a kind of "formal faith" that laid claim to some content. This story essentially concerns the theologians. In secret Leibniz comes alive again, and behind Leibniz — Plato. Concepts as ἀνάμνησις[57] etc. This initially skeptical movement is indeed directed against skepticism, *it takes pleasure in subservience*

34[83]

NB. The most annoying quality of the writings of obscure, poorly trained and unphilological spirits is not even their inadequate capacity for inference and the unsteady, wobbly gait of their logic. It is the unsteadiness of the concepts themselves, for which they make use of words: these people have only shapeless floating splotches of concepts in their heads. — But the good author is distinguished not only by the strength and concision of his sentence structure: but one notices, one smells, if one is a man of subtle nostrils, that such a writer constantly compels himself and practices first to *establish* his concepts in a rigorous manner and make them *firmer*, thus to connect unequivocal concepts with his words: and, until this is done, he will not write! — Moreover there is some charm also in the uncertain, twilight, half-light: this perhaps was Hegel's effect on foreigners mostly through his art of speaking like a drunkard of the most sober and cold things. In the great realm of intoxications this was really one of the rarest ever invented — and quite uniquely a matter of *German* ingenuity! For wherever Germans and German "virtues" have penetrated, we have also brought along and transported the lust and desire for crude and refined types of alcohol. — Perhaps even the captivating power of our German music belongs here.

34[84]

NB. What Plato and at bottom all post-Socratics did: that was a certain legislation of *concepts*: — they firmly established for themselves and their disciples "this and that **should** be *thought* and sensed with this word": — therewith they freed themselves most definitively from their time and environment. This is *one of the kinds* of subtle disgust with which superior, more demanding natures rise up against the obscure crowd and their conceptual chaos:

34[85]

What is this tremendous power that for 2 thousand years has made fools of philosophers and toppled the reason of the reasonable? That instinct, that belief as it is demanded by Christianity: this is the herd instinct itself, the herd belief of the animal "human," the herd longing for complete subservience to an authority — (the same thing that *Kant* christened the "categorical imperative" out of German herd instinct.) In fact it is the greatest relief and boon to endangered vacillating tender weak herd animals to get someone who *commands* absolutely, a bellwether: it is their first condition of life.[58] The Brahmans knew this relief well, likewise the Jesuits, in nearly all monasteries the basic tendency is this: to finally rid oneself of the eternal agitation that commanding oneself brings with it. This instinct for faith is also the genuine feminine instinct; and when women find one implacable teacher who wants obedience and subservience from them, or even only one artist who shows woman in the attitude of her "perfection," as an adoring worshipping devoted creature, as victim, like e.g., R⟨ichard⟩ W⟨agner⟩, then they are "beside themselves" for joy: namely sated and satisfied before herself in her ultimate instinct. — In a weaker form one sees this in the French, who as the most good-natured Europeans are also the most herdlike: they only feel good when they are allowed by their *esprit*[59] "to obey unconditionally" for once: as in the presence of Napoleon. Or also in the presence of "the ideas of the French Revolution" — or also in the presence of Victor Hugo (who throughout his whole long life always adorned this most beautiful of all herd instincts with beautiful words and coats of pomp in the name of *freedom*). — When Christianity came along antiquity was inwardly torn back and forth by opposites of valuations (as a result of the physiological conditioning of the nonsensical equality concept *civis romanus* or by that nonsensical state expansion of the *imperium romanum*[60]) and Christianity provided the great *relief*.

34[86][61]

Words are acoustical signs for concepts: but concepts are more or less definite groups of recurring sensations that arrive together. In order to understand one another it does not yet suffice that people use the same words: one must also use the same words for the same species of inner experience — and *this* one must have **in common**. This is why representatives of a single people understand each other better: or, when human beings have lived together for a long time under similar conditions of climate, activities, needs, then a certain variety of experiences that are most *closely* understood by them all gains the upper hand: the result is a *quick* comprehension of one another. And marriage and inheritance are again the result of it. It is the need to convey one's needs quickly and easily that binds human beings most firmly to one another. On the other hand nothing holds a friendship, a love affair together when it is discovered that one *means* something different with words. *Which* groups of sensations are in the foreground is determined by valuations: but valuations are the result of our innermost needs. —

This is said to explain why it is difficult to understand writings like mine: the inner experiences, valuations and needs are different in me. For years I have interacted with people and taken my resignation and courtesy so far as to never speak of things that were in my heart. Indeed I have lived with people almost exclusively so. —

34[87]

We *imagine to ourselves* that the commanding, supreme thing lies in our consciousness. Ultimately we have a double brain: our capacity *to will, to feel and to think* something of our willing, feeling, thinking ourselves is what we summarize with the word "consciousness."

34[88]

NB. Those law-giving and tyrannical spirits who are in a position to *firmly* establish a concept, *firmly maintain* it, people with this spiritual strength of will who know how to ossify for a long time and nearly eternalize the most fluid of things, the spirit, are commanding human beings in the highest sense: they say "I want to know this and that was seen, I want it precisely *thus*, I want it *for this* and only for this." This kind of law-giving human being necessarily exerted the strongest influence in all ages: we have them to thank for all typical elaborations of the human being: they are the sculptors — and the rest ("most" p⟨eople⟩ in this case —) compared to them are only *clay*.

34[89]

The most firmly established movements of our intellect, our law-like gymnastics e.g., in representations of space and time, or in the need for "justification": this *philosophical* habitus of the human intellect is our actual potency: therefore such that in many intellectual things we *can no longer do otherwise*: which is called psychological necessity. This has *become*: and to believe *our* space, *our* time, *our* causality instinct is something that has meaning even apart from mankind is well-nigh a childishness.

34[90]

I am hostile 1) toward *desensualization*: it stems from the Jews, from Plato, who was ruined by Egyptians and Pythagoreans (and these by Buddhists)

We have the Provençal spirit that remained pagan, I mean "*not* Germanic," to thank for the *spiritualization of the amor*[62] of sexual love: whereas antiquity had brought things only as far as a spiritualization of pederasty.

2) toward all doctrines that focus on an end, a calm, a "Sabbath of all Sabbaths." Such ways of thinking characterize seething, suffering, often also dying races, e.g., such verses as are in R⟨ichard⟩ W⟨agner's⟩ "Nibelungs."[63]

34[91]

"Habit": this means something different in a slavishly minded person than in a noble one.

34[92]

What we owe the Christian church

1) a spiritualization of *cruelty*: the idea of hell, tortures and heretic trials, the auto-da-fés are indeed a major advancement over the magnificent but semi-idiotic slaughter in the Roman arenas. Much spirit, much ulterior motive has gotten into cruelty. — It has invented many pleasures.

2) it has made the European spirit *subtle* and *flexible* through its "intolerance." One sees immediately how in our democratic age, with freedom of the press, thought is getting *clumsy*. The Germans invented gunpowder — hats off! But they canceled it out: they invented the printing press.[64] The ancient *polis* was of a very similar mind. The Roman Empire, on the other hand, allowed great freedom in faith and nonfaith: more than any empire allows today: the result was immediately the greatest possible degeneration oafification and crudening of the spirit. — How good Leibniz and Abelard, Montaigne, Descartes and Pascal look! It is a pleasure to see the supple daring of such

spirits, for which we have the church to thank. — The intellectual pressure of the church is essentially the inflexible rigidity by virtue of which concepts and values are treated as *fixed*, as *aeternae*.[65] Dante provides us with a singular pleasure in this: one need in no way be *limited* under an absolute regime. If there were limits, then they were stretched around a tremendous space, thanks to Plato: and within them one could move *very freely*, like Bach within the forms of counterpoint. — Baco{n} and Shakespeare almost repulse us if we have thoroughly learned to taste *this* "freedom under the law." Likewise the most recent music compared to Bach and Handel.

34[93]

As Frederick the Great constantly ridicules the "*féminisme*"[66] in the regency of his neighbor states, so Bismarck "parliamentarianism": it is a new means to do what one *wants*.

34[94][67]

The sight of today's European gives me a great deal of hope: what is taking shape here is a daring ruling race, across the breadth of an extremely intelligent herd mass. It is imminent that the movements for absorption[68] of the latter no longer stand alone in the foreground.

34[95][69]

Against *false idealism*, where the best natures of the world alienate themselves through exaggerated subtlety. What a shame that the whole of southern Europe has been deprived of its inheritance of that subdued sensuality, by the abstinence of the clergy! And that such Shelleys, Hölderlins, Leopardis are destroyed is fair, I do not regard such people very highly at all. It amuses me to think of the revenge that the rough naturalness of nature takes on this kind of human being e.g., when I hear that L⟨eopardi⟩ engaged in on⟨anism⟩ when young, was later impotent.

34[96][70]
NB. A great human being, a human being whom nature built up and invented in grand style, what is that? First: in his entire activity he has a long logic which due to its length is hard to survey, and consequently is misleading, an ability to stretch his will across great expanses of his life and to despise and throw away everything petty in himself, even if among them are the most beautiful "divine" things in the world. *Second*: he is *colder, harder, more unscrupulous* and without *fear of "opinion"*; he lacks the virtues associated with "respect" and being respected, in generally everything that belongs to the "virtue of the herd." If he cannot *lead*, then he goes alone; it then happens that he grunts at many things he encounters along the way. 3) he does not want a "sympathetic" heart, but servants, tools, in his interaction with people he is always out to *make* something of them. He knows himself to be uncommunicable: he finds it tasteless when he becomes "familiar"; and usually when someone considers him to be so he is not. When he is not talking to himself he has his mask. He would rather lie than tell the truth: it requires more spirit and *will*. There is a solitude in him, as something unreachable for praise and blame, as a jurisdiction of one's own, which has no higher court above it.

34[97]
What I like to perceive in Germans is their Mephistopheles nature: but, to tell the truth, one must have a higher concept of the G⟨erman⟩ M⟨ephistopheles⟩ than Goethe, ⟨who⟩ found it necessary to *diminish* his M⟨ephistopheles⟩ in order to magnify his "inner Faust." The true German Mephistopheles is much more dangerous, bolder, more evil, more crafty and *therefore* more candid: consider the inwardness of Frederick the Great. Or of that much greater Frederick, of that Hohenstaufen Frederick 2. — The genuine German Mephistopheles climbs over the Alps, believes that everything there belongs to *him*. This is why he thrives as Winckelmann thrived, as Mozart. He regards *Faust*

and *Hamlet* as caricatures invented for ridicule, likewise *Luther*. Goethe had good *German* moments in which he laughed inwardly about all that. But then he himself fell back into the humid moods.

The astonishment of Napoleon when he saw a German poet and — found a *man*! He had expected to find a German poet![71] —

The German is extensive: a second soul has built itself onto the first, there are caves, corridors, he can appear superficial, frankness and decency belong to the skills of the German. — "Good-natured and devious" is an impossibility in other p⟨eople⟩; but just try living for a time among Swabians! —

34[98]

An age of democracy propels the actor to the heights, in Athens, likewise as today. R⟨ichard⟩ W⟨agner⟩ has so far surpassed everyone in this, and awakened a high concept of the actor, which can be awe-inspiring. Music, poetry, religion, culture, books, family, fatherland, social life — all *art* for the time being, that is to say stage attitude!

34[99]

Pig-German! Excuse me! Newspaper-German! Here ⟨I⟩ read Friedrich Albert *Lange*, a good horse whom one should even recommend to German youths in the absence of better horses: but he writes for example: "The cult of reality binds itself with the praise of the present. What is ideal has no course; whatever cannot legitimize itself through the natural sciences and historically is condemned to decline."[72] Why do we learn Latin and Greek in German schools anyway: if we do not even learn to be disgusted by such a filthy mishmash! And what enthusiasm precisely the real German spoilers have aroused, formerly *Hegel*, more recently *Richard Wagner*, most recently Eugen Dühring!

34[100]

It is terrifying to think that my thoughts on woman could drive some lady writer to the vengeful idea of having children after she has already tortured herself and the world sufficiently with her books!

34[101]

"When a woman wants to have children, she usually does not let the little children come to her, but the men!"[73] said an old midwife.

34[102][74]

— We should pay attention to whether what the Germans call their literature does not for the best part hark back to their pastors' sons. — Now from the start in this origin of German prose lies the probability that the solemn, dignified, *slow*, grave genres have been cultivated best: that *allegro*[75] or even *presto*[76] will be missing. The extraordinary vivaciousness of a style, like *il principe*[77] (quite apart from the seriousness of its task), the brevity strength, a kind of joy in the thronging of difficult thoughts, gives an echo of Florentine eloquence, namely of advocates. In Voltaire too the advocate's skill is first rate, advocate's *tempo*. The fastest tempo I found in a writer is in Petronius: he runs like a swift wind and consequently is not lascivious: he is too funny for that.

34[103][78]

The Germans.
Suspicions and Desires
by
F. N.

34[104][79]

NB. The only Germans of whom I am speaking here, are something young and becoming: I separate them from the Germans of the Reformation and the Th⟨irty Years⟩ War and do not wish to participate in the historical falsification that ignores this chasm: as if nothing had happened back then. That something like the decline of an earlier race was going on with them in the

16th century is difficult to deny: this appearance of discouragement, of cowardice, of extreme old age, of the Chinese pigtail, to speak metaphorically — on the whole that must have been the result of a terrible corruption of the blood considering that the manly men went off and away into foreign lands and died or were ruined in foreign lands. On the other hand at that time an involuntary mixing with remotely related races took place: the fornication of war was disastrous beyond measure according to all descriptions. Here and there of course there were still remnants of a stronger race: e.g., the musician Handel, our most beautiful type of *man* in the realm of art, is proof of that: or, to name a woman — Professor Gottsched's wife, who with complete justification held the scepter for a good long time over German professors — just look at the portraits of those two! Some regions purified themselves more quickly and on the whole returned to health, e.g., Hannover Westphalia Holstein — there still to this day sits a sturdy peasant-like and phlegmatic race. — The worst off were surely the German nobility: it was damaged most profoundly. Whatever of it remained at home suffered from alcoholism, what went away and came back, from syphilis. To this day it has spoken only little in spiritual matters; and even as concerns Bismarck, his great grandmother came from the Leipzig professor class. —

34[105][80]

The *German* — not to mention the idiotic Teutonizing of youths who even today still prattle about "Teutonic virtues" — his *mystical* nature. There has never yet been a German culture: there were hermits who knew how to disguise themselves with astonishing skill, in the midst of the crudest barbarism.

34[106][81]

The German writing style.
Mephistopheles.

34[107]

Brutality and right next to it sickly tenderness of sensual feeling in R⟨ichard⟩ W⟨agner⟩ — is highly Parisian.

34[108]

I take the democratic movement as something unavoidable: but as something that is not unstoppable, but instead can be slowed down. However, on the whole the rule of the herd instinct and ⟨of⟩ herd valuations, *Epicureisme*[82] and benevolence together are increasing: humans are becoming weak, but good and cozy.

34[109]

NB. Parliaments may be extremely useful for a strong and flexible statesman, there he has something on which he can support himself — each such thing has to be able to *resist*! — a place to which he can shift much responsibility! On the whole, however, I wish that the numbers nonsense and the superstitious belief in majorities would not yet take hold in G⟨ermany⟩ as in the Latin races; and that they finally invent something in politics too! It makes little sense and is very dangerous to allow the habit of universal voting rights to put down deeper roots, still recent as it is and easily eradicable: whereas its introduction after all was only an emergency and momentary regulation.

34[110]

To me the inventive faculty and the accumulation of strength of will seems greatest and least used up in the Slavs, thanks to an absolutist regime: and a *Slavic* earth-regime is not the most improbable of things. The English do not know how to overcome the consequences of their own pigheaded "self-glorification," in the long run they will increasingly have the *homines novi*[83] at the rudder and ultimately women in parliament. But practicing politics is ultimately also a matter of *heredity*: no one begins to become a man of tremendous horizon from a private man.

34[111][84]

The Germans should cultivate a ruling caste: I confess that there are qualities inherent in Jews that are indispensable to their serving as an ingredient in a race that is supposed to practice world politics. The sense for money has to be learned, inherited and inherited a thousand fold: even now the Jew is a match for the American.

34[112][85]

I point out something new: certainly for such a democratic nature there is the danger of barbarians, but one sees them only in the depths. There is also a *different* kind of *barbarian*, they come from the heights: a kind of conquering and ruling nature that looks for a material that they can shape. Prometheus was such a barbarian. —

34[113]

Not a people of "professional politicians," of newspaper readers!

34[114][86]

— — — The smallness and pitifulness of the German soul was and is not at all a result of a plurality of small states: it is well known that people in much smaller states have been proud and self-aggrandizing and it is not large states in themselves that make the soul more free and manly. When the slavish imperative "you should and must kneel!" commands in someone's soul an involuntary bowing of the neck before honorary titles, medals, favorable glances from the top down, in an "empire" he will only bow deeper and lick the dust before his great sovereign more fervently than he did before the smaller one: there is no doubting this. — It can still be seen today in the lower classes of the Italians that aristocratic self-confidence and manly discipline and certainty of themselves belongs to the longest history of their city and has been *modeled* best for them; a poor gondolier in Venice is still a better figure than a real privy councilor in Berlin, and ultimately even a better man: this is palpable. Just ask the women about it.

34[115][87]
The Servant's Soul.
The Corruption of the Blood.
Moral Tartuffery.
The "Mind."[88]
Lack of Clarity
The Vacillators.
Conjecture on the Southern Lands.
Ugliness
The Hinter-Soul.
The Dependence on France.
The German Professor and the Officer.
The *niaiserie allemande*.[89]
The German Writing Style.
The Hermit.
The "Eternal Feminine" in the German Man.
Intoxication and Music.
The "Historical Sense."
The Actor.
Convenience (Philistines) and War.
The Philosophers.
Pessimism. (Comparison with France).
More herd animal than ever — but there are favorable conditions for individuals as well.

34[116]
What is most admirable about Kant is that he got over his Leibnizian seduction and retained the best of the previous century, sensualism.[90]

34[117]
NB. Schopenhauer, in his youth seduced by the romantics and diverted from his best instincts, was at bottom a Voltairean in body and soul, and really a child of the previous century — for the rest however led beyond French taste by the Greeks and by Goethe —and above all — *not* a theologian! The "immutability

of character," in plain language perhaps laziness, and on the other hand his faith in the infallibility of genius (in plain language perhaps vanity) prompted him to prematurely pronounce *holy* the "sin of his youth," I mean his metaphysics of the will; and to no longer "develop" himself. A h⟨uman being⟩ of his talent and inner *discordia*[91] had the substance for five "better" systems in his head, and one ever truer and falser than the other.

34[118]

We do not understand a "causal" relationship, but we see that a factum, in order to be established, ⟨should⟩ comprehend several *facta*[92] in itself. Our *analysis* sets up a succession. The numbers that are generated by this mean nothing for the relationship of those phenomena *among themselves*, but could lead astray: because humanity is *fixed* in some instincts, a similarity of numerical ratios is yielded with respect to *him*.

34[119]

Do our thoughts stand in a causal direct relationship to others? Or is their logical connection an illusion? I mean a result of the fact that the instigating events of each of these thoughts stand in a relationship that presents itself to us as "conclusion" and the like. They are purely final links? — Or is there a direct effect of a thought on another? A "causing" here at least?

34[120]

The world of appearance "empty illusion and deception," the need for causality that produces connections between appearances likewise "empty illusion and deception" — with this moral *condemnation* of the deceptive and the illusory voices itself. One has to get beyond this. There are no things in themselves, also no absolute knowing, the perspectival, deceiving character belongs to existence.[93]

34[121][94]

That *my* appreciation or condemnation of a person does not give another person a right to the same appreciation or condemnation: — unless he is equal to me and of the same rank. The opposite manner of thinking is that of newspapers: that the appreciation of people and things is something "in itself," for which anyone is allowed to reach as if for *his* property. Here is simply the assumption that *all* are *of equal rank*. — Being truthful is a distinction

34[122]

That something that originated is not known when one knows its origin[95] (father and mother): but instead that one *must already know* it in order to discover something "related" in the conditions of origin — and that mostly this is an *illusion*: — for in truth the recognition of the paternal and maternal element in the child is possible only in an *aggregate*, and involuntarily we seek, in order to *explain*, to comprehend something new *only* as an aggregate, an ordering-together i.e., the *analysis* refers not to the real origin, but to a fake "mechanistic" ordering-together and addition that did not happen at all. The explainer takes the facts as more stupid and simpler than they are.

34[123]

That a human being is a multiplicity of forces that stand in an order of rank, so that there are commanders, but that the commander must also create everything that serves the preservation of the obeyers, such that he is *conditioned* by their existence. All these living beings must be of a related kind, otherwise they could not serve and obey one another so: the commanders[96] in some sense must also be obeyers, and in more subtle cases the role between them must change temporarily, and he who otherwise commands must obey for once. The concept "individual"[97] is false. These beings do not exist at all in isolation: the center of gravity is something changeable; the constant *producing* of cells etc. yields a constant change in the number of these beings. And by *adding* nothing at all is accomplished. Our arithmetic is something too crude for this relationship and only an individual arithmetic.

34[124]

The logic of our conscious thinking is only a crude and simplified form of that thinking which is required by our organism, indeed by its individual organs. A simultaneous thinking e.g., is needed, of which we scarcely have an inkling. Perhaps an artist of language: the reckoning back with the heaviness and lightness of syllables, the reckoning ahead, simultaneously the analogy-seeking of the weight of the thought with the tonal or the physiological or larynx conditions happen simultaneously — but of course not as *conscious.*

Our causality feeling is something quite crude and isolated compared to the real causal feelings of our organism. In particular the "before" and "after" are a great naïveté.

Lastly: we must first gain everything for *consciousness*, a temporal sense, a spatial sense, causal sense: after it had existed much more richly for a long time without consciousness. And of course a certain most simple plain reduced form: our *conscious* willing, feeling, thinking is in the service of a much more comprehensive willing feeling and thinking. — Really?

We are constantly still growing, our temporal-spatial sense etc. is still developing.

34[125]

Nothing can be prophesied, but with a certain enhancement of the type human being a *new* force can reveal itself, of which we knew nothing so far. (Namely a synthesis of opposites?)

34[126][98]

The sigh of *Kleist* over ultimate unknowability — [99]

34[127]

We are beginners at *learning e.g.*, with our kind of logic. Or our passions. Or our mechanics. Or our atomism, which is the most honest attempt to construct the world for our eyes, and for our counting arithmetical understanding (thus *intuitive and calculable*)

34[128]

Our "means and purposes" are very useful abbreviations for making events manageable, surveyable for ourselves.

34[129][100]

1. The Will to Truth.
2. Beyond Good and Evil.
3. The Human Being as Artist.
4. Of Superior Politics.
5. The Cultivating Thought.

34[130]

Abstract thinking is for many a toil, for me, on good days, a celebration and an intoxication.

34[131]

Just as a general does not want to hear about many things and must not hear about them, in order not to lose his total overview: so too in our conscious intellect *above all* there must be an *excluding* drive that *scares things away*, a selecting one, which only permits *certain facta* to present themselves. Consciousness is the hand with which the organism reaches about itself most widely: it must be a firm hand. Our logic, our temporal sense, spatial sense are tremendous abbreviatory capacities for the purpose of commanding. A concept is an invention that does not correspond *entirely* to anything; but to many things a little bit: a sentence like "2 things, equal to a third, are equal to themselves" presupposes 1) things 2) equalities: both do not exist. But with this invented rigid world of concepts and numbers humans gain a means to master tremendous quantities of facts as if with signs and to inscribe them on their memory. The superiority of this sign mechanism is precisely that it distances itself from the individual fact as far as possible. The reduction of experiences to *signs*, and the ever greater quantity of things that can therefore be comprehended: is its *highest force*. "Intelligence"[101] as the capacity to master a tremendous quantity of facts in signs. *This intellectual world, this sign-world is pure "illusion and deception,"* likewise every "phenomenal thing" — *and the mo⟨ral⟩ h⟨uman being⟩ certainly is outraged*! (as with Napoleon only the essen⟨tial⟩ instincts of humanity came into consideration during his calculations and he had a right not to take notice of the exceptional ones e.g., of compassion — at the risk of miscalculating here and there)[102]

34[132]

What then is "perceiving"?[103] *Taking*-something-*as-true*: saying Yes to something.

34[133]

NB. There is something pathological about the whole type of philosopher up till now, there may be much in him that is failed. Instead of leading themselves and human beings higher, the philosophers prefer to step aside and seek whether there might not be a *different* way: this is perhaps in itself already the sign of a *degenerating* instinct. The human being who turns out well takes pleasure in the fact "human being" and in humanity's path: but — he goes *farther*!

34[134]

What *my* value judgment is, is not so for another. Yet the adoption of value judgments as of items of clothing is the most frequent fact: thus from the outside originate first skin, then flesh, finally character: the *role* becomes truth.

34[135]

I often watched these German idealists, but not they me! — they know and smell nothing of what I know, they take their gentle stroll, they have a heart full of different things than I: they seek different air, different nourishment, different pleasure. They look up, — I look out — we never see the same thing.

— It annoys me to interact with them. They may love the cleanliness of their bodies: but their spirit is unwashed, their "consequently" smells rotten to me, they are outraged where joyful curiosity begins in me, they have not cleaned their ears when I am ready to sing my song.

34[136]

— This Socrates who looked for sly reasons to act in accordance with what *custom* demanded was entirely after the heart of the "*Delphic priesthood*"! and his conversion of Plato was the masterpiece of his art of seduction. The learned concepts as *divine* in origin, the folk valuations as *eternal* and everlasting: — but to dress them up *anew* for a finer generation, to season them with the pepper and mugwort of dialectic joy, to use them on loquacious and enamored youths for the enflaming ⟨of⟩ their competitive spirit in word and deed —

34[137]

— They are so strange to me: in order to live with them I would always have to teach them precisely what is most opposite of what I regard as true and what seems invigorating to me: and among them I thought up the proverb "not only gold, but leather also glitters."

34[138]

In Germany there has always been a lack of spirit, and the mediocre minds there receive the highest honors because they are already rare. What is most appreciated is industriousness and persistence and a certain cold-blooded critical gaze; and for the sake of such qualities German philology, German military science have become master over Europe.

34[139]

NB. For subtler and smarter ears nearly any praise of a virtue sounds ridiculous: they do not hear a virtue e.g., when someone is called "*modest*" (in the event he evaluates himself honestly!) or that someone is called "*truthful*" (in the event he does not want to be deceived!) or "*sympathetic*" (in the event he has a soft yielding heart) ⟨or⟩ chaste (in the event he is a frog and yet on the other hand does not like to live in swamps)

34[140]

NB. There is ⟨a⟩ guilelessness of scien⟨tific⟩ p⟨eople⟩ that borders on idiocy: they have no nose for how dangerous their trade is, they believe from the bottom of their hearts that "love for truth" and "the good, beautiful and true" is their actual concern. I do not mean "dangerous" with respect to the disintegrating effects, but with respect to the tremendous center of gravity of responsibility that someone feels upon himself who begins to notice that all valuations according to which people live in the long term *drive people to destruction*.

34[141]

NB. The *demasculinizing* and perhaps *emasculating* effect of much *praying* also belongs to the damages of the German nature since the Reformation. It is a matter of bad taste under all circumstances to beg much instead of to give much: the mixture of humble servility with a courtly-rabble-like obtrusiveness, with which e.g., Saint Augustine grovels before God in his *Confessions*, reminds us that human beings perhaps are not alone among animals with religious feelings: dogs have a similar "religious feeling" for human beings. — The praying interaction with G⟨od⟩ cultivates a demeaning mood and attitude that demands its right also in impious times, through heredity: it is well known that Germans were awestruck by princes or by party leaders or by the phrase "as your most humble servant." There should be an end to this.

34[142]
NB. It never occurred to me to "deduce" all virtues from egoism. I first want to have proven that they are "virtues" and not only occasional instincts of preservation of certain herds and communities.

34[143]
This flaccid fear of "horrible fanaticism"

34[144][104]
NB. — he stirred and closed his lips again and looked like someone who still has something to say and hesitates to say it. And it seemed to those who watched him that his face had reddened slightly. This lasted for a short while: then however, all at once, he shook his head, voluntarily closed his eyes — and died. —

Thus it happened that Zarathustra perished.[105]

34[145][106]
He leads his friends ever higher, even to his cave and finally to the high mountain: there he dies.

blessing: cave of the island of tombs.

The *stations*: and each time speeches.

Noon and Eternity
By
Friedrich Nietzsche.

First Part:
The Herald's Cries.

Second Part:
The Proclamation.

Third Part:
The Vow Makers.

Fourth Part:
Rise and Fall.

34[146][107]

Someone who has a stake in knowing under which conditions the plant "human being"[108] grows most robustly — for someone occupied in this manner the appearance of a new political power, in case it is not based on new ideas, is not yet an event: he scarcely has time to look more closely.

Do not misunderstand me: with this book I wanted to explain why I have remained indifferent about the emergence of the German empire: I see one step further in the democratization of Europe and also one step further in the mo⟨ral⟩ mendacity of Europe.— nothing more, nothing new. But democracy is a form of *decline* of the state, a degeneration of races, a preponderance of failed people: I have already said this once before.

34[147][109]

Someone for whom nearly all books have become superficial, who still has the belief about a few people of the past that they possessed enough profundity to — not write what they knew.

I have thought so many forbidden things and have been reconciled and have always been at home where even righteous and capable spirits lose their breath: thus I am always amazed when I still find something to communicate. Even though I know full well and right away that my dashes are dearer to me than my communicated thoughts.

How many scholars I could occupy; and if in isolated cases I have perhaps done this —

The drawback of driving scholars out into regions where freedom, subtlety and unscrupulousness are required lies in the fact that they cannot see beyond *themselves* — that they have no eyes where they ⟨have⟩ no experience. In order e.g., to portray what is the moral conscience, for this one would have to be deep and wounded and monstrous like the conscience of Pascal and then even possess that expansive sky of bright and malicious spirituality that surveys, orders and laughs at this chaos of experiences from on high.

When I was younger I believed I was lacking a few hundred scholars whom I could drive into the bushes like bloodhounds — I mean into the history of the human soul — in order to hunt *my* game. Meanwhile I learned that assistants, too, are hard to find for the things that pique my curiosity.

34[148]

I think I feel that Socrates was profound — his irony was above all the need *to feign* superficiality in order to be able to interact at all with people — ; that Caesar had profundity: likewise perhaps that Hohenstaufen Friedrich the Second: certainly Leonardo da Vinci; to a not minor degree Pascal, who died only thirty years too early to scornfully laugh about Christianity itself from his magnificent bitter-malicious soul, as he had done it about the Jesuits earlier when he was younger.

34[149]

NB. I honor M⟨ichel⟩angelo higher than Raphael because through all the Christian veils and biases of his time he saw the ideals of a nobler culture than the Christian-Raphaelian one: whereas Raphael loyally and modestly glorified only the valuations given to him and did not bear in himself any further-seeking, longing instincts. M⟨ichel⟩angelo however saw and perceived the problem of the legislator of new values: likewise the problem of the triumphantly perfected one who first needed to conquer even "the hero in himself;" the human being who is elevated most highly, who was also beyond his compassion and pitilessly smashes and annihilates whatever does not belong to him — brilliantly and in serene divinity. M⟨ichel⟩a⟨ngelo⟩ was so high and so outside his age and Christian Europe only in moments, as is only fair: mostly he related condescendingly toward the eternal-feminine of Christianity; indeed it appears that he even ultimately broke down precisely before it and *gave up* the ideal of his highest hours. For it was an ideal to which only the human being of the strongest and highest fullness of life can be equal, but not a man who has grown old! At bottom he would have had to annihilate Christianity from the vantage point of his ideal! But for that he was not thinker and philosopher enough. — Among those artists L⟨eonardo⟩ da Vinci alone perhaps had a real supra-Christian eye. He knows "the East," the inside as well as the outside. There is something super-European and secretive about him, as it distinguishes anyone who has seen an excessively large compass of good and bad things.

34[150]
NB. *Schopenhauer*, a thinker of integrity and likewise not a bad writer on philosophical issues, even though in himself no philosopher: with respect to today's youth (and also to those elders who are modest in their claims to sharpness, brightness of sky and — academic rigor) irreplaceable, for he teaches *veneration* where he himself venerated, for the critical spirit of Kant, for Goethe, for the Greeks, for the free-spirited French; in his time he was perhaps the best-educated German, with a European horizon: there are even moments in which he sees with Eastern eyes. Pessimism as he understood it is likewise no small teacher of *veneration* in regions where veneration was not at home: e.g., for Indian antiquity, for *the* ancient genuine Christianity, Catholicism, against which Protestant schooling tends ⟨to⟩ turn its taste.

34[151]
On "genius." How little talent e.g., in R⟨ichard⟩ W⟨agner⟩! Was there ever a musician who was so poor in his 28th ⟨year⟩ (not so undeveloped, closed-minded, but so poor) that he was jealous of Meyerbeer — so bitterly jealous as to be bothered by it his whole life long? and consequently, with the consistency of "beautiful souls," to hold it against *him* his whole life long? On the other hand one learns how Kant justifiably praises industriousness and tenacity as that etc.

34[152]
Among good musicians Verdi counts as rich weighed against W⟨agner⟩: who had reasons to be thrifty and to "make good investments" with his "inventions," to practice usury with "leitmotifs" and to keep his "gold" to himself, so that in anticipation of it he can enjoy credit that is a thousand times *too big*: did W⟨agner⟩ learn this from the Jews?

34[153]
NB. A woman wants to be a mother; and if she does not want this, even though she could do it, then she nearly belongs in jail: so great then usually is her inner degeneration.

34[154][110]
NB. Germany produced only a single poet besides Goethe: that is Heinrich Heine – and on top of that he is a Jew. But in France just as in Italy, Spain and England and wherever people only — — — ; he had the finest instinct for the blue flower[111] "German," and of course also for the gray jackass "German." The Parisians[112] assert in addition that along with 2 other non-Parisians he represented the quintessence of the Parisian spirit⟨.⟩

34[155][113]
On Philosophers.
On Women.
On Musicians.
On Peoples.
On Scholars.
On Writers.
On the Pious.
On Herds — and Herd-Instincts.
"the good human being"
On those who Rule.
On the Ancient Greeks.
Dionysus — Diabolus.

The Good Europeans.
A Contribution to the Description
of the European Soul.

34[156][114]

A preface on order of rank.

These are *my* judgments: and in printing them, I give no one the right to voice them as their own: least of all do I consider them "public common property," and I will rap the knuckles of anyone who tries to steal them. In an age of "equal rights for all" there is something that sounds unpleasant: this is order of rank.

34[157][115]

NB. For explaining that inner daring skepticism in Germany, where it is greater and more sure of itself than in any country of Europe, we must include the fact that the Protestant clergy has always been fruitful in children and like Luther has not had its strength only in the pulpit: and for the same reason from which Machiavelli infers the skepticism of the Italians — they have always had God's deputy and his court too closely in view — all too many German philosophers and scholars as children of preachers and other kinds of church apparatus have *watched* the "priest" — and *consequently* they no longer believe in God. Protestantism is from the start *essentially* non-faith in the "saints"; German philosophy is essentially non-faith in the *homines religiosi*[116] and the second-rate saints, in all the provincial and city pastors, including the theologians of the university — and in this sense German philosophy may be a continuation of Protestantism.

34[158][117]

NB. The external world is the work of our organs, consequently our body, a piece of external world, is the work of our organs — consequently our organs are the work of our organs. This is a complete *reductio ad absurdum*:[118] consequently the external world is not the work of our organs.

34[159][119]

Arrows.
Thoughts About and Against the
European Soul

The Right of Prerogatives.[120]

34[160]

Arrows.
Thoughts
About and Against the German Soul.
By
Friedrich Nietzsche.

34[161][121]
NB. A capable craftsman or scholar looks good when he takes pride in his art and is content with it, gazing at life with satisfaction; and on the other hand nothing is more miserable to behold than when a shoemaker or schoolteacher indicates with his mournful expression that he really is born for something else. There is nothing better at all than the good! and it is: to have some kind of capability and to create from it, *virtù*,[122] in the Italian Renaissance sense.

34[162][123]
NB. Today, in an age when the state has an absurdly fat belly, in all fields and disciplines there are "representatives" in addition to the real workers e.g., in addition to scholars the literati, in addition to the suffering classes of people the babbling boasting good-for-nothings who "represent" that suffering, not to mention the politicians by profession who do quite well and with their strong lungs give "representations" of "distress" before a parliament. Our modern life is extremely *expensive* due to the quantity of intermediaries; in an ancient city, on the other hand, and then as an echo still in some cities of Spain and Italy, someone presented himself[124] on his own and would not have given anything to such a modern representative and intermediary — unless it were a kick![125]

34[163]

The ecclesiastical pressure of millennia has created a magnificent *tension* of the bow, likewise the monarchical: the two attempted slackenings (instead of shooting with the bow) are 1) Jesuitism 2) democracy.[126] Pascal is the glorious sign of that terrible tension: he laughed the Jesuits *to death.* — I am satisfied with despotic conditions provided that we are dealing with mixed races, where a tension exists anyway. To be sure: the danger of such attempts is great. — European democracy is *not* or ⟨is only⟩ to the smallest extent an unleashing of *forces,* rather above all an unleashing of letting-oneself-go, of wanting to have it easy, of inner *laziness.* Likewise the press.

34[164][127]

European d⟨emocracy⟩ is to the smallest extent an unleashing of forces: above all it is an unleashing of laziness, of weariness, of *weaknesses.*

34[165][128]

The Mirror.
An Opportunity for Self-Reflection
for Europeans.
By
Friedrich Nietzsche.

34[166]

What is shared in the development of the *European soul* is e.g., noticeable in a comparison between Delacroix and R⟨ichard⟩ W⟨agner⟩, the one *peintre-poète,*[129] the other composer, according to the difference of French and German talent. But otherwise the same. Delacroix by the way also *very much* a musician — and Coriolan overture.[130] His first interpreter *Baudelaire,* a kind of R⟨ichard⟩ W⟨agner⟩ without music. The *expression* expression[131] foremost in both, everything else is sacrificed. Both dependent on literature, highly educated and themselves people who write. Nervously-pathologically-afflicted, without sun.

34[167]

In every sense-judgment the entire organic prehistory is active: "that is green" e.g., *memory in instinct*, as a kind of abstraction and simplification, comparable to the logical process: what is most important is repeatedly underscored, but also the weakest traits *remain*. In the organic realm there is no forgetting; but surely a kind of *digestion* of what is experienced.

34[168]

The good, their relationship to stupidity.
Education and cultivation.
The *liberum "nego."*[132] "for the time being No!"
Reverence, anger and bravery

34[169]

The *countability* of certain processes e.g., many chemical ones, and a calculability of them still does not provide a reason to touch "absolute truths" here. It is always only a number in relation to human beings, to some firmly established inclination or measure in human beings. Number itself is *our* invention through and through.

34[170]

A *logical* process, of the kind "found in books," *never occurs*, as little as a straight line or two "identical things." Our thinking runs fundamentally differently: between one thought and the next reigns a middle world of quite a different kind e.g., drive to contradiction or to subservience etc.

34[171][133]

Synthetic judgments a priori are probably possible, but they are — *false* judgments.

34[172]

Nux et *Crux*.[134]
A Philosophy for Good Teeth.

34[173]

Every philosophy, however it may have originated, serves certain educational purposes e.g., for encouragement or for calming etc.

34[174]

The good a pre-stage of evil; a mild dose of evil: —

34[175]

When someone is concerned about others and *not* concerned about himself, this can be a sign of *stupidity*: this is how "the people"[135] think of *bonhomie*.[136]

34[176][137]

Moralities and religions are the major means with which one can fashion from human beings what one wishes: supposing that ⟨one⟩ has an excess of creating powers and can assert his creating will over long periods of time, in the form of law-giving and customs.[138] In reflecting on how to make humanity stronger and deeper than it was so far, above all I considered which morality to date has accomplished something like this. The first thing I grasped was that for this purpose the morality common in Europe cannot be used, which of course the philosophers and moralists of Europe believe is morality itself and alone — such a unison of philosophers is indeed the best proof that that morality really rules. — For this morality is the genuine *herd*-instinct that yearns for comfort, safety, easiness of life and even has as its ultimate most secret wish that of being able to dispense with all leaders a⟨nd⟩ bellwethers. Its two best preached teachings are: "equality of rights" and "compassion for all suffering" — and suffering itself is taken by all herd-animals as something that should be *abolished*. But whoever reflects on where and how the plant human being[139] grew most robustly and beautifully into the heights will extract from history, in contrast to European herd-morality and falsification of history, that for this purpose the danger of its situation must be intensified, its spirit of invention and dissembling must be challenged by long pressure and compulsion, and that consequently harshness, cruelty, secrecy, unpleasantness, inequality of rights, war, cataclysm of all kinds, in sum, the opposite of all herd ideals is required. That a morality with such opposite intentions could only be taught and planted in association with the existing moral law and under its words and pomp cloak, that therefore many forms of transition and deception have to be invented, and that, because the life of a human being is much too short for the implementation of such a long-lasting will, human beings will have to be cultivated in whom such a will is guaranteed duration by many generations: this is as well understood as the not easily articulated and-so-forth of this thought. Preparing a reversal of values in a specific strong kind[140] of human being and unleashing among them a large quantity of reined-in and slandered instincts: reflecting on this I considered which kind of human being so far involuntarily and unconsciously already worked on the prescribed task. I found the pessimists, since their dissatisfaction with everything *at least* logically compels them to dissatisfaction with present circumstances: this is why I favored Schopenhauer and the knowledge of Indian philosophies slowly dawning over Europe. Even a nightmare is a means for suddenly *waking* human beings. — Likewise I had a predilection for certain insatiably dualistic artists, who like Byron believe unconditionally in the privileges of higher human beings and under the seduction of art deaden the herd instincts in select human beings and enliven their opposite. Thirdly I honored the philologists and historians who continued the discovery of antiquity because in the ancient world a different morality ruled than today and indeed the human being back then was stronger more evil and deeper under the sway of its morality: the seduction of stronger souls by antiquity is prob⟨ably⟩ the most subtle and unnoticeable of seductions.

For my part I named this entire manner of thinking the philosophy of Dionysus: a view that recognizes in creating and shaping human beings and things the highest pleasure of existence and in "morality" only a means for giving the ruling will such strength and flexibility to impress itself on humankind in this manner. I regard religions and educational systems with an eye to how far they accumulate and bequeath strength; and nothing seems more essential to me to study than the *laws of cultivation*, in order not to lose again the greatest quantity of strength, through inappropriate connections and ways of living.

34[177][141]

I am disinclined toward 1) socialism, because it dreams entirely of the herd nonsense of the "good true beautiful" and equal rights: anarchism too wants the same ideal, only in a more brutal way 2) parliamentarianism and the press, because these are the means by which the herd animal makes itself master.

34[178][142]

My attention is on which points in history give rise to great h⟨uman beings⟩. The significance of long *despotic moralities*: they tense the bow, when they do not break it.

34[179]

That there could be one *development* for all of humankind is nonsense: also not even to be desired. The constant shaping *of* people, to extract the kind of *diversity* of people, to break them when a kind of type has had its zenith — therefore creating and annihilating — seems to me the highest pleasure that humans can have. Plato was certainly not so limited when he taught the concepts as *fixed* and *eternal*: but he wanted this to be believed.

34[180]

Not to place more reason into the whole history of human beings than there is in the rest of the world: *much* is possible, but one must not want it for too long a period. Chance smashes everything again.

The human being as a *spectacle*: that is the **historical sense** — but it contains a dangerous element, the human being learns to feel himself as the *shaping one* who not only looks on and wants to look on. The German — — —

— it is self-evident that publicly and secretly all organic fundamental intentions of h⟨uman beings⟩ are spoken of only under a thousand masquerades: just read a speech by Bismarck.

NB. — the *intelligent* human being who occasionally has seen behind the masks and knows how to see, who has *comprehended* generally how much everything is a mask — is in the *best of moods* about this, as is only fair. Intelligence is the thrill of an eternal carnival, whether we ourselves play along or are only played.

— the historical sense and geographic-climatic exoticism side by side.

34[181][143]

Thus as an idle person who has nothing better to do, I just want to tell my friends what I am thinking under the philosophy of Dionysus: for that gods too philosophize seems to me a worthy and pious idea, in which even the most pious can delight. Perhaps, according to the taste of my friends, I will go too far in the frankness of my narrative: but this god himself, in dialogues with me, has gone much further and if I were permitted to ascribe beautiful hypocritical honorific titles to him I would have to sing the praises of my courage, of my honesty truthfulness integrity "love for truth" and so on. But such a god does not know what to do with all this beautiful junk and splendor – for my justification two words suffice, which of course in Germany are not easily translated "into German": *gai saber.*

Keep this for yourself and your kind: I have no reason to cover my "nakedness."[144] Enough, it is a quite shameless kind of deity.

It was spring and all the trees were freshly in sap: as I walked through the woods and reflected on some childish thing, I carved myself a whistle without really knowing what I was doing. But as soon as I put it to my lips and whistled, the god appeared before me whom I have long since known.

Well, you pied piper, what are you doing here? You half Jesuit and musician — almost a German!

I was surprised that the god tried to flatter me in this way: and I resolved to be wary of him.

I did everything to make them stupid, had them sweating in bed, gave them dumplings to devour, commanded them to drink until they dropped, made them into stay-at-homes and scholars, inspired them with pitiful feelings of a servant's soul

You seem to be up to something wicked, driving h⟨uman beings⟩ to ruin?

Perhaps, answered the god: but in such a way that I get something out of it for myself.

— What then? I asked, curious. —

Who then? you should be asking. Thus spoke Dionysus to me.

34[182][145]

Dionysus.
Attempt at a Divine Way of
Philosophizing.
By
Friedrich Nietzsche

34[183]

How is it anyway that women bear their children alive? I always thought the poor creatures would come into the world suffocated, given the meager constitution of their powers of resistance. "Strait is the gate, and narrow is the way," as it is written:[146] or, how are live children a priori possible? — And inasmuch as I asked thus, I awoke completely from my dogmatic slumber,[147] gave the god a poke in the belly, and asked, with the seriousness of a Chinese from Königsberg: "In summa: how are synthetic judgments a priori possible?" "By means of a faculty for them" answered the god,[148] holding his belly.

34[184]

Hegel: the inclination of Germans to contradict themselves — from this a *Gothic*,

Wagner: who did not know how ⟨to⟩ find an end and made this, too, into a principle: also a Gothic.

34[185][149]

Not to falsify the real *historical* effect *of Kant*! He himself was proud of his table of categories and having *discovered* the faculty for it: his successors were proud to discover such faculties, and the fame of German philosophy abroad was associated with this: namely *it was the intuitive and instinctive comprehension of "truth"* that constituted the fame of Germans. Its effect belongs to the great *reaction*. A kind of *saving* of scientific work, a more direct taking on of the "things" themselves — an abbreviation of the way of knowledge: *this* dream intoxicated them! — In the main Schopenhauer produces *the same delight*: only not in satisfied Spinoza-inclined p⟨eople⟩ but in the dissatisfied: he grabs "the will" or rather the velleity the "random willing,"[150] desirability or sense and understanding

34[186]

"Calmly leaning on graces and muses" *Schiller* "The Artists."[151]

34[187]

The development of consciousness as an *administrative apparatus*: only accessible for *generalizations*. That which the eye reveals already enters consciousness as *generalized* and *contrived*.

34[188][152]

Preface: *The Order of Rank of Human Beings.*

1. *Knowledge as Will to Power.*
2. *Beyond Good and Evil*
3. *The Hidden Artists.*
4. *The Great Politics.*
5. *The Hammer.*

34[189]

the sensuality that seems so ridiculous in little pale Jews or Parisians, and nearly *comme une neurose*[153] —

34[190]

in the previous century *bonté*[154] was favored with the good conscience that for a long time resided in other feelings

34[191][155]

Noon and Eternity.
A Philosophy of the Eternal Recurrence.

By
Friedrich Nietzsche.

Preface: on Human Order of Rank
Part One: Science and Conscience.[156]
Part Two: Beyond Good and Evil.
Part Three: The Hidden Artists.
Part Four: Superior Politics.
Part Five: The Hammer (or Dionysus).

34[192][157]

Preface. For whom?
The Inventive.
The Scope of the Soul.
Profundity.
The Force of Transformation.
The Commanding Force.
Hardness.
Knowing:[158] Joy of the Conqueror
The Great Responsibility.
The Art of Masks. Transfiguration.
The Force of Communication.
— The Dionysian —

34[193]

The skeptics of morality do not consider how much moral valuation they carry in their skepticism: their condition is nearly a suicide of morality and perhaps even a transfiguration of it.

34[194]

From where should we *take* our valuations? From "life"? But "higher, deeper, simpler, more manifold" — are estimations that *we* first *place* into life. "*Development*" in every sense is also always a loss, a damage; even the specialization of each organ. The optics of self-preservation and of growth.

Optics of Growth.

That the destruction of an illusion still does not produce truth, but only one *more piece of ignorance*:

Science and Conscience.
A Morality for Moralists.
By
Felix Fallax.[159]

34[195][160]

The philosophers 1) had from time immemorial the wondrous capacity for *contradictio in adjecto.*[161]

2) they trusted concepts just as unconditionally as they mistrusted the senses: they did not consider that concepts and words are our inheritance from times when things were very murky and unassuming in our minds.

NB. The last thing to dawn on philosophers: they must no longer allow concepts to only be bestowed on them, not only purify and illuminate them, but first of all *make*, *create* them, posit and persuade people to them. So far on the whole concepts were trusted as if they were a wondrous *dowry* from some wonder-world: but ultimately they were the inheritance of our most distant ancestors, the most stupid as well as the most clever. Perhaps this *piety* toward *what is given in us* belongs — to the *moral* **element** in **knowing**. — What is needed first of all is absolute skepticism toward all concepts handed down (as it *possibly* was possessed already by a single philosopher — Plato: naturally ⟨he⟩ *taught the opposite* — —)

34[196]

Here a philosophy — one of my philosophies — speaks up, which absolutely does not want to be called "love of wisdom" but, perhaps out of pride, asks for a more modest name: even an offensive name that for its own part might contribute to its remaining what it wants to be: a philosophy for me – with the motto: *satis sunt mihi pauci, satis est unus, satis est nullus.*[162] — For this philosophy calls itself: the *art of mistrust* and inscribes above the door to its house: μέμνησ' ἀπιστεῖν.[163]

34[197]

Based on the misery of woman you demonstrate that her situation must be improved: but I wish you would do this on the basis of her better situation and strength

34[198]

The great virtues, responsibility.

"The good" as a background of the democratic socialist movement.

34[199][164]

1) Zarathustra captured —
   Prosecutor's speech charging him with being a seducer
   great contrast between tremendous uncertainty and the small human being
   Zarathustra praises the escapees (great *crisis* in him)
   he persuades the fathers to a festival of memory
   All aristocrats from all ends of the earth stream to that place
   In the end the children themselves come.[165]
2) the order of rank of human beings: he divides the people streaming in according to groups, in this way he simultaneously

distinguishes the degrees of education of human beings (by generations)

3) Before the smallest selection: the lawgivers of the future, with the *great virtues* (responsibility), the hammer.

4) the farewell: recurrence as the religion of religions: comforting.

Zarathustra captured, criticizes the situation of the escapees.
people stream to him (immediately dividing his public)
in the end the swarm comes.[166]

Order of rank as stages in the education of human beings (through many generations)

the highest lawgivers, with the hammer.
Presentation of the *great virtues.*

the farewell.

34[200]

The philosopher requires many foreground virtues and especially pompous words: such as truthfulness, honesty, love of truth.

34[201][167]

The Lawgiver of the Future.
Human Order of Rank.

Beyond Good and Evil.

The Philosopher as Artist.

Dionysus.

34[202][168]

The Rulers of the Earth.
Thoughts on Today and Tomorrow.
By
Friedrich Nietzsche.

34[203]

The state of Europe in the next century will again cultivate the manly virtues: because people will live in constant danger. "Universal military duty" is today already the strange antidote to the softness of democratic ideas: emerged from the struggle of nations (nation — people who speak one language and read the same newspapers today call themselves "nations" and also want much too eagerly to be of common ancestry and history: but which has not succeeded even with the most brazen falsification of the past.)

34[204]

My friends, what has occupied me for many years? I have endeavored to think pessimism to the depths, a⟨nd⟩ to free it from the half Christian, half German narrow-mindedness and simplicity in which it first appeared to me in ⟨the⟩ philosophy of Schopenhauer: so that the human being of this way of thinking is also equal to the highest expression of pessimism. I likewise sought an opposite ideal — a way of thinking that is the most exuberant lively and world-affirming of all possible ways of thinking: I found it in thinking the mechanistic world-view to the end; it truly takes the very best humor in the world to tolerate such a world of eternal recurrence as I have taught through my son Z⟨arathustra⟩ — hence we ourselves included in an eternal *da capo*.[169] In the end I decided that for me the most world-denying of all possible ways of thinking is the one that denounces becoming, originating and passing away as bad in themselves and that affirms only the unconditional, the one, the certain, being: I found that *God* is the most annihilating and life-inimical of all thoughts, and that the knowledge of this "truth" has had to wait so long due only to the tremendous obscurity of the good-old pious ones and metaphysicians of all ages.

Forgive me that I myself am in no way willing to forgo one of these two ways of thinking – for I would then have to forgo my task, which requires opposing means. For the destruction or for the delaying and deepening of people and peoples, occasionally (in some cases for a couple of millennia) a pessimistic way of thinking is of the highest value; and whoever lays major claim to being a creator will also have to claim to be an annihilator and in some cases will have to teach annihilating ways of thinking. In this sense I welcome existing Christianity and Buddhism, the two most comprehensive forms of contemporary world-negation; and, in order to give the death-thrust to degenerating and dying-out races e.g., the Indians, and the Europeans of today, I myself would defend the invention of an even stricter, genuinely nihilistic religion or philosophy.

After what I said previously I certainly leave no doubt as to which meaning I would ascribe to the idea of "God" in such a religion. The best nihilists among the philosophers so far were the Eleatics. Their god is the best and most thorough portrayal of Buddhistic nirvana; being and nothing are identical here.

34[205][170]

As concerns Richard Wagner: I did not overcome my disappointment of summer 1876, the amount of imperfection, in the works and in the man, was too big for me all of a sudden; — I ran away. Later I understood that the most thorough separation from an artist is that one has *viewed* his *ideal*. After such a glance as I had in my younger years — proof of which is my surviving little treatise[171] on Richard Wagner — I had no choice, gritting my teeth and beside myself, but to take leave of this intolerable "reality" — as I saw it all of a sudden. — That he changed in his old age does not concern me: nearly all romantics of this kind end up under the cross — I loved only the Wagner whom I knew, i.e., a righteous atheist and immoralist who had invented the character of Siegfried, a very free human being. Since then he gave everyone to understand, from the modest nook of his *Bayreuther Blätter*,[172] how highly he was able to prize the blood of the redeemer, and — they understood him. Only since then have many Germans, many clean and unclean fools of all kinds, believed in R⟨ichard⟩ W⟨agner⟩ as their "redeemer." All of this offends my taste. —

It goes without saying that I do not easily cede to anyone the right to make this my valuation into his own; and the whole disrespectful rabble that swarms like lice on the body of today's society should not even be allowed to utter such a great name as R⟨ichard⟩ W⟨agner⟩'s, neither in praise nor in contradiction.

34[206][173]

Century of fairs:[174]

34[207][175]

The lawgiver of the future.
Europe's characteristic as decaying. Fairgrounds.
The great millennia-long ebb in the invention of values.

My occasional encouragement through music: what I understood by "Dionysian." R⟨ichard⟩ W⟨agner⟩.
The separation from morality.

Think pessimism to the end and likewise optimism.

The Germans.	Hartmann
	Dühring
	Bismarck
	R⟨ichard⟩ W⟨agner⟩

34[208]

NB. "The struggle for existence" – this characterizes an exceptional state. The rule on the contrary is the struggle for *power*, for "More" and "Better" and "Faster" and "More Frequently."

34[209][176]

this our world of today, our age of the great boom-boom, which with its fairgrounds-taste[177] allows the enormous, the noisier to hold sway even in events and ultimately: produces such events

34[210]

Is there a 19th century? Or on the contrary only a diluted dumbed down and terribly stretched out eighteenth? What great things happened, and were created, that did not happen and were not created *before* 1800? Although many a fruit that grew and ripened in the 18th century only fell from the tree in this one. Take the French Revolution and Napoleon out of politics — therewith you take out of philosophy democracy and the — — —, French sensualism and hedonism, along with German-English skepticism — — —

34[211]

The powerful echo of the tragic events of that French generation of the thirties and forties, with which Richard Wagner also allies himself, with correct instincts, that magnificent and pathological kind of insatiable people that Beethoven preluded in notes and Byron in words: the effect of the enormous on p⟨eople⟩ whose nerve- and will-power were already too weak for it

34[212]

— the great silence — in the age of fairs[178]
— the *blessing* of the lawgivers (also "thou shalt be enemies to *yourselves*")
— from the soul of their development: how they want to *escape* their tremendous task.
— analysis of the herd animal. More humans than ever must be sacrificed, for wars
— the great horrific memorial festivals.
— sympathy for the *great* human beings of all ages, let us not climb down!
— since there is no God anymore, loneliness is no longer bearable: the superior human being *must* get to work.
— do you want the body, the senses etc.
— praise of cool reason, as refreshment for people of the labyrinth

— the master of *many* philosophies, powerful for the deepest pessimism and highest world-transfiguration.
— melancholics need cheerfulness.

34[213][179]

Gai saber.
Attempt at a Divine Manner of
Philosophizing.
By
Friedrich Nietzsche.

1. Science and Conscience.
2. Morality for Moralists.
3. Thoughts on Today and Tomorrow.
4. On Order of Rank.

34[214]

Self-Transfiguration.
The Good and the Evil
The 20th Century.

34[215]

Eugen Dühring, festooned with all the virtues and flaws of a stay-at-home scholar and rabble man, to which also belongs the bad taste of all his attitudes.

34[216]

NB. A) There are hours, very bright fun festive hours of good conscience, where we do not know any better way to characterize the whole magnificent babble of previous people of morality than with the words: "higher swindle."

The Reich-foolishness[180]

B) The ignorance in all our praising and blaming, esteeming and judging, loving and hating causes shame: this is the suffering of every deep human being. One step further: and this shame also causes shame: and *finally* — we laugh at ourselves.

34[217]
NB. We are standing right in the midst of discovering that appearance and the closest best probability least deserve faith: everywhere we learn the reverse: e.g., that sexual reproduction in the realm of all living things is only the exceptional case:[181] that at bottom the male of the species is nothing more than a degenerated decaying female:[182] — or that all organs in animal beings originally performed different services than those on the basis of which we call them "organs": generally that everything has originated differently than its ultimate *application* leads us to conjecture. The portrayal of that which *is* still does not teach us anything about its origin: and the history of the origin[183] still does not teach us anything about what is there.[184] Historians of all kinds deceive themselves in this almost to a person: because they proceed from the existing and look backward. But the existing is something *new* and not at all *something deducible*: no chemist could predict what would *become* of 2 elements in their combination if he did not already *know* it!

34[218][185]
NB. It is not at all possible that a human being might not have the qualities of his parents and ancestors: whatever appearance may say to the contrary. Supposing we know a bit about the parents, then an *inference* regarding the child is permitted: thus e.g., some kind of beastly intemperance, some oafish envy — both together constitute the oafish type — will have to be transmitted to the child as surely as tainted blood, and the child will have trouble concealing such an inheritance. Therefore the talent for acting is greater in people of lower descent than in the noble: and likewise the tartuffery of "virtue."

34[219]
To those superficial and oafish scholars who are shameless enough to feel themselves to be "free spirits," everything that belongs to the medical case history of superior human beings:

that subjugation of oneself, fear of oneself — — — is cowardice or betrayal of the truth, weakness of the will

34[220]

To *reconcile* Christian feelings with Greek beauty and possibly even with modern parliamentarianism — that may perhaps call itself "philosophy" in Rome today. — For this much subtlety of mind is needed and on the other hand much more fanaticism.

34[221][186]

The best that Germany has given, *critical rigor* – Kant, F. A. Wolf, Lessing, Niebuhr etc. Warding off of skepticism — rigor and robust courage, certainty of the hand that wields the scalpel, joy in No-saying and dissecting. *Countermovement*: romanticism, with Richard Wagner as the last romantic synthetic, — — —

34[222]

NB. The diversity of human beings is so great.

The judgments I have heard throughout my life about people I knew were usually so far from what I personally considered true that finally I created a maxim for my domestic use: "it is indiscreet *not* to lie about people." It is especially annoying to me that something on whose account I like s⟨omeone⟩ would also immediately cause damage to his "reputation" as soon as I attempt to give it a name.

34[223][187]

NB. Principle: there is something like decline in everything that indicates modern human beings: but right beside the illness are the symptoms of an untested strength and mightiness of the soul. *The same reasons that produce the diminution of the majority drive the stronger and rarer upward to greatness.*

34[224]

Oh to hell with this croaking! The Germans are boasting again of their famous "German virtue," of which history knows absolutely nothing. The worst is perpetrated by a few anti-Semites, including whatever remains sitting in the swamp of the Bayreuth master.[188]

34[225]

Motto: I have no time for myself — forward!

34[226]

NB. *Sphinx.*

Reduction to the judgment: "this is not true." The imperative follows: "consequently you *may* not hold it to be true!" Or does it really mean: "consequently you *can* no longer hold it to be true"? — Now we constantly e.g., see the sunrise and sunset and believe what we know to be untrue. It is entirely this way everywhere. A "you may not" would be an imperative that denies life. Consequently one must deceive and allow oneself to be deceived.

34[227]

That R⟨ichard⟩ W⟨agner⟩ who is revered today in Germany and revered with all the boastful junk of the worst Teutonomania: that R⟨ichard⟩ W⟨agner⟩ I do not know, indeed — if I were to express my hunch — that one never existed: it is a phantom.

34[228]

To the bad taste of today's G⟨erman⟩ I count: the virtuous Teutonomania that has history against it and *ought* to have shame against it

34[229]

NB. *Fundamental error* of all historians: the *facta* are all much too small to be grasped.

34[230][189]

The Tempter.

There are many kinds of eyes. The sphinx also has eyes: and consequently there are many kinds of "truths," and consequently there is no truth.

34[231]

The subtlest most agile spirituality with a hundred thousand tiny feelers, shaped and blown away by every breath, with the complete splintering of the will — is something *very* ridiculous. As in the fine Parisians who sigh because everything storms in on them.

34[232][190]

When I was young I encountered a dangerous deity and I wish to tell no one what crossed my mind back then — neither the good nor the bad things. Thus in time I learned to be silent, as well as that one must learn to speak in order to properly be silent: that someone with backgrounds needs foregrounds, be it for others, be it for himself: the foregrounds are needed to recover from himself, and in order to make it possible for others to live with us.

34[233]

Signs of an *un*scientific person: he holds an opinion to be true if it flatters him, and he looks good in its light.

34[234]

NB. The counterevidence has still not been produced for whether being good is not a sign of intellectual regression and whether virtue, as emotion and elation, does not belong to the symptoms of incipient idiocy, at least to its attacks. In an overview of history we find intellectual regression wherever the herd animal human being gets the upper hand, and the conditions of life for individual human beings or those who roam in packs are made difficult: we always find the "good" people at the same point of development. In all peoples "stupid to the point of sanctity."[191]

34[235]

NB. Every morality is a habit of self-glorification: by means of which one kind of human being enjoys its kind and its life: it defends against the influence of people of another kind by feeling these others to be "beneath them."

34[236]
NB. That a woman constantly has to have in her head much that is too small and odd and necessarily perceives herself to be comical next to the task of men — excluding ugly women, who are spared many worries in kitchen bed and nursery and nowadays "lay" books as a hen lays eggs — and that it is a boon to all enterprising and profound men to encounter beings who are superficially cheerful and good at pleasant desires, so that life's gloomy appearance is mitigated for them. One has to experience in all its depth what a boon woman is.

34[237]
Anti-Semites and other outright lying rabble that need big words, before themselves even more than before the whole world

34[238]
And better to sit alone on one's mountain like a black half-destroyed fortress, pensive and silent enough; such that the birds themselves are afraid of this silence:

34[239][192]
That it is moral *to do what our interest demands*, this is what the English try to prove to themselves from Bentham on, who adopted it from Helvétius. And that alone is supposed to be morality, and toward that goal morality is supposed to have originated. Which, historically, is entirely nonsensical: and even now taste is opposed to it. Conversely: earlier all philos⟨ophers⟩ tried to prove that *neminem laede, immo omnes quantum potes juva*[193] was the foundation of ethics, which for thousands of years people have sought like the philosopher's stone. — The English try to persuade themselves that the actual behavior of humans is *moral*. That the *herd instinct* is morality itself and alone, formerly — —

Important NB. – from Helvétius on!

34[240]

The Problem "Human Being."
By
Friedrich Nietzsche.

1. The Wrong Path of Philosophers.
2. The Wrong Path of the Preachers of Morality.
3. The Order of Rank of Human Beings.
   according to what? how much they have the strength to bear the terrible natural fact human being and nevertheless —
4. The Problem — where to? A new terrorism is needed.

34[241]

NB. How many false *interpretations* of things there have already been! Consider what all people who *pray* must think about the connection between cause and effect: for no one will persuade us to expunge the element "prithee"[194] from the prayer and the belief that it makes *sense* to request something, that it could be "heard." Or that other interpretation in which someone's fate is "sent"[195] to him for his improvement, admonishment, punishment, warning; or that third interpretation that in the course of things themselves there is right and righteousness,[196] and behind all causal events a kind of criminalistic ulterior motive. — Thus the entire *moral⟨istic⟩* interpretation *of our behavior* could be only a tremendous misunderstanding: as quite obviously the moral⟨istic⟩ interpretation of all natural events has been.

34[242]

An upright sensible kind-hearted capable h⟨uman being⟩, a man with his "heart in the right place" — it does us good to be in his proximity. But why should this *undangerous* h⟨uman being⟩, who does us good, be of more value to us than the dangerous, unrecognizable, unpredictable one who forces us to be on our guard? Our sense of well-being proves nothing. Question: whether among the *great* h⟨uman beings⟩ there was ever one of the undangerous kind described above?

34[243]
NB. The human being of highest intelligence and strength feels himself equal to every chance, but also entirely in the midst of the snowflakes of chance; he denies the reasonableness of every succession and scornfully sheds light on its accidental qualities. — Formerly people believed only in purposes: it is the switching of one error for another that people today believe only in *causae efficientes*.[197] There are neither *causae finales*[198] nor *causae efficientes*: in both we have made a false conclusion from a false self-observation: 1) we believe we are active through willing 2) we at least believe ourselves to be *acting*. Of course: without this belief there would be no living thing: but must it therefore — be *true*?

34[244]
NB. "*Cognition*"[199] is the way to bring us to the point of feeling that we *already know*[200] something: hence the *struggle against a feeling of something new and transformation of the apparently new into something old.*

34[245]
"criminals of the highest order are just as close to the Capitol as to the Tarpeian Rock"[201] I believe was said by Mirabeau.[202]

34[246]
Life as a waking *dream*; the subtler and more extensive someone is, the more he feels the coincidence, equally as horrific as it is sublime, in his life, will, success, happiness, intention: he shudders like the dreamer who feels for a moment "I am dreaming." Belief in the causal necessity of things rests on the belief that *we* are acting; if one acknowledges the unverifiability of the latter, then one loses somewhat faith in the former. Add to this that "appearances" cannot possibly be causes. To trace an unaccustomed thing back to already accustomed things, to lose the feeling of strangeness — our emotions *regard* this as *explaining*. We do not want to "discern" at all, but instead not be disturbed in the belief that we already *know*.[203]

34[247]

Something can be irrefutable: it is not yet true on that account.

The whole of the organic world is a stringing together of beings with made-up[204] little worlds around them: inasmuch as they posit their strength, their desires, their habits out of themselves and into their experiences, as their *external world.* The ability to create (shape invent make up) is their fundamental ability: naturally they have only this false made-up simplified conception of themselves as well.

"A being with the habit for a kind of regulated dreaming" — that is a living being. In the end tremendous quantities of such habits have become so hardened that *species* live on their account. They probably stand in a favorable relation to the conditions of existence of such beings.

Our world as *illusion, error*[205] — but how are illusion and error possible? (Truth does not represent an opposite of error, but the position of certain errors to other errors, perhaps that they are older, more deeply incorporated, that we cannot live without them and so on.)

The creative aspect of every organic being, what is it?

— that everything that is the "external world" for everyone represents a sum of valuations, that green, blue, red, hard, soft are inherited *valuations and their markers.*

— that valuations must stand in some relation to the conditions of existence, but by no means such that they would be *true* or *precise.* The essential thing is their very impreciseness indefiniteness, by which a kind of *simplification of the external world* comes to pass — and precisely this sort of intelligence is favorable to preservation.

— that it is the will to power that also guides the inorganic world, or rather that there is no inorganic world. The "effect at a distance" cannot be set aside: *something pulls something else to itself, something feels itself pulled.* This is the fundamental fact: on the other hand the mechanistic notion of pressure and thrust is only a hypothesis on the basis of *appearance* and the *sense of touch*, although it may serve us as a regulative hypothesis for the world of appearance!

— that in order for this will to power to be able to express itself, it must perceive those things it pulls, that it *feels* when something assimilable by it approaches it.

— the alleged "laws of nature" are formulas for "power relationships" of — — —

The mechanistic way of thinking is a foreground philosophy. It trains people to determine formulas, it is accompanied by a great relief,

— the different philosophical systems can be regarded as *training methods* of the spirit: they have always best *educated* a particular strength of the spirit; with their one-sided demand to see things precisely so and not otherwise.

34[248][206]

Dionysus.

Dionysus as Educator.
Dionysus as Deceiver.
Dionysus as Annihilator.
Dionysus as Creator.

34[249]

The model of a complete *fiction* is logic. Here a thinking is *made up* where a thought is posited as the cause of another thought; all affects, all feeling and willing are thought away. This kind of thing does not occur in reality: the latter is unspeakably and differently complicated. By applying that fiction as a *scheme*, hence by *filtering* the actual event during thinking through a simplification mechanism, as it were: we arrive at a *sign hieroglyphics* and *communicability* and *retainability* of logical events. Therefore: to regard intellectual events *as if they corresponded to the scheme of that regulative fiction*: this is the *basic will*. Wherever there is "memory" this basic will was in charge. — In reality there is no logical thinking, and no principle of arithmetic and geometry can be taken from it because no such principle exists.

My view of ignorance and uncertainty is different. My worry is not that something remains unknown: I am *glad* on the contrary that a kind of knowledge *can* exist and admire the complexity that enables this. The means are: the introduction of complete fictions as schemata, according to which we think intellectual events to be simpler than they are. Experience is only possible with the help of memory: memory is only possible by virtue of an abbreviation of an intellectual event into a *sign*.

Hieroglyphics.

Explanation: this is the expression of a new thing by means of the signs of already known things.

34[250]

That we are *acting*[207] beings, forces, is our basic belief. *Free*: means "not thrust and pushed, without **feeling** *of compulsion*." NB. Where we encounter resistance and must yield to it, we feel ourselves *unfree*: where we do not yield to it but compel it to yield to us, *free*. I.e. it is the *feeling of our* **More** *of force* that we describe as "freedom of will": the consciousness that our force *compels*, in relation to a force that is compelled.

34[251]

In willing there is an affect.

34[252]

Knowledge: the enabling of *experience*, by means of tremendously simplifying real events both on the part of effecting forces as well as on the part of our shaping forces: *so that there appear to be similar and identical things. Knowledge is the* **falsification** *of the diverse and innumerable into the same, similar, numerable.* Thus *life* is only possible by virtue of such a *mechanism of falsification*. Thinking is a falsifying reshaping, feeling is a falsifying reshaping, willing is a falsifying reshaping — : in *all* of this lies the force of assimilation: which presupposes a will to make something the same as *us*.

34[253][208]

Truth is the kind of error without which a certain species of living being could not live. Ultimately the value for *life* decides. Very vulgar and virtuous p⟨eople⟩ — — —

34[254][209]

I loved him and no one else. He was someone after my heart, so immoral, atheistic, antinomian, who walked a solitary path and never liked to believe that — — —

34[255]

NB. A new way of thinking — which is always a new way of measuring and presupposes the presence of a new standard, a new scale of sensations, which is always a genuine b⟨elief⟩ — wants to assert itself and with the fire of its first love says to everything that resists it: "that is false." In this struggle it refines itself, learns to defend itself and in order to win needs to trick the opponent out of his weapons and to copy his art. "That is false" originally means "I do not believe in it"; examined more closely "I feel nothing for it, it means nothing to me."

34[256][210]

I have made many not inconsiderable attempts to lure human beings to me to whom I could speak of such rare things: all my writings so far were nets cast: for this I wished to catch human beings with deep rich and exuberant souls.

To whom could I turn? I made my longest attempt on that manifold and mysterious human being whose soul, of all the human beings of this century, had perhaps encountered the most good and bad things, on R⟨ichard⟩ W⟨agner.⟩ Later I thought about "seducing" German virtue — for I have well known how dangerous things are in a German in his twenties. Still later I crafted a language for daring manly heads and manly hearts who might be waiting somewhere in a corner of the earth for my odd things. Finally — but no one will believe what kind of "finally" I ended up with. Enough, I composed "Thus Spoke Zarathustra."

Shall I confess? So far I have found no one, but again and again some odd form of that "raging stupidity" that even wants to be worshipped as *virtue*: my favorite name for it is "the moral tartuffery," I honor it as the vice of our century and am prepared to accompany it with a hundred curses.

34[257][211]

Deep and distant h⟨umans⟩ have their foregrounds: and at times they find it necessary to pretend as if they were only foreground.

34[258][212]

Lonely amidst good friends and loyal neighbors, smiling and amazed by their "raging stupidity," by their intrusive benevolence.

34[259]

Deep and exuberant spirits!

34[260][213]

Struggle as the basis of *commanding and obeying*
The will to power.
as the basic will of all living things
1. in knowledge and philosophy.
2. in ethics and education and politics.
3. in art and religion.

the two most extreme ways of thinking, the mechanistic and the Platonic converge in the *eternal recurrence*: both as ideals[214]

34[261]

The estimation of the inorganic as *inferior* is a narrowness. What is lacking is pain, error. The will to power there is *true* and *painless*.

34[262]

Pure thinking could not think: the unconditional cannot condition.

Pure knowledge is like the thing in itself a *contradictio* ⟨*in adjecto*⟩[215]

34[263]

But if you no longer acknowledge any morality, why do you seek truth? And if being moral drove you to seek truth, why do you *deny* morality, once being moral no longer compels you? Precisely now you *could* allow it to be: a prerogative of the skeptic!

34[264]

By morality I mean a system of valuations that touches on the vital conditions of a being[216]

Are there moral forces and valuations in inquiry?

The criterion of truth is in the intensification of the feeling of power.[217]

"It shall be so and so" stands at the beginning: From this later, often after a lengthy series of generations, a "so it is" develops. Later it is called "truth"; at first it was a will to see something so and so, to call something so and so, to say a Yes to one's own value-creation. —

We compare something to that which we hold to be true according to the method in which we are accustomed to believe.

34[265]

A ⟨moralist⟩ is a thinker who takes morality as a problem i.e., as questionable: in order to do this with any measure of cleanliness, he must be able to think without moral secondary or ulterior motives: *but is an extramoral thinking possible*?

So that we do not fall victim to that famous *niaiserie allemande*[218] that has immortalized the name of Kant (he answered the question —): one has a faculty for it

A being that does not want to be deceived is by no means one that does not want to d⟨eceive⟩: and whoever does not want to deceive usually likes to allow himself to be cheated.

34[266]

Sources of *compassion: imitation* and *cruelty.*

34[267]

Freedom in relation to *deed* as different as to the *work* (the artist to his work, and the woman to her child)

What is essential in creating is the commanding aspect.

34[268]

The criterion of *truth* is not in every "I like it" (in pleasure), but per⟨haps⟩ in *one* variety of pleasure (feeling of power)?

34[269]

My problem: the legislator.

34[270]

The Legislator.

The venerator.
The denier.
The attempter.
The commander.

34[271]

Even the morality of the just is still possible: as "I *want* justice" — but at a steep price. *One* such ideal lives at the expense of another; has no right in itself, no god for itself, laughs at the *Yes's* and *No's* of conscience.

34[272]

One must not speak too loudly if one wants to be heard by refined ears, I also hate noise. One must *not* say many things and say many things differently than one thinks; and I nearly believe that even as a teacher one must always teach the opposite of what one considers to be true. If someone thinks differently today: what does it matter? What does it matter today that paper gets printed for everybody? "Paper for everybody" can still be used for different things than reading: in this it has its justification.

[35 = W I 3a. May–July 1885]

35[1]

A moralist is the opposite of a preacher of morality: namely a thinker who regards morality as questionable, questionmarkable, in sum as a problem. I regret to have to add that the moralist for precisely this reason belongs to the questionable beings himself.

35[2][1]

The historical sense: the ability to quickly guess the order of rank of valuations according to which a people, a society, an individual lives — the relations of these valuations to the conditions of life, the relation of the authority of values to the authority of acting forces (the alleged relationship for the most part even more than the actual): to be able to *reproduce* all of this in oneself constitutes the historical sense.

35[3]

Some of the aesthetic valuations are more fundamental than the moral ones, e.g., the pleasure in what is ordered, surveyable, limited, in repetition — these are the good feelings of all organic beings in relation to the dangerousness of their situation, or to their difficulty in acquiring food. The known gives pleasure, the sight of something that one hopes to *master* with ease gives pleasure etc. The logical, arithmetical and geometrical good feelings form the ground floor of aesthetic valuations: certain conditions of life are felt as so important, and the contradiction of reality against them so frequent and great, that pleasure arises upon perceiving such forms.

35[4][2]

The refinement of cruelty belongs to the sources of *art.*

35[5]

Morality is the doctrine of the order of rank of humans, and consequently also of the significance of their actions and works *for* this order of rank: therefore the doctrine of human valuations concerning everything human. Most philosophers of morality represent only the *present* ruling order of rank; on the one hand lack of historical sense, on the other hand they themselves are dominated by morality that teaches the present as what is eternally valid. The unconditional importance, the blind selfishness with which every morality treats itself wants that there cannot be *many* moralities, it wants no comparison, nor any criticism: but instead unconditional faith in itself. Therefore by nature it is anti-scientific — and already for this reason the perfect moralist would have to be *immoral*, beyond good and evil. — But then is science still *possible*? What is searching for truth, truthfulness, honesty if not something moral? And without these valuations and their corresponding actions: how would science be *possible*? With conscientiousness in knowing[3] gone — where did science go? Is skepticism in morality not a contradiction, insofar as the highest refinement of moral demands is active precisely here: as soon as the skeptic no longer feels these subtle value estimations of the true as binding, he no longer has any reason to doubt and to explore: *therefore the will to know must have a completely different root than truthfulness.* —

35[6]

"*Soul*": for characterizing a system of valuations and *value affects.*

35[7]

When philosophers gather among themselves they start to spew a lot of beautiful junk; above all they no longer call themselves "philosophers" and they hang "love of wisdom" on a nail like a stiff official robe and costume. "*We are* friends of mistrust," so they speak to one another, "*we do not want to be deceived. That we do not want to deceive anyone* — of course this is what people should *believe* about us, we must solemnly *convince* everyone of this. For between you and me: — — —

35[8]

The Strong and the Weak.

Thoughts and Dashes[4]
of a Good European.

35[9][5]

These good Europeans that we are; what distinguishes us from the p⟨erson⟩ of fatherlands?

First: we are atheists and immoralists, but for now we support religions and moralities of the herd instinct: for with them a kind of human is prepared that will one day have to fall into our hands, that will have to *yearn* for our hand.

Beyond good and evil, but we demand that the herd morality be held unconditionally sacrosanct.

We reserve for ourselves many kinds of philosophy that will have to be taught: under certain circumstances the pessimistic, as hammer; a European Buddhism could perhaps not be dispensed with.

We probably support the development and maturation of the democratic character: it trains weakness of the will: we see in "Socialism"[6] — a goad, that {protects} against convenience — — —

Stance toward peoples. Our preferences; we pay attention to the results of interbreeding.

Aloof, well-off, strong: irony toward the "press" and its culture. Concern that the scientific men do not become literati. Our stance is contemptuous of any notion of culture that coexists with reading newspapers, let alone writing them.

We take our incidental positions (like Goethe, Stendhal) our experiences as shelter huts, as a wanderer uses and accepts them — we guard against feeling at home.

We have the advantage of a *disciplina voluntatis*[7] over our fellow human beings. All strength expended on *development of strength of will*, an art that allows us to wear masks, of understanding *beyond* the affects (also thinking in a "supra-European" manner, sometimes)

Preparation for becoming the rulers of the earth; the law-givers of the future. At least from our children. Fundamental consideration for marriages.

35[10][8]

The same conditions that drive the development of the herd animal also drive the development of the leader animal.

35[11]

In the "emancipation of woman" those women who do not get spouses and children want to influence considerably the *overall position* of woman to man i.e., the *failed* elements (who in *numbers* have the upper hand *everywhere*) want to change the position of the species i.e., for the sake of numbers the quality of the species is supposed to be diminished. (Think of only one consequence of this: that now even the *ugly* women *demand* the satisfaction of their drives by men — the unconscious reason driving this movement) Or, in G⟨eorge⟩ Sand, who never had enough men and who quickly tired of those she had.

35[12]

The nonsense of the greatest number as of the greater reason shows its most disastrous side when one considers to what extent everything that is good, turns out well, happy, intelligently spiritual on earth, in sum everything whereby the average failing and miswilling — — —

35[13]

In the end Europe is a woman: and the fable tells us that such a woman under certain circumstances can be dragged away by certain animals. Formerly, in the time of the Greeks, by a bull. Today — heaven protect me from naming the animal.

35[14][9]

What are these good Europeans of whom you speak and remain silent even more than you speak? What distinguishes them from us, the good fatherlanders?

35[15]

For the plan. *Introduction.*

1. organic functions translated back into the basic will, the will to power — and split off from it.
2. thinking, feeling, willing in all living things
   what else is desire than: a stimulation of the feeling of power by an impediment (even more strongly by rhythmic inhibitions and obstacles) — so that it swells up: Therefore in all desire pain is included. — If the desire is supposed to be very great, then the pains have to become very long and the tension of the bow tremendous.
3. the will to power specializing as will to nourishment, to possessions, to *tools*, to servants —
   Obeying and ruling: the body.
   — the stronger will directs the weaker one. There is no other causality at all than that of wills to wills. So far there has not yet been any kind of mechanistic — — —
4. the mental functions: Will to shaping, to assimilating etc.[10]

Appendix. The great misunderstandings of the philosophers.

35[16]

Just once perhaps one is tempted to pose the question, whether all great humans cannot be counted among the evil humans.

35[17]

Humans, in whatever situation they may find themselves, need a kind of valuation by virtue of which they justify i.e., *self-glorify* their actions, intentions and conditions before themselves and especially before their environment. Every natural morality is the expression of satisfaction of a kind of human with himself: and if one ⟨has⟩ need of praise, one also has need always of a *corresponding* table of values in which those actions are valued most highly of which we are most capable, in which our actual *strength* expresses itself. Where our strength is, that is where we also want to be seen and honored.

35[18][11]

Whether we do not have a right to count all *great* humans among the *evil*? Individually it cannot always be demonstrated. Often they have been capable of a masterful hide-and-seek, so that they took on the gestures and appearances of great virtues. Often they honored the virtues earnestly and with a passionate severity against themselves, but out of cruelty — that kind of thing is deceiving, viewed from a distance. Some understood themselves wrongly as they — — — not seldom a great task demands great qualities e.g., justice. The essential thing is: the greatest perhaps also have great virtues, but precisely then their opposites as well. I believe that out of the presence of opposites, and from their feelings, arises precisely the great human, *the bow with great tension.*

35[19]

One has to free oneself from the question: what is good? what is compassionate? — ask rather "what is *the* good person, the compassionate person?"

35[20]

So far in the first instance a morality was the expression of a conservative will to cultivate a same kind, with the imperative:

"All variations should be prevented; the only thing that should remain is enjoyment of our kind." Here a number of qualities are *maintained* and *cultivated* for a long time, and others sacrificed; all such moralities are *harsh* (in their education, in the selection of the female, generally toward the rights of youth etc.) Humans with few but very strong and always the same characteristics are the result. These characteristics stand in relation to the foundations on which such communities are able to persevere and assert themselves against their enemies.

All of a sudden the bond and the compulsion of such a discipline tear (— for the time being there are no more enemies —): the individual no longer has any such limitation, it shoots up wildly, a tremendous destruction stands side by side with a magnificent, multifarious, jungle-like growth. For the new humans in whom now the *most diverse things* are inherited a need arises to make an *individual legislation* for themselves, commensurate with their distinctive conditions and *dangers*. The moral philosophers appear, who usually represent some more frequent type and with their *disciplina* create advantages for a certain kind of human.

35[21]

I have never wasted intellect and effort on questions like: what is good? what is bad? — Each of these philosophers took himself to be a typical human and wanted to assert *himself* against all who were different: they embark on a struggle with this their faith in their ideal. Even their morality is that of *self-satisfaction*, but of the individual's self-satisfaction.

35[22]

We know from the experiences of breeders that species which are provided with an excess of nourishment and every kind of care and protection tend in the strongest manner to variation of the type and are rich in freaks and monstrosities (also in m⟨onstrous⟩ vices). Now just look at an aristocracy as an arrangement for the purpose of breeding: for a long time it is lacking that excess of favorable conditions, it has a difficult time asserting itself at all, it is constantly beset by the danger of maintaining fear. To this end it feels it is essential that a certain kind of qualities (virtues) must be preserved above all and primarily: it *suppresses* all others for the sake of these virtues, it feels these virtues as conditions of existence. Finally a successful situation emerges, the great compulsion is no longer necessary: and immediately, in the greenhouse of its culture, a *tremendous number of variations* and monsters (including geniuses) appear: meanwhile as they struggle the community perishes.

The species-*variations* (as deviance, partial degeneration) emerge where favorable conditions of life exist: but the species itself emerges, becomes *sturdy* and *strong* under the long struggle with always the same unfavorable c⟨onditions⟩.

Concern for the *preservation* of the species, its faithful repetition, its essential uniformity is instilled by love for this species, admiration for it by comparison with its environment, hence *satisfaction* with it: foundation of all aristocracies, one is happy with one's kind and wants to continue *oneself* through the same progeny: but one must be maintained in this position by constantly recurring endangerment, and by comparison with neighboring beings of lower standing. The notion of "progress" and likewise the notion of "equal rights for all" must be lacking: preservation of the species, *enjoyment* of all *typical* qualities and otherwise aversion (also against everything foreign) *to resemble* the ancestors as much as possible serves as the controlling morality: mourning at the thought of change and variation.

But now there are suffering, oppressed, semi-misfit, sick species dissatisfied with themselves: when they too thirst for teachers, consolers and physicians as it were, when they too create a morality: what will they most like to reach and long for? Above all not for the preservation of their suffering species, or its condition. Rather "away *from it*! And preferably anywhere else!" On the whole therefore their morality will behave like a kind of self-negation: its favorite practice will become "selflessness," disgust with themselves, rejection of the egoistic — and their greatest hatred will turn itself against the happy, proud, victorious! Along with this the delights of emotion that lie in devotion, renunciation, in forgetting-oneself, in love: from the doglike tail-wagging of the slave up to the mystical "union with God." In fact just this kind of sufferer and semi-misfit *will be kept alive*, and to a certain extent made *viable*: and insofar as it primarily learns to adapt to one another, a *low* but a viable type emerges. For example the European of today, as well as the Chinese. The *diminution* of humans: but when all their powers are put together, they will become *master* over the noble race: and because the latter themselves are often seduced by their noble instincts into throwing away their harsh existence (also by their happiness-seeking instincts), or are degenerate themselves, so that they no longer believe in themselves, then e.g., such great follies occur as the preludes to the French Revolution. Then a kind of preponderance of the many, consequently of the least kind of human over the select a⟨nd⟩ rare sets in, a democratic fundamental taste of all valuation, in which ultimately belief in great things and humans transforms into mistrust, in the end into disbelief and becomes the cause for the fact that greatness is dying out.

35[23]

The thirst for great and profound souls — and always encountering only the herd animal!

35[24][12]

1) is the "philosopher" today still *possible*? Is the scope of what is known too great? Is the improbability not very great that he will never achieve an *overview*, especially the more conscientious he is? Or *too late*, when his best time has passed? Or damaged, coarsened, degenerated, so that his *value judgment* means nothing anymore? — Otherwise he will become a "*dilettante*" with a thousand little feelers and lose the great pathos, the respect for himself — the good subtle conscience too. Enough, he will no longer lead, he will no longer command. If he wanted

to, then he would have to become a great actor, a kind of philosophical *Cagliostro*.

2) what does *living* philosophically being wise mean to us anymore today? Is it not almost a means of *extricating* oneself well from a bad situation? A kind of escape? And whoever lives aloof and simply in this manner, is it probable that in so doing he has shown his knowledge what is the best way? Must he not have experimented with his life in a 100 ways in order to be able to speak of its value? Enough, we believe that someone would have to have lived completely and totally "unphilosophically," according to previous notions, above all not as a timid virtuous person — in order to judge from *experiences* on the great problems. The human being of the most extensive experiences, who compresses them into universal conclusions: must he not be the most powerful human being? — For too long we have mistaken the wise man for the scientific man, and even longer for the religiously elevated man.

35[25][13]

Problem: many kinds of *great human beings* are perhaps *no longer possible*? E.g., the *saint*. Perhaps also the *philosopher*. Finally the *genius*? Perhaps the tremendous distance-ratios between human and human have diminished? At least the *feeling* of this distance has diminished, and as an effect this carries with it a less brusque demeanor and discipline, by virtue of which humans also no longer elevate themselves, as before. — We need a new concept of the *greatness* of human beings; of which we are capable, and from which most of us are deeply separated. *Voilà*: this democratic world transforms everyone into a specialty, *therefore* today greatness is *being-universal*. It weakens the will, *therefore* strength of will is greatness today. *It* develops the herd animal, therefore standing alone and living according to one's own rules must be counted as greatness today. The most extensive human being, going it alone, without herd instincts, and with an indomitable will allowing him to have many transformations and to submerge himself insatiably into new depths of life. — We must seek the *greatness of humans* where we are least at home. For ages of energy the gentle resigned contemplative human is the great *exception*; it required great inner discipline and hardness to become a Socrates from a half-wild animal. The indifferentism[14] of Epicurus acts almost as a transfiguration. We arrive at opposing *ideals*: and first we have to demolish the old ideals for ourselves.

35[26][15]

Dionysus.
Book of Prophecy.

35[27][16]

Our psychologists, whose focus involuntarily remains stuck only on the symptom of *décadence*, again and again throw suspicion on the intellect.

35[28][17]

New barbarians. One always sees only the weakening tenderizing debilitating effects of the spirit:

but now come:	The cynics.	Combination of intellectual
	The tempters.	superiority with well-being
	The conquerors.	and excess of forces.

35[29]

The Epochists, the Ephectics.

He likes to linger before open problems and is ironic toward hasty hypotheses; he rejects the kind of satisfaction that making-round, making-full, stuffing a hole with some kind of oakum involves. Thus he behaves not on the basis of his weakness but his strength: *he does not perish right away* when he is missing the *support* of those "railings" which e.g., today the pessimists use as their prop. — Basic fact: that in the moral spheres *all science* is still lacking, even more *all material for science.* The practical ulterior-intentions ligate the veins of the researcher. It is time for seeking the widest possible regulative hypotheses, in order to gather material from them.

Therefore actual strict ephexis of science is not yet possible here by a long shot; we are in the *pre-stage*. The sharpening of methodical demands will come later. The sciences by no means develop simultaneously: rather, just as the organs have their faster or slower growth and maturation, so it is here. It is self-evident that the science that will be furthest behind is the one that has been resisted longest, with the belief that *here* we should not be exploring at all. Here the truth exists, here belief in it is our duty — even now the "moral consciousness" itself recoils from time to time in the garb of a kind of "philosophy" against the right of an analysis of morality. And our most recent researchers of morality are thoroughly convinced of precisely this: here science only has to establish the facts, not to *criticize*.

35[30][18]

1. to *see* and *show* the problem of morality — this seems to me the new task and main thing. I deny that this has happened previously in moral philosophy.

35[31][19]

One must not feign scientism where it is not yet time to be scientific; but even the real researcher has to rid himself of the vanity of feigning a kind of method that at bottom is not yet timely. Likewise not to "falsify" things and ideas upon which he has come by other means with a false arrangement[20] of deduction and dialectic. Thus Kant in his "morality" falsifies his innermost psychological inclination; a more recent example is Herbert Spencer's ethics. — One should not conceal and ruin the *fact* of how our thoughts have come to us. The profoundest and most inexhaustible books will probably always have something of the aphoristic and abrupt character of Pascal's *Pensées*. The *driving* forces and valuations have been beneath the surface for a long time; what emerges is effect.

35[32][21]

I resist all tartuffery of scientism:

1) with respect to *demonstration*, if it does not correspond to the *genesis* of the thoughts,

2) in the claims to *methods*, which perhaps are not even possible at a certain time of science,

3) in the claims to *objectivity*, to cold impersonality where, as in all valuation, we speak with every word about ourselves and our inner experiences. There are ridiculous kinds of vanity e.g., Saint-Beuve's, who was bothered his whole life long to have had real warmth and passion here and there in "pro" and "contra" and would have liked to have lied it out of his life.

35[33][22]

(51)

Today people like to put on the *veneer* of a very colorful and multiform affectation of scientism—understandable in such a fake century, where "equal rights" also attract "the feeling of equal demands"[23] e.g., the demand to be able to be scientific if only one *wants* to. Almost all literati believe it of themselves; even more, it is now part of the ambition of novelists.

35[34]

Nothing more lamentable than the moralistic literature in today's Europe. The utilitarian English at the forefront, plodding clumsily as cattle in the footsteps of Bentham, just as he himself plodded in the footsteps of Helvétius; no new thought, not even a real history of what had been previously thought, but always the same old moral tartuffery, the English vice of cant[24] beneath the new form of scientism alongside the secret warding-off of stings of conscience as they tend to afflict a race of former Puritans. —They want to *convince* themselves at any price that one *must* pursue one's own advantage, insofar as precisely in this manner the general advantage, the happiness of the greatest number would be best served: therefore that the striving for English "happiness," I mean for comfort[25] and fashion[26] is on the right path to virtue:

indeed that, as far as there has been virtue in the world, it consisted in their kind of striving for their own happiness consequently also general happiness: none of all these ponderous, conscience-troubled herd animals — for that is what all of them are —wants to know anything of the fact that there is an order of rank of human beings, consequently that one morality for all is an impairment of the highest human being, that what is fair for one absolutely cannot be fair for another; that on the contrary the "happiness of greatest number" is a nauseating ideal for anyone ⟨who⟩ has the distinction of not belonging to the greatest number. — From France recently Comte's superficial juxtaposition of altruism and egoism — but there is no altruism at all! — has made its way to England; and now we see e.g., in Herbert Spencer the attempt to reconcile again with this too, but with such bad will toward taking any concept seriously anymore that henceforth in England even **urinating** would count among the altruistic activities. In Germany — where they do not even know what to do with the moral naïveté of Schopenhauer, E. von H⟨artmann⟩ recently held forth on the Comtean idea — held forth to the tune of 871 pages[27] — ; and, without a single German bursting into laughter, solemnly and formally threw egoism out the door at the front, only to welcome it again in the name of "altruism" at the back. Indeed, there is no better way to visualize the uncanny fact of an almost sudden dumbing down of Europe's peoples — visible in today's Germany and England as well as in France and Italy — than by leafing through their moralistic books. At best I could highlight 3 small texts as exceptions (although even in these nothing fundamental is said):

One is the book of a German Jew, Paul Rée, which bears the title[28] — On account of its *form* it deserves distinction and carries something of that genuine philosophical habitus to which Stendhal once gave a sharp formulation:[29] — — — Rée adopts once more, with a subtle hand, the more rigorous habits of taste of the old French moralists — his book comes like a refreshing aroma from that "good old time," far from all the edifying ulterior motives of which morality books written in German tend to smell — : unfortunately he also has the same defects as those French, the narrow horizon, the wretchedness of knowledge; his hypotheses are cheap and a waste of breath; he completely lacks "the historical gaze and tact," that is to say, the actual and single virtue that German science of the 19th century has over all older sciences. In the end it is a book that "stimulates the appetite."

Secondly I name the subtle, melancholy-robust book of a Frenchman[30] — — — , which, to be sure, like nearly everything that comes from Paris makes it all too plain *where* pessimism is really at home today: (namely *not* in Germany) And what good is all positivism and resolute kneeling before the "*petits faits*"![31] In Paris they suffer as if from cold autumn winds, as if from a frost of great disappointments, as if winter were coming, the final, ultimate winter — and the best and the bravest, like that fine fellow Guyau, ⟨tremble and shudder the while, even when they put on such a brave face with their "*positivisme*":[32] who believes that to which they want to persuade us with irony, that that trembling and shuddering even belong to the *charms* and seductive arts of life? To be sure: "shuddering is the *finest* portion of humanity"[33] — Goethe said that, and Goethe — *was allowed* to say it! But a Parisian? — Finally I single out the polemic book of a German half-Englishman, which contains enough spirit, acid and science to thoroughly "break down" that combination of *bêtise*[34] and Darwinism that Herbert Spencer put into the world under the title *Data of Ethics*: Rolph, *Biologische Probleme* 1881.[35] To be sure, apart from the polemics there is nothing to praise in this book; and at bottom what offends us here, just as in the book that it contests, is the chiming-in of insignificant people on areas where only a select kind of knower and "experienced one" speaks without immodesty.⟩[36]

35[35][37]

What separates me most thoroughly from the metaphysicians is: I do not grant them that the "I" is what thinks: on the contrary I take the *I itself as a construction of thinking*, of the same rank as "material," "thing," "substance," "individual," "purpose," "number": therefore only as *regulative fiction* with whose help a kind of constancy, consequently "knowability" is posited into, *fictionalized into* a world of becoming. The belief in grammar, in the linguistic subject, object, in verbs has so far subjugated the metaphysicians: I taught that this belief should be abjured. The I is first posited by thinking: but up till now it was believed, as the people believe, that in "*I* think" there existed something of direct certainty and this "I" was the given cause of thinking, by analogy with which we "understood" all remaining causal relations. However habitual and indispensable that fiction may be now, this offers no proof against its fictitiousness: something can be a condition of life and be *false nevertheless*.

35[36]

Having freed myself from the tyranny of "eternal" concepts, I am on the other hand far from therefore plunging myself into an abyss of skeptical arbitrariness: on the contrary I ask that concepts be regarded as experiments with whose help certain kinds of humans {can be} cultivated and for their preservability and duration — — —

35[37][38]

The falseness of a concept is for me not yet an *objection* to it. Perhaps our new language sounds strangest in this respect: the question is, how far is it life-promoting, life-preserving, species-preserving. I am even fundamentally of the belief *that the falsest assumptions are* precisely *the most indispensable to us*, that without an acceptance of logical fiction, without measuring reality against the *invented* world of the absolute, self-identical, human beings cannot live, and that a renunciation of this fiction, a practical dispensing with it, would amount to the same thing as a renunciation of life. *To admit untruth as a condition of life*: this truly means to rid oneself in a terrible way of the accustomed value emotions — and here, if anywhere, what matters is not "bleeding to death" from the "known truth." In this supreme danger one must immediately summon the creative basic instincts of humans, which are stronger than all value emotions: those which are the mothers of value emotions themselves and enjoy their sublime consolation in eternal birthing over the eternal perishing of their children. And finally: *what power was it* that forced us to abjure that "belief in truth," if not life itself and all its creative basic instincts? — so that we therefore do not need to conjure up these "mothers": — they are already *up here*, their eyes look at us, we simply execute that to which their magic has persuaded us.[39]

35[38][40]

— And as concerns act⟨ual⟩ philos⟨ophy⟩ in France today: no one should believe that these stout positivists that is to say empiricists from the school of Comte, or the successors of Stendhal Montesquieu Condillac — heirs of the best that the 18th century had — like Taine, constitute a contrast to the skeptical mood of the century.

35[39][41]

Noon and Eternity.

1. On the Order of Rank.
2. The Legislators. (Cultivation of new ruling castes)
3. On the Ring of Rings. Or: "The Mirror."
4. The Great Blessings.

35[40][42]

Noon and Eternity.
Visions and Prophecies.

35[41][43]

Noon and Eternity.
Prophecies
of a Man of the Future.

Part One:
On the Order of Rank.

Part Two:
On the Rulers of the Earth.

Part Three:
On the Ring of Rings.

Part Four:
On the New Dying.

35[42][44]

— until we, too, are capable of calling out with sufficient pride the words that Pericles called out to his Athenians in that funeral oration: to every land and sea our boldness has broken a path, everywhere founding timeless memorials for things good and wicked.

35[43][45]

In the end let us guard against the knowledge of human nature of these Sainte-Beuves and Renans, against this kind of sounding-out and sniffing-out of the soul as it is practiced by these unmanly and spineless hedonists of the spirit: it seems shameful to us when they fumble around with curious fingers on the secrets of humans or ages that were higher, stricter, deeper and in every respect nobler than they themselves: such that they would not have readily opened their doors to any such roaming half-women. But this nineteenth century, which has sacrificed all the finer instincts of order of rank, no longer knows how to rap the fingers of these unwanted interlopers and gate crashers; indeed, it is proud of its "historical sense," by virtue of which the sweating plebeian is allowed, providing he comes with scholarly instruments of torture and questionnaires, to penetrate even into the company of the supremely unapproachable, among the saints of conscience as well as among the eternally disguised rulers of the spirit. More skepticism lies hidden beneath its historical sense and knowing than one sees at first: an insulting skepticism aimed at the difference in rank between human beings, and the same shameless demand for "equality" is even extended to include the dead, whom the paid servants of public opinion now presume to use against any of the living.

But we are no skeptics — we still believe in an order of rank of human beings and problems and wait for the hour when this doctrine of rank and of order will once again inscribe itself plainly on the faces of this rabble-like society of today. Perhaps this hour is also our hour.

Is it possible, if we are not skeptics, that we are critics or "criticists"? And if in our name we particularly underscored experiment and the joy in experimenting, does this perhaps occur because we love to avail ourselves of experiments in a broad and dangerous sense, but for the sake of a more deeply understood critique? Are we perhaps secretly, to the best of our knowledge, compelled to go further as experimenters than the soft-hearted and coddled taste of our century can condone? Indeed, we do not wish to forgo all those qualities that separate the critic from the skeptic: the certainty of value standard, the conscious application of a unity of method, cunning courage, standing alone and being able to answer to oneself; indeed we confess to a joy in no-saying and dissecting, a certain cruelty of the hand that steadily wields the scalpel even if it is the heart that bleeds. We are harder — and perhaps not only toward ourselves — than "humane" people may wish; we do not get mixed up with "truth" because it "pleases" or "elevates" or "inspires" us — on the contrary our faith is small that truth could ever bring with it such pleasant feelings. It sounds awkward to many ears when we say: our suspicion is aroused precisely where our emotion rises up in beautiful surges; we smile if someone believes anything is *proved* by saying: "but this thought elevates me: how could it not be true?" Or: "this work delights me: how could it not be beautiful?" Or: "this artist enlarges me: how could he not be great?"[46] On the contrary with critics we have —

35[44][47]

Superstition about the philosopher, confusion with the scien⟨tific⟩ person. As if values inhered in things and one only needed to determine them. To what extent they explore among *given* values (their hatred of appearance, body etc.) Schopenhauer with respect to morality. (Scorn for the utilitarian) In the end the confusion goes so far that Darwinism is regarded as philosophy: and now dominance is held by the *scientific* people.

Even the French like Taine seek or think they seek without already having the value standards. Bowing down before the "facts," a kind of cult. In fact they *annihilate* the existing valuations.

Explanation of this misunderstanding. The commander emerges rarely, he misinterprets himself. One thoroughly *wants* to divert authority from oneself and posit it into *circumstances.* — In Germany appreciation for the critic belongs to the history of awakening *manliness*. Lessing etc. (Napoleon regarding Goethe) In fact this movement was cancelled out again by German romanticism: and the *reputation* of German philosophy hinges on it, as if the danger of skepticism were eliminated by it, and *faith* could be *proven*. Both tendencies culminate in Hegel: at bottom he generalized the fact of German criticism and the fact of German romanticism — a kind of dialectic fatalism, but in honor of the spirit, actually with the submission of the philosopher *under* reality. — *The critic prepares the way*: nothing more!

With Schopenhauer the task of the philos⟨opher⟩ dawns, that what is at stake is a determination of *value*: always still under the domination of eudaemonism (scorn for Hartmann) the ideal of pessimism.

35[45]

The philosopher as legislator, as attempter of new possibilities, his means. He *uses* religion. The New Testament — what Christianity *can do.*

His opposite: the morality of the herd animal.

Likewise the freethinkers etc.

How the herd animals today imagine the "Superior Human": to be demonstrated using V. Hugo.

Those who prepared the way for me: Schopenhauer.

the extent to which I deepened pessimism and first made it entirely palpable to myself by inventing its highest opposite.

Then: the ideal artists, those offspring from the Napoleonic movement.

Then: the higher *Europeans*, forerunners of the *great politics*.

Then: the Greeks and their emergence.[48] I gave hints in the *Birth of Tragedy* about the relationship between "necessity" and "art."

The *Germans* and the *spirit*.

The personal education of the philosopher: solitude.

The Dionysian.

35[46]

Paete, non dolet![49] Paete, this pessimism does not hurt! Paete, Eduard does not bite! Paete, look at me: am I not friendly blue, yes even Prussian blue; Paete, indeed, I leave nothing at all to be desired

Paete, non dolet! Paete, this pessimism does not hurt! Paete, your Arria does not bite! Paete: Eduard is full of knowledge, cozy, humane, friendly, even friendly to the empire, even Prussian blue, in sum Eduard is a girl Friday and his pessimism leaves nothing at all to be desired

I was in error back then: I thought E⟨duard⟩ v⟨on⟩ H⟨artmann⟩ was a subtle superior mind and joker who was making fun of the pessimistic embarrassment of the age; I found the invention of his "unconscious" so malicious, so witty, it seemed to me a real mousetrap for the doleful and dumb of philosophical dilettantism as it spreads more and more across Germany. But now they insist on assuring me that he means it *seriously*: and they are practically forcing me to believe in it: but is it supposed to stop being entertaining for me? Am I supposed to have to stop laughing when this Arria again and again tries to encourage her Paetus not to be *afraid* of the *dagger*, I mean of Hartmannian pessimism? *Paete*, she calls tenderly, *non dolet!*

35[47]

§ No critics. Embarrassment. Finally "the scientific human being." *The English.*

§ Neither pessimists nor optimists. Schopenhauer's great position — that the destruction of an illusion still does not yield truth, but one *more piece of ignorance*, an expansion of our "empty space," a growth of our inner "desolation" —[50]

§ Basic thought: the new values must first be created — we are not *spared* this! The philosopher must be like a legislator. New types. (How the highest types (e.g., the Greeks) were cultivated so far: to *consciously* **will** this kind of "chance")[51]

§ His means: Religions, moralities

§ Meaning of Christianity.

§ Meaning of the democratic way of thinking.

§ Freethinkers, included in this movement? Victor Hugo.

§ Unconscious counter-movements: Napoleon, the 30s, R⟨ichard⟩ W⟨agner⟩.

§ The new philosopher can only emerge in connection with a ruling caste, as their highest spiritualization. Great politics, rule of the earth are near; complete *lack* of *principles* for this[52] — (irony toward the *empty* German spirit)

§ The European and his education.

§ Period of grand *experiments.* Humans with their own canon of values. Institutions for the cultivation of superior humans.

§ The "for the time being" of philosophers. Their solitude.

§ Prepare the "Beyond Good and Evil." State of "morality."

15 § Dionysus.

15: 110 | 6

3 big pages for each section

35[48][53]

Preface.

It matters little to me today whether I was right or wrong with respect to R⟨ichard⟩ W⟨agner⟩ and Schopenhauer: if I erred, well, my error accrues to the dishonor neither of those mentioned nor myself. What is certain is that in those early days it was a tremendous boon to me to be able to paint my idealist colors, in which I viewed the images ⟨of the⟩ philosopher and ⟨the⟩ artist, not entirely upon the unreal but as it were upon previously sketched figures; and if I was accused of having looked at the aforementioned with a *magnifying* eye, then I am *glad* to be so accused — and glad, too, for my eyes. At least the reader of the second *Unfashionable Observation* should not be in doubt as to how little I was always concerned about the truth and — — —

What I wrote at that time — and wrote less than *painted*, and on top of that heatedly and, as it seems to me today, in a daring and not unobjectionable alfresco: this would not become *more true* if I portrayed it again more gently, colorfully and rigorously now that my hand and eye have perhaps learned something in the meantime. Each period of life understands "truth" in its own way; and whoever steps up to that painting with youthful and stormy senses and great demands will find as much truth in it as he is capable of seeing.

My first four *U⟨nfashionable⟩ O⟨bservations⟩*, to which I now add a fifth, sixth and seventh after ten years, were attempts to lure to myself the kind of humans who belong to me: thus fishhooks cast to hook "my kind." Back then I was young enough to go fishing in such a way with impatient hope. Today — after a hundred years if I may measure time according to my standard! — I am *still not old enough* to have lost all hope, all patience. How strange it sounds to my ears even today when an old man compresses his experience into these words: — — —

Thus speaks Goethe: could he be right? Then how unreasonable it would be to grow as old a⟨nd⟩ as reasonable as Goethe!

And it would be fair like the Greeks to heed their judgment concerning old age: — they hated growing old more than death, and loved to die when they felt themselves becoming reasonable in that manner. Meanwhile youth, too, has its own kind of reason: a reason that believes in life, love and hope

35[49][54]

As concerns R⟨ichard⟩ W⟨agner⟩: there was a moment in my life when I vehemently pushed him away from me. Away from me! — is what I cried. This kind of artist is untrustworthy precisely where I tolerate no joking. He tried to come to an "arrangement" with existing Christianity by extending his left hand to Protestant communion — he spoke to me of the delights he was able to experience from this communion — but at the same time his right hand to the Catholic Church: he offered it his *Parsifal* and let himself be known as a "creature of Rome" *in partibus infidelium*[55] by all who had ears.

35[50]

The laws of thinking as results of organic development — a fake positing force must be assumed — likewise inheritance and continuation of the fictions.

35[51]

In a world of becoming in which everything is conditioned, the acceptance of the unconditional, of substance, of being, of a thing etc. can only be an error. But how is error possible?

35[52]

To show succession ever more clearly means *explanation*: nothing more!

35[53]

To concede *perception* even for the inorganic world and moreover with absolute accuracy: there "*truth*" reigns! With the organic world begin *indefiniteness* and *illusion*.

35[54][56]

That a state of equilibrium is never achieved proves that it is not possible. But in an indefinite space it must have been achieved. Likewise in a spherical space. The **shape** *of space* must be the cause of eternal motion and ultimately of all "imperfection."

That "force" and "inertia" "remaining self-identical" are in conflict with one another. The extent of force as magnitude as fixed, but its essence fluid, tense, compelling, — — —

35[55][57]

"Timeless" to be refuted. In a specific moment of force the absolute conditionality of a new distribution of all its forces is given: it cannot stand still. "Change" belongs to its essence, therefore also temporality: but by this only the necessity of change is once again conceptually posited.

35[56][58]

Time is *not* a priori given. Spir 2, p. 7.

illogical character of our knowledge of bodies, cf. 2 p. 93.

35[57][59]

That there are identical things, identical cases, is the *basic fiction* already when making a *judgment*, then when making an inference.

35[58]

In the chemical world reigns the sharpest *perception* of difference in force. But a protoplasm, *as a multiplicity of chemical forces*, has an *uncertain and indefinite* overall-perception of a foreign object.

35[59]

The transition from the world of the inorganic into that of the organic is that from the firmest perceptions of force values and power ratios into that of *uncertain, indefinite* ones. because a multiplicity of warring beings (= protoplasm) feels itself in opposition to the external world.

35[60]

The restless will to power or to constant creation or to transformation or to self-overpowering

35[61][60]

"so-called time a mere abstraction, neither existing objectively nor a necessary and original representational mode of the subject" ⟨Spir⟩ 2, p. 15.

35[62]

The Germans have no culture: they are *dependent* on Paris now as before — the cause is they still have no character.

Our great human beings do not constitute a race, but individuals.

But what is it that I formerly set aside and on which I founded my hopes, *German music*?

35[63]

NB. Misunderstanding about Richard Wagner is enormous in Germany today: a⟨nd⟩ since I have contributed to increasing it, I want to pay my debt and attempt to decrease it

35[64]

NB. For two centuries there was only one contrast between French and Ital⟨ian⟩ music.

In the struggle between Gluck and Piccini it sharpened and came to a head: here Gluck was perceived entirely as a representative of *French taste* — as a representative of the noble, pompous and rationalistic.

The Germans as musicians listened in turn in the direction of France and Italy: even today the Germans do not yet have their own taste in music

It seems to me that Wagner once again brought *French taste* to predominance over Italian, i.e., over Mozart, Haydn, Rossini, Bellini, Mendelssohn, but it is the taste of 1830s France: literature become dominant over music as over painting. "Program-music," with the "*sujet*"[61] in the forefront!

35[65]

Beethoven belongs to Rousseau and to the humanitarian current which partly anticipated the Revolution, partly succeeded it transfiguratively, but even more he belongs to the main event of the last century, the appearance of Napoleon.

Mozart presupposing the society of the Rococo age

35[66]

Difference between actors, like Schiller and Wagner and — — —

Goethe isolated, between Pietism and Hellenism, doubtful whether he should not write in French.
Lessing — Bayle
Frederick the Great keen on France
Frederick II on Moorish-Eastern enlightenment
Leibniz between Christianity Platonism and mechanics.

Bismarck learning from Napoleon III and Cavour

35[67]

If mechanics is only a logic, then what follows for it is also what applies for all logic: it is a kind of spine for vertebrates, nothing true-in-itself.

35[68][62]

On the Ring of Rings.

NB. An *inside* belongs to the power that transforms and always remains the same, a kind of character of Proteus-Dionysus, disguising itself and enjoying itself in transformation. To comprehend the "person" as *deception*: in fact *heredity* is the main objection, insofar as innumerable formative forces from much earlier times assert their constant existence: in truth they struggle in it and are ruled and tamed — a will to power cuts through persons, it requires the *diminution* of perspective, "*egoism*," as an *occasional condition of existence*; on every step it looks out for an even higher one.

The diminution of the effective principle to a "person," to the individual.

35[69]

NB. How much someone bears of the *truth*, without *degenerating*, is *his standard*. Likewise how much *happiness* — — likewise how much *freedom* and *power*!

On the order of rank

35[70]

The *most rigorous school* needed, misfortune, illness: there would be no spirit on earth, also no delight and jubilation. — Only great-spirited, tense souls know what *art*, what cheerfulness are.

35[71][63]

Z⟨arathustra⟩ can only succeed when he has first established the *order of rank*.

35[72][64]

NB. There must be many superhumans: all goodness develops only among its kind. *One* god would always be a *devil*! A *ruling race*. On "the rulers of the earth."

35[73][65]

I. Zarathustra can only *succeed* after the order of rank has been established. At first this will be *taught*.
II. The order of rank executed in a system of earthly rule: the rulers of the earth last, a new ruling caste. Springing up from them here and there, quite Epicurean god, the superhuman, the transfigurer of existence.

III. The superhuman interpretation of the world. Dionysus.
IV. Lovingly returning to the closest and smallest things from this greatest *alienation*, Zarathustra *blessing* all his experiences and dying as a blesser.

35[74][66]
Z⟨arathustra⟩ 5.

1. Great trumpet-herald's noise. *Happiness* of loud notes! Zarathustra I. I am that *predestined human* who determines values for thousands of years. A hidden one, one forced to go everywhere, a human without friends who has rejected every homeland, every rest. What makes the *grand style*: Becoming **master** over one's *happiness* as well as one's *unhappiness*: a — — —
2. My *gift* will only be received when there are receivers: *for this* order of rank. The greatest events are the latest to be comprehended. — To this extent I must be a legislator.
3. *The time of its appearance*: the most dangerous *middle*, where it can go over to "last human," but also —
— characterized by *the greatest event*: God is dead. Only humans do not yet notice anything of the fact that they are living only on inherited values. The general negligence and squandering.
4. — *Basic insight*: "good" and "evil" are now observed as from the eye of the "*herd animal*." Equality of humans as *goal*. Against this *me*: (The One God as preparation for herd morality!)
the *teacher* of the order of rank.
5. Leaders, herds and isolated ones. The tempters.
6. Complete humans and fragments.
7. Those who turned out well and turned out badly.
8. Creators and those who were shaped. Difference in strength.
9. Artists and small completers.

10. the scientific people as describers and most comprehensive organs.
11. the lordly people, as attempts at cultivation.
12. the religion founders; as attempts at new universal value positing.
13. the feeling of imperfection: the penitents
14. The strain in the direction of perfection: the pious, the beautiful souls, the great longings
15. The force to *do* the perfect somehow (master-artisans artists officials scholars etc.
16. the earth now lying there as a marble workshop: a *ruling race* is *needed*, with absolute power.

35[75][67]

1. Zarathustra awakening on the old fortress. Hears the drumming of the heralds.
2. The test. "Do you belong to me?"
3. The rose festival parade.
4. The doctrine of the order of rank.
5. Nighttime on the bridge.

35[76][68]

(49)

What is *noble*? *Preface* to "*Mixed Opinions and Maxims*"

— meticulousness in the most external things, even the fr⟨ivolous⟩ ap⟨pearance⟩, in word, clothing, demeanor, insofar as this meticulousness sets apart, keeps at a distance, protects from being confused for someone else.

— the slow gesture, also the slow gaze. There are not too many valuable things: and these automatically come to and want to go to the valuable ones. We have a hard time admiring.

— the bearing of poverty and of neediness, also of illness.

— the avoidance of small honors, and suspicion of everyone who easily praises: for the praiser believes that he understands what he praises: but to understand — Balzac revealed it, this typical ambitious one — *comprendre c'est égaler*.[69]

— Our doubt about the communicability of the heart goes deep; solitude, not as chosen but as given,

— the conviction that one has responsibilities only to one's kind, behaves toward others as he pleases: that only *inter pares*[70] can justice be hoped for (unfortunately not counted on in the least).

— irony toward the "talented"; belief in nobility of birth even in moral matters. "Aristocrats of the spirit" — is a euphemism for Jews.

— to always feel oneself as someone who has to *forgive* honors: whereas it is not very often that someone is found who is allowed to honor him.

— always disguised: the higher the type, the more a human needs the incognito. God, if there were one, should be permitted, for purposes of decency, to reveal himself in the world only as a human.

— the capacity for *otium*,[71] the absolute conviction that a trade in any sense does not disgrace one, to be sure, but certainly disennobles. Not "industriousness" in the bourgeois sense, as highly as we esteem it, or like those insatiably cackling artists who do as the hens — cackle and lay eggs and cackle some more.

— we *protect* the artists and poets and whoever is a master in anything: but as beings who *are* of a superior kind than these who are only *skilled* at something, than the merely "productive people," do not confuse us with them.

— enjoyment of *forms*; the taking-under-protection of everything related to form, the conviction that courtesy is one of the great virtues; suspicion of all kinds of letting-oneself-go including all freedom of the press and thought, because under them the spirit becomes comfortable and oafish and relaxes.

— pleasure in *women*, as in a perhaps smaller, but subtler and lighter kind of being. What happiness to encounter beings who always have dance and folly and finery on their minds! They have been the delight of all very tense and profound manly souls, whose lives are burdened with great responsibilities.

— pleasure in princes and priests, because even in the assessment of the past at least *symbolically* and on the whole even literally they uphold the belief in a difference of human values, in sum in the order of rank.

— the ability to keep silent: but not a word of this before listeners.

— bearing of long hostilities: the lack of easy reconciliation.

— disgust with demagoguery, with the "Enlightenment," with "coziness," with rabble-like intimacy.

— the collecting of precious things, the needs of a higher and more selective soul; wanting to have nothing in common. *His* books, *his* landscapes.

— we revolt against bad and good experiences and do not so quickly generalize. The individual case: how ironic we are toward the individual case when it has the bad taste to behave like a rule.

— we love what is naïve and the naïve, but as observers and higher beings, we find Faust to be just as naïve as his Gretchen.

— we have a lowly estimation of the good, as herd animals: and know how among the worst most malicious harshest human beings often an inestimable gold drop of goodness keeps itself hidden, which all mere kindliness and milky soul — — —

— we do not consider a human of our kind refuted either by his vices, nor by his follies. We know that we are hard to recognize, and that we all have grounds to give ourselves foregrounds.

35[77][72]

Letters of Count — — —
Edited
by
J. v. A.

After the death of my mother.

Invent anecdotes.

35[78][73]

Preface.

Is one permitted to publish letters? — A venerable friend of mine was accustomed to pronouncing the word "public" never without malice. The nineteenth century, he once said, loves truth, as everyone knows: well, with precisely *this* taste it offends my taste! I fear that if this continues, people will write only *public* letters from now on. Yes, he said on another occasion, it could come to pass that at some time a decent human being would summarize his entire morality in a single sentence: thou shalt — lie! Sir, you shall absolutely and always lie! Or you, too, are what everyone else already is — "public"! — This was his secret opinion of the taste of our century. As I contemplated giving a title to his collection of letters and opinions, it crossed my mind to characterize them thus: "*The Mirror.* An Opportunity for Self-Reflection. For Europeans." May one glean from this tasteless idea of mine at least how much value *I* personally ascribe to these letters — and why I give myself the *right* to publish these letters precisely out of hatred for everything that is called "public" today.

35[79]

Century of minstrels (t⟨he⟩ p⟨eople⟩ of the dishonest burial) (Galiani) murderers boredom.

35[80][74]

The Germans

of Yesterday and of the Day After Tomorrow

A Contribution to the Critique of the German Soul

35[81]

The demagogues in art. — Hugo Michelet Sand R. Wagner

35[82]

A pessimistic way of thinking and doctrine an ecstatic nihilism can be indispensable to precisely the philosopher under certain circumstances: as a powerful pressure and hammer, with which he smashes races that are degenerating and dying out and clears them out of the way, ⟨in order⟩ to pave the way for a new order of life or in order to impart a longing for the end to what is degenerate and wants to die out.[75]

For the delaying and deepening of peoples and races a pessimistic way of thinking, a religion of negation and escape from the world, an ecstatic desensualization and uglification of life can — — —

35[83]

But, insofar as I have these kinds of worries and prepare a long answer to such a question — oh, maybe I myself am nothing more than a long answer to this question? — I already hear that broken and malicious voice

35[84][76]

Gai Saber.
Prelude to a Philosophy of the Future.
By
Friedrich Nietzsche.

To the Mistral.[77]
Introduction.
Book One: The Prejudices of the Philosophers.
Book Two: Beyond Good and Evil.
Book Three: To the Artists.
Book Four: The Mirror. An Opportunity for Self-Reflection for Europeans.
Book Five: The Noble Soul.
Among Friends: An Aftersong.[78]
the ideal cloister, for the preservation of delicate plants
the future of music — Europeans' music
music of grand style
the snares of language
Wagnermania and Hegelmania as intoxicants
"classic" — inapplicable word in music

the hermits, like Goethe, Beethoven, and the demagogic or courtly or ecclesiastical artists.
education of *musicians*.
against the "nationalistic" ambitions in art
concept of culture; — style etc.
rejection of *pessimisme*, likewise of all eudaemonistic points of view.

III To the Artists. New concept of the creator; the *Dionysian*. New festivals. The transfiguration.
"Perfected Infinity"
pain and joy
purpose
value judgments in perceptions of taste, colors, sounds
establish concepts
the *re-interpretability* of the world — but holding on to the basic features
what is pathological about philosophers
cause and effect
the economy of affects
the "persona"

Luther's discourse, the Bible as the foundation of a new poetic form.

[36 = W I 4. June–July 1885]

36[1][1]

Gai Saber.
Prelude to a Philosophy of the Future.
By
Friedrich Nietzsche.

Appendix

The Modern Soul.
Attempt at an Elucidation concerning Today and Tomorrow.

36[2]

Never has more been demanded of living creatures than with the emergence of terra firma: accustomed to and equipped for life in the sea, now they had to turn around and overturn their body and their customs and act differently in all things than they had been accustomed up till then — so far there has been no more remarkable transformation on earth. —Just as back then the sea descended into the faults caves pits and acquired *depth* through cave-ins, through a slow breaking down of the earth: so, too, what now transpires among human beings perhaps offers the precise opposite, to speak metaphorically: namely humans are becoming whole and rounded, the faults caves and pits are disappearing and consequently also — terra firma is disappearing. For a human made rounded and whole by my way of thinking, "everything is in the sea," the sea is everywhere: but the sea itself has lost its depths. — Yet I was on my way to a quite different metaphor and only got lost! I wanted to say: like everyone I was born a land animal — and now nevertheless I *must* be a sea animal!

36[3][2]

Germany, which is wealthy in talented and highly educated scholars, for a long time has lacked great souls, powerful spirits to such an extent that it appears to have forgotten what a *great* soul, what a *powerful* spirit is: and nowadays human beings who are mediocre and turned out badly take themselves to market, almost in good conscience and devoid of all embarrassment, and praise themselves as great men, reformers; as does for example Eugen Dühring, a talented and well-educated scholar, but who reveals with almost every word that he harbors a petty soul and is crushed by narrow jealous feelings; also that he is not driven by a powerful, brimming, benevolently squandering spirit — but by ambition! But to thirst for honors in this age is far unworthier of a philosopher than in any earlier age: today where the rabble rules, where the rabble bestows the honors!

36[4]

When the philosopher joins the *homines bonae voluntatis*,[3] the good-natured, compassionate, gentle, everyday people, then it is as if he landed in humid air and beneath a cloudy sky: for a short time it does him good, he feels relieved, as it were; but if he pays close attention, he notices how he himself is becoming comfortable and negligent in this false environment; vain too — but above all melancholy. In order to quickly learn how weak and meager is the constitution of this good-natured human material, with all their obliging appearance, he might irritate and wound their vanity, let him get them to the point where they become abusive: then the "undeepness" of these waters will betray itself soonest, and also surely what kind of sand and filth or presumptuousness lies hidden beneath all this well-mannered light azure surface.

36[5]

The women in Europe, quite aside from their real business ("laying children") are useful for many good things. It is pleasant to dance with Viennese women. With a French woman one can *causer*, with an Italian *poser*, with a German — *oser*.[4] Among Jewish women are the best prattlers of all: the model for this, all wrapped up in Goethean lace and smugness, was Rahel.[5] A Russian woman has usually experienced something, occasionally thought something. English women know how to blush in the most feminine and heavenly manner, almost without a reason, like the angels; in sum, we would never finish if we once tried to stiffly and steadfastly *prove* the usefulness of woman —something that everyone *believes* in — using the m⟨odel⟩ of E⟨nglish⟩ u⟨tilitarians⟩.

36[6][6]

Gai saber.
Prelude to a Philosophy of the Future.

To the Mistral. A Dance Song.

Part I. 1. "Without a passionate pleasure
Conclusion. "And do you know what 'the world' is to me?

Part II.
Conclusion. "When I was very young, Dionysus.

Part III. On the Future of the Arts.

Part IV. The Mirror.

Part V. Among Free Spirits.

36[7][7]

My "compassion." — This is a feeling for which no name suffices for me: I sense it where I see a waste of precious capabilities, for example at the sight of Luther: what strength, and what tasteless backwoods-problems (at a time when in France the courageous and cheerful skepticism of a Montaigne was already possible!) Or where I see someone fall short of what he could have become, due to the influence of a stupidity of chance. Or even when thinking of the fate of humankind, as when I watch, with fear and contempt, the European politics of today which under all circumstances is also working on the fabric of the future *of all* human beings. Indeed, what could become of "humans" if — — ! This is a kind of "compassion"; even if there is no suffering one *with* whom I might suffer here.[8]

36[8][9]
Moralia[10]

Just as from time immemorial humans have lived in profound unfamiliarity with their *bodies* and allow a few formulations to suffice for communicating about their well-being, so too is the case with our judgments on the value of humans and deeds: privately we cling to a few external and incidental symbols and have no feeling for *how* deeply unfamiliar and foreign we are to ourselves. And as concerns judgment about others: how *quick* and "certain" even the most cautious and the fairest are to judge!

36[9][11]
Moralia.

Sparse reflection is required to expose the fact that there is no "good in itself" — that something good must be thought only as "good for what," and that what is good in one purpose necessarily will at the same time be "evil and harmful" in many other purposes: in sum that each thing to which we apply the predicate "good" is likewise characterized as "evil" for precisely that reason.

36[10][12]

How long has it been that I have made an effort to prove the complete *innocence* of becoming in myself![13] And what strange paths I have already walked in doing so! Once the right solution seemed to me that I decreed: "existence, as something resembling a work of art, is not at all under the *jurisdictio*[14] of morality; on the contrary morality itself belongs in the realm of appearance." Another time I said: all guilt-concepts are objectively completely worthless, but subjectively all life is necessarily unjust and alogical. A third time I extracted from myself the denial of all purposes and perceived the unknowability of causal combinations. And why did I do all this? Was it not to provide myself with the feeling of complete irresponsibility — to position myself outside of any praise and blame, independent of all formerly and today, in order to pursue my goal in my way? —

36[11][15]

At bottom morality is *hostile* toward science: already Socrates was this — and moreover because science takes things as important that have nothing to do with "good" and "evil," and consequently *take importance* away from the feeling for "good" and "evil." For morality wants the whole human being and his entire strength to be at its service: it regards it as a squandering of someone who is *not rich enough* to squander when a human seriously concerns himself with plants and stars. This is why in Greece things rapidly went downhill with scientism when Socrates dragged the illness of moralizing into science; a height such as that in the mentality of a Democritus, Hippocrates and Thucydides was not achieved for a second time.

36[12][16]

Human Being in Relations with Others

It is a sign of a lack of noble-mindedness when someone on the street responds to a greeting before he has recognized the person who greeted: — greeting and kind of greeting should be distinctions, after all — with the sole exception that a prince (or he *qui range aux souverains*[17]) goes his way and is greeted. It is his prerogative not to have to know anyone, but to have to be known by all. A parable.

36[13][18]

The H⟨uman Being⟩ *By Oneself Alone*:

How differently one perceives the business and the work of his life if he is the first in his family to do it or when the father and grandfather have already been active in the same way! In the former case, where one is the first, one has much more inner distress from it, also a much more sudden pride; good conscience is not yet wedded to such an activity, and *something* about it will readily be felt as arbitrary, as incidental.

36[14][19]

What value Wagner might have for the non-musician, and might also retain going forward, the question should be spared us for now. Without any doubt Richard Wagner gave the Germans of this age the most comprehensive notion of what an artist *could* be: — respect for "the artist" suddenly shot up: everywhere he awakened new valuations, new desires, new hopes; and perhaps not least through the merely heralding, incomplete, imperfect nature of his artistic creations. Who did not *learn* from him! And even if not so directly, like the artists of elocution and the poser-humans[20] of every kind, then certainly at least indirectly, "occasioned by Richard Wagner," as one may be allowed to say. Even philosophical knowledge gained no meager impulse from his appearance, of this there is no doubt. Today there is an abundance of aesthetic problems of which even the subtlest minds had no whiff *before* Richard Wagner — above all the problem of the actor and his rel⟨ation⟩ to the different arts, not to mention psychological problems as they are copiously provided by Wagner's character and W⟨agnerian⟩ art. To be sure: insofar as he himself ventured into the realm of knowledge he deserves no praise, on the contrary an unconditional rejection; in the gardens of science he always distinguished himself only as the most immodest and untalented intruder. The "philosophizing" of Wagner belongs to the most illicit kinds of dilettantism; that people did not even know enough to laugh at it is German and belongs to the old German "cult of obscurity." But if one absolutely wants to assist him in the acquisition of honors and statues even as a "thinker" — the good will and the subservience of his disciples will not be able to forgo this — so be it! then I recommend he be depicted as the *genius of German obscurity* itself, with a smoking torch in hand, inspired and in the act of stumbling over a stone. When Wagner "thinks," he stumbles. — But we will be concerned with Wagner the m⟨usician⟩.

36[15][21]

If the world had a goal then it must have been reached. If an unintended final state existed for it, then it likewise must have been reached. If it were generally capable of stopping and becoming fixed, of "being," if it had this capacity for "being" for only a single moment in all its becoming, then in turn all its becoming would have ended long ago, therefore also all thinking, all "spirit." The fact of a "spirit" *as a form of becoming* proves that the world has no goal, no final state and is incapable of being. — But the old habit of thinking of goals with every event that happens and of a guiding creative God with the world is so powerful that a thinker has trouble in not thinking to himself that even the aimlessness of the world is a purpose. This notion — namely that the world deliberately *avoids* a goal and even knows how to artificially guard against getting caught in an orbit — must occur to all who wish to decree upon the world the capacity for *eternal novelty*, that is for a finite, specific, unchangeable force of constant size as is "the world" — the miracle-capacity for *infinite* restructuring of its forms and states. The world, even if no longer a god, is still supposed to be capable of divine creative force, of infinite transformational force; it is supposed to willfully *resist* falling back into one of its old forms, it is supposed to have not only the intention but also the *means to protect* itself from every repetition, thus in every moment it is supposed to *control* each of its movements with respect to avoiding goals, final states, repetitions — and whatever else may be the consequences of such an unforgivably insane manner of thinking and desiring. That is still the old religious way of thinking and desiring, a kind of longing to believe that *in some way* the world is indeed the same as the old beloved, infinite, boundlessly creative God — that in some way "the old God still lives" after all — that longing of Spinoza's which expresses itself in the phrase "*deus sive natura*"[22] (he even felt "*natura sive deus*" —). But what then is the proposition and belief with which the decisive turn, the now attained *upper hand* of the scientific spirit over the religious god-creating spirit is most distinctly formulated? Is it not: the world, as force, must not be thought as unlimited, for it *cannot* be thought thus — we forbid ourselves the concept of an *infinite* force *as incompatible with the concept "force."* Therefore — the world also lacks the capacity for eternal novelty.

36[16]

If I could have my way: then it is time to declare war on European morality, and likewise on everything that has sprouted from it. This temporary order of the peoples and states of Europe must be smashed. The Christian-democratic way of thinking favors the herd-animal, the diminution of human beings, it weakens the great motivating forces (evil —), it hates compulsion, harsh discipline, great responsibilities, great risks. The mediocre win the day and assert their value standards.

36[17]

But to whom do I say this? Where then are these "free spirits"? Is there even such a thing as "between ourselves"? —

I look around me: who thinks, who feels as I do about this? Who wants what my most concealed will wants? But so far I found no one. Perhaps I only searched badly? Perhaps those who suffer from my kind of new plight and new happiness must conceal themselves in the same way that I do — ? And don masks as I did? — And consequently are not much good at seeking their kind?

We new philosophers, we tempters, think otherwise — and we do not want to leave it at thinking. We think more *freely* — perhaps the day will come when people see with their own eyes that we also act more freely. Meanwhile we are difficult to recognize; people have to mistake us. Are we "freethinkers"?

In all European countries and likewise in North America there are now "freethinkers": do they belong with us? No, gentlemen, you want almost the *opposite* of that which lies in the intentions of those philosophers whom I call tempters; they sense little temptation to trade mendacious pleasantries with you. Indeed, if you "freethinkers" had only a whiff of what one can free himself *from*, and *where* one is then driven! I believe you would be among the most raging opponents of that which I call my "freedom of spirit and my "Beyond Good and Evil."

That I no longer need to believe in "souls," that I deny "personality" and its alleged unity and in each human being find the material for very different "personae" (and masks), that to me "absolute spirit" and "pure knowing" signify mythical creatures behind which a *contradictio in adjecto*[23] clumsily conceals itself — with this I am perhaps on the same path as many of those "freethinkers," not to mention at all the denial of *God*, with which even today a few self-satisfied Englishmen assume they are providing a tremendous sample of free-mindedness. What separates me from them are valuations: for they all belong to the democratic movement and want equal rights for all, they see in the forms of our previous old society the causes for human deficiencies and degenerations, they enthuse about smashing these forms: and sometimes they imagine the most humane thing they could do is to help all human beings to reach their degree of spiritual "freedom." Briefly and plainly, they belong to the "*levelers*" — to that kind of human being who crudely offends my taste in every way, and offends my reason even more: I want war and opposites even in matters of the spirit; and more war than ever, more o⟨pposites⟩ than ever; I would sooner condone the harshest despotism (as a school for the flexibility of the spirit) than the humid tepid air of an age of "freedom of the press," in which all spirit becomes comfortable and stupid and stretches its limbs. In this matter I am still today what I was — "untimely."

But we new philosophers: we are not only beginning with the portrayal of factual order of rank and value differences in humans, but we also want precisely the opposite of an assimilation, an equalization: we teach estrangement in every sense of the word, we tear open chasms as they have never existed before, we want humans to be more evil than they ever were. For the time being we ourselves still live as strangers to one another and concealed. It will be necessary for us for many reasons to be hermits and even to don masks — consequently we will be in a poor position to seek our kind. We will live alone and probably know the agonies of all seven solitudes. But if we do cross one another's path, by accident, then you can bet that we will fail to recognize one another or mutually deceive ourselves.[24]

36[18][25]

I am wary of speaking of chemical "laws": this has a moral aftertaste. On the contrary what is at stake is an absolute determination of power relationships: the stronger gains mastery over the weaker, at least as far as the latter cannot assert its degree of independence — here there is no mercy, no sparing, even less a respect for "laws"!

36[19][26]

It is improbable that our "knowledge" should reach further than is just required for the preservation of life. Morphology shows us how the senses and nerves, as well as the brain develop in proportion to the difficulty of finding nourishment.

36[20][27]

Even in the realm of the inorganic, for an atom of force only its own neighborhood comes into consideration: the forces in the distance even themselves out. Herein lies the kernel of the perspectival, and why a living being is "egoistic" through and through.

36[21][28]

The weaker presses itself upon the stronger, from a need for nourishment; it wants to find shelter, wants to become *one* with it if possible. The stronger on the contrary fends things off, it does not want to perish this way; on the contrary, in growing it splits itself in two and into several parts. The greater the pressure for unity, the more one can infer weakness; the greater the pressure for variety, difference, internal dissolution, the more strength is there.

The drive to approach — and the drive to repel something are the bond in the inorganic and well as the organic world. The whole separation is a prejudice.

The will to power in every combination of forces, *fending off the stronger, pouncing on the weaker* is *more correct*. NB. *Processes* as "beings."[29]

36[22][30]

The connection between the inorganic and the organic must lie in the repelling force that every atom of force exerts. Life would be defined as an enduring form of the *process* of *force determinations*, where the different combatants for their part grow unequally. The extent to which a resistance lies even in obeying; one's individual power is by no means surrendered. Likewise in commanding there is a concession that the absolute power of the opponent is not vanquished, not incorporated, dissolved. "Obeying" like "commanding" are forms of jousting.

36[23][31]

Continuous transitions do not allow us to speak of "individual" etc.; the "number" of beings is itself in flux. We would not speak of time and know nothing of movement if we did not, in a crude manner, believe we saw "things at rest" beside "things in motion." Just as little would we speak of cause and effect, and without the erroneous conception of "empty space" we would not have arrived at all at the conception of space.

The principle of identity has as background the "appearance" that identical things exist. A world of becoming could not be "comprehended," not "known" in the strict sense: only insofar as the "comprehending" and "knowing" intellect finds an already created crude world, pieced together entirely from illusory things, but become firm, insofar as this kind of illusion has preserved life — only to this extent does something like "knowledge" exist: i.e., a measuring of earlier and more recent errors against one another.

36[24]

The sun: its movements are results 1) of the drive to pounce on the planets 2) this brings forth an approach to all 3) defending itself against a stronger sun

36[25][32,33]

I believe in absolute space, as a substratum of force: the latter limits and structures. Time eternal. But in itself there is no space, nor time: "changes" are only appearances (or sense-processes for us); if we nonetheless posit regular recurrence among these, then nothing is *proven* thereby but this simple fact, that it has always happened this way. The feeling that the *post hoc*[34] is a *propter hoc*[35] is easy to deduce as a misunderstanding; it is understandable. But appearances cannot be "causes"!

36[26]

"Subject" "object" "predicate" — these separations are *made up* and are now slapped like schemata on all apparent facts. The false fundamental observation is that I believe *I* am the one who does something, who suffers something, who "*has*" something, who "*has*" a quality.[36] This "doing" "suffering" "having" — — —

36[27]

Philosophy, in the only way I still grant it validity, as the most universal form of history, as the attempt to somehow describe Heraclitean becoming and abbreviate it in symbols (to *translate* it so to speak into a kind of illusory being and to mummify it)

36[28][37]

That "heredity," as something quite unexplained, cannot be used for explanation, but only for describing, for fixing a problem. Precisely this applies to the "capacity for adaptation." In fact nothing is *explained* through morphological representation, supposing it were completed, but a tremendous fact is *described*. How an organ can be used to some purpose, *that* is not explained. In these things as little would be explained with the assumption of *causae finales*[38] as with *causae efficientes*.[39] The concept "*causa*" is only a means of expression, nothing more, a means for describing.

36[29][40]

There are analogies, e.g., to our memory another memory that makes itself noticeable in forms in heredity and development. To our inventing and experimenting, an inventing in the application of tools for new purposes etc. That which we call our consciousness is innocent of all essential processes of our preservation and our growth; and no mind could be so subtle that it could construe more than a machine — which is far exceeded by every organic process.

36[30]

One is unfair toward Descartes if one takes lightly his invocation of God's credibility. In fact, from the start it is only with the assumption of a God who is morally similar to us that "truth" and the search for truth are something that promises success and has meaning. Leaving this God aside, it is permitted to ask whether being deceived does not belong to the conditions of life.

36[31][41,42]

The triumphant concept "force" with which our physicists have ousted God from the world requires one more enhancement: an internal world must be attributed to it, to which I refer as "will to power," i.e., as an insatiable demand for displaying power; or application, exertion of power, as creative drive etc. The physicists cannot rid the "effect at a distance" from their principles: just as little as a repelling force (or attracting one) There is no helping it: one must grasp all motion, all "appearances," all "laws" only as symptoms of an internal event and use to the limit the analogy of the human being.[43] In the animal it is possible to deduce all its drives from the will to power: likewise all functions of organic life from this single source.

36[32]

Leibniz is dangerous, as a proper German who needs foregrounds and foreground-philosophies, daring and mysterious to the extreme in himself, but without nobility

Spinoza is deeper more comprehensive more hiding in caves than Descartes: Pascal in turn deeper than Spinoza. Measured against such hermits of the spirit and conscience Hume and Locke are humans of the surface; — — —

36[33][44]

On the Critique of the German Soul.

36[34][45]

Of the world interpretations that have been attempted so far, the mechanistic today seems to stand triumphantly in the foreground: clearly it has good conscience on its side; and no science believes for itself in progress or success unless it is won with the help of mechanistic procedures. Everyone knows these procedures: one leaves "reason" and "purposes" out of it, as much as possible, one shows that in due time everything can evolve from everything, one does not conceal a gloating grin when once again the "apparent intentionality in the fate" of a plant or an egg yolk is traced to pressure and thrust: in sum, one wholeheartedly honors, if a humorous expression is permitted in so serious a matter, the principle of the greatest possible stupidity. Meanwhile precisely in these distinguished intellects who belong to this movement a premonition, an anxiety can be detected, as if this theory had a hole that before too long could become its final hole: I mean the hole that is their rock bottom[46] from which they will leak when they are in their moment of highest need. Pressure and stress themselves cannot be "explained," one cannot be rid of the *actio in distans*.[47] — we have lost our belief in even the ability to explain and we admit with a peevish expression that describing and not explaining, that the dynamic world interpretation with its denial of "empty space," of particle atoms, will soon hold sway over physicists: whereby of course in addition to *dynamis*[48] an inner quality — — —

36[35][49]

Using the Body as a Guide. —

Supposing that "the soul" was an attractive and mysterious idea from which philosophers justifiably parted only with reluctance — perhaps that which they are now learning to exchange for it is even more attractive, more mysterious. The human body, in which the entire most distant and most recent past of all organic development again becomes lively and embodied, through which and over and beyond which a tremendous inaudible stream appears to flow: the body is a more amazing idea than the ancient "soul."

36[36][50]

At all times people have believed better in the body as our most certain being, in sum as the ego, than in the spirit (or the "soul" or "the subject," as school discourse now says instead of soul). No one ever hatched the notion that his stomach could be understood as a foreign, perhaps divine stomach: but his thoughts as "given from beyond," his valuations as "inspired by a god," comprehending his instincts as demonic activity: for this tendency and taste of human beings there are testimonies from all the ages of humanity. Even today, especially among artists, there is abundant evidence of a kind of amazement and reverential suspension of judgment when they are presented with the question of how they succeeded in their best throw and from which world the creative idea came to them: when they ask in this manner, they have something like innocence and childish shame, they scarcely dare to say "this came from me, this was my hand that threw the dice." — Conversely, even those philosophers and religious people who had the most compelling grounds in their logic and piety to take their corporeality as a deception, and indeed as an overcome and dispensed-with deception, were not able to avoid recognizing the stupid fact that the body has not gone away: for which the most remarkable testimony is to be found partly in Paul, partly in the Vedanta philosophy.

But what ultimately does *strength of belief* mean! Therefore it could still be a very stupid belief! — What needs contemplating here: —

And in the end, if the belief in the body is only the result of an inference: supposing it were a false inference, as the idealists maintain: is it not a question mark against the credibility of the spirit itself that it is the cause of such false inferences? Supposing multiplicity, and space and time and motion (and whatever else may be the presuppositions of a belief in corporeality) were errors, what suspicion will be aroused against the spirit by that which occasioned such presuppositions in us! Enough, the belief in the body is for the time being still a stronger belief than the belief in the spirit; and whoever wants to undermine it, at the same time most thoroughly also undermines the belief in the authority of the spirit.

36[37][51]

1.

Human All Too Human: with this title the will to a great *separation* is signaled, the attempt of an individual to free himself from all kinds of prejudices that speak in *favor* of human beings and to walk all paths that lead high enough, at least for a moment, to look *down* on humans. Not to despise the despicable in humans, but instead to question deep down to the ultimate grounds whether even in the highest and the best and in everything of which humans so far have been proud, whether in this pride itself and the harmless superficial confidence of its valuations there is not something still left to despise; this not innocuous task was one means among all the means to which a *greater*, a more comprehensive task compelled me. Does anyone want to walk these paths with me? I *advise* no one to do so. — But you want to? Then let's go.

36[38]

Goethe is an exception: he lived among Germans in a subtle manner sheltered and disguised; Schiller belongs to those Germans who loved the big gleaming words and pomp gestures of virtue (— even his taste for Kantian morality and its absolute command-tone belongs here —) It hurts the Germans to admit to themselves how much they have been the Germans of Kotzebue[52] (and to a good extent not yet —); and that life-threatening fanatic Sand perhaps only took his revenge in the wrong place, as so often happens.

Jans⟨s⟩en

36[39]

If there is anything that accrues to the honor of contemporary Germans it is that they no longer tolerate the big gleaming glittering Schillerian words that their grandfathers — — —

36[40]

The small German towns as Kotzebue painted them — and the painting was good — are made in the image of Weimar-dwellers, at the time of Schiller and Goethe.

36[41]

The pettiness and pitifulness of the German soul, its partly hedonistic, partly jealous sitting-in-the-corner, its incarnate "small town atmosphere," to invoke Kotzebue, its "frog-perspective" for all higher things, to use the language of painters — how painful — — —

36[42]

If intellect, industriousness and capability alone were considered, the Prussian Jews would already be in possession of the higher state offices, especially in the administrative sector: in sum, they would also have the "power" *in their hands* (just as they already have it — judging by manifold evidence — "in their pockets"). What excludes them from this is their inability to represent power: the Jews even in their fatherland have not been a *ruling* caste: their eye does not convince, their tongue easily runs too swiftly and trips itself up, their anger does not know the deep honest roaring of a lion, their stomach does not tolerate great feasting and their understanding does not tolerate strong wine — their arms and legs do not permit them any proud affects (often twitching in their hands is I know not what kind of — memory —); and even the manner in which a Jew mounts a horse (or a Jewish musician arrives at his theme — "the Jewish leap" —) is not innocuous and lets us know that the Jews have never been a *knightly* race. If the Jews are frequently perceived as unfit for the dignity of serving as judges, then what is condemned here is not their morality, but only their inability to represent this morality. Now from this it immediately follows that the Jew of Prussia must be a diminished and atrophied kind of Jew; for in itself the Oriental understands representation incomparably better than, say, a north German: — Delacroix. This degeneration of the Jew is connected to a wrong climate and being neighbors of ugly and oppressed Slavs Hungarians and Germans: among Portuguese and Moors the higher race of Jews is preserved, indeed on the whole the solemnity of tone and a kind of *sanctifying* of passion has perhaps never on earth been more beautifully portrayed than by certain Jews of the Old Testament: even the Greeks could have learned something from them!

36[43]

The dangers of the Jewish soul are: 1) it seeks to nest itself parasitically somewhere 2) it knows how to "adapt," as the natural scientists say, in this manner they "have become born actors, like the octopus," which as Theognis sings, borrows its color from the cliff to which it adheres.[53] Their talent and even more their tendency and inclination to both seem tremendous; their habit of expending much spirit and persistence on very small gains has left a fateful furrow in their character: so that even the most respectable wholesalers of the Jewish money market cannot bring themselves, if the circumstances warrant, to ⟨not⟩ cold-bloodedly reach for little *mesquinen*[54] overcharges of the kind that would make a Prussian financier blush.

36[44]

The future of German culture rests on the sons of *Prussian officers*

36[45][55]

A. The Jews the oldest and purest race. *Beauty* of the women.
B. The Jews the *actors*: in a democratic age: reduction of the literary man to the actor
C. Problem of merging the European aristocracy or rather the young Prussian nobleman with Jewesses.

36[46]

German atheism.
the school master culture.
German pessimism.

36[47]

The dangers of the Jewish soul: parasitism and acting
The Jew does not "represent"
The school master culture.
German pessimism.
The hermit:
Teutonomania.
German music.
The literary men.

The women.
Mistrust of modern ideas.
German anarchism.

36[48]

Hostility toward everything that smacks of literary men and popular enlightenment, especially toward everything that ruins women, deforms women — for *spiritual enlightenment* is an infallible means of making humans insecure, weaker willed, more dependent and needy of support, in sum of developing the *herd animal* in human beings: which is why so far all great artists of governing (Confucius in China, the *imperium romanum*,[56] Napoleon, the papacy at the time when it successfully had power and not only the will to power where the ruling instinct *culminated* so far, also made use of spiritual enlightenment; at least they allowed it to *reign* (like the popes of the Renaissance) The self-deception of the masses on this point e.g., in all democracies, is extremely valuable: the diminution and governability of humans is striven for as "progress"![57]

36[49][58]

On German Pessimism. —

Dimming, pessimistic coloring necessarily follow as a result of the Enlightenment. Around 1770 one already noticed a decrease in cheerfulness; women believed, with that feminine instinct that always sides with virtue, that immorality was to blame: Galiani hit the mark: he quotes Voltaire's verse.[59] — If I now presume to be out in front of Voltaire and even Galiani — who was something much profounder — by a couple of centuries in terms of enlightenment: how far therefore must I have come in terms of dimming! This is also true: and early on I was cautious with a kind of regret of German and Christian narrowness and the logical inconsistency of Schopenhauerian or even Leopardian pessimism and looked for the most principled forms (— Asia —) I do *not* count E⟨duard⟩ v⟨on⟩ H⟨artmann⟩ among the continuators of pessimism, on the contrary among the "pleasant literatures" — — — etc. But in order to bear *this* extreme pessimism (as it echoes forth from time to time from my *Birth of Tragedy*) living alone "without God and morality," I had to invent a counterpart for myself. Perhaps I know best why only humans laugh: they alone suffer so deeply that they *had to* invent laughter. The unhappy and melancholy animal is, as is only fair, the most cheerful.

36[50]
On the German Lyric Poets, —

36[51]
South and East.

36[52]
Brahms, no "event," no exception, no breach in the chain before Wagner, on the contrary one link *more,* a — — —

If one excludes what he occasionally sacrificed so to speak to a hospitable genius of foreign ways and human beings — also sacrifices of piety for great teachers, old and new, included — then he alone is the musician who so far has claim to the characterization "the *north German musician*"

36[53][60]
The Germans *are* nothing yet, but they are *becoming* something; therefore they still have no culture — therefore they *cannot* yet have a culture! This is my proposition: let it offend whomever it must: namely whoever has Teutonomania in his head (or on his shield)! — They are nothing yet: that is: they are everything. They are *becoming* something: that is, they will someday stop being everything. The latter is at bottom only a wish, scarcely still a hope; fortunately a wish according to which one can live, a matter of will, of work, of discipline, of cultivation as well as a matter of unwillingness, of longing, of renunciation, of discontent, even of embitterment: in sum, we Germans *want* something that before us no one yet has wanted — we want something *more*!

That this "German who becomes and not yet is" — deserves something better than today's German "education," that all "who are becoming" have to be enraged wherever they perceive a satisfaction in this sphere, a brazen "resting on one's laurels" or "anointing oneself": this is my second proposition, concerning which I have also not changed my thinking.

36[54]

How a theologian today can have a good conscience with his Christianness is incomprehensible and inaccessible to me; but there is adequate good conscience in him — it seems there must not be much to this "good conscience"!

36[55][61]

"*German.*"
Questions and Dashes.[62]

Thoughts on Discipline and Cultivation.

36[56]

Offended pride, annoyance at having loved where one could have despised, an added melancholy over the resulting emptiness and gap, finally the bite of intellectual vanity that said "you let yourself be cheated" — : this was the next experience. But a philosophical human being drives all he has experienced into the universal, all that is individual grows into chains

36[57]

The Asiatic h⟨umans⟩ are a hundred times more magnificent than the European

36[58][63]

The jungle-vegetation "human being" always appears where the struggle for power has been waged longest. The *great* humans.

36[59]

Even the development of the *highest forms* of intelligence has been cultivated under *unfreedom* and counter-pressure. So far we have nothing to thank the "liberal spirit" for. One underestimates what refinement for the *spirit* has accompanied the agony of conscience of a simultaneously Christian and scientific-logical interpretation of the world.

36[60]

"*On the Critique of the Modern Soul.*"

[37 = W I 6a. June–July 1885]

37[1][1]

Many a hearty objection could be made to that which I dare to present in this book, certainly from up close, and even more from a distance. I have anticipated one part of these objections myself, thanks to my manifold practice in interrogating and in dueling with myself but unfortunately I have also always answered them in advance: so that up till now the *entire* burden of my "truths" has rested on me. One will understand that it has been a matter of *burdensome* truths here; and if there is one faith that makes us blessed, well then, here is a faith that does *not* do that! But why should things be organized t⟨o⟩ bring us pleasure? — Even though precisely this time, speaking frankly, I would enjoy the pleasure of being *refuted*. — And if on the other hand knowledge — — — us, what is knowledge for? —

Ultimately perhaps this, too, is only a question of time: in the end we get along even with the devil. And if things are not supposed to be organized to bring us pleasure, who could prevent us from — organizing them to that end?

37[2][2]

It is bad taste to want to agree with many. At bottom my friend *Satis* is enough for me: surely you know who that is? *Satis sunt mihi pauci, satis est unus, satis est nullus.*[3] And in the end this is what remains: the great things are left over and preserved for the great, the abysses for the profound, the delicacies and shudders for the refined, and on the whole and in sum, everything rare for the rare. My judgment is *my* judgment: anyone else does not easily have a right to it. — And you, my dear Mr. Neighbor, you who are just now peeking over my shoulder at my book, you even insist on agreeing with me on this? You look into this book and say Yes to it? Away with you! I absolutely do not want to become suspicious, on account of you, of what I just wrote. For I, too, love truth, like all philosophers: all philosophers so far loved their truths — —

37[3][4]

I forgot to say that such philosophers are cheerful and that they like to sit in the abyss of a perfectly bright sky: — they need different means to endure life than other people, for they suffer differently: (namely just as much from the profundity of their contempt for humans, as from their love). — The most suffering animal on earth invented for itself —*laughter*.

37[4]

Morality and Physiology. — We consider it a hastiness that precisely human consciousness has been regarded for so long as the highest stage of organic development and as the most amazing of all earthly things, indeed as their blossom and "goal" so to speak. What is more amazing on the contrary is the *body*: one cannot cease to admire how the human *body* has become possible: how such a tremendous unity of living beings can grow and for a time exist, each one dependent and subservient and yet in a certain sense on the other hand commanding and acting from its own will — : and this occurs obviously *not* through consciousness! Compared to this "wonder of wonders" consciousness is just a "tool" and no more — in the same sense that the stomach is a tool for it. The magnificent binding together of the most manifold life, the order and arrangement of the higher and lower activities, the thousand-fold obedience which is not a blind, even less a mechanistic but rather a selecting, circumspect, considerate, even resisting obedience — this whole phenomenon "body," measured by intellectual standards, is as much superior to our consciousness, our "spirit," our conscious thinking, feeling, willing as algebra is to multiplication tables. The "nerve- and brain-apparatus" for producing thinking, feeling, willing in the first place is *not* as subtle and "divinely" constructed: on the contrary to me it seems that precisely for this, for thinking, feeling, willing, really no "apparatus" at all is needed, rather that this, this precisely — is "the thing itself." On the contrary a tremendous synthesis of living beings and intellects such as this, which is called "human being," will only be able to live when that subtle connecting- and mediating-system, and through it lightning-fast communication among all these higher and lower beings are created — and moreover exclusively by living mediators: but this is a moral and not a mechanistic problem! Today we have forbidden ourselves to fantasize about "unity," about the "soul," about the "person": with such hypotheses we only *complicate* the problem, so much is clear. And even those smallest living beings that constitute our body (more accurately: whose working-together is the best metaphor for that which we call "body" —) are not regarded by us as soul-atoms, but instead as something growing, struggling, self-increasing and again dying out: so that their number changes erratically, and our life like any life is simultaneously a continuous dying. Therefore there are as many "consciousnesses" in a human being as there are beings, in every moment of his existence, that constitute his body. What we usually conceive of as a singular "consciousness," the intellect, is distinguished precisely by the fact that it remains protected and closed off from the innumerable multiplicity in the experiences of these multiple consciousnesses and, as a consciousness of a higher order, as a ruling multiplicity and aristocracy, it is presented with only a *selection* of experiences, moreover only those that are simplified and rendered surveyable and comprehensible, hence *falsified* experiences — so that for its part it can continue this process of simplifying and rendering surveyable, hence of falsifying, and can prepare that which we commonly call "a will" — each such act of will presupposes as it were the appointment of a dictator. But that which presents this selection to our intellect, which already simplified, compared, interpreted the experiences in advance, is in any case not this intellect: just as little as it is that which *executes* the will, which picks up a pale, thin and extremely imprecise value- and power-representation and translates it into living power and precise value-standards. And precisely the same kind of operation that plays out here must continuously play out on all deeper levels in the behavior of all these higher and lower beings toward one another: this same selecting and presenting of experiences, this abstracting and thinking in unison, this willing, this translating back of the always very imprecise willing into precise activity. Using the body as a guide, as I mentioned, we learn that our life is only possible through an interplay of many intelligences of very unequal value and therefore only through a constant thousand-fold obeying and commanding — morally spoken: through the incessant exercise of many *virtues*. And how could one cease to speak morally! —

— Prattling in this manner I surrendered myself in unbridled fashion to my didactic streak, for I was blissful to have someone who could tolerate listening to me. And yet, at precisely this point Ariadne could tolerate it no longer — you see, the story took place during my first stay on Naxos — : "but sir," she said, "you are speaking Pig-German!" —"German," I answered cheerfully, "simply German! Leave the pig out, my dear goddess! You underestimate the difficulty of saying subtle things in German!" — "Subtle things!" cried Ariadne, appalled: "but that was just positivism! Philosophizing with tusks! Conceptual-mishmash and muck from a hundred philosophies! What is that supposed to mean!" — and here she played impatiently with her famous thread, which once guided her Theseus through the labyrinth. — Thus it came to light that Ariadne was around two millennia behind in her philosophical education.

37[5]

In books of aphorisms like mine strictly forbidden lengthy things and thought-chains stand between and behind short aphorisms; and some of it may be questionable enough for Oedipus and his sphinx. I do not write essays: they are for asses and readers of newspapers. Speeches even less. My *Unfashionable Observations* I aimed as a young person at young people to whom I spoke of my experiences and vows, in order to lure them into my labyrinth — at German youths: but I have been persuaded to believe that German youths have died out. Well then: now I no longer have any reason to be "eloquent" in that former manner; today — I would probably no longer be able to do it. Whoever has sat together days a⟨nd⟩ nights and year-in, year-out with his soul in the most intimate discord and dialogue, whoever in his cave — it could be a labyrinth a⟨nd⟩ also a gold mine — turned into a cave-bear or gold digger, whoever like me allowed and allows all kinds of thoughts, second thoughts and questionable matters[5] to run through his head and over his heart, which he would not always communicate, even if he had kindred spirits and boisterous brave comrades around him: even his concepts ultimately acquire their own twilight color, an aroma as much of profundity as of mold; something incommunicable and recalcitrant that chills any curious bystander: — and a hermit-philosophy, even if it were written with a lion's claw, would still only look like a philosophy of "quotation marks."

37[6][6]

In the writings of a hermit one also hears something of the echo of the wasteland, something of whispered tones and the shy looking-around of loneliness: his strongest words and even screams still sound as it were like a new and more dangerous kind of silence, of concealment.

37[7][7]

Supposing one were to imagine a philosopher as a great educator, powerful enough to stand on his lonely heights and pull long chains of generations up to him: then one would also have to grant him the uncanny prerogatives of the great educator. An educator never says what he himself is thinking, but always only what he thinks about a thing in relation to its use to the one he is educating. He must not be detected in this dissemblance; it is part of his mastery that we believe in his honesty. He must be capable of all means of discipline and castigation: some natures he advances only through the whiplashes of scorn, others, lethargic, indecisive, cowardly, vain, perhaps with exaggerated praise. Such an educator is beyond good and evil; but no one is allowed to know it.

37[8][8]

It is approaching, irrefutably, hesitatingly, terrible as fate, the great task and question: how should the earth as a whole be governed? And *for what* should "the human being" as a whole — and no longer a people, a race — be bred and cultivated?

The legislative moralities are the major means by which one can shape the human into what a creative and profound will prefers: supposing that such an artist-will of the highest order holds the power in his hands and can assert his creating will over long stretches of time, in the form of legislations, religions and customs. Such humans of great creativity, the truly great human as I understand it, will be sought in vain today and probably for a long time to come: they are *missing* — : until finally, after much disappointment, one has to begin to understand why they are missing and that there is nothing more hostile standing in the way of their emergence and development for now and for a long time than what today is straightforwardly called "*the* morality" in Europe: as if no other existed and no other were allowed to exist — that herd-morality referred to earlier, which strives with all its powers for universal green pasture-happiness on earth, namely security, absence of danger, comfort, ease of living and to top it off, "if all goes well," even hopes to get rid of every kind of shepherd and bellwether. Its two most abundantly preached doctrines are: "equal rights" and "sympathy for all who suffer"

— and suffering itself is construed by them as something that must absolutely be *abolished*. That such "ideas" can still be modern sends a bad message about — — — But whoever has thoroughly reflected on where and how the plant human being has so far grown most robustly, has to surmise that this occurred under the *reverse* conditions: that for this the danger of its situation must grow immensely, its power of invention and dissimulation must struggle to the top under long pressure and compulsion, its life-will must be intensified to the point of unconditional will to power and to super-power, and that danger, harshness, violence, danger in the streets a⟨nd⟩ in the heart, inequality of rights, stealth, stoicism, tempter-arts, a⟨nd⟩ devilishness of every kind, in sum, the opposite of all herd-desiderata are essential for the *elevation* of the *type* human being. A morality with such inverted aims, that seeks to cultivate humans into the heights, instead of into comfort and mediocrity, a morality with the aim of cultivating a ruling caste — the future *rulers of the earth* — must, in order to be taught, introduce itself in association with the existing moral code and under its words and appearances; but that for this many transition- and deception-methods have to be invented, and that, because the lifespan of a single human means practically nothing with respect to the execution of such long-term tasks and aims, above all first *a new species* must be cultivated, in which that specific will, that specific instinct will be guaranteed longevity through many generations: a new ruler-species and caste — this is just as understandable as the long and not easy to articulate et cetera of this thought. To prepare an *inversion of values* for a specific strong species of human of the highest spirituality and will-power and for this purpose to slowly and cautiously unleash in them a large quantity of reined-in and slandered instincts: whoever reflects on this belongs among us, to the free spirits — to be sure to a newer kind of "free spirit" than previous ones: for the latter desired roughly the opposite. To this group belong, it seems to me, above all the pessimists of Europe, the poets and thinkers of an outraged idealism, insofar as their dissatisfaction with existence on the whole also forces them at least *logically* into dissatisfaction with the current human; likewise certain insatiably ambitious artists who heedlessly and unconditionally fight for the special rights of higher humans and against "the herd animal," and who, using the seductive methods of art, lull to sleep all herd instincts and herd caution in the more select spirits; thirdly, finally, all those critics and historians by whom the successfully begun discovery of the old world — it is the work of the *new* Columbus, of the German spirit — is courageously *continued* — for we are still at the beginning of this conquest. For in the ancient world there ruled indeed a different, a more ruler-oriented morality than today; and the ancient human under the educating sway of his morality was a stronger and deeper human than the human of today: — he alone so far was "the human who turned out well." However, the seduction that is exerted by antiquity on humans who have turned out well, i.e., on strong and enterprising souls, is even today the finest and most effective of all antidemocratic and antichristian seductions: as it was already at the time of the Renaissance.

37[9][9]

I see beyond all these national wars, new "empires" and whatever else stands in the foreground: what concerns me — for I see it preparing itself slowly and hesitatingly — this is the One Europe. Among all more comprehensive and profound humans of this century the real total work of their soul was to prepare that new synthesis and to experimentally anticipate "the European" of the future: only in their weaker hours, or when they became old, did they fall back into the national narrowness of their "fatherlands" — then they were "patriots." I am thinking of people like Napoleon, Goethe, Beethoven, Stendhal, Heinrich Heine, Schopenhauer; perhaps Richard Wagner also belongs here, about whom, a type of German obscurity who turned out well, absolutely nothing can be said without such a "perhaps." But by way of explanation, standing alongside that which stirs and takes shape in such spirits as a need for a new unity or already is a new unity with new needs, is a great economic fact: the small states of Europe, I mean all our current states and "empires," must in a short time become economically untenable given the absolute drive of big commerce and trade for a final limit, for world commerce and world trade. (Money alone is already forcing Europe to gather itself together into a single power at some time.) But in order to join the struggle for governing the earth with decent prospects — it is plain as day against whom this struggle will be aimed — Europe probably needs to come to a serious "understanding" with England: the colonies of England are needed for that struggle just as much as today's Germany needs the colonies of Holland for practicing its new mediator and broker role.[10] For no one believes anymore that England itself is strong enough to maintain its old role for even fifty years; it will be destroyed by the impossibility of excluding the *homines novi*[11] from government, and there must be no such change of parties if these long-lasting things are to be — — — today one must first be a soldier in order not to lose one's credit as a merchant. Enough: in this as in other things the next century will be found in the footsteps of Napoleon, the foremost and most highly anticipatory human being of modern times.

For the tasks of the next centuries "public" and parliamentarianism are the least suitable forms of organization.

37[10][12]

I differentiate, among superior humans as well as among peoples, those who want to have the world round, whole and firm — big perhaps, *very* big but whole and not at all "infinite" — and those who love the clouds: because clouds veil, because clouds make us "intuit." To the latter, among peoples, belong the Germans; and therefore it is not advisable for a thinker of the opposite disposition to build his cottage among them. The air is too cloudy for him there. German "simplicity," German faith in the "pure fool": he always translates that into French and calls it *la niaiserie allemande*.[13] The German "*mind*":[14] by that he literally means what Goethe meant by it: "Indulgence toward weaknesses of others and oneself." German bad taste: he finds it hair-raising, — I had an opportunity once to point this out in the case of a senile book by Strauss.[15] Seen from abroad, one is allowed to doubt whether Germany can come up now with ten men who are discerning in matters of literary form and have profundity. For profundity is necessary in order to grasp the delicate needs for form generally; only from the depths, from the abyss does one enjoy all the happiness found in bright, confident, colorful, superficial things of all kinds. But the Germans believe they are profound when they feel grave and melancholy: — they sweat when they think, sweating to them is regarded as proof of their "seriousness." Their spirits are clumsy, the spirit of beer is powerful even in their thoughts — and this they even call their "idealism"! To be sure, the Germans, at least as they themselves believe, have taken precisely this idealism far, "as far as the stars," and they might be allowed, if only German modesty permitted, to boldly seat themselves beside the Greeks in this regard, as the famous people of "poets and thinkers." Or, to let this self-confidence speak immodestly for once, and moreover in the verses of a great idealist:

"Why praise the Greeks to excess!
"*They must slink into darkness*,
"When softly stirs the German muse.
"Horace in Flemming simmers,
"In Opitz Naso shimmers,
"In Greiff the gloom of Seneca."

Leibniz.[16]

37[11][17]

Socialism — as a form of *tyranny* of the paltriest and stupidest, of the shallow, of the jealous and the three-quarters-actors, thought through to the end — is in fact the ultimate conclusion of modern ideas and their latent anarchism: but in the tepid air of democratic well-being the capacity for coming to conclusions or even coming *to conclusion* withers away. One follows — but one no longer draws conclusions. Therefore socialism on the whole is a hopeless, sour affair: and nothing is more fun to watch than the contradiction between the poisonous and desperate faces made by today's socialists — and what pitiful crushed emotions are betrayed by their style! — and the harmless little-lamb-happiness of their hopes and desires. In many places in Europe it can lead to occasional coups and attacks on their part: the next century will thoroughly "rumble" here and there in its stomach, and the Paris Commune, which also has its mouthpieces and advocates in Germany (e.g., in the philosophical grimace-maker and swamp-salamander E⟨ugen⟩ D⟨ühring⟩ in Berlin), was possibly only a milder case of indigestion, compared to what is coming. Nevertheless there will always be too many property owners for socialism to be anything more than an attack of sickness: and these property owners are to a man of one belief: "you have to own something to *be* something." But this is the oldest and healthiest of all instincts: I would add "you have to want more than you have in order to *become* more." For thus rings the doctrine that is preached by life itself to everything that lives: the morality of development. Possessing and wanting to have more, in a word, growth — this is life itself. In the doctrine of socialism a "will to denial of life" is badly concealed; it has to be failed humans or races who think up such a doctrine. Indeed, I wish it would be demonstrated by a few big experiments that in a socialist society life denies itself, cuts off its own roots. The earth is big enough, and human beings are still unexhausted enough, that a practical lesson and *demonstratio ad absurdum*[18] of this kind still has to seem desirable to me, even if it were gained and paid with a tremendous expenditure of human life. Still, even as the restless mole under the soil of a society rolling into stupidity, socialism can be something useful and healing: it delays "peace on earth" and the whole good-nature-izing of the democratic herd animal, it forces Europeans to preserve spirit, namely cunning and caution, to not entirely swear off the manly and warrior virtues, and to maintain a modicum of spirit — of clarity, dryness and coldness of the spirit

— it protects Europe for the time being from the *marasmus femininus*[19] that threatens it.

37[12]

In the main matter I consider the artists to be right more than all philosophers so far: they did not lose the great trail on which life walks, they loved the things "of this world" — they loved their senses. To strive for desensualization: that seems to me a misunderstanding or an illness or a cure, where it is not merely hypocrisy or self-deception. I wish for myself and for all those who live, who *are allowed* to live — without the anxieties of a Puritan-conscience an ever greater spiritualization and multiplication of the senses; indeed we want to be grateful to the senses for their subtlety, fullness and power, and in exchange offer them the best of the spirit that we have. What do the priestly and metaphysical denunciations of the senses concern us! We no longer need this denunciation: it is a sign of having turned out well when someone clings like Goethe with ever greater joy and heartiness to "the things of the world": — for that is the way he holds on to the great conception of the human being, that the human being becomes *the transfigurer of existence* when he learns to transfigure himself.[20] — But what are you saying? someone objects. Are not precisely today the worst pessimists among the artists? What do you think for example of Richard Wagner? Is that not a pessimist? — I have to rub my ears: ⟨you are right, I forgot something for a moment.⟩

37[13]

Historians today want too much and they all sin against good taste: they force themselves into the souls of humans to whose rank and in whose company they do not belong. What for example does such an agitated sweating plebeian like Michelet have to do with Napoleon! It makes no difference whether he hates or loves him, but because he sweats, he does not belong in his vicinity. What does that mediocre animal, elegant in the worst sense of the word, have to do with this same Napoleon! he makes us laugh, the little man, when he measures the great man against Caesar, Hannibal and Frederick with the mien of a wise judge. I value it higher when someone acknowledges even as a historian when the ground is too hot or too holy for his foot; but a historian who "removes his shoes" at the right time, or *puts them on* and walks away is a rare bird today, in this age of ingenuous shamelessness. The German historians among whom the "historical sense" was invented — now the French are rehearsing it — reveal, each and every one of them, that they do not come from a ruling caste: as knowing ones they are intrusive and show a lack of finer shame.

37[14]

I have named my unconscious workers and way-pavers. But where could I seek with a bit of hope for my kind of philosopher himself, at least for *my need for new philosophers*? Only where a *noble* way of thinking reigns, one that believes in slavery and in many degrees of bondage as the prerequisite of any higher culture; where a *creative* way of thinking reigns, which does not set the world's goal as the happiness of repose, the "Sabbath of all Sabbaths" and honors peace itself as a means to new wars; a way of thinking that prescribes laws for the future, which treats itself and everything of the present harshly and tyrannically for the sake of the future; a heedless, "immoral" way of thinking that wants to cultivate to greatness the good and wicked qualities of humans equally, because it trusts in its strength to deploy both in the right place — in the place where both are essential to one another. But whoever seeks philosophers in this manner today, what prospects does he have to find what he seeks? Is it not probable that he, searching with the best Diogenes-lantern, would run around day and night in vain? Our age has the *opposite* instincts: above all and in the first place it wants comfort; secondly it wants publicity and that grand noise of actors, that grand boom-boom that corresponds to its fairground-taste; thirdly it wants everyone to crawl on their belly in deepest subservience before the greatest of all lies — this lie is called "equality of human beings" — and it honors exclusively the virtues that *make equal* and *assign equal rights*. But in this way our age fundamentally opposes the emergence of the philosopher as I understand him, even though it believes in all innocence that it promotes him. Indeed, everyone today is lamenting about how bad the philosophers *used to* have it, jammed between the stake, bad conscience and presumptuous church father wisdom: but the truth is that precisely these circumstances provided for *more favorable* conditions for the education of a powerful, comprehensive, devious and audaciously daring spirituality than the conditions of contemporary life. Today a different kind of spirit, namely the demagogue-spirit, the actor-spirit, perhaps even the beaver- and ant-spirit of scholars has favorable conditions for its emergence. But for superior artists things are already even worse; for do not almost all of them perish from an inner lack of discipline? They are no longer tyrannized from the outside by the absolute value tablets of a church or a court: so they no longer learn to nurture their "inner tyrant," their *will*. And what is true of artists is true in a higher and more fateful sense of philosophers. After all, where *are* the free spirits today? Just show me a free spirit today![21] — Well, let's not talk too loudly! Solitude today is full of secrets and more solitude than ever. — — Indeed, I learned in the meantime that the free spirit has to be a hermit.

37[15][22]

Another demagogical talent of our time is Richard Wagner: but he belongs in Germany. — Really? Let an opposing estimation have a chance to speak for once. The Parisians may block and bristle against Wagner as much as they want: in the end he belongs more in Paris than to G⟨ermany⟩, and in any case more in it than in any other capital of Europe. Admittedly, the kind of French who are most closely related to him might have become scarce even there: — I mean those offspring of the *romantisme*[23] of the thirties, among whom he *wanted to live* in the most decisive period of his life. There he felt more related to and at home with himself than in Germany, with his tremendous appetite for exotic smells and colors and untested new excesses of the sublime, with his sunless, tortured happiness in the discovery of the ugly and the horrific. What else did these romantics seek, what else did they find and invent[24] besides Richard Wagner? Were they not all intelligently sick like him, violent and unsure of themselves, dominated by literature up to their eyes and ears, most of them even writers, poets, artists of expression at any cost — I make an exception for Delacroix — mediators and collectors of the arts and the senses themselves, jumped-up plebeians who, like Balzac, showed ⟨themselves⟩ to be insatiable in their longing to shine and for fame and incapable of a noble tempo in living and creating — of a *lento*[25] —? We should just admit it to ourselves: *how much* Wagnerian there is indeed to this French romanticism! Even that hysterical-erotic feature that Wagner especially loved in woman and set to music is best at home precisely in Paris: just ask the psychiatrists — ; and among the women of Paris, better than anywhere else, there is "appreciation" for the hypnotizing tricks and laying-on of hands with which our musical magus and Cagliostro compels and persuades his little women to lustful sleep-walking with open eyes and closed minds. The proximity of pathological desires, the ardor of senses gone raving mad, where one's gaze is deceived in a dangerous way by mists and veils of the supersensual: where does this belong more than in the romanticism of the French soul! Here a magic is at work that will yet inevitably convert even the Parisians to Wagner. — But Wagner is supposed to be the thoroughly *German* artist: thus it is decreed today in Germany, thus he is venerated in a time that once again elevates boastful Teutonomania. This "genuine German" Wagner *does not exist at all*: I suspect *he* is the spawn of very dark German youths and virgins who want to glorify themselves with this decree. It is probable enough that something in Wagner might be German: but what? Perhaps only the degree, not the quality of his willing and talents?

Perhaps only that he made everything stronger, richer, more daring, harsher than any Frenchman of the nineteenth century could make it? That he was more severe toward himself and for the longest part of his life he lived in the German way, on his own initiative as an implacable atheist, antinomist and immoralist? That he created the figure of a *very* free human being, of Siegfried, who in fact may be too free, too harsh, too cheerful, too unchristian for the Latin taste? — Of course in the end he knew how to make up for even this sin against French romanticism: the late W⟨agner⟩ in his old age with his Siegfried-caricature, I mean with his Parsifal, accommodated not only Roman taste but downright Roman-Catholic taste: until ultimately he went so far as to genuflect before the cross and bid his farewell with a not ineloquent thirst for "the blood of the redeemer." Farewell from himself too! For among romantics who have grown old there is an unpleasant rule that at the end of their life they "renounce" and disavow themselves and — *cross out* — their own life! — Finally let me ask: if that generation of the thirties in its blood and nerves was the heir and even more the *victim* of those tragic convulsions of the Napoleonic period — Beethoven served as the prelude to this generation in sounds and Byron in words — is it not permitted to think of a similar lineage of the soul for Richard Wagner? He was born in 1813.

37[16]

I observe that among those who now travel around in the world, no one likes to see himself regarded as a Frenchman if this is not what he is. To be considered an Englishman appears to be a source of pleasure for some northerners, e.g., the Swedes: the Englishman is proud. The German abroad now enjoys a boost of amazement and respect, compared to earlier times, but he is no pleasure; the Prussian in particular is still awkward in the southern countries of Europe, not because of his pride — for he is not proud — rather because of his immodesty and his bad, harsh, often obtrusive manners. The southern German is clumsy, peasant-like, good-natured and yet not trust-inspiring: with him one senses the famous "two souls in one breast."[26]

37[17][27]

One cannot think highly enough of women: but that is no reason to think falsely of them. In this one needs to be thoroughly on one's guard. That they themselves would be in a position to enlighten men about "the eternal feminine" is improbable; perhaps they are too close to themselves for this — and moreover all this *enlightening* itself — at least up till now — has been a man's affair and man's skill. Finally one should reserve a good mistrust for everything that women write about woman: namely in case quite involuntarily a woman, even when she writes, ultimately must not do what — up till now at least — has been eternally feminine: namely "*to dress up*"! Has one ever conceded *profundity* to a female mind? And to a female heart — justice? But without profundity and justice — what good is it when women make judgments "about woman"! With love and praise even when one loves and praises oneself certainly the danger of being unjust and shallow is not lessened. Some women may have a good reason for thinking that men do not approach them with praise and love: taken as a whole it seems to me *that up till now "woman" has been disrespected mostly by women* — and absolutely not by man!

37[18]

A human being who strives for greatness regards everyone he encounters along the way either as a means or as a delay or as a temporary resting place. His unique and superior *graciousness* toward fellow human beings is only possible when he is at his height and dominating. Impatience and the feeling that up till now he has been condemned to comedy ruins every relationship for him: this kind of human being knows solitude and what is most poisonous in it.

[38 = Mp XVI 1a. Mp XVI 2a. Mp XV 2b. June–July 1885]

38[1]

A thought in the shape in which it comes is an ambiguous sign that needs interpretation, more precisely, needs an arbitrary narrowing-down and limitation, until finally it becomes unambiguous. It surfaces in me — from where? through what? I do not know. It comes, independent of my willing, usually surrounded and obscured by a throng of feelings, desires, dislikes, also by other thoughts, often enough scarcely distinguishable from a "willing" or "feeling." One pulls it out of this throng, purifies it, stands it on its own feet, one sees how it stands there, how it walks, everything in an amazing *presto*[1] and yet entirely without the feeling of haste: *who* does all this — I do not know and am certainly more of a spectator in this than originator of this process. Then one sits in judgment of the thought, one asks: "what does it mean? what can it mean? is it right or wrong?" — one summons the help of other thoughts, one compares it. Thinking proves in this manner to be nearly a kind of practice and act of justice in which there is a judge, an opposing party, even an interrogation of witnesses, to which I am allowed to listen a bit — to be sure only a bit: most of it, it seems, escapes me. — That every thought first comes ambiguously and floating and in itself only as the occasion for the attempt of interpretation or for arbitrary determination, that with all thinking a multiplicity of persons seems to be involved — : this is not at all so easy to observe, we are at bottom trained for the opposite, namely not to think of thinking while thinking. The origin of the thought remains hidden; the probability is great that it is only the symptom of a much more comprehensive state; insofar as precisely *it* comes and no other, that precisely it comes with this greater or lesser clarity, sometimes confident and commanding, sometimes weak and in need of a prop, on the whole always exciting, questioning — for consciousness namely every thought functions like a stimulus — : in all of this something of our total state expresses itself in signs. — The same can be said of every feeling, it does not mean something in itself: when it comes it is first interpreted by us and often *how strangely* interpreted! Just think of the urgency of the bowels that is almost "unconscious" to us, of the blood pressure strains of our lower body, of the pathological states of the *nervus sympathicus*[2] — and how much is there of which we scarcely have a shimmer of consciousness through our *sensorium commune*![3] — In the case of such uncertain feelings of aversion only someone trained in anatomy guesses the correct species and *region* of causes; but all others, therefore on the whole nearly all people, as long as people have existed, do not seek a physical, but rather a psychical and moral explanation for pains of this kind and foist a *false justification* on the actual irritations of the body, in that within the vicinity of their unpleasant experiences and tribulations they seize upon a reason to feel as badly as they do. Under torture nearly everyone confesses guilt; with pain whose physical cause one does not know, the tortured one questions himself so long and so inquisitorially until he himself or others are *found guilty*: — as was done by the Puritan for instance, who habitually gave moral interpretations to a spleen that is associated with an unreasonable life style, namely as the bite of his own conscience. —

38[2]

The logical thinking of which logic speaks, a thinking where the thought itself is posited as the *cause* of new thoughts — is the model of a complete fiction: *a thinking of this kind never occurs in reality*, but it is applied as a schema of forms and filtering apparatus, with the help of which we dilute and simplify thinking's actual, extremely manifold occurrence: so that in this form our thinking becomes comprehensible, noticeable, communicable in signs. Therefore: to regard mental occurrence as if it really corresponded to that regulative scheme of a feigned thinking, this is the trick of falsification by virtue of which something like "knowledge" and "experience" exists. Experience is only possible with the help of memory; memory is only possible by means of an abbreviation of a mental process to a sign. "Knowledge": this is the expression of a new thing through the signs of already "known," already experienced things. —Today of course people even drivel about an *empirical* origin of logic: but what does not exist in reality, like logical thinking, cannot be derived from reality either, no more than some law of numbers as long as there has not yet been a case in which reality coincided with a mathematical formula. The mathematical formulas are likewise only regulative fictions with which we simplify and adjust real occurrence, for the purpose of practical exploitation, to our standard — to our stupidity —.

38[3][4]

— — — through thinking the ego is posited; but hitherto one believed, like the common people, that "I think" was some kind of immediate certainty, and this "I" was the given *cause* of thinking, according to whose analogy we understood all remaining causal relationships. However highly accustomed and indispensable that fiction may now be — *This* alone does not yet prove anything against its fictionality: a belief can be a condition of life and *nevertheless* be *false.*

38[4][5]

"Truth": within my way of thinking this describes not necessarily an opposition to error, but in the fundamental cases only a disposition of different errors to one another: perhaps that the one is older, deeper than the other, perhaps even inextinguishable, insofar as an organic being of our kind could not live without it; while other errors do not tyrannize us to this extent as conditions of life, rather, measured against such "tyrants," can be set aside and "refuted." An assumption that is irrefutable — why must it on this account already be *true*? This proposition probably outrages the logicians, who posit *their* limits as the limits of things: but I declared war on this logician-optimism long ago.

38[5][6]

Even now France is still the seat of the most spiritual and sophisticated culture in Europe and the preeminent school of taste: but one has to know where to find this "France of taste." Whoever belongs to it keeps himself well hidden: a dumbed-down and coarsened France wallows in the foreground today — recently at the funeral of Victor H⟨ugo⟩ it celebrated a veritable orgy of bad taste — they may be few in number, and include people who do not stand on the strongest of legs, some of them fatalists, some pampered (those who have reasons to hide themselves) — they as a whole recognize roughly the following higher spirits as their forefathers and masters. First *Stendhal*, the last great event of the French spirit, who marched through his undiscovered Europe with a Nap⟨oleonic⟩ tempo and ultimately found himself alone — horrifyingly alone: for it took two generations to even come close to him. Now he commands, as I said, a commander for the most elite; and whoever is gifted with subtle and daring senses, curious to the point of cynicism, a logician nearly from disgust, riddle guesser and friend of the sphinx like every born European, he will have to follow in his steps. May he also follow him to that place, full of shame for the secrets that great passion has *when it stands still*! This noblesse of *being able to* be silent, *being able to* stand still is his advantage for instance over Michelet and especially over German scholars. — His disciple is *Mérimée*, a noble withdrawn artist and despiser of those spongy emotions praised by a democratic age as its "noblest emotions," austere toward himself and full of the harshest demands on his artistic logic, constantly prepared to sacrifice small beauties and impulses to a strong will to necessity: — a genuine although not rich soul in a fake and dirty environment, pessimist enough to play along with the comedy without vomiting. — Another disciple of Stendhal is *Taine*, now the foremost living historian in Europe, a decisive, brave human being even in his despair, whose courage did not fall to pieces any more than did his will power under the fatalistic pressure of knowing, a thinker not diminished either by Condillac with respect to profundity nor Hegel with respect to clarity, rather someone who knew how to *learn* and for a long time will know how to *teach*: — the French of succeeding generations will have their spiritual drill sergeant in him. It is he primarily who pushes back the influence of Renan and Sainte-Beuve, who are both insecure and skeptical down to the bottom of their hearts: Renan, a kind of Catholic Schleiermacher, cloying, candy, feigning sensitivity for landscapes and religions: Sainte-Beuve, a burned-out poet who devotes himself to sniffing out souls and all too gladly would like to hide that he has no foothold either in the will or in philosophy, indeed, not surprisingly after both of these, he lacks a genuine *solid* taste *in artibus et litteris*.[7] In the end one notices in him the intention of even turning this lack into a kind of principle and method of critical neutrality: but his annoyance betrays itself too often, at one point because he in fact was not neutral, but instead really enthused a few times about certain books and human beings — he would like to strike out and lie away these terrible "*petit faits*"[8] from his life — but then because of the much more unpleasant *grand fait*[9] that *all* great French connoisseurs of humanity also genuinely possessed their own will and character, from Montaigne, Charon, La Rochefoucauld up to Chamfort and Stendhal: — compared to all of them Sainte-Beuve is not without envy and in any case without preference or pre-understanding. — Much more benevolent, one-sided, more able in every sense is the influence of Flaubert: with his preponderance of character that even endured solitude and failure — something extraordinary among French people — he rules at the moment in the realm of the aesthetics of the novel and of style — he brought resounding and colorful French to the pinnacle. Of course he too lacks philosophical discipline, like Renan and Sainte-Beuve, likewise a genuine knowledge of scientific procedures: but in him a deep need for analysis and even for scholarliness along with an instinctive pessimism paved the way, oddly perhaps, but strongly enough to provide a model for the current novel writers of France. In fact the new ambition of the most recent school goes back to Flaubert, namely that of displaying themselves in scientific and pessimistic attitudes. — Whatever blossoms now in France by way of poets stands under the influence of Heinrich Heine and Baudelaire, perhaps with the exception of Leconte de Lisle: for in the same manner as Schopenhauer is now already loved and read more in France than in Germany, the cult of Heinrich Heine has relocated to Paris. As concerns the pessimistic Baudelaire, he belongs to those scarcely believable amphibians who are just as German as Parisian; his poetry has something of what in Germany is called *Gemüt*[10] or "endless melody" and sometimes also "caterwauling."[11] For the rest Baudelaire was a human being of perhaps ruined but very specific and sharp taste, sure of itself: with this he tyrannizes the insecure of today. Though in his day he was the first prophet and advocate of Delacroix: perhaps today he would be the first "Wagnerian" of Paris. There is much Wagner in Baudelaire.

38[6][12]

Victor Hugo, an "ass of a genius" — the expression is from Baudelaire — who always had the *courage* of his bad taste: with it he knew how to command, he, the son of a Napoleonic general. In his ears he had the requirements of a kind of military rhetoric, he imitated in words the firing of cannons and the bursting of rockets; the French *esprit*[13] appears in him obscured by smoke and din, so to speak, often to the point of naked stupidity. Never has a mortal written such dull, bursting antitheses. At other times he even gives the painter's visual desires mastery over his intellect: he bristles with picturesque insights and often does nothing more than to accurately copy what he *sees*, what the painter's hallucination places in front of his eyes. He, the plebeian, who with his strong sensual desires, I mean his ears and eyes, does the will's bidding even with his intellect — This after all is the basic fact of French *romantisme*, as a plebeian reaction of taste — : with this he is on the opposite track and wants precisely the inverse of what the poets of a noble culture wanted of themselves, for instance Corneille. For these had their pleasure and ambition in overwhelming their perhaps more strongly natured senses with the *concept* and in helping a subtle bright spirituality to victory against the brutal demands of colors, sounds and shapes: with which, it seems to me, they were on the trail of the great Greeks, despite how little they might have known about it. Precisely that which today causes us to be displeased about the ancient Greeks and the older French, offending our clumsy sensual and naturalistic taste — was the *purpose* of their artistic willing, also their triumph: for they fought against and conquered precisely this "sensual rabble" whom our poets, painters and musicians aspire to help to some form of art. Victor Hugo's political and moral designs correspond to this artistic one: he is shallow and demagogical, on his belly before all big words and gestures, a flatterer of the people who speaks with the voice of an evangelist to all lowly, oppressed, deformed, crippled people and does not have a whiff of what discipline and honesty of the spirit are, what intellectual conscience is — on the whole an unconscious actor, like nearly all artists of the democratic movement. His genius affects the masses as does an alcoholic drink that simultaneously makes one drunk and stupid. — The same species of sympathies and antipathies and something similar by way of talent were possessed by another advocate of the people, the historian Michelet, only in place of painter's eyes an admirable capacity to reproduce states of mind within himself, in the manner of musicians: — today in obscure G⟨ermany⟩ we would therefore refer to him as a human being of *compassion*.

This "compassion" in any case is something obtrusive; in his interactions and even in his veneration of past human beings there is much immodesty, indeed it sometimes seems to me as if he takes to his emotional work with a zeal that requires him to remove his coat. His eyes do not see into the depths: all easily "inspired" spirits were superficial so far. He is too excited for me: justice is just as inaccessible to him as that graciousness that only flows from the highest superiority. At a certain elevation of excitement he is overcome each time by an attack of the tribunes, he also knows from his own experience the rabble's predatory fits of rage. It sufficiently characterizes the ignobility of his morality that Napoleon as well as Montaigne is foreign to him.[14] It is unusual that even he, the industrious straight-laced scholar, richly shares in the sexually lascivious curiosity of his race: and the older he got, the more this kind of curiosity grew. — Finally, democratic and therefore likewise thespian is the talent of George Sand: she is eloquent in that wicked manner whereby her style, a colorful, unbridled exaggerating female style, runs away with her emotions every half page — not the opposite, as much as she wishes that people believe the opposite of her. Indeed, people believed much too much in her feeling: whereas she was rich in that cold skill of the actor who knows how to spare his nerves and makes everyone believe the opposite. One should concede that she has a great talent for narrating; but she ruined everything and forever with her heated female coquetry of showing herself only in men's roles that did not suit precisely her height — her spirit was short-legged — : so that her books were taken seriously only for a brief time and already today have fallen into the realm of involuntarily comical literature. And if it was not only coquetry but cleverness as well that drove her to always drape herself in men's problems and masculine appurtenances, including pants and cigars: ultimately the very female problem and misfortune of her life nevertheless leaps into view, namely that she needed too many men and that even in these demands her senses and her spirit were divided. What could she do about the fact that whenever her spirit found pleasure in men, they were too sickly to satisfy the needs of her senses? Hence the eternal problem of two lovers at the same time and an eternal coercion of female modesty to deceive about this circumstance and to pretend that entirely different, much more general, much more impersonal problems stood in the foreground for her. For instance the problem of marriage: but what did she care about marriage!

38[7][15]

People everywhere now are making an effort to divert attention from the actual great influence Kant exerted on German philosophy — and especially to wisely sidestep the value he attributed to himself. Kant was above all and chiefly proud of his table of categories, saying with this table in his hands: "this is the most difficult task that *could* ever be undertaken for the benefit of metaphysics"[16] (let us make sure we understand this "could be"!) — he was proud of having discovered a new faculty in human beings, the faculty for synthetic judgments a priori. It does not concern us here how greatly he deceived himself about this: but German philosophy, as it has been admired and as it has influenced people throughout Europe for a hundred years, depended on this pride and on the rivalry of the younger generation to possibly discover something even prouder — and in any case new faculties! It has so far constituted the actual *fame* of German philosophy that through it people were taught to believe in a kind of "intuitive and instinctive comprehension of truth"; and Schopenhauer too, as much as he scorned Fichte, Hegel and Schelling, was at bottom on the same course when he discovered in an old, well-known faculty, the will, that it had a new faculty — namely to be the very "thing in itself." This required one to reach in boldly indeed, and not spare one's fingers, right into the "essence"! Bad enough that this essence turned out to be unpleasant, and, as a result of burned fingers, pessimism and denial of the will appeared to be absolutely necessary for living! But this fate of Schopenhauer is an incident that remained without influence for the overall significance of German philosophy, for its higher "effect": in the main namely it signified throughout Europe the *jubilating* reaction against the rationalism of Descartes and against the skepticism of the English, in favor of the "intuitive," "instinctive," and everything "good, true and beautiful." One thought the way to knowledge was henceforth *abbreviated*, one could get directly to the heart of "things," one hoped "to save labor": and all the happiness that noble idlers, the virtuous, dreamers, mystics, artists, three-fourths-Christians, political obscurantists and metaphysical concept-spiders are capable of perceiving accrued to the honor of Germans. The good *reputation* of Germans was suddenly manufactured: by their philosophers! — I hope people still know that in fact the Germans in Europe had a bad reputation? That people took them to have servile and pitiful qualities, an inability to have "character," a famous servant-soul? All of a sudden, however, they learned to say: "the Germans are profound, the Germans are virtuous — just read their philosophers"! In the last analysis it was the suppressed and long obstructed *piety* of the Germans that finally exploded in their philosophy, unclear and uncertain, to be sure, like all things German, namely now in pantheistic vapors, as in Hegel and Schelling, as gnosis, now mystically and life-negating, as in Schopenhauer: in the main however a Christian piety, and not a pagan one — toward which Goethe and before him Spinoza had shown so much good will.

38[8][17]

The will. — In every willing there is a plurality of *sensations*, namely the sensation of the state *away from which*, the sensation of the state *toward which*, the sensation itself of this "away" and "toward," the sensation of duration, finally then an accompanying sensation in the muscles that comes into play through a kind of habit as soon as we "will," even without our having to move our arms and legs. Secondly therefore, just as sensation and in fact many kinds of sensations are to be recognized as ingredients of the will, so too *thinking*: in every act of will there is a commanding thought — and we had better not believe that this thought can be separated from the "willing" as if will would still be left over. Thirdly the will is not only a complex of sensation and thinking, but above all an *affect*: and specifically that affect of command. What we call "freedom of the will" is essentially the affect of superiority with respect to the one who must obey: "I am free, he must obey" — this consciousness lies in every will, and likewise that straining of attention, that clear gaze that fixes on one thing exclusively, that unconditional valuation "now this is essential and nothing else," that inner certainty that something will be obeyed, as all this belongs to the disposition of the commander. Someone who *wills* — commands something in himself that obeys or which he believes obeys. But now let us observe what is the most wondrous thing about the "will," about this very complicated thing for which the people have only one word: insofar as in this case we are simultaneously the commanders and the obeyers, and as obeyers we know the sensations of resisting, pushing, pressing, *moving*, which usually begin immediately after the act of willing; and insofar on the other hand as we have a habit of disregarding and *deceiving* ourselves about this duality by virtue of the synthetic concept "I," a whole chain of erroneous conclusions and consequently of false valuations has attached itself to willing: — to such an extent that the willing individual believes in good faith that his will itself is the actual and sufficient *mobile*[18] for the entire action. And because in most cases by far there has only been willing where the effect of command, of obedience, therefore action could be expected, the appearance has translated into sensation, as if there were a necessity of effect there: enough, someone who wills believes with a considerable degree of certainty that will and action are somehow one — he attributes the success of executing the will to the will itself and in doing so enjoys an increase in that feeling of power that comes with all commanding. "Freedom of the will": that is the word for that very mixed state of the one who wills, who commands and simultaneously as the executor also enjoys the triumph of superiority over obstacles, but thinks to himself that it is his will alone that really overcomes the obstacles: — he takes the pleasurable sensations of the executing successful tool — the useful will and sub-will — and adds them to his pleasurable sensation as commander. — This interwoven nest of sensations, states and false assumptions, which is described by the people with one word and as one thing because it is suddenly and all "at once" there and belongs among the most frequent, consequently the "best known" experiences: *the will* as I have described it here — can we believe that it has never before been described? That this clumsy prejudice of the people so far has rightfully existed untested in every philosophy? That there was no difference of opinion among philosophers regarding what "willing" is, because they all believed that precisely here one had an immediate certainty, a fundamental fact, here opining was not at all in order? And that all logicians still teach the trinity "thinking, feeling, willing" as if "willing" included no feeling and thinking? — After all of this Schopenhauer's major blunder seems less crazy and arbitrary, when he took the will as the best-known thing in the world, indeed as the actual and solely known thing: he simply took over a tremendous prejudice of all previous philosophers, a popular prejudice, and as philosophers generally do, *exaggerated* it. —

38[9]

There is no small danger in extraordinary spirits that at some time they will learn to strive for the horrific pleasures of destroying, of ruining, of slowly ruining: namely when they are absolutely denied the creative deed, perhaps through a lack of tools or some other mischief of chance. In the economy of such souls there is no longer an either-or; and perhaps they must ⟨corrupt⟩, with the pleasure of a devil and in a subtle protracted manner, precisely what they have loved most up till then.

38[10]

The human being is a form- and rhythm-constructing creature; in nothing is he better practiced and it appears that he takes pleasure in nothing *more* than in the *inventing* of shapes. Just observe what our eye immediately becomes occupied with as soon as it no longer gets to see anything: it *creates* itself something to see. Presumably in the same case our hearing does no differently: it *practices*. Without the transformation of the world into shapes and rhythms there would be no "sameness" for us, therefore nothing recurring, therefore also no possibility for experience and appropriation, for *nourishment*. In all perceiving, that is, in the most original appropriation, the essential occurrence is a doing, or better yet: an imposition of forms: — only the superficial speak of "impressions." Human beings get to know their force here as a resisting and even more as a determining force — rejecting, selecting, forming to suit, arranging into their schemata. There is something active in the fact that we even adopt a stimulus and that we adopt it as *such* a stimulus. It is characteristic of this activity not only to posit forms, rhythms and series of forms, but also to evaluate the created formation with respect to incorporation or rejection. Thus our world emerges, our entire world: and this world that belongs to us alone, first created by us corresponds to no alleged "actual reality," no "in-itself of things": instead, it is itself our sole reality, and "knowledge" turns out to be, regarded in this manner, only a *means of nourishment*. But we are hard-to-nourish beings and have enemies everywhere and indigestible things, as it were — : this is why human knowledge has become *refined* and ultimately so proud of its refinement that it does not like to hear it is not a goal, but a means or even a tool of the stomach — if not a kind of stomach itself! — —

38[11][19]

The superior philosophical human being, who has solitude around himself, not because he wants to be alone but because he *is* something that does not find his equal: what dangers and new sufferings are reserved just for him today, when one has unlearned belief in order of rank and consequently does not know how to honor and understand this solitude! Formerly a wise man almost sanctified himself for the conscience of the masses through such stepping-aside — today the hermit sees himself as if surrounded by a cloud of gloomy doubt and suspicions. And not only perhaps on the part of the envious and the pitiful: he has to perceive misjudgment, neglect and superficiality emanating from every benevolence that he experiences, he knows those treacheries of narrow compassion that feels itself to be good and holy when it seeks to "rescue" him from himself, perhaps through more comfortable circumstances, through more orderly, more trustworthy company — indeed, he will have to marvel at the unconscious drive to destruction with which all mediocre of spirit are active against him, and what is more, in the best belief in their right to it! It is necessary for humans of this incomprehensible solitude to wrap themselves skillfully and heartily even in the mantle of external, of spatial solitude: this belongs to their prudence. Even cunning and disguise will be needed today for such a human being to sustain himself, to hold himself *up* amidst the sweeping, dangerous rapids of the times. For every attempt to endure it *in* the present, *with* the present, for every approach to these human beings and goals of today he must do penance as if for an actual sin: and he might marvel at the hidden wisdom of his nature, which always immediately called him back to himself after all such temptations through sickness and wicked accidents.

38[12][20]

And do you also know what "the world" is to me? Should I show it to you in my mirror? This world: a colossus of energy, without beginning, without end, a firm, unshakable magnitude of energy that does not get bigger, does not get smaller, that does not expend itself but only transforms itself, as a whole unchangeable in size, an economy without expenditures and losses, but likewise without growth, without income, encased by "nothingness" as by its border, nothing blurring, wasted, nothing infinitely extended, but laid into a definite space as a definite force, and not a space that would be "empty" anywhere, rather as force everywhere, as play of forces and waves of forces simultaneously one and "multiple," increasing itself here and at the same time decreasing itself there, a sea of forces storming and flooding together, eternally transforming, eternally receding, with tremendous years of return, with an ebb and flow of its configurations, from the simplest striving outward into the most complex, from the stillest, most rigid, coldest out into the most glowing, wildest, most self-contradictory, and then returning home again from abundance to the simple, from the play of contradictions returning to the joy of accord, affirming itself even in this sameness of its courses and years, blessing itself as that which must recur eternally, as a becoming that knows no satiety, no tedium, no weariness — : this my *Dionysian* world of eternal self-creating, of eternal self-destroying, this mystery-world of the doubly voluptuous, this my beyond good and evil, without goal, if a goal does not lie in the happiness of the circle, without will, if a ring does not have good will for itself — do you want a *name* for this world? A *solution* for all its riddles? a *light* for you too, you hiddenmost, strongest, most intrepid, most midnightly? — *This world is the will to power — and nothing else*! And you yourselves are also this will to power — and nothing else![21]

38[13][22]

When I was younger I worried about just what a philosopher actually is: for I believed I perceived contradictory features in the famous philosophers. Finally it occurred to me that there are two different kinds of philosopher, first those who have to hold on to some great factual legacy of valuations, that is previous valuations and value creations (logical or moral), then those who themselves are legislators of valuations. The former seek to master the present or past world by summarizing and abbreviating it through symbols. It is the duty of these researchers to make all previous events and everything that has been valued so far surveyable, thinkable, comprehensible, handy, to overpower the past, to abbreviate everything that is long, indeed time itself, a great and wonderful task. The actual philosophers *however are commanders and legislators*, they say: it *shall* be so! they alone determine the where-to and what-for of human beings and in so doing dispose of the preliminary work of the philosophical laborers, those who overpower the past. This second kind of philosopher rarely turns out well; and in fact their situation and danger are tremendous. How often have they purposely blindfolded themselves, in order simply not to have to see anymore the narrow ledge that separates them from abyss and plunge: for instance Plato, when he convinced himself that the good as he wanted it was not Plato's good, but the good in itself, the eternal treasure that some human being named Plato happened to find along his way! This same will to blindness reigns in a much cruder form in the founders of religion: their "thou shalt" must absolutely not sound like "I want" to their ears — only as the command of a god do they dare to comply with their task, only as "inspiration" is their legislation of values a *bearable* burden under which their conscience does *not* shatter. — Now as soon as those two consolations, those of Plato and Mohammed, have fallen away and no thinker can ease his conscience anymore with the hypothesis of a "god" or "eternal values," the claim of the legislator's new values rises to a new and never before attained level of terribleness. From now on those hand-picked ones on whom the inkling of such a duty begins to dawn will make the attempt to see whether they might be able to escape it at just "the right time," as their greatest danger, through some kind of leap to the side: for instance, by convincing themselves that the task has already been solved, or it is unsolvable, or they do not possess the shoulders for such burdens, or they are already overburdened with other more immediate tasks, or even this new distant duty is a seduction and temptation, a distraction from all duties, a sickness, a kind of madness. Some may indeed succeed in evading it: the trace of such evaders and their bad conscience runs through the whole of history. But for the most part that redeeming hour came for these fateful human beings, that autumn hour of ripeness when they had to do what they did not even "want" to do: — and the deed they previously feared more than anything fell to them easily and unbidden from the tree, as a deed without arbitrariness, almost as a gift. —

38[14]

What separates us most thoroughly from all Platonic and Leibnizian ways of thinking is: we do not believe in any eternal concepts, eternal values, eternal forms, eternal souls; and philosophy, insofar as it is science and not legislation, for us means only the broadest extension of the concept "history." On the basis of etymology and the history of language we take all concepts as *having become*, many as still becoming; moreover in such a way that the most universal concepts, as the *falsest*, must also be the oldest. "Being," "substance," and "absolute," "sameness," "thing" — : thinking invented these schemata, which in fact most thoroughly contradicted the world of becoming, as the first and the oldest, but which *appeared* from the start to correspond with it, given the dullness and monotony of the incipient, still sub-animal consciousness: every "experience" seemed always to underscore it anew and underscore it entirely alone. Sameness and similarity were admitted ever more rarely with the sharpening of the senses and of attention, with the development and the struggle of the most manifold life: whereas for the lowest beings everything seemed "eternally the same," "one," "permanent," "absolute," "without qualities." Eventually the "external world" multiplied itself in this way; but through tremendous stretches of time a thing on earth was considered identical and corresponding with a single characteristic, for example with a certain color. The multiplicity of characteristics of a single thing was admitted only with the greatest slowness: we still see a resistance against the multiplicity of predicates in the history of human language. But the longest confusion is that the predicate symbol is posited as equal to the thing itself; and the philosophers, who have best reproduced in themselves precisely the oldest instincts of humanity and also the oldest fears and superstitions (like the superstition of the soul) — one can speak of an atavism par excellence in them — pressed their seal upon this confusion when they taught that precisely the symbols, namely the "ideas" were what truly existed, what was unchanging and all-valid. Whereas in fact, in the perception of a thing, thinking navigates a series of symbols offered to him by memory, and looks for similarities; whereas a human being with a similar symbol posits, grasps, *apprehends* the thing as "known": for a long time he simply believed he *comprehended* it in this manner. Seizing and grasping, appropriating already meant knowing for him, a knowing-to-the-end; for a long time even the words in human language seemed — and today still seem to the common people — to be not symbols but truths with respect to the things they signify. The more refined the senses, the more rigorous the attention, the more manifold the tasks of life became, the harder it was to admit the knowledge of a thing, of a fact, as definitive knowledge, as "truth"; and in the very end, at the point to which our methodical mistrust has driven us today, we no longer give ourselves the right at all to speak of truths in the absolute sense — we have sworn off the belief in the knowability of things just as much as the belief in knowledge. The "thing" is only a fiction, the "thing in itself" even a contradictory unpermitted fiction: but knowing, too, of the absolute and consequently also the relative kind, is likewise only a fiction! With this, the necessity also disappears for positing a something that "knows," a subject for knowing, some pure "intelligence," an "absolute spirit": — this mythology not yet completely given up by Kant, which Plato prepared for Europe in a disastrous manner and which, using the fundamental Christian dogma of "God is a spirit," threatened all science of the body and therewith also the continued development of the body with death — this mythology has now had its time.

38[15]

I have experienced strange things with respect to the effect of my books. Recently I received the letter of an old noble Dutchman[23] who regards *Human, All Too Human* as his most faithful life companion; the *Birth of Tragedy* perhaps produced the greatest sound of happiness in the life of R⟨ichard⟩ W⟨agner⟩, he was beside himself, and there are wondrously beautiful things in the *Twilight of the Gods* that he produced in this state of an unexpected greatest hope. (Back then — — —

I would like to know if this book has been understood by anyone: its backgrounds belong to my most personal property. *Zarathustra* has the value estimations of a couple of millennia against it; I absolutely do not believe that anyone today is in a position to hear the ringing of its overall tone: understanding it also presupposes a kind of philological and more than philological work that no one today would invest in it, out of a lack of time.

I myself am very satisfied with the fact that my taste *in musicis* and *philosophicis*,[24] which in 1865 (when I was perhaps the only German who, just as Sch⟨openhauer⟩ and W⟨agner⟩ and — — — now belongs to German taste.

The choice that people make with respect to my books gives me food for thought.

38[16]

the unhesitating use of stop-gaps and of spiritual expenditure and wealth in order to give a weakness here the attribute of strength: what nearly gives Wagnerian style its character —

38[17]

Schopenh⟨auer's⟩ perversity of mentality and my *Birth of Tragedy*!

38[18]

"he could have acted differently" — this viewpoint on the emergence of the sense of justice is falsely applied by Rée.[25]

38[19][26]

In surveying my life, the first trace of philosophical meditation that I can lay my hands on I encounter in a small text from my 13th year: it contains an insight concerning the origin of evil. My assumption was that for a God thinking something and creating something are one and the same. Now I reasoned thus: God thought himself at the time when he created the second person of the divinity: but in order to be able to think himself he first had to think his opposite. Thus in my representation the devil had the exact same age as the son of God, even a clearer origin — and the same *descent*. Regarding the question of whether it was possible for a God to think his opposite, I finessed this by saying: but everything is possible for him. And secondly: *that* he did it is a fact, in case the existence of a God-son is a fact, consequently it was also possible for him, — — —

38[20]

Without a passionate pleasure in the adventures of knowledge someone will scarcely endure very long in its dangerous realm; and anyone who is too cowardly or too timid for such "dissipations" should in fairness acknowledge making a virtue and a commendation of it, too. But for the stronger spirits, the demand that one should indeed be a human being of passion, but also the *master* of his passions, also applies with respect to their passion for knowledge. Just as Napoleon, to the astonishment of Talleyrand, allowed his anger to bark and roar at the chosen time and then later, just as suddenly, silenced it, so too the strong spirit must do with his wild dogs: at the chosen time, no matter how urgent the will to truth is in him — it is his wildest dog — he must *be able* to be the incarnate will to untruth, the will to uncertainty, the will to ignorance, above all to *foolishness*.

38[21]

The decline of grace. — Belonging among the symptoms of general uglification as it accompanies an age that increasingly makes the rabble its master, not the least is the growing letting-herself-go of woman and a kind of "return to nature" i.e., to the rabble: even in places where noble and rigorous habits were formerly maintained like a privilege: e.g., at court. One stands amazed before the lack of refinement even in dealings with the most amiable of women: and we help ourselves — — —

38[22]

A garden in which even the lattice is gilded has to defend itself not only against thieves and rascals: its worst dangers are presented by its meddlesome admirers, who everywhere would like to break off something and all too gladly take away this or that as a memento. — And do you not notice, you idlers in my garden, that you cannot *justify* yourselves even next to my herbs and weeds, that they say to your face: be gone, you intruders, you — — —

[39 = N VII 2a. Z I 2b.
August–September 1885]

39[1][1]

The Will to Power.

Attempt
at a New Interpretation
of All Events.

By
Friedrich Nietzsche.

39[2][2]
"milky spirit"

Like a child encountering other people's public holidays: shyly it stands there — never before has it heard this bell, never before did it see these decorations and festive costumes.

Am I then a mirror that becomes cloudy and blind right away because a stranger's breath breathes on me, seethes at me?

Why do you want to scrape the down from such things? —

Truths that no smile has gilded.

39[3][3]
Zarathustra 5 (*youth as the basic tone*)
martial in the highest degree

On an old *fortress* — the drumming of heralds.
(Finale) — at night as on the Rialto.[4]
the rose festival.

Zarathustra the godless hermit, the first solitary one who did not pray.

Are you strong enough for my truths?

Who belongs with me? what is noble?

"*Are you such?*" (as refrain) the order of rank:

and you must have everything in you in order to be able to rule, but also *under* you!

Refrain: "a⟨nd⟩ if you are not able to speak: "we honor them, yet we are of a superior kind" —then you are not of *my* kind.

The rose festival.
At night on the bridge.

Zarathustra happy about the fact that the struggle of the classes is *over* and now finally it is time for an order of rank of individuals.

Hatred for the democratic leveling-system is only *in the foreground*: actually he is very glad that **this** *has gone so far*. Now he can solve his task. —

His teachings so far were directed only at the future ruling caste. These rulers of the earth are now supposed to **replace** *God* and create for themselves the profound unconditional confidence of the ruled. First: *their new holiness*, their *renunciation* of *happiness and pleasure*. They give the *lowliest* the prospect of happiness, not *themselves*. They redeem the misfits with the doctrine of the "quick death," they offer religions and systems according to the order of rank.

39[4]

The self-mirroring of the spirit, the creaking of the logical clockwork, the unwinding of the instincts

Supposing you had resolved everything into formulas: what would happen then? Are we supposed to *live* with bad conscience?

I admire the great *falsifications* and *interpretations*: they elevate us above the happiness of animals.

The overestimation of truthfulness in the circles of the herd animal makes good sense. To not allow oneself to be cheated — and consequently — to not cheat.

That the truthful one is of more value than the liar cannot be proved by anything: and supposing that life is based on a consequential being-deceived, then a consequ⟨ential⟩ liar could achieve highest honors under certain circumstances. That one harms by not "telling the truth" is a naïveté. If the value of life lies in well-believed errors, what is harmful resides in "telling the truth."

39[5]

Life in the hereafter gone? — the *pointe*[5] of life has been taken away.

39[6][6]

Just as the matador fig[7] pursues its goals, ruining that which it wants only as a support: so too reason in relation to the philos⟨ophers⟩. What does every philosophy mean for the life of a human being? Whether as enhancement of the feeling of power: Or as a means of masking an unbearable existence? Behind consciousness the *drives* are working.

39[7]

Nourishment property reproduction sexual lust (as a narcotic work (overcoming of oscillations)

The sublime human being has the highest value, even when he is quite delicate and fragile, because an abundance of quite difficult and rare things has been cultivated and kept together through many generations.[8]

Primeval forest animals the *Romans*.[9]

39[8]

The deification of the devil — how did this heavenly illusion occur!

The belief in goodness justice and truth at the bottom of things has something hair-raising about it.

The masks of the devil.

39[9]

The interpretation of nature: we interpret ourselves into it.

— the terrible character.

39[10][10]

Zarathustra 1. the beginnings of the differentiation.

All "happiness" permitted only as cure or resting. Against the "happy" and "good" and the herd animals.

Zarathustra 2. The *"self-overcoming" of the human being.*

Greatest of all struggles and longest cultivation.

As a means the "tempters" are conjured up.

Zarathustra 3 on the ring
the *primeval forest*, everything in terrible magnification

39[11]

In order not to express the opposite about the essence of the world, one must hold firm that every moment signifies a necessary total-displacement of all changes; but as a thinking and creating thing it must of course compare, consequently also be able to be *timeless* vis-à-vis its own inner conditions.

39[12][11]

Chap. Nourishment.
Procreation.
Adaptation.
Heredity.
Division of labor.
} Traced back to will to power.

Chap. The *juxtaposition* of consciousness with that which actually *drives* and *rules.*

Chap. The reversal of the temporal order: also in embryonic growth (organic development reversed, as it is stored in memory: simultaneously the oldest as the strongest in front). Just as the oldest errors constitute the spine, so to speak, to which everything else attaches itself.
Chap. The development of the logical

39[13][12]

The qualities of the organic being.
The development of organic beings.
The union of the organic and the inorganic.
"Knowledge" in relation to the conditions of life. The "perspectival."
"Laws of nature" as determination of power relations.
"Cause and effect" an expression for the necessity and inexorability of this power determination.
Freedom of the will and power.
Pain and joy in relation to the will to power.
"Person" "subject" as deception. A ruled community. Using the body as a guide.
Ruling and obeying as expression of the will to power, in the organic.
Emergence of the logical. "Rationale."
Against self-mirroring. Mathem⟨atics⟩.
The physical world like the psychical both false, but enduring errors.
The artist and the will to power. The impression of neutrality is mesmerizing for herd animals. Palazzo Pitti[13] and Phidias. Art depending on morality, for herds or leaders: — — —
the *refutation* of God, actually only the mor⟨al⟩ God is refuted.
Rights and duties.
The punishments.
Point of departure. Irony toward Descartes: supposing that at the bottom of things there were something deceitful from

which we derived, what would it help *de omnibus dubitare*![14] It could be the most beautiful means of deceiving ourselves. Moreover: is it possible?

"Will to truth" as "I do not want to be cheated" *or* "I do not want to cheat" *or* "I want to convince myself and become firm," as a form of the will to power.

"Will to justice"
"Will to beauty"   } all will to power.
"Will to help"

on goodness.

39[14][15]

For the preface.

Human *comprehension* — which is ultimately always an interpretation according to us and our needs — stands in relation to the *rank* that the human being assumes in the order of all beings. Let it serve as an example, how much the finger knows what the piano player executes with it. It will sense nothing but mechanical processes and logically combine these. Even among humans the lowly exert their power without awareness of what purpose they serve in the big picture. The whole physical causality is *interpretable* in a hundred ways, according to whether a human or another being interprets it. — For cruder types of human being the *human* kind of goodness or justice or wisdom was *verifiable* from nature. Inasmuch as finer more spiritual human beings now reject this verifiability, they do it because their concept of goodness justice and wisdom has grown. Atheism is the result of an *elevation of the human being*: at bottom he has become more bashful, deeper and more modest before the fullness of the whole; he has *better* understood his order of rank. The *farther* our knowledge grows, the more the human being perceives himself in his *corner*. The most shameless and firmest articles of faith that we bear in us stem from the period of our greatest ignorance, e.g., that our *will* is *cause* etc. How naïvely we carry our moral valuations into things, e.g., when we speak of *laws of nature*! It might be useful once to conduct an experiment of a *completely different* manner of interpretation: so that through an embittered contradiction we come to understand how very unconsciously *our moral canon* (preference for truth, law, rationality etc.) *reigns* in our *entire so-c⟨alled⟩ science.*

Put popularly: God has been refuted, but not the devil: and all divine functions are also part of his nature: the opposite did not work!

He deceives, he creates deceiving intellects
He prefers to destroy
He ruins insofar as he spurs the highest to ennoblement
In the woods: he allows his innocence to be worshipped
Ultimately: why do we hate such a being?

39[15][16]

For the *introduction.*

The great danger is not pessimism (a form of hedonism), the calculating of pleasure and pain,[17] and whether perhaps human life includes an excess of painful feelings. Instead, the *meaninglessness* of all events! The moral interpretation has become invalid at the same time as the religious interpretation: this they do not know of course, the superficial! The more impious they are, the more instinctively they cling with their teeth to moral valuations. Schopenhauer as atheist uttered a curse upon anyone who divests the world of its moral significance. In England they strive to associate morality with physics, Mister von Hartmann morality and the irrationality of existence. But the actual great fear is: *the world no longer has a meaning*

To what extent the previous morality has also fallen away with "God": they mutually supported one another.

Now I bring a new interpretation, an "immoral" one, in relation to which our previous morality appears as a special case. Put popularly: God has been refuted, but not the devil. —

39[16]

With the foolish and immodest question of whether pleasure or pain is preponderant in the world, one stands in the midst of philosophical dilettantism: such things should be left to yearning poets and little women. On a nearby planet there could be so much happiness and amusement that it would outweigh "the entire misery of humanity"[18] ten times over: what do we know! And on the other hand we really only want to be the inheritance of Christian profundity and sensitivity, so that we do not condemn suffering in itself: whoever no longer knows how to use it morally, for the "salvation of the soul," is supposed to at least accept its aesthetic validity — be it as artist or observer of things. The world, suffering thought away, is unaesthetic in every sense: and perhaps pleasure is only a form and rhythmic variety of the same!

I meant to say: perhaps suffering is something of what is essential to all existence.

39[17]

One is permitted to hope that the human being will rise so high that the formerly highest things, e.g., the previous belief in God, will seem childlike-childish and touching, indeed that he will *once again* do as he has done with all myths, namely transform ⟨them into⟩ children's stories and fairy tales.

39[18]

NB. The credibility of the body first is the basis according to which the *value of all thinking* can be evaluated. Supposing we had *thought* nothing but things that do not exist! (as e.g., Teichmüller assumes!) etc. The body proves itself *less and less* to be illusion! Who until now has had *reasons* to think the body as *illusion*? The perfect Brahman-worshipper.

39[19]

Woman

And wherever a woman comes to be conscious of any kind of talent: how much ridiculous self-admiration, how much "goose" is unleashed each time at the same time!

39[20][19]

Jew.

— I highlight with distinction Siegfried Lipiner, a Polish Jew who knows how to reproduce the most diverse forms of European lyric in the most delicate manner — "nearly genuine," as a goldsmith would say —

39[21]

Hellwald, Natural History of Human Beings.

Hermann *Müller*
Burmeister } on plants.

39[22][20]

Zarathustra 4.

says to his own: watch out, whoever speaks *against* suffering, illusion, foolishness

> — *he belongs to the common people*, even as a philosopher. How does one best speak to the masses? *I do not know*, it does not belong to my task. It seems to me that one must make their lives very *hard* through the demands of strict virtues: otherwise they become lazy and voluptuous, also in their thinking.

For the *lower* human beings the opposite valuations apply: it is a matter of planting the virtues in them. The absolute commands, terrible tyrants, tear them away from the easy life[21]

the significance of religions

Zarathustra as seducer of youth, the vengeance of the fathers, he commands them to wait.

Zarathustra walking on the ramparts of the fortress: — he hears someone preaching absolute pessimism. The city is surrounded. He remains silent.

[40 = W I 7a. August–September 1885]

40[1]

The weary, suffering, fearful mean peace, mean immovability, calm, something similar to deep sleep when they think of the supreme happiness. Much of this has gotten into philosophy. Likewise fear of the uncertain, ambiguous, changeable has brought to favor its opposite, the simple, what remains the same, the predictable, the certain. Another kind of being would bring the opposite conditions to favor. But as I, ten years ago — — —

40[2][1]

The Will to Power.

Attempt at a New Interpretation of all Events.

(Preface on the threatening "meaninglessness." Problem of pessimism.)

Logic.
Physics.
Morality.
Art.
Politics.

40[3][2]

For whom this interpretation is important. New "philosophers." There might be someone here and there who loves his independence in a similar way — but we do not crowd together, we do not "long" for one another.

40[4]

We are the *heirs* of the imperfect bad variety, the *longest* variety of observing and inferring. Our most thorough and incorporated concepts will probably be the falsest: namely to the extent that we have been able to live with them! But conversely one can ask: would life even be possible at all with a finer observation and a more rigorous cautious process of inference? Even today the practical portion of our life is still *experimental* in the crudest sense, hit-or-miss: just look at what most people know about nutrition! That the expediency of means in the overall history of organisms has increased (as Spencer believes) is an English-superficial judgment, in relation to the complexity of our aims the stupidity of means has probably *stayed the same*.

40[5]

The *increase* of **stealth** in the order of rank of beings (in the inorganic power against power quite crudely, in the organic world *cunning* etc.) the highest human beings like Caesar Napoleon (Stendhal's quote about him) likewise the higher races (Italians etc.). Should we not consider it possible that the most thousand-fold slyness belongs in the nature of higher creatures? Naturally the sense of truth (to see *what is*) would also have to increase, as a means of being able to appear. The actor. Dionysus.

40[6]

How impoverished have the philosophers been so far when language, or at least grammar, on the whole that which is their inner "common people" has prompted[3] them! There are truths in words, at least inklings of truth: this is what they all believe rigidly and firmly: hence the tenacity with which they cling to "subject" "body" "soul" "spirit." What disaster lies in the single mummified error concealed by the word "abstraction"! As if by omitting, and not on the contrary by underscoring, emphasizing, strengthening, we could give rise to that which is described in such a manner! Just as every image, every form emerges in us and becomes possible, through coarsening!

40[7]

Just as the emergence of arithmetic had to be preceded by a long practice and preschooling in seeing the same, in wanting to take things as the same, in positing identical cases and in "counting," so likewise logical inference. Judgment is originally more than the belief "this and that *is* true," rather "thus and such is precisely how I *want* it to be true!" The drive to assimilation, that organic basic function on which all growth is based, also adapts internally what it appropriates from its vicinity: the will to power functions in this comprising of the new under the forms of what is old, previously experienced, still alive in memory: and then we call it — "comprehending"!

40[8]

The concept "individual" "person" contains a great relief for naturalistic thinking: which above all feels good when doing multiplication tables. In fact prejudices are found there: but unfortunately we do not have words to describe what really exists, namely the degrees of intensity on the way to the individual, to the "person." Two derive from one, one from two: this can be clearly seen in the procreation and propagation of the lowest organisms; mathematics is constantly contradicted in real events, counter*lived*, if the expression is permitted. I once used the expression "many mortal souls":[4] just as everyone has the stuff for many personas.

40[9]

There are schematic minds, those who hold a thought-complex to be *truer* if it can be sketched into previously drafted schemata or categorical tables. There are countless self-deceptions in this area: nearly all great "systems" belong here. But the *basic prejudice* is: that order, surveyability, the systematic must cling to the *true being* of things, and conversely disorder, the chaotic, the unpredictable come to the fore only in a false or imperfectly known world — in sum are errors — : — which is a moral prejudice, drawn from the fact that the truthful confidence-inspiring human being tends to be a man of order, of maxims, and on the whole something predictable and pedantic. Now it is however quite unverifiable that the in-itself of things comports with this recipe of a model bureaucrat.

40[10]

— Descartes is not radical enough for me. With his craving for certainty and "I do not want to be deceived" one needed ⟨to⟩ ask "why *not*?" In sum, moral prejudices (or utilitarian justifications) in favor of certainty against appearance and uncertainty. It is in this context that I look at the philosophers, from the Vedanta philos⟨ophy⟩ to the present: why this hatred for the untrue, evil, painful etc.? — For the preface. First take care of the mor⟨al⟩ valuations!

— For the "categorical imperative" it takes an imperator!

40[11]

— The children of innocence who believe in the "subject" predicate and object, the grammar believers who have not yet heard of our apple of knowledge!

40[12]

Teichmüller p. 25[5] "it is a conclusion when we declare so-called things as being, thus we must therefore *know* in advance which nature (*terminus medius*[6]) the being (*terminus major*[7]) possesses, in order to be able to agree with or dispute this concept of things" Against which I say: "*think* we know in advance."

"Logical laws" in Spir I p. 76[8] defined as "universal principles of affirmations about objects i.e., an inner necessity to believe something about objects."

My basic ideas: "the absolute" is a regulative fiction that cannot be ascribed any existence, existence does not belong to the necessary qualities of the absolute. Likewise "being," "substance"

— all things that *should* not be drawn from experience, but in fact *due to an erroneous interpretation of experience are drawn from it.*

Concluding Chapter	The previous interpretations all had a certain meaning for life — preserving, making it bearable, or alienating, refining, probably even separating out what is sickly and bringing it to dying out my new interpretation gives the future philosophers as rulers of the earth the necessary uninhibitedness.

1. Not so much "refuted" as incompatible with what we now chiefly consider "true" and believe: to this extent the religious and moral interpretation is impossible for us.

40[13][9]

Logic is bound to the condition: *supposing there are identical cases.* In fact, so that thinking and inferring can logically take place, *this* condition *must* first be feigned as fulfilled. This means: the will to *logical truth* can only enact itself after a fundamental *falsification* of all events has been undertaken. From which it follows that here a drive reigns that is capable of both means, first the falsification and then the execution of a single point of view: logic does *not* stem from the will to truth.

40[14]

One could say, the complexity of ways (e.g., of a plant to come to fertilization) would be an argument *against* intentionality: for here an ingenious spirit would have to be thought, who chooses detours that are too big, clever with respect to the way, stupid regarding precisely the choice of this *way* — hence a contradictory kind of spirit. But against this interpretation I would point to our human experience: we must exploit this accidental and disrupting element and adopt it into each of our drafts, so that everything we execute bears the same character, of a spirit that executes its plan despite many obstacles, therefore with many crooked lines. Let us think of this case translated into tremendous proportions: then the seeming stupidity of the course of the world, the character of wastefulness, of useless sacrifices would perhaps be only an observation from the *corner*, a perspectival observation for small beings such as we are. In consideration of the fact that we do not know the *purposes*, it is childish to criticize the means on the basis of their rationality. What is certain is that they are not precisely "humane."

40[15][10]

Judgment, this is the belief: "this and this is so." Therefore judgment harbors the admission of having encountered an identical case: it presupposes comparison therefore, with the help of memory. The judgment does *not* succeed in making it appear that an identical case is there. Instead, it believes it perceives such a case; it works under the assumption that identical cases exist generally. Now what do we call that function that is much *older*, and must be working earlier, that equalizes and assimilates cases that in themselves are dissimilar? What do we call that second one which, based on the first one etc. "What arouses the same sensations is the same": but what do we call that which makes sensations the same, "takes" them to be the same? —There could be no judgments at all if a kind of equalization were not practiced first within the sensations: memory is only possible with a constant underscoring of the already accustomed, experienced — — *Before* there is judging *the process of assimilation must already have been done*: therefore here, too, an intellectual activity ⟨is⟩ present, that does not fall under consciousness, as with pain resulting from a wound. Probably there is an inner event corresponding to all organic functions, hence an assimilating, secreting, growing etc.

Essential, proceed from the body and use it as a guide. It is the much richer phenomenon that allows for clearer observation. Belief in the body is better established than belief in the spirit.

"No matter how strongly a thing may be believed: there is no criterion of truth in it." But what is truth? Perhaps a kind of belief that has become a condition of life? Then of course strength would be a criterion. E.g., with respect to causality.

40[16][11]

What then does all recent philosophy do at bottom? it makes, secretly or openly, an assassination attempt on the old concept of the soul — that is, on the foundation of Christianity, on the "I": it is antichristian in the most subtle sense. Formerly one believed unconditionally in grammar: one said: "I" is condition, "think" is predicate. One tried with an admirable tenacity to see if one could escape from this net — whether first of all the opposite might not be true: "think" condition — and "I" conditioned, as a synthesis that embarks on thinking. Kant wanted at bottom to prove that the subject could not be proven from the standpoint of the subject, nor the object either. The possibility of an *illusory existence* of the "subject" is dawning: an idea that has already been on earth once, as in the Vedanta-philosophy. If one wants a new, albeit very provisional expression for it, then read ⟨*The Birth of Tragedy*⟩

40[17]

Coarsening as a basic means of allowing return, identical cases to appear; thus before anything was "thought" something must have already been *made up*, the forming sense is more original than the "thinking" one

40[18]

On morality. *We behave in accordance with the rank order to which we belong*: even if we do not know it, even less are able to demonstrate it to others. An imperative "behave according to the rank order to which you belong" is nonsensical: because we would *have to* know 1) ourselves 2) that order, neither of which is the case — — and 3) because it is superfluous to command something that happens anyway. Rank order: not only in relation to our neighbors, rather in certain cases to posterity, likewise to the inhabitants of other planets; for we do not know whether anyone is there who compares us with themselves. — All that is imperatival in morality addresses itself to the *multiplicity of masks* that we wear in ourselves, and it wants us to display this and not that, hence *change our appearance*. "Improvement" is: to display something of that which the good humans like — nothing more!

40[19]

And as concerns descendants: one has to decide in a clever and timely way — *aut libri aut liberi*.[12]

40[20][13]

Apart from the governesses who even today still believe in grammar as *veritas aeterna*[14] and consequently as subject predicate and object, no one is so innocent today as to still posit the subject "I" as the condition of "think" in the manner of Descartes; instead, through the skeptical movement of recent philosophy assuming the reverse has become more credible to us, namely thinking as cause and condition of "subject" and "object," as well as of "substance" and of "matter": which is perhaps only the reverse kind of error.[15] This much is certain: — we have let go of the "soul" and consequently also the "world soul," the "things in themselves" as well ⟨as⟩ a world-beginning, a "first cause." Thinking is not for us a means of "knowing," but of describing occurrence, of ordering, of making things handy for our use: this is how we think today about thinking: tomorrow perhaps differently. We do not properly comprehend anymore how "comprehending" is supposed to be necessary, still less how it is supposed to have emerged: and though we ⟨already⟩ constantly get into the plight of having to help ourselves with language and the habits of the popular understanding, still the appearance of constant self-contradiction does not yet testify against the justification of our doubt. Also we are not so easily satisfied anymore with respect to "direct certainty": we do not even find "reality" and "appearance" to be opposite, rather we would speak of *degrees* of being — and perhaps even more preferably of degrees of appearance — and that "direct certainty" e.g., of the fact that we think and that consequently thinking has reality we would still sour with the doubt of what degree this being has; whether perhaps as "ideas of God" we are indeed real, but fleeting and illusory like rainbows. Supposing that in the nature of things there were something deceptive silly something fraudulent, then the very best will *de omnibus dubitare*[16] in the manner of Descartes would not guard us from the traps of this nature; and precisely that Cartesian method could be a major trick to thoroughly fool us and take us for fools. Indeed, already insofar as we would actually have reality, in the opinion of Descartes, we as reality would have to share somehow in that fraudulent deceptive ground of things and its grounding-will: — enough, "I do not want to be deceived" could be the method of a deeper more subtle more thorough will, that wanted precisely the reverse: namely to deceive itself.

In summa:[17] it is to be doubted whether "the subject" can prove itself — for this it would simply have to have a firm point outside and *that* is lacking!

40[21][18]

Point of departure from the *body* and from physiology: why? — We gain the right idea of the nature of our subject-unity, namely as regents at the head of a community, not as "souls" or "vital forces," likewise of the dependence of these regents on the ruled and of the conditions of rank order and division of labor as enablement of individuals and the whole simultaneously. Likewise how living unities constantly emerge and die and how eternity is not part of the "subject"; likewise that struggle also expresses itself in obeying and commanding and a fluid determination of power limits is part of life. The certain *ignorance* in which the regent is kept regarding the individual arrangements and even disturbances of the community belongs to the conditions under which ruling can take place. In brief, we gain an appreciation for not-knowing, too, for seeing on the whole and coarsely, for simplifying and falsifying, for the perspectival. But the most important thing is: that we understand the ruler and his subjects as *identical in kind*, all of them feeling, willing, thinking — and that we also learn to infer a corresponding subjective invisible life wherever we see or detect movement in the body. Movement is a symbolism for the eye; it signifies that something has been felt, willed, thought. — Direct questioning of the subject about the subject, and all self-mirroring of the spirit has its dangers in the fact that for its activity it could be useful and important to falsely interpret itself. This is why we ask the body and reject the testimony of the sharpened senses: if you wish, we look into whether the subordinates themselves are capable of establishing contact with us.

40[22]

NB. "Something is thought: consequently there exists something that thinks" — this is what Descartes's argumentation amounts to — but it is not the reality of a thought that Descartes wanted. He wanted to get beyond "imagination" to a *substance* that thinks and imagines.

40[23]

Let us be more careful than Descartes, who got caught up in the trap of words. *Cogito*[19] is only a word to be sure: but it means something manifold: many a thing is manifold, and we grab at it crudely believing full well that it is one thing. In that famous *cogito* there is 1) it thinks 2) and I believe that it is I who is thinking here, 3) but even assuming that this second point remains hanging, as a matter of faith, then also that first "it thinks" contains another belief: namely, that "thinking" is an activity for which a subject, at least an "it" must be thought: — and the *ergo sum*[20] means nothing more than this! But this is the belief in grammar, here "things" and their "activities" are already posited, and we are far away from direct[21] certainty. Let us therefore leave that problematic "it" out and let us say *cogitatur*[22] as fact without articles of faith mixed in: thus we deceive ourselves again, for the passive form also includes articles of faith and not only "facts": *in summa*, precisely the facts of the case cannot be set forth nakedly, "believing" and "presuming" are harbored in the *cogito* of *cogitat*[23] and *cogitatur*: who will guarantee that with *ergo* we do not extract something out of this believing and presuming and that what remains: something is believed, therefore something is believed — a false form of deduction! Ultimately one would have to know what "being" is in order to extract a *sum* from the *cogito*, one would likewise already have to know; what *knowing* is: one proceeds from faith in logic — in the *ergo* above all! — and not only from the setting forth of a fact! — Is "certainty" possible in knowing? is direct certainty not perhaps a *contradictio in adjecto*?[24] What is knowing in relation to being? But for someone who brings already finished articles of faith to all these questions, the Cartesian cautiousness no longer has any meaning at all: it comes much too late. Before the question of "being" the question of the value of logic would have to be decided.

40[24][25]

One should not embellish and tidy up the naïveté of D⟨escartes⟩, as e.g., Spir does.

Consciousness is directly certain to itself: the existence of thinking cannot be denied, nor doubted, for this very denial or this doubt are themselves conditions of thinking or of consciousness, their own existence therefore proves what they deny, and consequently they are deprived of any significance." Spir I, 26. "Something is thought," therefore something is, namely "thinking." Was *this* the meaning of Descartes? Teichmüller p. 5 and 40 there are *passages*. "Something that is directly certain to itself" is nonsense. Supposing e.g., God thought through us, and our thoughts, insofar as we felt ourselves as cause, were an illusion, then the existence of the thoughts would not be denied or doubted, but certainly the *ergo sum*. Otherwise he would have to have said: *ergo est.* — There are no direct certainties: *cogito, ergo sum* presupposes that one knows what "thinking" is and secondly what "being" is: therefore, if the *est* (*sum*) were true, it would be a certainty on the basis of two correct judgments, with the added certainty that one has a right generally to the conclusion, to *ergo* —therefore in any case no "direct" c⟨ertainty⟩. Namely: in *cogito* is harbored not only some kind of event, which is simply acknowledged — this is nonsense! — but a judgment that it is this and that event, and whoever e.g., did not know how to distinguish between thinking feeling and willing could not establish the event at all. And in *sum* or *est* is still harbored such a conceptual *imprecision* that not even *fit*[26] or "it is done" are refuted. "Something is happening there" could be substituted for "there is something there, there exists something, there is something."

40[25]

The belief in the direct certainty of thinking is one more belief, and no certainty! We moderns are all opponents of Descartes and resist his dogmatic carelessness in doubting. "Doubting must be done better than Descartes!" We find the opposite, the countermovement against the absolute authority of the goddess "reason" wherever there are profounder human beings. Fanatical logicians managed to convince us that the world is a deception; and that only in thinking the path to "being," to the "absolute" is given. By contrast I take pleasure in the world *if* it is supposed to be deception; and among more complete h⟨umans⟩ there has always been ridicule about the common sense of the most sensible.

40[26][27]

Apparently contradictory the 2 qualities that distinguish modern Europeans: the *individualistic* and the *demand for equal rights*: I finally understand this. Namely the individual is an extremely vulnerable vanity: — the latter demands, with its awareness of how quickly it suffers, that every other is regarded as equal to it, that it is only *inter pares*.[28] Therewith a social race is characterized in which in fact the talents and strengths do not vary considerably. Pride, which wants solitude and few appreciators, is completely beyond comprehension; the very "great" successes exist only through masses, indeed one scarcely comprehends that a mass-success is really always a *small* success: because *pulchrum est paucorum hominum*.[29] — All the moralities know nothing of the "rank order" of human beings; the law teachers nothing of the community-conscience. The individual-principle rejects the *truly great* human beings and among those who are roughly equal it demands the most subtle eye and the fastest recognition of a talent; and because everyone has something in the way of talents, in such late and civilized cultures, and accordingly can expect to win back his share of honors, today therefore an emphasizing of the small merits is taking place as never before: — it gives the age a patina of *unlimited fairness*. Its unfairness consists of a rage without bounds *not* against the tyrants and demagogues, also in the arts, but against the *noble* h⟨umans⟩ who despise the praise of the many. The demand for equal rights (e.g., to be allowed to sit in judgment over everything and everyone) is *anti-aristocratic*. Likewise foreign to it is the vanished individual, the submerging into a large type, the will-to-be-a-nonperson: in which the distinction and the ambition of many superior human beings formerly consisted (among them the greatest poets); or "city existence" as in Greece; Jesuitism, Prussian officer corps and bureaucracy; or being a disciple and continuator of great masters: for which unsocial conditions and the lack of *petty vanity* are necessary

40[27]

Just as mathematics and mechanics for long periods were regarded as sciences with absolute validity and only now the suspicion dares to unveil itself that they are nothing more and nothing less than applied logic based on the specific unverifiable assumption that there are "identical cases" —but logic itself a consequential hieroglyphics on the basis of the executed assumption (that there are identical cases) — : so too the *word* formerly qualified as the knowledge of a thing, and even now the grammatical functions are the best-believed things, against which one cannot sufficiently guard oneself. It is possible that the same kind of human being who later thought up Vedanta-philosophies, thousands of years earlier probably thought up a philosophical language on the basis of imper⟨fect⟩ languages, *not*, as they believed, as hieroglyphics, but as "knowledge of the world" itself: but whatever "this is" may have been postulated so far, a later and subtler age has discovered again and again that it is nothing more than "this means." Even today most philos⟨ophers⟩ do not have even an *inkling* of the actual critique of concepts or (as I once described it) a real "history of the emergence of thinking." One should uncover and reevaluate the *valuations* that lie around logic: e.g., "the certain is of more value than the uncertain" "thinking is our highest function"; likewise the optimism in the logical, the triumphal awareness in every inference, the imperatival in judgment, the innocence in the belief in the comprehensibility of the concept.[30]

40[28]

There must have been thinking long before there were eyes: "lines and shapes" therefore are not given from the beginning, rather, thinking has occurred for the longest time based on sensations of touch: but this, *not* supported by the eye, teaches degrees of pressure sensation, not yet shapes. Hence prior to the practice of understanding the world as moved shapes lies the period in which it was "grasped" as changeable and degree-differential pressure sensation. There is no doubt that thinking can occur in images, in sounds: but also in pressure sensations. The comparison with respect to strength and direction and sequence, memory etc.

40[29][31]

We must relearn with respect to memory: here lurks the major seduction of assuming a "soul," which timelessly reproduces, recognizes etc. But what is experienced[32] continues to live "in memory"; that it "comes" is beyond my control, for this the will is inactive, as in the coming of any thought. Something happens of which I become aware: now something similar comes —who calls it? awakens it?

40[30]

The great danger inheres in the assumption that there is direct knowing (therefore "knowing" in the strict sense generally!) Teichm⟨üller⟩ p. 35.[33]

40[31]

This would have to be something, not subject, not object, not energy, not material, not spirit, not soul: — but someone will tell me that something of this kind would have to look like the spitting image of a hallucination? I believe this myself: and bad if it did not do that! Indeed: it must also look like the spitting image of everything else that there is and that could be, and not only of the hallucination! It must have the great family feature by which everything recognizes itself as *related* to it — —

40[32]

Supposing you were to ask: "Did the tree already look green 50,000 years ago?" then I would answer: "perhaps not yet: perhaps back then there were only the two main contrasts of *valeurs*,[34] darker and lighter masses: — and gradually colors evolved from them.

40[33]

Before logic, which operates everywhere with equations, equating, assimilating must have reigned: and it continues to reign, and logical thinking is itself an ongoing means of assimilation, of *wanting*-to-see identical cases.

40[34]

Our "memory," whatever it might be, may serve us as a metaphor for describing something impor⟨tant⟩ with it: in the development of every organic being a prodigy of memory for its overall prehistory reveals itself, to the extent organic beings have a prehistory — and to be sure a reproducing memory that reproduces the earliest and longest-embodied forms sooner than the recently experienced: reaches back in this manner and does not go step by step, as one would have to assume, with a *regressus*[35] from the most recent to the most-distantly experienced, rather precisely the *opposite* way round it leaves aside for the time being everything more recent and freshly imprinted. Here an amazing arbitrariness exists: — Even the "soul," which is usually called upon to help in all philosophical predicaments, is incapable of helping here: at least not the individual-soul, but a soul-continuum that reigned in the entire process of a certain organic series. Then again: because not everything is reproduced, but only basic forms, then in every memory a subsuming thinking, simplifying, reducing must constantly take place: enough, something analogous to what we describe as "logic" from the standpoint of our consciousness. — And how far might this reproduction go of the previously experienced? Certainly also as far as the reproduction of trains of feeling and thought. But how do ⟨we⟩ regard the "innate ideas" that Locke called into question?[36] There is certainly much *more* true than only this, that ideas are innate, assuming one does not underscore the act of birth in the word "innate."

40[35]

The universal mendacity of human beings about themselves, the mor⟨al⟩ interpreting of what they do and want, would be despicable if it were not also something very funny: and it really would require spectators — so interesting is the spectacle! *Not* by the kind of gods Epicurus imagined! But by Homeric gods: as distant and near to humans and watching them as Galiani perhaps stood in relation to his cats and monkeys: — thus related a bit to humans, but of a higher species!

40[36]

Mathematical physicists cannot use the particle-atom for their science: consequently they construct themselves a force-points-world with which one can reckon. Exactly the same, on a crude scale, has been done by humans and all organic creatures: namely they positioned, thought, and fictionalized the world to suit themselves for so long that they were able to use it, until they were able to "reckon" with it.

40[37]

Should it not suffice for us to think of "force" as a unity in which willing sensing and thinking are still mixed and undifferentiated? And the organic beings as approaches to separation, so that all the organic functions are still together in that unity, thus self-regulation, assimilation, nourishment, excretion, metabolism? Ultimately nothing is given as "real" except thinking and sensing and drives: is it not permitted to attempt whether this given does not *suffice* to construct the world? I do not mean as appearance: but precisely as real as our willing feeling thinking are — but as a more primitive form of them. In the end the question is this: whether we acknowledge the will really as *effecting*? If we do this, then naturally it can only have effect on something that is *of its kind*: and not on "materials." *Either* one must interpret all effect as illusion (for we have formed our idea of cause and effect only according to the model of our will as cause!) and then nothing at all is comprehensible: *or* one must attempt to think all effects as being of the same kind, like acts of will, hence make the hypothesis as to whether all mechanical events, insofar as there is a force in them, are not simply force of will. —

"Mortal souls" with resp.{ect} to the impossibility of transferring the *numerical* relationship to these things. *Against* the individual. "Counting" is only a simplification, like all concepts. Namely: wherever something should be thought purely arithmetical, *quality* is calculated away. Likewise in everything logical, where the *identity of cases* is the assumption, therefore the actual spec⟨ial⟩ *character* of each event is simply thought away (the *new*, not to be understood from the conditions of emergence — or r⟨espectively⟩ included.)

40[38]

What it boils down to is properly characterizing the unity in which thinking willing and feeling and all affects are combined: obviously the intellect is only a *tool*, but in whose hands? Certainly the affects: and these are a multiplicity behind which it is not necessary to posit a unity: it suffices to construe it as a regency. — That the organs have everywhere taken shape, as is shown by morphological development, may also certainly be used as a metaphor for the intellectual: so that something "new" is to be construed always only through the separation of a single force from a synthetic force.

Thinking itself is the kind of action that *takes apart* what is actually One. Everywhere is the *appearance* that there are countable multiplicities, already in thinking as well. There is nothing "added" in reality, nothing "divided," a thing half and half is not equal to the whole.

40[39]

Physicists are now of one mind with all metaphysicians that we live in a world of deception: fortunate that one no longer needs to settle up with a God on this issue, about whose "truthfulness" one could come to odd ideas. The perspectival nature of the world goes as deep as our "understanding" of the world reaches today; and I would dare to apply it even where human beings generally should in fairness be allowed to look away from understanding — I mean where metaphysicians ⟨posit⟩ the realm of the seeming certain-to-itself, understandable-to-itself, a⟨nd⟩ in thinking. That number is a perspectival form, as well as time and space, that we no more harbor "one soul" in a breast than "two souls,"[37] that "individuals" like material "atoms" can no longer be maintained, except for the daily-domestic use of thinking, and ⟨have⟩ fled into a nothingness (or into a "formula"), that nothing living and dead can be added together, that both concepts are false, that there are not three faculties of the soul, that "subject" and "object" "*activum* and *passivum*"[38] "cause and effect" "means and purpose" are always only perspectival forms, *in summa* that the soul, substance, number, time, space, ground, purpose —stand *and fall* together. But supposing now that we are not so foolish as to value truth, in this case the x, higher than appearance, supposing we have resolved to *live* — then we do not want to be dissatisfied with this seemingness of things and only firmly embrace that no one pauses at any kind of ulterior motives in the representation of this *perspectivity*: — which in fact has happened so far to nearly all philosophers, for they all had ulterior motives and loved *their* "truths" — Indeed: here we have to throw open the problem of truthfulness: supposing we live as a result of error, what then can the "will to truth" be? Would it not have to be a "will to death"? — Would the striving of philosophers and scientific people perhaps be a symptom of degenerating dying-out life, a kind of life-weariness of life itself? *Quaeritur*:[39] and here one could really become contemplative.

40[40]

Skepticism Toward the Skeptics. — What happiness a delicate down gives to things! How all of life glows with beautiful appearances! So far it was the great falsifications and explanations that raised us up above the happiness of animals — into the human! And conversely: what so far has the creaking of the logical clockwork, the self-reflection of the intellect, the unwinding of the instincts brought with it? Supposing you had reduced everything to formulas and your faith to degrees of probability: because you could not live according to them, what? are you supposed to live with bad conscience? And once human beings perceive their belief in goodness justice and truth in the ground of things as *hair-raising falsification*: how are they *themselves* supposed to feel, insofar as they ⟨are⟩ indeed part and parcel of this world? As something hair-raising, false: — — —

40[41]

There are no direct sensations Spir 2 p. 56.[40]
no direct pain feelings
no direct thoughts

If there were a direct knowing, then one could not speak, like J. S. Mill, of the "relativity of knowing."

40[42][41]

The assumption of a *single subject* is perhaps not necessary; perhaps it is equally permissible to assume a multiplicity of subjects, whose working together and struggle underlie our thinking and generally our consciousness? A kind of *aristocracy* of "cells" in which ruling resides? Certainly of *pares*,[42] who together are accustomed to ruling and know how to command?

My hypotheses:

The subject as *multiplicity*

pain as intellectual and dependent on the judgment "harmful": projected

effect always "unconscious": the inferred and imagined "cause" is projected, *follows* after time.

pleasure as a kind of pain.

the single *force* that exists is of the same kind as the will's, a commanding of other subjects, who change themselves accordingly.

the constant transitoriness and fleetingness of the subject, "mortal soul"

number as perspectival form.

40[43][43]

Within a herd, every community, therefore *inter pares*, the *overestimation* of truthfulness makes good sense. Not to let oneself be deceived — and *consequently*, as personal morality, not to practice deception oneself! A mutual obligation among equals! It is to the *outside* that danger and caution demand us to be *on guard against deception*: as a psychological precondition for this also *inside*. Distrust as the source of truthfulness.

40[44]

Supposing the world were false, life were understandable only on the ground of delusion, under the protection of delusion, based on delusion: what then would "live according to nature" mean? Could the exhortation not be precisely: "*be* a deceiver"? Indeed, how could one prevent oneself deceiving? We err about ourselves and are incomprehensible to ourselves: how much more are we this for our "neighbors"! But they do not believe themselves to be deceived by us — and it is *with that in mind* that all dealings with mutual rights and obligations are based. — That deceiving is not part of my *intention*, admitted! But looked at more closely: I also do nothing to enlighten my neighbors about the fact *that* they deceive themselves about me. I do not prevent their error, I do not fight it, I let it happen — : in this sense I am indeed the deceiver in the end *on purpose*. But I also behave exactly the same toward myself: self-knowledge does *not* belong among the feelings of obligation; even if I seek to know myself, it happens for reasons of utility or a more refined curiosity — but *not* out of the will to truthfulness. — That the truthful one is more valuable than the liar in the economy of humanity would still have to be proven. The very great and powerful *were* deceivers so far: their task demanded it of them. Assuming it turned out that living and getting ahead were only possible on the basis of a consistent and lengthy period of being deceived: then the consistent deceivers could achieve highest honors as ones who condition life and promote life. That one *harms* by not telling the truth is the belief of the naïve, a kind of frog-perspective of morality. If life and the *value* of life rest on well-believed errors, then precisely the truth-teller, the truth-willer could be the harmful one (as the unwinder of illusions).

40[45][44]

The Philosopher of the Future.
Thoughts on Discipline and Cultivation.[45]

40[46]

NB. Our distant future determination reigns over us, even if we do not yet have an eye open for it; for long periods of time we experience only riddles. Our choice of people and things, our selection of events, the pushing away of what is most pleasant, often of what is most revered — it frightens us, as if here and there chance, a random act were bursting out of us like a volcano: but it is the higher reason of our future task. Seen forwards everything that happens to us might seem like only the unanimity of chance and nonsense: seen backwards I for my part am no longer able to find anything of either of them in my life.

40[47]

Descent. What is noble? The emergence of the nobility. The imitating talents as in Voltaire.

The great separation.

The seven solitudes.

The will to power.

40[48][46]

On the Order of Rank.
Prelude to a Philosophy of the Future.

Book One: Cultivation and Discipline.
Book Two: The Great Separation.
Book Three: The Seven Solitudes.
Overcoming Morality.
Book Four: The Will to Power.

40[49]

Let us be suspicious of all seeming "simultaneity"! Time fragments insert themselves here, which can only be called small according to a crude standard, e.g., our human standard of time; but in abnormal circumstances, e.g., as hashish smokers or in a moment of mortal danger, even we humans have a sense of how in one second of our pocket watch a thousand thoughts can be thought, a thousand experiences experienced. When I open my eyes the visible world stands there, apparently immediately: but in the meantime something tremendous has happened, multifarious things have occurred: — first second third: but here the ph⟨ysiologists⟩ should speak!

40[50][47]

Herewith under the not undangerous title "The Will to Power" a new philosophy or, spoken more clearly, *the attempt at a new interpretation of all events*, should have its say: as is fair only provisionally and as an attempt, only in preparation and questioningly, only "as prelude" to an earnestness for which initiated and chosen ears are required, as goes without saying, incidentally — or at least *should* go without saying — for everything that a ph⟨ilosopher⟩ says *publicly*. But today, thanks to the superficial and presumptuous spirit of an age that believes in the "equality of all rights," it has gotten to the point that one absolutely no longer — — — For every philosopher should have the virtues of an educator to the extent that before he undertakes to convince, he must first know how to persuade. Indeed, before proving anything the seducer has to undermine and shock, before any commanding and leading he must first ascertain the extent to which he also knows how to seduce.

40[51]

Concepts are something that lives, consequently also something now growing, now receding: many concepts have died a miserable death. As a metaphor they would probably have to be described as cells, with a cell nucleus and a surrounding body that is not firm and — — —

40[52]

There are fateful words that seem to express a knowledge and in truth prevent a knowledge; to them belongs the word "appearances." Let these propositions I have borrowed from various modern philosophers reveal what chaos these "appearances" can perpetrate.

against the word "*appearances.*"

40[53]

NB. *Appearance*[48] as I understand it is the actual and single reality of things — that which first merits all existing predicates and which relatively speaking is best described with all, therefore even the most opposing predicates. But with this word nothing more can be expressed than its *inaccessibility* for logical procedures and distinctions: therefore "appearance" as opposed to "logical truth" — but which itself is only possible in an imaginary world. Thus I do not posit "appearance" in opposition to "reality" but conversely take appearance as the reality that resists transformation into an imaginary "truth-world." A specific name for this reality would be "the will to power," namely described from the inside and not from the standpoint of its incomprehensible fluid protean nature.

40[54]

The *deliberateness* of actions is nothing decisive in morality (belongs to the myopic *individualistic* tendency). "End" and "means" in relation to the entire species from which they grow are only symptomatic, ambiguous in themselves and nearly incomprehensible. Animals and plants show their moral character according to the life conditions in which they are placed. What is decisive lies only behind "deliberateness." One will never be allowed to isolate the individual: "Here, one must say, is a growth with such a prehistory."

40[55]

Nature's conformance to law is a false humanitarian interpretation. What is at stake is an absolute determination of power relationships, the whole brutality, without the alleviation brought along by the anticipation of the future, caution and cunning and prudence, in brief by the intellect in organic life. The absolute momentariness of the will to power reigns; in the human being (and already in the cell) this determination is a process that continually displaces itself in the growth of all participants — a struggle, assuming that one understands this word broadly and deeply enough still to understand the relationship of the ruler to the ruled as one of wrestling, and the relationship of the obeyer to the ruler as one of resisting.

40[56]

1. *On Noble and Common Morality.*
   "The ethical": a *type* of human being is supposed to be *preserved*. Noble morality.
   What is human is supposed to be preserved to some kind of degree: common morality.
2. *The intentionality of actions.*
3. *Evil in the virtues.*
4. *The bad drives* and their utility.

40[57]

NB! But is something at rest really happier than everything in motion? Is the immutable really and necessarily more valuable than a thing that changes? And if someone contradicts himself thousands of times and walks many paths and wears many masks and finds in himself no end and ⟨no⟩ final line on the horizon: is it more probable that such a man experiences less of the "truth" than a virtuous stoic who has placed himself on his spot once and for all, like a pillar and with the hard hide of a pillar? But these kinds of prejudices have sat at the threshold to all philosophy so far: and especially the one that certainty is better than uncertainty and open seas, and that appearance is what a philosopher has to fight as his actual enemy.

40[58]

There is little importance now in people knowing *what* I really wanted back then from Richard Wagner (although the reader of my *Birth of Tragedy* will not be in the dark about that), indeed, that I, through a longing of this kind, definitely proved in the most thorough manner how seriously I erred about him and his talent. Enough, that my error — including my belief in a shared and compatible destiny — does dishonor neither to him nor me and, in any case, was no small refreshment and boon to us both at the time, as two men isolated in very different ways.

The moment came when I sensed to what extent I had wanted *much too much* with respect to Richard Wagner: and, somewhat later, the even worse moment when he my — — —

40[59][49]

Conclusion of "*In Relations with Others*"
Preface and Prequestion:
"what are free spirits?"
⟨1.⟩

"Through its health, a soul in which dwells the wisdom of the world must make even the body healthy": thus says Montaigne,[50] and today I gladly say my Yes to that, as someone who has experience in this sphere. "There can be nothing more cheerful, more alert, I would almost have said more fun than the world and its wisdom": thus likewise I speak with Montaigne — but under what pale and horrific masks did wisdom pass me by at that time! Enough, I was afraid of it often enough and did not like being alone with it like that — — — and embarked, alone and in silence, but with a tenacious "will to wisdom" and to the south — on wandering. Back then I privately called myself a "free spirit," or "Prince Vogelfrei"[51] and if anyone had asked me: where is your home anyway, I would have answered him "maybe beyond good and evil, otherwise nowhere." But I insisted firmly that I had no wandering comrades: then one day I cast my fishing line in search of other "free spirits" — with precisely this book, to which I have already given the title "A Book for Free Spirits."

Today of course — what does one not learn after all in ten years! — I scarcely know any more whether I am seeking companions and "wandering comrades." For in the meantime I learned what few now understand, to bear solitude, "understand" — solitude, and today I would place it right there among the essential characteristics of a "free spirit" that he would rather walk alone, rather fly alone, indeed, if he happened to have sick legs, rather *crawl* alone. Solitude kills if it does not heal: this is true; solitude is part of a wicked and dangerous art of healing. But it is certain that *when* it heals it also sets up a human being in a healthier and more self-affirming way than a human being could ever stand in society, or a tree in its woods: solitude tests most thoroughly, more than any illness itself, whether someone is born and destined for *life* — or for death, like most people. Enough, I first learned from solitude how to think to the end the complementary concepts "free spirit" and "health."

2.

We "free spirits" live apart and here and there on earth — this cannot be changed; we are few — and this is fair. It belongs to our pride to think that our kind is a *rare* and *unusual* kind; and we do not crowd together, we probably do not even "long" for each other. To be sure: if we happen to meet once, like today, then there is a celebration! When we use the word "happiness" in the sense of *our* philosophy, then we are not thinking above all like the weary, fearful and suffering among the philosophers of external peace, of painlessness, immobility, undisturbedness, of a "Sabbath of Sabbaths," of something that might resemble deep sleep in value. On the contrary, *our* world is the uncertain, the changing, capable of transforming, ambiguous, a dangerous world! certainly more than the simple world that always stays the same, predictable, fixed, to which philosophers so far have given highest honors, as heirs of the herd instinct and herd valuations. Known in many lands of the spirit and driven about etc.

3.

Have these words described you? Or have they only *concealed* you in a new way? I do not know: but you tell me in any case that you think I have *erred* in using this name? That the name "free spirit" has been anticipated? That it misleads? That people will mistake us on the basis of this name? — But why, among us, my friends, why indeed should we *not* mislead? What does it matter that *people* mistake us? Will we therefore mistake *ourselves*? And in the end: would it perhaps not be worse if — — ?

Well then, I understand you: you absolutely want another, a new name! "Out of pride" you tell me: the best argument on which to base any stupidity. Thus I will start over again: now open your ears to my novelties!

— But here you interrupt me, you free spirits. "Enough, Enough! I hear you shouting and laughing — we cannot take it any more! Oh you horrific fool! You virtuous traitor and slanderer! Do you want to ruin our reputation throughout the world? Blacken our good name? Saddle us with nicknames that eat their way into not only our skin? Be quiet, you disturber of the conscience's peace! And why, on a bright sunny day, these gloomy grimaces, these gurgling noises, this whole raven-black music? If you speak truths: there are no feet that could *dance* to these truths, therefore they are no truths for *us*. *Ecce nostrum veritatis sigillum*![52] And here is lawn and soft ground: what would be better than to swiftly chase away your mopey thoughts and make ourselves a good day after your 'night'? But someone has to strike up the tune for us! And first let's get rid of all these storm clouds! It is high time that a rainbow stretched itself again over the land, some colorful beautiful bridge of lies upon which only spirits, very free, very airy merry spirits can walk! And lastly and firstly: have you no *milk* to drink? You yourself have made us thirsty for your milk!"

— "As much as you want, my friends. There you see my herd leaping, all my tender sunny sheltered lambs and rams:

and here standing waiting for you already is a whole pail full of milk, a pail full of freshly milked truths, still warm enough to make you warm again. *Incipit*:[53] 'Human All Too Human: Good Milk for Free Spirits.' Do you want to drink some?

It is lovely to be silent together — — —[54]

40[60]

Artist-pessimism. — There are very different kinds of artists. If Richard Wagner must be a pessimist, then he is forced into it by his aversion to himself, the worm of manifold self-contempt, the necessity of intoxicants, including his art, in order to tolerate life at all, and again disgust behind the intoxication, added to all this the consciousness of thespianism, the pressure of unfreedom from which everyone suffers who must disguise himself because he cannot tolerate himself naked — on the other hand his insatiable hunger for praise and noise, because such comedians must always have their belief in themselves bestowed first from the outside and only for moments at a time: — they are not in the least free to renounce praise and noise! But what help are even the most blissful moments of *vanitatum vanitas*,[55] what help is all incense, all self-deification! Immediately afterwards the old grief stirs anew! and above all the storms of passion, or the intemperance masked as passion, in the end an inner weak hesitating voice will always sound forth once more, a *sentencing* voice: — Such artists involuntarily and unavoidably glorify their "non-ego" in their art, and everything that constitutes the extreme opposite of themselves: those therefore, in the case of Wagner, all extravagant virtues, e.g., absolute loyalty or absolute chastity or the simplicity of a child or ascetic self-sacrifices: so that up to a certain point one would have a right to be suspicious of the character of every artist who always glorifies precisely only extravagant virtues: for that way he wants to get free of himself and he denies himself! But let *us* be satisfied with this even so! In the end such an artist for all his will to world denial actually praises and extols something that *is possible in this world: art can be nothing other than world-affirmation*! — And my objection, my friends, was no objection.

Therefore my friend: one will have noticed from his judgment, even if one does not agree with it, that he loved Wagner very much: for an opponent never takes his subject so profoundly as he does. There is no doubt that insofar as he suffers from Wagner, he also suffers with Wagner.

40[61][56]

For the Plan.

Our intellect, our will, likewise our sensations are dependent on our *valuations*: these correspond to our drives and their conditions of existence. Our drives are reducible to *the will to power.*

The will to power is the last factum to which we are able to get down.

{ Our intellect a tool
Our will
Our feelings of malaise { already dependent on valuations
Our sensations

40[62]

The *embellishing* style of historiography of *Ranke*, his *pussy-footing*, in all those passages where what is needed is to record a terrible nonsense of chance as such; his belief in an immanent finger of God as it were, that occasionally pushes and shifts something in the clockwork: for he no longer dares, the super-anxious one, to regard him either as clockwork or as the cause of the clockwork

40[63][57]

Preface to "Mixed Opinions and Maxims"

What kind of human might that be who takes joy in such notations? — Allow me to quickly paint my picture of this kind on the nearest best wall: here, on the pages of my "preface." The last thing I want to do is lay claim to a characterization, a single word for it, even though there might be such a thing: — perhaps someone who sees my picture will find the word himself — the "right word"!

This kind of human protects the artist and philosopher but does not mistake himself for them. They are idle, they have the reasonableness for *otium*[58]

40[64][59]

For a long time I tried as hard as I could to see a kind of Cagl⟨iostro⟩ in R. W⟨agner⟩: one must forgive me this far from innocuous idea, which at least was not inspired by hatred or by revulsion, but by the charm that this incomparable human being exerted on me: add to this that according to my observations the real "geniuses," the genuine ones of the highest order, all do *not* "charm" in this manner, so that "genius" alone did not seem to me to suffice as an explanation for that mysterious influence.

40[65][60]

Preface

Whoever has the desires of a high and selective soul will at all times be in great danger: but today it is extraordinary. Thrown into a noisy, rabble-like age with which he does not want to eat from the same bowl, he could easily perish of hunger and thirst, or, in the event he finally "digs in" after all, of disgust. Such a human being must be helped at the right time by a pair of strokes of fortune that somehow manage to balance out whatever harm may have befallen him through an unsatisfied, yearning and isolated youth: for instance that a rigorous occupation is found for him, in whose service he temporarily becomes estranged from himself and his illness, and has to live totally and completely according only to the demands of a brave spirituality. Or that he opens his ears to a ph⟨ilosopher⟩ who leads him away from everything timely and time-flattering back to "more enduring" goals than the present, yet without damaging his pupil's sense of respect through an excess of denial: that he becomes a friend of good music and even better of good musicians themselves — a great solace (for the good musicians are all hermits and "outside of time") and a good antidote against an all-too-martial a⟨nd⟩ wrathful inclination that likes to pounce on the human beings and things of today.

It happened late — I was already beyond my twenties in years — when I realized what I was still entirely lacking: namely justice. "What is justice? And is it possible? And should it not be possible, how then would life be bearable?" — this is what I asked myself relentlessly. Wherever I dug in myself, it alarmed me deeply to find only passions, only corner-perspectives, only the unscrupulousness of those who were already lacking the preconditions for justice: but where was the presence of mind? — namely presence of mind from comprehensive insight. The only things I admitted to myself were *courage* and a certain *hardness*, which are the fruits of a long self-mastery. In fact it already took courage and hardness to admit so much to myself and moreover so late. Enough, I found reasons and ever better reasons to distrust my praise as well as my blame and to laugh about the judicial dignity that I had presumed for myself: indeed I finally *forbade* myself, with shame, any right to Yes and No; at the same time a sudden and intense curiosity awakened for the unknown world in me — in brief, I resolved to go into a hard and long new school and as far as possible away from my corner. Perhaps justice itself would meet up with me for once along the way! Thus began for me a period of *wandering*.

What was really happening to me back then? I did not understand myself, but the stimulus was like a command. It seems that our distant future determination disposes over us; for a long time we experience only riddles. Our selection of events, what we seize and suddenly crave, the pushing away of what is most pleasant, often of what is most revered: it frightens us as if here and there chance, a random, mad act were bursting out of us like a volcano. But it is only the higher reason and caution of our future task. The long sentence of my life wants perhaps — thus I asked myself restlessly — to be read *backwards*? Forwards, there is no doubt of this, at that time I read only "words without meaning."

A great, ever greater *separation*, a voluntary going-abroad, an "alienation," cooling off, sobering up — this alone, nothing more was my desire in those years. I tested everything to which my heart had generally attached itself up to that point, I turned around the best and most beloved things and looked at their other sides, I did the opposite with everything on which the human art of slander and defamation had so far been practiced most subtly. Back then I walked around many things that had so far remained foreign to me with a sparing, even loving curiosity, I learned to perceive our time and everything "modern" — more fairly. On the whole it might have been an uncanny and wicked game; — I was often ill because of it. That separation comes suddenly like an earthquake: the young soul has to see what is happening to it. At the same time it is an illness that can destroy human beings: this first outbreak of strength and will to self-determination; and much more pathological are the first peculiar and wild experiments of the spirit to henceforth shift the world into place on one's own. But my decision remained standing; and, even ill, I put the best face on my "games" and maliciously defended myself against every conclusion in which illness or loneliness or the exhaustion of wandering *could* have played a part. "Forward," I said to myself, "tomorrow you will be healthy, today it suffices for you to feign health." Back then I gained mastery over everything "pessimistic" in me; the *will* to health itself, the play-acting of health was my cure. What I perceived and *wanted* as "health" at the time is expressed comprehensibly and treacherously enough in these sentences (p. 37 of the first edition[61]): "a stable, mild, and basically cheerful soul, a mood that does not need to be on guard against pranks and sudden outbursts and whose expressions have no grumbling in their tone, nor any sullenness — those familiar, burdensome traits of old dogs and people who have been on a chain for a long time" — and "as the most desirable condition that free, fearless hovering above people, customs, laws, and traditional appraisals of things." — Indeed a kind of bird freedom and bird panorama, something of curiosity and contempt at the same time, whose like is familiar to anyone who surveys a tremendous multifariousness without being involved. — "A free spirit" — ⟨this⟩ cool word does a person good in any condition, it nearly warms; a human being has become the opposite of those who worry about things that do not concern them; the free spirit — was concerned purely about things that no longer "worry" him.

It is of no use that it immediately becomes a hard nut that must be cracked here: — the superior human being, the exceptional human being *must*, unless he — — —

Back then the personal result of all that was (*Human, All Too Human*, p. 31) as I described it, logical world-denial: namely the judgment that the world *that concerns us at all* is false. "It is *not* the world as thing in itself" — this is void, void of meaning and worthy of Homeric laughter! — "but the world *as error* that is so rich in meaning, deep, and wonderful, bearing happiness and unhappiness in its lap":[62] thus I decreed at the time — . The "overcoming of metaphysics," "which requires the greatest possible exertion of human presence of mind" (p. 23)[63] I regarded as achieved: and at the same time I posed myself the challenge of *maintaining* a great grateful meaning for these overcome metaphysics, insofar as "the greatest advancement of humanity" derived from them.

But in the background stood the will to a much broader curiosity, indeed to a tremendous experiment: the thought dawned in me as to whether all values did not permit themselves to be reversed, and the question always came back: "what do all human valuations mean anyway? What do they reveal about the conditions of life — your life, and furthermore of human life, ultimately of all life generally? —

40[66][64]

Draft for 2) of the preface: whoever has not experienced similar things does not belong here. A book of preparation. One must write a preface not only to invite, but to scare away.

"Our highest insights must and should etc.

To avoid being mistaken,[65] I added many things in order to enhance the *state* to which back then I

: it is a *necessary* transition-state for a few human beings. — Now I could say some things *more comprehensibly*.

Rejection of "freethinkers."

Against the *scabies anarchistica*.[66] It is a book through which natures that are destined to rule a⟨nd⟩ lead the way under certain circumstances should be brought to terrible conclusions, to reflection regarding the *discipline* toward themselves, the kind of superiority and accessibility to many ways of thinking (flexibility) and that tremendous health that even does not want to do without illness for a higher purpose.

That discipline and self-mastery of the spirit that is just as much a flexibility of the heart as an art of the mask: that inner comprehensiveness and pampering that permits the walking of paths to many and opposing ways of thinking, without our running the danger of getting lost in or falling in love with them; that tremendous health that even does not want to do without illness, that excess of plastic healing imitating restoring powers

40[67][67]

It was at that time that I first developed an eye for history: Ranke. Ignorance in the natural sciences and medicine makes our historians into modest advocates of *facta*:[68] as if for us something good "came of it" after all, some little "finger of God" at least.

40[68][69]

No. 1 of H. All Too H: *The Sphinx*. —

Conclusion of section I: *the new Oedipus*.

40[69]

Our "spirit" including feelings and sensations is a tool that is at the service of a many-headed and multifaceted master: this master is our valuations. But our valuations reveal something of what our *life-conditions* are (for the least part the conditions of the person, to a greater extent those of the species "human being," and to the greatest and widest extent the conditions under which *life* generally is possible).

40[70][70]

"*German.*"
Questions and Dashes.[71]

German Pessimism
German Romanticism.
The Rediscoverers of the Greeks.
German Anarchism.
The Dangers of the Jewish Soul.
The Literati.
Women.
Hermits.
The Demagogues in Art.
German Style.
German Music. The South The East (two souths: Venice and Provence)
The "Enlightenment" and Modern Ideas.
The School Master Culture.
Wagnerianism.
The Europeans.
The German Spirit.
The Jews
Voilà un homme.[72]
"Profundity."
The Christian European.

[41 = W I 5. August–September 1885]

41[1]

Sils-Maria end of August 1885

Friedrich Nietzsche, Collected Writings.

Early Works. The Birth of Tragedy.
Unfashionable Observations.
Address on Homer.

Human, All Too Human: A Book for Free Spirits.
"*Between Ourselves*": Mixed Opinions and Maxims.
Dawn: Thoughts on the Presumptions of Morality
Gai Saber: Prelude to a Philosophy of the Future.
Thus Spoke Zarathustra: A Book for All and None.
Noon and Eternity: Bequest of a Soothsayer.

"*Exultabit Solitudo et florebit quasi lilium.*"[1]

Isaiah.

41[2][2]

New Unfashionable Observation. —

1.

In our youth we admire and despise like a fool and probably bring forth our tenderest and highest feelings for the interpretation of people and things that do not belong to us, as little as we belong to them. *Youth* itself is something falsifying and deceiving. It seems that the reverence and the anger suited to youth are unwilling to rest at all until they have "falsified" people and things in such a way that it can unleash its emotions on them. Later on, when we have become stronger, deeper, also more truthful, we are startled to discover how little we had our eyes open at the time, when we sacrificed at these altars. We are angered at not having seen all that is vain, exaggerated, fake, varnished, thespian in our beloved idols — we are angered on account of this self-blinding, as if it had been a dishonest blindness. In this transition we take vengeance on ourselves through distrust; we are on guard against our enthusiastic feelings — indeed we feel even "a good conscience" to be a danger, like a self-veiling and weariness of one's own honesty. One decade later again: and we understand that all this too still — was *youth*. —

2.

— What I myself once, in my "young years," wrote about Schopenhauer and Richard Wagner, and not so much wrote as *painted* — perhaps in an all too daring super-exuberant and super-youthful *al fresco*[3] — that is what I want least to scrutinize today with an eye toward "true" and "false." But supposing I had erred back then: my error at least accrues to the dishonor neither of those mentioned, nor of myself! It *is* something to err *thus*; it *is* also something to seduce precisely *me* to error in this manner. In any case it was also an invaluable boon to me, back then when I decided to paint "the philosopher" and "the artist" and my own "categorical imperative" so to speak — to be able to paint my new colors not entirely onto the unreal but as it were on sketched-out figures. Without my knowing it, I spoke only for myself, indeed at bottom only about myself. Meanwhile: Everything that I experienced at the time, those are typical experiences for a certain kind of human being, which in order to be expressed — — — And whoever reads those writings with a young and fiery soul will perhaps guess the solemn oaths with which I bound myself for my life at the time — with which I resolved myself to *my* life: may he be one of those few who is *allowed* to resolve himself to a similar life and to similar oaths!

3.

There came a point in time when I secretly began to laugh about Richard Wagner, back then when he embarked on his last role and appeared before his beloved Germans with the gestures of a miracle man, salvation preacher, prophet, indeed even philosopher. And because I had not yet stopped loving him, my own laughter bit into my heart: as belongs to the story of anyone who becomes independent of his teacher and finally finds his own way. In this period arose the lively essay that follows below, from which, it seems to me, even today many a young German can profit: — I myself, in my current frame of mind, would wish to have said everything more patiently, also more cordially and considerately. In the meantime I guessed all too much about the painful and horrific tragedy that lies hidden behind the life of such a human being as was Richard Wagner.

4.

Richard Wagner has without any doubt Germans etc.

5.

But the musician Richard Wagner? — "Richard Wagner and No End":[4] this is the watchword today.

But with that we friends of music are at the end of our patience. For so long we have had to grin and bear the Wagnermania, and with the help of all virtues and kinds of aesthetic we have encouraged and exhorted ourselves throughout a very long rainy day: "how beautiful is even this nasty weather! How many charms lie concealed in the wrinkles of the thunderstorm! How subtly the rain plays the 'endless melody'! How incomparably the lightning flashes in the midst of long gray gloom! And especially the thunder: how beautiful is the chromatics of the thunder!" But finally, finally we also want to see the clear sky again and at least have the *beautiful evening* that we deserve after such a virtuous, but so wicked day! — Really? The evening? Is it really "becoming night" already? Is even our best art, music, beginning to nod now? My friends, here is someone who no longer believes in it! It is by no means time for the evening! And Wagner signified neither the day nor the night of our art — but only a dangerous interval, an exception and a question mark *that put our conscience to the test*! We still learned to say No! at the right time: any righteous and profound musician says No to Wagner today and to himself insofar as he still "wagnerizes" — and to be sure the more thoroughly if precisely he was schooled by Wagner, learned from him.

6.

Of course it may be all the worse for the musicians who are less skilled, also for those who crave money and honor: precisely for them there are exquisite seductions in Wagner's manner of making music. For it is *easy* to compose with Wagnerian methods and tricks, it may also be, given the demagogic craving of today's artists for excitement of the "masses," more lucrative, namely "more full of effects," "more overpowering," "more striking," "more gripping" and however else the treacherous favorite words of the theater rabble and the dilettantish fanatics put it. But ultimately, what do noise and the enthusiasm of the "masses" mean in matters of art! *Good* music never has a "public": — it is and can never be "public," it belongs to the most exquisite, it should always and only — speaking in metaphors — exist *for the "chamber*!"[5] "Masses" can sense the one who knows best how to flatter them, in their way they are grateful for all demagogic talents and return it in kind to the best of their abilities. (How "masses" are able to *thank*, with what "spirit" and "taste," for this the death of Victor Hugo provided edifying testimony: in all the centuries of France together, has there been so much France-demeaning nonsense printed and spoken as on this occasion? But also at the burial of Richard Wagner the flatteries of gratitude spiraled as high as this "pious" wish: "Redemption to the Redeemer!"[6] —)
NB. There is no doubt that W⟨agnerian⟩ art today has an effect on the masses: that it can do that — should this not constitute a testimonial about this very art? For three good things in art "masses" have never had a sense, for nobility, for logic and for beauty — *pulchrum est paucorum hominum*[7] — : not to speak of an even better thing, of *grand style*, to which so far even the

most highly evolved artists of modern times were allowed to say neither Yes nor No: — they have not had a right to it yet, they felt distant and ashamed before it, and this shame was in fact precisely their highest height! Wagner stands farthest from grand style: the excessive and heroically ostentatious aspects of his artistic methods stand in direct *contrast* to grand style; and likewise the tenderly seductive, the manifoldly charming, the restless, uncertain, suspenseful, momentary, mysteriously effusive, the whole "supersensual" masquerade of sick senses, and whatever else might be called "Wagnerian" in the typical sense. And nonetheless, despite his most thorough inability for it: Wagner *leers* at the grand *style*, he who is incapable of even ordinary, proper, genuine *logic*! He knows this well enough, he recognized it early on: but immediately he set about, with the ruthless actor-adroitness that constitutes his mastery, interpreting his deficiency as an advantage. In the illogical, semi-logical there is much that is seductive: — this is what Wagner thoroughly divined — : namely for Germans with whom obscurity is perceived as "profundity." He was denied the manliness and rigor of a logical development: but he found "something more full of effect"! "Music," he taught, "is only ever a means, the end is drama."[8] Drama? No, the gesture![9] — *thus* at least Wagner personally understood it. Above all and first the gripping gesture! Something that knocks you down and makes you shudder! Who cares about "sufficient reason"! A kind of ambiguity even in the rhythmic phrasing likewise belongs among his favorite artistic methods, a kind of drunkenness and sleepwalking that no longer knows how to "infer" and unleashes a dangerous will to blind following and giving in.

Just look at our *women* when they are "wagnetized":[10] what "unfreedom of the will"! What fatalism in their extinguishing gaze! What letting-go, what submission! Perhaps they even intuit that in this condition of the "unhinged" will they possess one *more* charm for some kind of men?: what *more* reason for their worship of their Cagliostro and miracle man! With the actual "maenads" of Wagner-worship one can even confidently diagnose hysteria and illness; something or another is not in order with their sexuality; or children are lacking, or in the most bearable case, men.

7.

As concerns the *youths* who pay homage to Wagner, generally speaking they are musically bad. (One of the best even once said to me ingenuously "I understand *nothing at all* about music, but Wagner unites everything good that exists today — he is an anti-Semite, vegetarian and abhors vivisection") Wagnerian youths, in many respects a very refreshing and noble kind of youth — revere in Wagner roughly the same thing that the passionate disciples of Victor Hugo around 1828 revered in their idol: above all the master of big words and gestures, the advocate of all swelling emotions, all sublime instincts, then the daring innovator and shackle-breaker in battle with and in opposition to older stricter, perhaps more restrictive artistic schooling, the opener of new portals, new vistas, new distances, new depths and heights, finally, and not least: these German youths revere in Wagner his commanding nature, the ability to noisily command, to stand on himself alone, to answer to himself alone, to obstinately say Yes to himself, and always in the name of the "chosen people," the Germans! — in brief, they revere what is tribunal and demagogic in Wagner. Such enthusiastic youths of course still see nothing of the bad, indeed abominable taste of this whole "self-staging" of Wagner's: youth simply *has* the right to bad taste — it is *their* right. But if one wants to learn *where* the innocence and the unhesitating readiness of youths can be led and seduced by an old drifting pied piper, then just cast a glance at that literary swamp from which ultimately the now aged master loves to sing with his "boys" (is "sing" the right word?) I mean the infamous *Bayreuther Blätter*.[11] That is really a *swamp*: Presumption, Teutonification and conceptual chaos all mixed in the gloomiest way, poured over with an intolerable sugar of "sweetest" compassion, and in between that already mentioned inclination for green vegetables and that purposeful anointing and sentimentality for the sake of animals, *close* beside the unvarnished genuine and thorough hatred for science and generally the scorn and defiling of everything that stands or stood in Wagner's way — how the *nobler* nature of Mendelsohn, the *purer* nature of Schumann stood in the way of his influence! — along with a prudent squinting for new reinforcements, an "accommodation" in the direction of powerful parties, for instance the completely impure playing and ogling with *Christian* symbols — Wagner, the old atheist, antinomian and immoralist, even at one point unctuously invokes the "blood of the Redeemer"! — on the whole the impudence of an old high priest enveloped by thick smoke, who discloses his obscure emotions like revelations about every conceivable realm of thought that is inaccessible and forbidden precisely to him; and all this in a German, a real swamp-German of obscurity and exaggeration such as perhaps not even the most "German"-hostile disciples of Hegel had achieved!

8.

Perhaps only now can it be made clear *where* Wagner belongs: namely *not* in the great series of the authentic and the genuine of the highest order, *not* at this Olympic "court of courts." Rather, Wagner is due an entirely different rank and an entirely different honor — and in fact, not a small and mean one: Wagner is one of those three actor-geniuses of art from whom the *mob* in this century — and it is after all the "century of the mob!" — practically *learned* its concept of "artist" in the first place: I mean those three odd and dangerous human beings, Paganini, Liszt, Wagner, dubiously positioned in the middle between "God" and "ape," who were predestined just as much for "imitation" as for invention, for creating *in the art of imitation itself*, and whose instincts divined everything that can be discovered and amplified for the purpose of performance, expression, effect, sorcery, seduction. As demonic mediators and art-interpreters they became — and *are* today the masters of all artists of interpretation generally: everyone in these circles learned from them; — this is why the seat and likewise the origin of the actual "Wagner-cult" must be sought among actors and practicing itinerant musicians of all kinds. But apart from these circles, to whom we must concede every right to their belief and superstition,[12] and with respect to the total appearance of those three actor-geniuses and their most secret and universal meaning I personally cannot get beyond raising the same question again and again: what is it in those three that seemingly expresses itself as new, is it perhaps only the old and eternal "Cagliostro" after all, only newly costumed, newly staged, "set to music," set to religion — as it might best correspond with the taste of the new century — the century of the *mob*, as mentioned? Therefore no longer like the last Cagliostro as the seducer of a noble and exhausted culture, but instead —as *demagogical* Cagliostro? — And our music, with whose help people are being "bewitched" here: — what, I beg and ask you, does our G⟨erman⟩ m⟨usic⟩ mean!

9.

— This *late* Wagner, at bottom a broken and conquered human being, but one who could not abandon his great playacting, this Wagner who in the end even spoke of the "thrills" that he knew how to extract from the Protestant holy communion while at the same time he stretched out his hands to everything *Roman* with his Parsifal music: this flatterer of all German vanities, obscurities and presumptions who offered himself everywhere — this *late* Wagner is supposed to be the ultimate and highest pinnacle of our music and the expression of the finally achieved synthesis of the "German soul," *the* German himself? — It was in summer 1876 that I recanted *this* faith; and therewith began that movement of the German conscience of which today ever more serious, ever more distinct signs are becoming visible — and the *decline* of Wagnermania!

41[3][13]

There is only nobility of birth, nobility of blood. (I am not speaking here of the little word "von" and the *Gothaische Kalender*:[14]

interpolation for asses.) Where people speak of "aristocrats of the spirit," usually grounds are not lacking for hiding something; it is a well-known favorite term among ambitious Jews. For spirit alone does not ennoble; on the contrary something is first required *that ennobles the spirit.* — What then is required for this? The blood.

41[4][15]

German philosophy as a whole — Leibniz, Kant, Hegel, Schopenhauer, to name the great ones — is the most thorough kind of *Romanticism* and homesickness that has ever existed: the longing for the best there ever was. One is no longer at home anywhere, ultimately one longs to return to where one can somehow be at home, because only there does one wish to be at home: and that is the Greek world! But precisely to that place all bridges are broken — *except* the rainbows of concepts! And they lead everywhere, to all homelands and "fatherlands" there have been for Greek-souls! Indeed: One must be very subtle, very light, very thin to step across these bridges! But what happiness lies already in this will to spirituality, almost to ghostliness! How distant one is here from "pressure and thrust," from the mechanistic silliness of the natural sciences, from the fairground din of "modern ideas"! People want to *return* to the Greeks through the church fathers, from the north to the south, from the formulas to the forms; they still enjoy the outcome of antiquity, Christianity, as an entrance to antiquity, as a good piece of the old world itself, as a gleaming mosaic of ancient concepts and ancient valuations. Arabesques, flourishes, Rococo of scholastic abstractions — still better, namely finer and thinner, than the peasant- and rabble-reality of the European north, still a protest of higher spirituality against the peasant war and rabble-insurrection that has become master of spiritual taste in the north of Europe and that had its ringleader in the great "unspiritual man," in Martin Luther: — In this sense German philosophy is a piece of counter-Reformation, even Renaissance, at least will to Renaissance, will, to *continue* in the discovery of antiquity, in the excavation of ancient philosophy, above all of the pre-Socratics — of the best-buried of all Greek temples! Perhaps a few centuries later one will judge that all German philosophizing has its genuine dignity in being a step-by-step reclamation of antiquity's soil, and that every claim to "originality" sounds petty and ridiculous in relation to that higher claim of the Germans to have newly tied the bond that seemed torn, the bond with the Greeks, hitherto the most highly constituted type of "human." Today we are again approaching all those fundamental forms of interpreting the world that the Greek spirit in Anaximander, Heraclitus, Parmenides, Empedocles, Democritus and Anaxagoras invented — we are becoming *more Greek* from day to day, at first, as is only fair, in concepts and valuations, as graecofying[16] ghosts, so to speak: but someday, hopefully also with our *body*! Herein lies (and has ever lain) my hope for the German character!

41[5]

One opens a female book: — and soon one sighs "another failed cook!"

41[6][17]

Only the very rarest and most highly evolved individuals achieve the highest and most illustrious human joys in which existence celebrates its own transfiguration, as is only fair: and even these only after they themselves and their ancestors have lived a long and preparatory life aimed at this goal, and without even knowing about this goal. Then an overflowing wealth of manifold forces and simultaneously the most agile power of "willing freely" and masterful commanding dwell lovingly together in a single human being, the spirit is then just as indigenous and at home in the senses as the senses are at home and indigenous in the spirit; and everything that plays out only in the spirit must also trigger a subtle extraordinary happiness and play in the senses. And likewise in reverse! — consider this reversal in the example of Hafiz; even Goethe, however faintly it shows in him, provides an inkling of this occurrence. It is probable that with such perfect and well-evolved human beings ultimately the most sensual tasks are transfigured by a symbol-frenzy of the highest spirituality; they perceive in themselves a kind of *deification of the body* and they are furthest from the ascetic-philosophy of the proposition "God is a spirit": whereby it clearly turns out that the ascetic is "the failed human being" who pronounces only a something in itself *good*, and precisely the judging and condemning something — and pronounces it "God." From that pinnacle of joy where human beings feel themselves totally and utterly to be a deified form and self-justification of nature, down to the joy of healthy peasants and healthy semi-human animals: to this entire long tremendous light- and color-scale of *happiness* the Greeks gave, not without the grateful shudders of someone who is initiated into a mystery, not without great caution and pious silence — the divine name: Dionysus. — What now do all modern humans, the children of a fragmented multifarious sick odd mother *know* of the *scope* of Greek happiness, what could they know about it! From where would the slaves of "modern ideas" even take their right to Dionysian festivals!

41[7][18]

When the Greek body and Greek soul "blossomed," and not to be sure in conditions of pathological effusion and madness, that mysterious symbol emerged of the highest world-affirmation and transfiguration of existence attained so far on earth. Here a *standard* is given according to which everything that has grown since is found to be too brief, too poor, too narrow: — merely pronounce the word "Dionysus" before the best modern names and things, before Goethe, perhaps, or before Beethoven, or before Shakespeare, or before Raphael: and all at once we feel our best things and moments *judged*. Dionysus is a *judge*! — Have I been understood? — There is no doubt that the Greeks attempted to interpret the ultimate mysteries "of the fate of the soul" and everything they knew about the education and purification, above all about the unbudgeable rank order and value-inequality from human to human, from their Dionysian experiences: here for all things Greek is the great depth, the great silence — *one does not know the Greeks* as long as the hidden underground entrance still lies here blocked by rubble. Obtrusive scholar-eyes will never see anything of these things, however much scholarship still has to be applied in the service of that excavation — ; precisely here even the noble zeal of such friends of antiquity as Goethe and Winckelmann has something forbidden, almost immodest. Wait and prepare oneself; wait for new sources to open up, prepare oneself in isolation for strange faces and voices; wash one's soul ever cleaner of the fairground dust and noise of this age; *overcome* everything Christian through something supra-Christian and not only cast it off —for the Christian doctrine was the counterdoctrine to the Dionysian — ; rediscover the *south* in oneself and spread out above oneself a bright gleaming mysterious southern sky; reconquer one's southern health and the hidden might of the soul; step by step become more comprehensive, more supranational, more European, more supra-European, more eastern, finally *more Greek* — for the Greek[19] was the first great bond and synthesis of everything eastern — : and therewith the very *beginning* of the European soul, the discovery *of our* "*new* world": — whoever lives under such imperatives, who knows what *he* can encounter some day? Perhaps even — *a new day*!

41[8][20]

In my early years I declared war on the conditions of German education and dutifully wielded my sword against them: there is no alternative. Away with the women, with the masculine women and sissies too! *they* know nothing about war and wail themselves half dead over a single drop of shed blood. People have reproached me for earlier having "killed" the aged David Strauss? I will probably have still other human lives on my conscience — but such are the fortunes of war. A thing that is ripe for dying: why artificially nurse, spare and coddle such a thing? But nothing in the conditions of German education deserves to be spared: that *is* "ripe."

41[9][21]

Preface

Whoever has the desires of a high and selective soul and only rarely finds *his* table set, *his* nourishment ready, is in no small danger today. Thrown into a noisy, rabble-like age with which he does not want to eat from the same bowl, he could easily perish of hunger and thirst, or, in the event he finally "digs in" after all — *of nausea*. This was the danger of my youth, an unsatisfied, yearning, solitary youth; and the danger reached its peak when I realized one day *which kind* of dishes I had ultimately consumed and *where* the impetuous hunger and thirst of my soul had lured me. It was in summer 1876. At that time, enraged by nausea, I pushed away all the tables at which I had eaten up till then, and I promised myself that I would rather live accidentally and meagerly, rather on grass and weeds and roaming about like an animal, rather not live at all anymore than share my meals with the "theater folk" and the "higher trick riders of the spirit"— I used such harsh expressions back then: — for I seemed to have ended up among sheer Cagliostros and ingenuine people, and I was angry and raging at the fact that I had loved where I should have despised.

After I finally became calmer, although definitely not more equitable and conciliatory, I slowly and without rudeness freed myself from my previous "company" and began wandering — sick, sick for many long years. A great, ever greater separation — for philosophical people like to pursue the particular into the universal — a voluntary "*alienation*" was my sole refreshment in that time: I tested everything to which my heart had generally attached itself up to that point, I turned around the best and most beloved things and looked at their other sides, I did the opposite with everything on which the human art of slander and defamation had so far been practiced most subtly.

It was a wicked game: I was often ill because of it — but my resolve stood firm. I "broke my venerating heart" itself and even looked at its broken pieces and their reverse sides — not without all kinds of new joy and curiosity: for one is cruel to the same degree that one is capable of love. Finally I arrived, step by step, at the last challenge of my inner hardness: I put on the best face for my wicked game, laughed at all "pessimism" in me and maliciously defended myself against every conclusion in which illness and loneliness *could* have played a part: "forward," I said to myself, "someday you will be healthy, today it suffices for you to *feign* health! The will to health is already the very best cure!"

Then I opened my eyes for the first time — and immediately saw many things and many colors of things, as they are never allowed to be seen by fearful loafers and spirits who are worried about themselves, and have always stayed home. A kind of bird freedom, a kind of bird panorama, a kind of mixture of curiosity and contempt as possessed by anyone who surveys a tremendous multifariousness without being involved — that finally was the newly achieved state with which I persisted for a long time. "A free spirit" and nothing more: thus I felt, thus I called myself at the time; and really I had become the opposite of those who worry about things that do not concern them; the free spirit — *I* was concerned purely about things that no longer — "worried me."

These were the years of *recovery*: multifarious years full of colorful and painfully magic events, of which the healthy, the stocky of spirit are permitted to grasp and smell just as little as the sickly, the condemned, those predestined for death and not for life. Back then I had not yet found "myself": but I was bravely underway to "myself" and tested a thousand things and people I passed along the way, as to whether they belonged to "me" or at least knew something about "me." What surprises there were! What horrors! What brief little nooks of happiness! What resting in the sun! What tendernesses! And again and again this harsh inner voice that commanded: "away from here! Forward, wanderer! There are many seas and lands left for you: who knows *whom* you must still encounter?"

In order to gratefully confess it then: at that time, when I began to study the rule known as "human being," I encountered and my path was crossed by strange and not undangerous spirits, including even *very* free spirits — and above all one, and this one repeatedly, none other than the god Dionysus himself: — the same one to whom I once, in much younger years, had made a reverential and innocent sacrifice. Perhaps I will once again find enough leisure and quiet to tell my friends everything that I retained from the philosophy of the god Dionysus: in undertones, as is only fair — since we are dealing with many secret things, and much that is uncanny.[22] But that Dionysus is a philosopher and that *gods* therefore also *philosophize* seems to me at least to be an important circumstance worthy of the most cautious communication, which has nothing against it except perhaps that it is not revealed at the right time: for these days people do not like to believe in gods. Perhaps, too, I will have to go further in the frankness of my narrative than is always endearing to the strict habits of my friends' ears. Certainly the god in question went further in our conversations and was always out ahead of me by several steps: he *loves* to go far! Indeed, if it were permitted to ascribe beautiful, solemn names of splendor and virtue to him, in keeping with human custom, I would have to greatly extol his explorer and discoverer courage, his honesty, truthfulness and love of wisdom. But such a god does not know what to do with all this venerable junk and splendor. "Keep this," he would say, "for yourself instead and for your kind and whoever else needs it! *I — have no reason to cover my nakedness.*"

As one sees, this kind of deity and philosopher is lacking in shame. Thus he said right away in his first conversation with me: "under certain circumstances I love the human being" — and with this he was alluding to Ariadne —: "it is a pleasant inventive animal without peers on earth, it can even find its way in any labyrinths. I often think about how I can advance it and make it stronger, more evil and deeper than it is." — "Stronger, more evil and deeper?" I asked, startled. "Yes," he said once more, "stronger, more evil and deeper: also more beautiful" — and at that the god smiled as if he had just uttered a charming compliment. Here we also see immediately: this deity is lacking not only shame — ; and there are generally good reasons to conjecture that in some matters all the gods could learn from us human beings. We are *more humane*.[23]

And herewith we have arrived and are at the right place: namely at the end. For by now one will have abundantly grasped what it is supposed to be called: *Human, All Too Human*. And why this book is "a book for *free spirits*."

2.

What the words *Human, All Too Human* in this title are supposed to mean I have already made clear — at least for those who have subtle ears. But what in all the world was I thinking back then by "free spirits," to whom I cast the fishhooks of my book? It seems I desired —company?

41[10][24]

— — — Therefore I cannot sufficiently praise the three fortunate events of my life that at the right time balanced out how I had come to harm through an unsatisfied, yearning and solitary youth. The first was that in my early youth I found a respectable and scholarly occupation that allowed me to make myself at home in the proximity of the Greeks: if one will excuse me this immodest but clear expression. In this manner off to the side and entertained in the best way, I could not easily bring myself to ⟨get⟩ vehemently angry about anything that happens today. In addition to this I was devoted to a philosopher who knew how to valiantly oppose everything in the present, yet without eradicating respect in his pupil through an excess of denial. Finally, ever since I was a child I have been a lover of music and at all times a personal friend of good musicians: all of this together resulted in my having little reason to concern myself about contemporary human beings: — for the good musicians are all hermits and outside of time.

I was already beyond my twenties when I discovered that I was lacking knowledge of human beings. Is it probable that someone could become a connoisseur of human beings by directing his thoughts neither to honors, nor high office, nor money, nor women, and spending the longest periods of every day by himself? Here there would be ample occasion for mocking if it were not contrary to good taste for the author of a book to abuse its preface for the purpose of mocking himself. Enough, I found reasons, and ever more and better reasons to mistrust my praise as well as my blame; at the same time a vehement and sudden curiosity for "the human being awakened in me: in sum, I resolved to enter a hard and long school.

41[11][25]

"Thinking" in its primitive state (pre-organic) is *the imposing of shapes*, as in crystal. — In *our* thinking the *essential* element is the ordering of new material into old schemata (= Procrustean bed), the *making*-same of what is new.

41[12][26]

Conclusion of I.

I see new philosophers coming up. If I know you, my friends, you free spirits, then these "coming ones," beautiful proud birds are flying among you too! — I — — —

41[13][27]

— — — But as concerns the above quoted imperative of the German instinct, that commands: "Admit no *more* Jews! And keep the doors barred to the east!" — then the circumspect calculation of the German Jews themselves should counsel them toward a similar "border-regulation": their task of growing into the German nature and achieving a more German type of expression and gesture, ultimately of "soul" — for *this* is the pathway, from the outside to the inside, from "appearance" to "reality" — should not be pushed back again and again into the insoluble by the horrific and despicable ugliness of newly immigrating Polish and Russian, Hungarian and Galician Jews. *Here* is the point where the Jews also for their part have to act, namely "to set borders" for themselves: — the single and last point in which Jewish and German advantage could still balance out to a common advantage: but of course it is time, indeed the highest time!

41[14][28]

So far there has been no German culture either. It is no objection to this proposition that there have been great hermits in Germany — Goethe e.g.,: for these had *their* own culture. But all around them in particular, as around mighty defiant randomly strewn boulders, lay the rest of German nature *as their opposite*, namely as a soft marshy unstable ground on which every foreign step and stride made its "impression" and created "forms": "German education" was a thing without character, a nearly limitless elasticity.

41[15][29]

— I publicly laughed to death a miserable presumptuous moldy book, with which "German education" had become infatuated — well now, on earth one can make a still *more dangerous* use of one's laughter! Perhaps in doing this I accidentally "killed" an old man, the old venerable David Strauss, *virum optime meritum*?[30] — that's what people lead me to believe. But such are the fortunes of war; and I want in good conscience to have yet other human lives "on my conscience"! Only away with the women, with the masculine wailing-women and sissies too! *They* know nothing about war-craft and wail themselves half dead over every "lack of mercy." In order for something else to begin, here one must first make an end: I certainly hope that here — I have been — understood? But nothing in "German education" deserves to be spared anymore: here one must not spare oneself and finally make an end — or something else cannot begin at all

41[16][31]
The Germans are deep.
the Christian European.
the German spirit
that unhesitating enthusiast.
the demagogues in art.
On the Decline of Wagnerianism.
How little the German style
the Jews
Ranke, the embellishing advocate of the fact

[42 = Mp XVII 2a. August–September 1885]

42[1][1]

The Mirror.

An Opportunity for Self-Reflection for Europeans.

Latent anarchism.
Varieties and causes of world-defamation.
III The Germans. Thoughts on discipline and cultivation.
Ulterior motives of logic.
The embarrassment of the physicists.
II What are "free spirits"?
The demagogues in art.
The eternal feminine.
Morality in Europe.
The discipline of *willing*.
On the order of rank.
Christ and Dionysus.
The historian.
I The philosophers of the future.
The decline of cheerfulness.
On solitude.
South and east. A word for musicians.
World-interpretation, not world-explanation.
(Literature and actor culture.)
The "late Wagner." —

The genuinely *royal* calling of the philosopher (according to the expression of Alcuin the Anglo-Saxon): *prava corrigere et recta corroborare et sancta sublimare.*[2,3]

Attempt at a Critique of the Modern Soul.

42[2]

Atheism and its causes.
Latent atheism.
Nationalism and the global economy.
On the order of rank and equality.
Moral skepticism
World defamation and the decrease of cheerfulness
North south
Music
The philosophers
The historians
The demagogues in art.
Woman.
The discipline of willing.
Nourishment.
Reading and literature press.

42[3][4,5]

Human, All Too Human. I *Metaphysica*

If the world had a goal then it must have been reached
Using the body as a guide
Whoever has pursued the history of any single science
What we experience in dream
What {separates} us from all Platonic and Leibnizian ways of thinking
The human being is a form- and rhythm-constructing creature
A thought is in the shape in which it comes
"How are synthetic judgments a priori
What distinguishes me most thoroughly from the metaphysicians,

Truth: this describes within
The logical thinking, of which logic speaks
There are truths that are best {}[6] by mediocre minds
Conclusion: In what strange *simplification*!
The new Oedipus.
Appearance, as I understand it.

Human, All Too Human II Section **Moralia**
"Our highest insights must — and should — like follies, indeed like crimes"
"Insofar as at all times, as long as humans have existed, herds also"
"Moralities are the main method"
"One is still offended, if someone,
"The old theological problem of faith and of knowledge"
"Crudeness. — Words are musical notes for concepts"
"Nothing more miserable than moralistic literature etc."
"The will. — In each will there is a plurality
"The diversity of human beings is revealed not only in the diversity of their tablets of good"
"At bottom morality is inimically disposed toward science"

Human, All Too Human. *Religiosa.*
"The human soul and its limits"
"The philosophers will also {use} religions"
"In the Jewish Old Testament — "
"The English, dark, sensual"
Conclusion "On the highest and most illustrious human joys"

Human, All Too Human. 4 *Art*
On the whole I agree more with the artists: pessimism.
Conclusion: Against R. Wagner. *On the decline of Wagnerianism*. —
How little the German style {corresponds} with the sound

Human, All Too Human. 5. *Higher Culture.*
German philosophy as romanticism

People call the Germans profound.
Wagner and Paris
Even today the finest culture is
Victor Hugo "*The demagogues of culture*
Kant's influence in Europe
Supposing one were to think of a philosopher as a great educator
On conviction and justice (penultimate)

In Relations with Others.

When the philosophers {mingle} with the *homines*[7]
Human, All Too Human. *Woman* and child.
The greater sensuality
One cannot think highly enough of women
The decline of *grace.* —

Human, All Too Human. *State.*
Socialism is the ultimate
Over all these national wars, new empires
There is a nobility of blood
That unhesitating enthusiast
The Germans, {compared} to their Germanic ancestors
The German Jews. — The good Europeans.
The Germans have not yet been anything, for they are becoming something

Human, All Too Human. By *oneself alone.*
— The danger with extraordinary spirits
A person who strives for greatness
— That many speak of things with respect to which
— The hermit, the higher philosophical human being.

I *followed by*: "*Freethinker*"
Third to last II "the free spirit" and solitude
III 2 (*At the end*) The *strong* spirit
IV Conclusion: In *Genoa*: Oh my friends, do you understand this "Nevertheless"? — —

42[4][8]

1 *The knowing one*
2 *Beyond what is good and evil*[9]
3 *New fables of God*
4 *Man and woman*
5 *Friend, Enemy* and solitude

42[5][10]

Alone or in twos — 6, 13, 14, 24, 36, 48
Victims — 19, 18
Contempt for woman — 20, 16, 17, 23, 37
Not too many words — 22, 15
Child man woman — 28
The creators — 29, 30
Against self-knowledge — 38, 45
In order to be loved — 46
Purposes — 57
Herd — 62
Marriage — 60, 53, 18, 17
Devil God — 47
Time and future — 76, 102

42[6][11]

P. 1. There is no common-good: — this word contradicts itself, for whatever can be common must always be of common value therefore not be good.

1 Dogmatists. Plato and the "pure spirit."
the magnificent tension through the dogmatists.
2 Skeptics.
The commanders rare. In the end the most mediocre rule in philosophy!
Where does the will still exist?
3 The critics:
Does German philosophy belong in the critical or the skeptical movement? Kant. No, it is a countermovement, at

bottom a theological one.
"without a passionate enjoyment."

4 The English and philosophy, entirely unsuited for the moralistic "hunt."
The French. Richard Wagner.

5 Herd-morality.
Christianity makes small ⟨the⟩ Old Testament. Socialism.
Free thinkers. "Enlightenment"

6 The philosopher as the experimenter of new possibilities
the value of immorality for upbringing.
his cruelty
his solitude.
Teichm⟨üller⟩

7 My antecedents.
On my *Unfashionable Observations*
a word about pessimism.
a word about artists: the Dionysian.
the shaping of the soul of Europe.
significance of the Greeks, their discovery
the historical sense

8 The Dionysian.

42[7][12]

— the spitting image of my hallucinations
— did the trees already look green 50 thousand years ago?
— prior to logic, temporally speaking, lies the production *of identical cases*, assimilation
— memory in the organic sequence
— "innate" ideas
— hypocrisy would be eliminated if it were not funny to look at. Not gods according to Epicurus, but according to Homer: or like Galiani
— the mathematicians who continue deducing until the atom becomes *useful* to them! But h⟨umans⟩ have always done it this way, in a cruder form. What does reality matter before it is useful for our house!

42[8][13]

Yes, the philosophy of right! This is a science which, like all moral sciences, is not even in diapers yet! E.g., the oldest *meaning* of punishment has yet to be recognized, not even among jurists who imagine themselves to be freethinking — it is completely unknown: and as long as jurisprudence fails to establish itself on new ground, namely in history and comparative studies of peoples, it will remain trapped in dreary battles between thoroughly false abstractions that fancy themselves these days to be "philosophy of right" and that are completely derived from the contemporary h⟨uman being⟩. Yet this contemporary h⟨uman being⟩ is such a convoluted web, even in regard to its leg⟨al⟩ valuations, that it allows for the most varied *interpretations*.

[43 = Z I 2c. Autumn 1885]

43[1][1]

Draft.

The first problem is: how deeply does the "*will to truth*" go into things? If one were to measure the entire value of ignorance connected with the means for preservation of life, likewise the value of simplifications *generally* and the value of regulative fictions, e.g., of the logical kind, if one were to consider above all the value of interpretations, and to what extent it is a matter not of "it is" but "it means" — — —

then one arrives at this solution: the "will to truth" develops in the service of the "will to power": on close scrutiny its actual task is helping a certain kind of untruth to victory and to duration, taking a coherent whole of falsifications as the basis for the preservation of a certain kind of life.

Problem: how deep down does the *will to goodness* go into the heart of things. One sees the opposite of this everywhere, in plants and animals: Indifference or harshness or cruelty. "Justice" "punishment." The development of cruelty.

Solution: Sympathy only exists in social constructs (to which the human body belongs, whose living individual beings sympathize with one another) as the consequence of the fact that one greater whole *wants to preserve* itself against another whole, and again because in the overall economy of the world, where there is no possibility of perishing and loss, goodness would ⟨be⟩ a *superfluous* principle.

Problem: how deeply reason reaches into the ground of things. According to a critique of ends and means (— no factual relationship, but always one that only gets interpreted into it), the character of squandering, of derangement is normal ⟨in the⟩ overall economy. "Intelligence" appears as a specific form of unreason, nearly as its most malicious caricature.

Problem: how far does the "will to beauty" reach. Ruthless development of forms: the most beautiful are only the strongest: as the triumphant they maintain themselves firmly, and take pleasure in their type, reproduction. (Plato's belief that even philosophy is a kind of sublime sexual and reproductive drive.)

Hence the things that we have so far valued most highly: as the "true," "good," "reasonable," "beautiful," prove to be isolated cases of the *converse* powers — I point my finger at this tremendous *perspectival falsification*, by virtue of which the species human being asserts itself. It is its condition of life that it enjoys itself this way (the human being takes joy in the means of its preservation: and they include that the human being does not want to let itself be deceived, that humans mutually help each other, ⟨are⟩ prepared to understand one another; that on the whole the successful types know how to live at the expense of the failed). In all of this the will to power expresses itself, with its unhesitating readiness to seize the means of deception: a *malicious pleasure* is conceivable, that a god senses when looking at a human being admiring itself.

Therefore: the will to power.

Consequence: if this idea is *hostile* to us, why do we give in to it? Bring on the beautiful phantoms! Let us be deceivers and embellishers of humanity! Fact, *what* actually a *philosopher* is.

43[2][2]

Misunderstanding of logic: it explains nothing, on the contrary

Misunderstanding of historical development: succession is a description

Superficiality of our causality-sense.

"Knowledge" — to what extent impossible in a world of becoming?

The organic world represents a perspectival sphere.

Knowability of the world — in itself an immodesty for human beings.

Dissolution of the instincts — transformation into formulas and formula human beings. Against naturalism and mechanism. The "calculability" of the world, whether it is desirable? with this even the creative act would be "calculable"?

Mechanics a kind of *ideal*, as regulative method — nothing more.

Mockery of the idealists who believe "*truth*" to be where they feel "good" or "elevated."

Classical: Renan, quoted by Bourget.

Denial of empty space and reduction of mechanics to tyranny of the eye and touch.

Denial of the *actio in distans*.[3] *Against* pressure and thrust.

The *shape* of the world as cause of its cycle process.

Not sphere!

Force continual.

Against Laplace-Kant.

Battle of the atoms, as of individuals, but with a certain difference in strength from two atoms one will form, and from two individuals one. Likewise inversely from one two will form if the inner state brings about a disgregation of the power-center. — *Therefore against* the absolute concept "atom" and "individual"!

The atom fights for its duration, but other atoms attack it in order to increase their strength.

Both processes: that of disintegration and that of compression to be understood *as effects* of the will to power. Down to its tiniest fragments it has the will to compress. But it is *forced*, **in order** to *compress* itself anywhere, to dilute itself at another spot etc.

Planetary bodies and atoms only different in magnitude, but *same laws*.

43[3]

The Germans, in whose Germanic ancestors no Tacitus was able to praise the spirit, or even only a pleasure in spirituality, perhaps an *argute loqui*,[4] in addition have done everything possible throughout many centuries to make themselves stupid; and a malicious God who was hostile to Germans — possibly in fear of their predestined atheism and twilight of the gods? — ruled over them and endowed them exclusively with the inclinations that a people uses to shut the doors to even the *arrival of the* spirit: e.g., by commanding them to sweat in overheated beds, to crouch in stuffy narrow rooms, to choose as their favorite foods nothing but undigestible dishes like dumplings and heavy fatty broths, above all to drink until they fell down: so that going to sleep and being drunk were for a long time neighboring concepts of a German mind. One is almost tempted to believe that, if there were something like "*German* spirit" after all, it was only made possible through de-Germanification, I mean through mixing with foreign blood. Who keeps a ledger of everything that the Slavs or the Celts or the Jews are owed for the spiritualization of Germany! But the blood-mixing itself may have been most important, in that it planted different instincts in the same p⟨erson⟩ and not always only "two but instead twenty souls" in a single breast,[5] that tremendous blood-corruption of the race, which has no equal in Europe and has made of the German an all-comprehending, all-sympathizing and accommodating people of the middle, of mediation — a ferment-race in whom henceforth "no thing is impossible." If one checks the history of the German soul, one grasps⟨, how⟩ these inwardly imbalanced, multifaceted, multifarious h⟨uman beings⟩ became outwardly weak, servile, comfortable, clumsy, inwardly a playground of spiritual temptations and struggles: how finally at least a kind of stirring peasant- and preacher-spirit sprang up (Luther is the most beautiful example of this, he who waged the peasant war of the spirit against the "superior human beings" of the Renaissance —), how this peasant- and preacher-spirit later transformed itself into the aggressive, cutting and biting citizen- and critic-spirit — Lessing is again the most beautiful example of this, he who waged a "citizens' war," the war of the German bourgeois against the aristocratic spirit of French culture: Lessing against Corneille, Lessing the advocate of Diderot): until finally our last double-type of the ever-developing spirit, Goethe and Hegel, manifested the all-encompassing boa constrictor "spirit in itself" and its ferment-nature, the cosmo- and theo-political all-accessibility of the German, the superiority of his abstractions, the clever suppleness of his accommodating historicizing: its last and most noble variation, that of a mandarinesque superiority and "beyondness" — — —

— all of Europe sank to its knees in admiration of it —

— of course to the same extent the complete lack of limits, of measure in the Greek sense, of any sense of "style," of a genuine *content* — I mean of *new* valuations, *value-creations.*

Nonetheless: compared to this last great European remarkable event, this "German spirit," the "German empire" that is being taken so seriously at the moment is no object of serious interest, at least in the eyes of a philosopher. Why in all the world a new empire if it does not rest on a new idea, or at least on a new stupidity? But once again this *old* stupidity — equal political rights, representation of the people, parliamentarianism, newspapers as the foundation of a state — once again the idiocy-producing European sickness of constant politicizing expanded to one *more* great people: what new things would a ph⟨ilosopher⟩ have to learn here — or even to despise! —

[44 = Mp XVII 2b. Autumn 1885]

44[1][1]

The chapters.

On Interpretation.
On the Order of Rank.
The Paths to the Saint.
The Eternal Recurrence.
The Superstition of the Critical Philosophers.
Critique of Pascal: he already has the Christian-*moral interpretations* in the nature of human beings and thinks he grasps the "facts." Sainte-Beuve too.

44[2]

Nothing has happened since Pascal, the German philosophers do not come into consideration compared to him.

44[3]

The Germans have no prose that rings and leaps.

44[4]

The classical prose of the French of 1648: *what* has to come together.

44[5]

The absence of mor⟨al⟩ cultivation; h⟨umans⟩ have been allowed to grow. Perhaps the h⟨umans⟩ of Port-Royal are like *artificial* gardens.

Authority is lacking.

Moderation within calm horizons is lacking; — infinity has been made into a kind of drunkenness.

Subtlety in judgment is lacking.

A chaos of contradictory valuations rules.

44[6]

What is this then, this struggle of the Christian "against nature"? We will certainly not let ourselves be deceived by his words and interpretations! It is nature against something that is nature. For many fear, disgust for some, a certain spirituality for others, love for an ideal without flesh and desire, for the highest types an "extract of nature" — the latter want to be like their ideal. It goes without saying that humiliation instead of a sense of self, fearful caution of desires, separation from the ordinary duties (whereby a higher sense of rank is again created) the stirring up of a constant struggle for tremendous things, the habit of emotional effusion — it all composes one type: in it *irritability* of an atrophying body predominates, but nervousness and its inspiration are *interpreted* otherwise. The *taste* of this kind of character focuses 1) on hair-splitting 2) on the flowery 3) on extreme emotions. — The natural inclinations do *indeed* satisfy themselves, but under a new form of interpretation e.g., as "justification before God," "feeling of redemption in grace" (— every undeniable *feeling of well-being* is interpreted this way! —) pride, lust etc. — General problem: what becomes of the human being who slanders the natural in himself and renounces and stunts it in practice? In fact the Christian proves to be an *exaggerated* form of self-mastery: in order to control his desires, he appears to need to annihilate or crucify them. —[2]

The *Epicurean kind of Christian and the Stoic kind* — to the former belongs François de Sales, to the latter Pascal

Triumph of Epicurus — but precisely this kind of human being is hard to understand and *must* be poorly understood. The Stoic kind (which needs to fight and *consequently* unduly treasures the value of the fighter —) always slanders the "Epicurean"!

44[7]

Graeco-Roman antiquity needed a tyrannical and exaggerating morality of anti-nature; the Teutons likewise, in a different respect.

Our contemporary kind of human being actually *dispenses* with rigor and strict discipline; the danger in this is not great because this kind of human being is weaker than earlier kinds and on the other hand because the unconscious disciplinarians (like industriousness, ambition to get ahead, bourgeois respectability) function very inhibitively and hold one in check. — But *how* people from the age of Pascal had to be held together!

Superfluous Christianity: where no extreme means are *necessary* anymore! There everything becomes false, and every word, every Christian perspective a tartuffery and cajoling.

44[8]

The New Japan.

I read with much malice of ulterior motives what a German anarchist {means} by the notion "free society" — — —

"Free society" — all features as grotesque word- and color-finery of a small kind of herd animal.

"Justice" and the morality of equal rights — the tartuffery of moral predicates.

"the press," its idealization.

"the abolition of the worker"

"the pre-Aryan race is breaking through": and generally the oldest kinds of society

the decline of woman

the Jews as ruling race.

Noble and vulgar culture.

the scholar overestimated: and a triumphing more loving and masterful fullness of heart

— how I saw all of this, perhaps without love, but surely also without scorn, and what probably causes amazement therefore — with the curiosity of a child that stands before the most colorful and ornamental of all peep shows. — — —

44[9][3]

Consider how all suffering forces a h⟨uman being⟩ back upon himself, damage, supposing it makes smarter certainly to the same degree also makes worse (narrow, petty, suspicious, loveless — — —

For their number is always small: but the others, the suffering, have nothing that heals them to *that* degree from the negative consequences of much suffering and — — —

[45 = W I 6b. Autumn 1885]

45[1]

Discipline of the *Heart.*

45[2][1]

Prince Vogelfrei
Songs and Thoughts.

By
Friedrich Nietzsche.

45[3][2]

Dedication and Closing Refrain.[3]

45[4][4]

Songs and Thoughts
Of Prince Vogelfrei

By
Friedrich Nietzsche.

45[5][5]

Misfortune overtakes the fugitive — whether
As golden grief of the impoverished hand,
As sadness of the eternally bestowing:
Misfortune captures the fugitive — whether

Unconcerned and not mindful of himself
He tossed the pearls away

That forces the conquered down
That turns every pride to tears:
Dishonest constellation,
You tossed the pearls into the sand —
The sea gulped them in its throat!
What does life owe the squanderer

45[6]

How one gets beyond self-destruction. The harpies. Breaking free. For the history of the "free spirit." Description of the free spirits.

2) *cheerfulness* 3) masks 4) nobility.

the woman question
Artist-pessimism.

45[7][6]

Day is fading, joy and light turn yellowy,
The noon hour is far.
How much longer? Then come the moon and stars
And wind and frost: no lingering for me,
Like fruit that a breeze breaks from the tree

Prefatory Note by Mazzino Montinari to *KSA* Volume 12

Volumes 12 and 13 of the *Kritische Studienausgabe* {*CW* 16 [in part], 17, and 18} together contain Nietzsche's unpublished fragments from autumn 1885 to the beginning of January 1889. The fragments are preserved in twenty-two handwritten manuscripts, more specifically fifteen larger booklets, three notebooks, and four folders.

The principles according to which the publication of Nietzsche's unpublished fragments proceed can be found in the prefatory note to *CW* 10, part of which is reproduced in the following six paragraphs.

The fragments from the *Nachlass* are published according to strictly chronological principles; the editors have refrained from any systematic arrangement. Accordingly, the manuscripts are published in the sequence corresponding to their date of origin. Every single page of a manuscript is reproduced either according to the arrangement of the pages made by Nietzsche himself or according to the sequence of pages that can be deduced with certainty on the basis of his transcriptional habits (e.g., his habit of writing in booklets from back to front). If both of these indications are lacking, then the archival numeration of the pages is taken as valid. The principle that the manuscripts are published individually is subordinated to the temporal sequence when a manuscript contains layers from different times; in this case the individual layers are published separately. The orthography and punctuation of the manuscripts are maintained in principle; unavoidable editorial interventions are indicated in the apparatus of *KSA* {and translated in this volume}.

The consecutive numbering of the manuscripts or of their layers derives from the editors; it is begun anew within each chronological section for the corresponding groups of *Nachlass* fragments. Every manuscript or every layer of a manuscript is supplied with a number corresponding to the chronological sequence; the fragments within a manuscript or within the layer of a manuscript are likewise numbered consecutively, so that next to the number indicating the manuscript or the layer of a manuscript is found another number in square brackets that indicates the sequence of the fragments as this can be determined in each case.

Words underlined by Nietzsche only once are printed in italics; ones underlined twice or more are printed in bold.

Angle brackets ⟨ ⟩ indicate supplements by the editors. Square brackets [ ] indicate titles in the *Nachlass* text that are provided by the editors. {Curly brackets { } indicate supplements by the translator or *CW* editors.}

The following symbols are also used in the *Nachlass* text: [—] an illegible word; [— —] two illegible words; [— — —] three or more illegible words; — — — incomplete sentence; [+] lacuna in the manuscript.

The classifications for Nietzsche's manuscripts introduced by Hans-Joachim Mette have been retained.[1]

Let the following be noted with respect to volumes 12 and 13 of *KSA* {volumes 16, 17, and 18 of *CW*}: these volumes take on a special meaning because — through their complete and manuscript-faithful reproduction of all fragments, drafts, plans, and titles from autumn 1885 until the end of Nietzsche's productivity in the beginning of 1889 — they constitute the foundation for a conclusive solution to the much-discussed problem of

1. Cf. *Sachlicher Vorbericht zur Gesamtausgabe der Werke Friedrich Nietzsches*, 1:xxxi–cxxvi, of the interrupted complete historical critical edition (Munich: Beck, 1933–40).

Nietzsche's alleged philosophical main work with the title *The Will to Power*. Read in their chronological sequence, the fragments yield a precise, almost seamless representation of his productivity and his literary intentions from autumn 1885 to the beginning of January 1889. They clearly reveal that and why the compilation of *The Will to Power* arranged by Peter Gast and Elisabeth Förster-Nietzsche, included in previously published editions of Nietzsche, is editorially untenable and objectively questionable in the extreme. The commentary (*KSA* 14 [pp. 383–400, {translated in *CW* 17}]) will explain this in detail and prove that and how Nietzsche changed his literary plans in the course of the years, until finally at the end of August 1888 he dispensed entirely with the publication of a work under the title *The Will to Power: Attempt at a Revaluation of All Values*.

It is the achievement of Karl Schlechta to have elevated to a principal editorial requirement the publication of the unpublished notes in chronological sequence.[2] Yet it is precisely this requirement that he did not fulfill in his edition of Nietzsche's unpublished notes from the so-called revaluation period, because he merely published the exact same material of the traditional *Will to Power* in a (seeming) chronological sequence. In other words: Schlechta unintentionally validated the *content* of the *selection* of Peter Gast and Elisabeth Förster-Nietzsche from the mass of unpublished fragments from the 1880s.

2. Cf. Friedrich Nietzsche, *Werke in drei Bänden* (Munich{: Carl Hanser,} 1954–56), 3:1393ff.

[1 = N VII 2b. Autumn 1885–Spring 1886]

1[1][1]

Really I should have around me a circle of deep and tender human beings who would protect me somewhat from myself and would also know how to cheer me up: because for someone who thinks such things as I must think, the danger is always very near that he will destroy himself.

1[2][2]

Let no one believe that a person lands accidentally and on both feet one day in such a robust state of the soul as seen in the testimony or metaphor of the dance song that was just concluded. Before one learns to dance in this manner one must have first learned thoroughly to walk and run, and even to stand on one's own legs is something for which, it seems to me, only a few are ever predestined. In the period when one first dares to go forth on his own limbs and without leading-strings and railings, in the periods of the first youthful strength and all the charms of one's own spring time, one is most endangered and often walks timidly, hesitatingly, like an escapee, like an exile, with a trembling conscience and with a bizarre mistrust of his path: — when the youthful freedom of the spirit is like a wine

1[3][3]

The Mirror.

Lack of a dominating way of thinking.
The actors.
Gleba.[4]
The new shamelessness (that of the mediocre, e.g., the English, also of women who write)
The will to prejudice (nations, parties etc.
Latent Buddhism.
The lack of solitude (and consequently of *good* company)
Alcohol, book and music and other stimulants.
The philosophers of the future.
The ruling caste and anarchism.
The curious difficulties of the unusual one who is disturbed by his plebeian modesty.
Lack of character-upbringing. Lack of higher monasteries
Gradual restriction of people's rights.

1[4]

— *The doctrine of opposites* (good, evil etc.) has value as an *educational* standard, because it makes people take sides.

— the most powerful, and dangerous passions of humanity, from which it is most easily ruined, have been outlawed so thoroughly that the most powerful human beings themselves have become impossible or would have to feel themselves to be *evil*, to be "harmful and forbidden." This loss is great, but so far it has been necessary: now that a quantum of counter-forces has been cultivated through temporary suppression of those passions (of lust to rule, joy in transformation and deception) their unleashing is again possible: they will no longer have their old wildness. We allow ourselves tame barbarism: just look at our artists and politicians[5]

— The synthesis of opposites and counter-drives a sign of the total strength of a human being: *how much* can it **control**?

— A new concept of holiness: Plato's naïveté — no longer the opposite of those drives branded heretical in the foreground

—To be demonstrated, to what extent the Greek religion was *higher* than the Jewish-Christian. The latter triumphed because the Greek religion itself had degenerated (*had* **regressed**).[6]

Goal: the sanctification of the most powerful terrible and best-discredited forces, or to say it old-fashionedly: the deification of the devil

1[5]

— I measure according to how far a human being, a people can unleash the most terrible drives in himself and turn them to his salvation, without perishing from them: on the contrary for his fruitfulness in deeds and works

— the interpretation of all mishaps as effects of unreconciled spirits is what has so far driven the great masses to religious cults. Even the higher moral life, that of the saint, has been invented only as *one* of the means of satisfying unreconciled spirits.

— the interpretation of our *experiences* as providential hints of a kindly, educating divinity, even of our mishaps: — Development of the *fatherly* concept of God, proceeding from the patriarchal family.

— the absolute corruption of humanity, the unfreedom for goodness and consequently the interpretation of all our actions with the interpretation of bad conscience: finally mercy. Miracle-act. Sudden reversal. Paul, Augustine, Luther

— the barbarization of Christianity by the Teutons: the intermediate beings, and the abundance of cults of atonement, in brief the pre-Christian standpoint returns. Likewise the composition-system.

— Luther restores the basic logic of Christianity, the *impossibility of morality* and consequently of self-satisfaction, the necessity of mercy and consequently of miracles and also predestination. At bottom an admission of being overcome and an outbreak of self-contempt.

— "it is impossible to pay one's *debts*," outbreaks of salvation craving and the cults and mysteries. "It is impossible to rid oneself of sins" Outbreak of the Christianity of Paul Augustine and Luther. Formerly the occasion to become religious was external misfortune; later the inner feeling of misfortune, being unredeemed, fear, uncertainty. What appears to distinguish Christ and Buddha: it appears to be inner happiness that would make them religious

1[6]

— the feeling of belonging to the higher order of rank is dominating in the moral feeling: it is the self-testimony of the higher caste whose actions and conditions afterwards pass again as the sign for a disposition with which one *belongs* in that caste or *should* belong in it —

1[7][7]

— at first the moral feeling is developed with respect to human beings (classes above all!), only later is it translated to actions and character traits. The *pathos of distance* is in the innermost ground of that feeling.

1[8]

— the unknowing state of human beings and their non-reflecting make for the fact that individual attribution is only made later on. One feels oneself too unfree, unspiritual, swept away by sudden drives, to think of oneself in any other way than with respect to nature: in us, too, *demons* are active.

1[9][8]

— Human, all too human. One cannot reflect on morality without involuntarily becoming morally occupied and indicating one's morality. Thus I worked at the time on that refinement of morality that already perceives "reward" and "punishment" as "immoral" and no longer knows how to interpret the concept "justice" as "affectionate *understanding*," at bottom *approval*. In this perhaps there is weakness, perhaps dissipation, perhaps also — — —

1[10][9]

— "punishment" develops in the narrowest space, as reaction of the powerful, of the lord of the house, as expression of his wrath toward the disrespect of his command and prohibition. — *Before* the morality of custom (whose canon wants "everything traditional should be honored") stands the morality of the ruling person (whose canon wants that "the commander alone should be honored") The pathos of distance, the feeling of rank differentiation lies at the ultimate bottom of all morality.

1[11]

— "Soul" ultimately as "concept of the subject"

11[12]

— If things are unknown, *then so too is the human being.* What's the use of praising and blaming here!

1[13]

— I do not grasp how one can be a theologian. I do not wish to think ill of such human beings, who are not after all just knowledge-machines

1[14]

— Every action of which a human being is not capable is misunderstood by him. It is distinguishing to always be misunderstood with one's actions. Then it is also necessary and no excuse for becoming embittered.

1[15]

— It is not *unselfish* when I prefer to reflect upon causality instead of the lawsuit against my publisher;[10] my gain and my enjoyment lie in the direction of knowledge, precisely there my tension, restlessness, passion have been active longest.

1[16]

Thoughts are actions

1[17]

— how we have *relearned* in fifty years! The whole of Romanticism with its belief in the "folk" has been refuted! No Homeric writing as folk-poetry! No deification of the great powers of nature! No inference from linguistic-affinity to racial-affinity! No "intellectual intuition"[11] of the supersensual! No truth veiled in religion!

1[18]

— The problem of truthfulness is entirely new. I am amazed: In this we regard such natures as Bismarck as guilty out of negligence, those like Richard Wagner out of lack of modesty, we would condemn Plato with his *pia fraus*,[12] Kant on account of the deduction of his categorical imperative, whereas faith certainly did not come to him on this path

1[19]

— Finally doubt also turns against itself: doubt about doubt. And the *question* of the *justification* of truthfulness and its scope *stands there* —

1[20]

— All our conscious motives are surface phenomena: behind them stands the struggle of our drives and conditions, the struggle for power.[13]

1[21]

— That this melody sounds beautiful is *not* imparted to children by authority a⟨nd⟩ instruction; no more so than the pleasant feeling at the sight of an honorable human being. *Valuations are innate*, despite Locke!, inherited; to be sure, they develop more strongly and beautifully when the people who protect and love us at the same time share the same valuations. What agony for a child to always posit his good and evil in contrast to his mother and to be scorned and despised wherever he venerates!

1[22]

— How manifold is that which we perceive as moral feeling: in it are veneration, fear, being touched as if by something holy and mysterious, in it speaks something that commands, that takes itself to be more important than we are; something that elevates, enflames or makes us calm and deep. Our moral feeling is a synthesis, a simultaneous-resounding of all dominating and subservient feelings that reigned in the history of our ancestors

1[23]

— *To the credit of the present.* Health is promoted, ascetic world-renouncing ways of thinking (with their will to sickness) scarcely comprehended. Everything possible is valid and allowed to be valid and acknowledged, moist mild air in which every kind of plant grows. It is paradise for all *petty* luxurious vegetation

1[24]

— Soul and breath and *existence* equated to *esse.*[14] What *lives* is being: there is no further being.

1[25][15]

— "The good people are all weak: they are good because they are not strong enough to be evil" said the Latuka chief Comorro to Baker.[16]

1[26][17]

gin is Arabic and means *spiritus*[18] (= g'inn)

1[27][19]

"For the faint-hearted there is no misfortune" one says in Russian[20]

1[28]

— all *movements are to be understood as gestures*, as a kind of language through which forces understand one another. In the inorganic world misunderstanding is lacking, communication appears perfect. In the organic world *error* begins. "Things" "substances" properties, activ-"ities" — all this should not be carried into the inorganic world! They are the specific errors by virtue of which organisms live. Problem of the possibility of "error"? The contrast is not "false" and "true," but "*abbreviations of the signs*" as opposed to the signs themselves. What is essential is: the formation of forms that *represent* many movements, the invention of signs for entire varieties of signs.

— all movements are *signs* of an inner occurrence; and every inner occurrence expresses itself in such changes of forms. Thinking is not yet inner occurrence itself, but likewise only a sign language for the power equalization of affects.[21]

1[29]

— the anthropomorphizing of nature — interpretation according to us.

1[30][22]

A. Psychological *point of departure*:

— our thinking and valuations are only an expression for cravings that reign behind them.

— the cravings become more and more specialized: their unity is *the will to power* (to apply the expression of the strongest of all drives that has so far directed all organic development)

— Reduction of all organic basic functions to the will to power

— question, whether it is not likewise the *mobile*[23] in the inorganic world? For in the mechanistic world-interpretation a *mobile* is still needed.

— "law of nature": as a formula for the unconditional production of power-relations and degrees.

— mechanical *motion* is only a means of expression of an inner occurrence.

— "cause and effect"

1[31]

— struggle as the means of equilibrium

1[32][24]

— the assumption of atoms is *only* a consequence of the concept of subject and substance: somewhere there must be "a thing" from which the activity proceeds. The atom is the last descendant of the concept of the soul.

1[33][25]

— the most terrible and thorough yearning of humanity, its drive for power — one calls this drive "freedom" — must be held in check for the longest time. This is why ethics to date, with its unconscious instincts of education and cultivation, has been intent upon keeping the greed for power in check: it disparages the tyrannical individual and underscores the herd-power instinct with its glorification of communal welfare and love of the fatherland.

1[34]

— According to nature the strengths of humankind should develop in such a sequence that the *undangerous* ones are developed (praised, approved) first off, that conversely the strongest ones remain slandered and branded longest as heretics.

1[35][26]

The Will to Power.
Attempt at a New Interpretation of all
Events.
By
Friedrich Nietzsche.

1[36]

the world of thought only a second degree of the world of appearance —

1[37]

— movements are not "*effected*" by a "*cause*": that would be the old soul-concept once more! — they are the will itself, but not entirely and completely!

1[38]

NB. The belief in causality goes back to the belief that it is I who effects, to the division of the "soul" from its *activity*. Therefore an ancient superstition!

1[39]

The tracing back of an effect to a cause is: back to a *subject*. All changes are regarded as produced by subjects.

1[40]

— the *current* stage of morality demands

a) no punishment! ⎫ no retaliation!
2) no reward — ⎭
3) no servility
4) no *pia fraus*!

1[41]

— we no longer bear the sight of them, *consequently* we do away with slaves

1[42][27]

It is a favorite expression of the indolent and those without conscience *tout comprendre c'est tout pardonner*:[28] it is also a stupidity. Oh if one always had to wait first for the "*comprendre*": it seems to me that one would then too seldom arrive at forgiving! And in the end, why should one forgive precisely if one had understood? Supposing I understood completely and thoroughly why this proposition bothers me, should I therefore not be allowed to *cross it out*? — There are enough cases where one crosses out a person *because* one has understood him.

1[43]

— the concept "change" already posits the subject in advance, *the soul as substance*

1[44]

— the offense that one takes at the doctrine "of the unfreedom of will" is this: it seems as though it were claiming "you do what you do not voluntarily but involuntarily i.e., forcibly." Now everyone knows how someone feels when he does something involuntarily. Thus the teaching that accompanies that doctrine seems to be: everything that you do you do involuntarily therefore *reluctantly*, "against your will" — and *this* one does not admit because one does many things *gladly*, even specifically many "moral things." Thus one understands "unfree will" as "compelled by a *foreign* will": as if the claim were: "everything that you do you do compelled by a foreign will." Your obedience to your own will is not called compulsion: for there is pleasure in it. *That you command yourself*, that is called: "freedom of will"

1[45]

Sapienta victrix.[29]
Prelude to a Philosophy of the Future.[30]

1[46]

Religions live for the longest time without being mixed with morality: morality-free. Consider what any religion really wants — it is still palpable even today: what one wants from it is not redemption from *distress*, but above all redemption from the *fear of distress*. All distress is considered to be the consequence of the evil, hostile reigning of spirits: all distress that afflicts someone is of course not "deserved," but it raises the thought *through which* a spirit might be irritated at us; the human being trembles before unknown roaming ungracious monsters and wishes to render them gracious. In so doing he examines his behavior:

and if there are any means at all to render friendly certain spirits that he knows, then he will ask himself *whether* he has really done everything that he could have done in this regard. As a courtier examines his own behavior toward the ruler when he has perceived an ungracious mood in him: — he looks for some omission etc. "Sin" is originally that whereby some spirit could be sorely offended, some omission, a — — — : there one must again *make* something *good*. — Only insofar as a spirit, a divinity also expressly sets forth certain moral commandments as means to please and serve *him*, does the moral valuation enter into "sin" as well: or rather: only then can an offense against a moral commandment be perceived as "sin," as something that separates from God, insults him and also has dangers and distress from him in its wake.

1[47]

Cleverness, caution and provision (in contrast to indolence and to living in the moment) — now one nearly means to *debase* an action if one names these motives. But what has it cost to cultivate these traits! To regard *cleverness* as *virtue* — is still Greek!

Likewise then sobriety and "presence of mind" in contrast to acting from violent impulses, to "naïveté" of acting.

1[48]

Absolute devotion (in religion) as reflex of slavish devotion or of the feminine (— the eternal-feminine[31] is idealized slave sense)

1[49]

Measuring the moral value of an action according to its intent: presupposes that the intent really is the cause of the action — which actually means regarding the intent as a perfect knowledge as "thing in itself." In the end it is only the consciousness a⟨nd⟩ the interpretation of a state (of malaise, desire etc.)

1[50]

— states and desires are supposed to be described with language: therefore concepts are signs for recognizing. The aim at logic is not in it: logical thinking is a dissolution. But each thing that we "comprehend," each state is a synthesis that one does not "comprehend," but can indeed describe: and even this only insofar as one recognizes a certain similarity to what has been. "Unscientific" indeed is every inner spiritual action, also *every* thinking.

1[51]

Thinkers of humble or dishonest lineage falsely understand the lust to rule, also the drive to distinction: they relegate both to vanity, as if it were a matter of standing there respected, feared or adored in the *opinion* of other human beings.

1[52]

Measured according to scientific standards, the value of each moral value judgment of humans over humans is very meager: there is a groping and fumbling and much delusion and ignorance in *every* word.

1[53]

These are separate tasks:

1) to grasp and determine the current (and in a limited cultural sphere) dominating kind of moral assessment of humans and actions
2) the entire morality codex of a period is a *symptom* e.g., as a means of self-admiration or dissatisfaction or tartuffery: secondly therefore, in addition to determining the current *character* of *morality*, the *meaning and interpretation of this character* still needs to be given. For in itself it is ambiguous.
3) to explain the emergence of this manner of judgment that is dominating right now

4) to give a critique of it or to ask: how strong is it? what does it affect? what *becomes* of humankind (or of Europe) under its sway? Which powers does it promote, which does it suppress? Does it make us healthier, sicker, braver, subtler, more art-needy etc.?

Here already it is presupposed that there is no eternal morality: this should be accepted as proven. As little as there is an eternal kind of judgment about nourishment. But new is the criticism, the question: is "good" really "good"? And what use perhaps is had by what is now neglected and maligned? Distances in time have to be considered.

1[54]

The character of the absolute will to power is present in the entire realm of life. If we have a right to deny consciousness, then hardly the right to deny the driving affects, e.g., in a rain forest.

(consciousness always contains a double mirroring — there is nothing direct —)

1[55]

Fundamental question: how deep does the ethical go? Does it belong only to what is learned? Is it a form of expression?

All profounder human beings are of one mind in this — it enters the consciousness of Luther Augustine Paul — that our morality and its events do not correspond to our *conscious will* — in sum, that the explanation from purpose-intentions *does not suffice.*

1[56][32]

Remaining objective, hard, firm, strict in asserting an idea — this is still best accomplished by artists; but if people are needed for this (like teachers, politicians etc.) then the calm and coolness and hardness quickly go away. In natures such as Caesar and Napoleon one can intuit something of a "disinterested" laboring on one's marble, regardless of any possible sacrifice of human beings. The future of the highest human beings lies on this path: to bear the greatest responsibility and *not collapse under it.* —Until now inspirational deceptions were almost always needed in order not to lose *faith in one's right* and one's *hand.*

1[57]

Transformations of the will to power, its elaborations, its specializations — to be represented as parallel to morphological development!

1[58]

From the standpoint of each of our fundamental drives there is a different perspectival assessment of all events and experiences. Each of these drives feels itself hindered, or promoted, flattered with respect to every other: each has its own law of development (its high and low, its tempo etc.) — and the latter is dying out when the former rises.

The human being as a multiplicity of "wills to power": each with a multiplicity of means of expression and forms. The individual *alleged* "passions" (e.g., human beings are cruel) are only *fictive unities* insofar as that which enters into consciousness as *homogeneous* on the part of the different fundamental drives is synthetically fictionalized to form a "being" or "faculty," a passion. In the same manner therefore as the "soul" itself is an *expression* for all phenomena of consciousness: but which we *interpret as the cause of all these phenomena* ("self-consciousness" is fictive!)

1[59]

Everything material is a kind of motion symptom for an unknown event: everything conscious and felt on the other hand is symptom of unknown — — — . The world that can be known to us from these two sides could have yet many other symptoms. No necessary relationship exists between spirit and material, as if they somehow exhausted the forms of depiction and solely represented them.

Movements are symptoms, thoughts are likewise symptoms: desires are verifiably behind both, and the fundamental desire is the will to power. — "Spirit in itself" is nothing, just as "movement in itself" is nothing[33]

1[60]

It is nearly comical that our philosophers demand that philosophy must begin with a critique of the knowledge faculty: is it not very improbable that the organ of knowledge can "critique" itself when one has become suspicious of the previous results of knowledge? The *reduction* of philosophy to a "will to a theory of knowledge" is comical. As if *certainty* could be found in this manner! —

1[61]

Everything that enters into consciousness is the last link of a chain, an ending. That one thought would directly be the cause of another thought is only illusory. The actual connected events play (themselves) out beneath our consciousness: the appearing series and sequence of feelings thoughts etc. are symptoms of what actually happens! — Beneath every thought an affect is hidden. *Every thought*, every feeling, every will is *not* born from one specific drive, but it is an *overall state*, an entire surface of the entire consciousness and results from the momentary power-determination *of all* the drives that constitute us — therefore of the currently ruling drive as well as the one that obeys or resists it. The next thought is a sign of how the overall power-situation has shifted in the meantime.

1[62]

"Will" — a false reification.[34]

1[63]

— How Goethe will look at some point later on! how insecure, how drifting! And his "Faust" — what an incidental and temporal, and insufficiently necessary and durable problem! A degeneration of the knowledgeable one, a sick person, nothing more! In no way the tragedy of the knowledgeable one himself! Not even of the "free spirit."

1[64]

<table><tr><td>love of humanity.
Justice.
cruelty.
reward and punishment.
self-satisfaction.
reasonableness.
order of rank.
slavery (devotion)</td><td>everything has already had its pro and contra</td></tr></table>

all praising and blaming is perspectival from the standpoint of a will to power.

"innate ideas"

the soul, the thing — false. Likewise "the spirit"

1[65][35]

Chapter on *interpretation*
reification
the *afterlife* of bygone ideals (e.g., slave sense in Augustine)

1[66]

The *love of humanity of the Christian*, which makes no distinctions, is only possible in the continuous beholding of God, in relation to which the order of rank between human and human is growing disappearingly tiny, and *the* human itself generally is becoming so insignificant that relative sizes are no longer of interest: as from atop a high mountain big and small become ant-like and *similar*. — One should not overlook this *underestimation* of the human being generally, which lies in the Christian feeling of love for humanity: "you are my brother, I already know how you feel, no matter who you are — namely bad!" etc. In fact such a Christian is an extremely obtrusive and immodest sort.

Conversely: if we let God go, then we are lacking a type of being that is higher than the human: and our eye becomes *refined* for the differences *of this* "highest being."

1[67]

— I am mistrustful of the contemplative, self-contained,[36] fortunate among the philosophers — what is lacking there is the shaping force and the subtlety in honesty that admits to itself lack as a force

1[68]

The transformation of morally depraved into morally revered — and vice versa.

1[69]

— some select an absolute obligation from within and at times make one up, others want to prove it and thus plant with it at the same time —

1[70][37]

— how immodest humans appear with their religions, even if they are groveling before God, like the saintly Augustine! What obtrusiveness! This fatherly or grandfatherly principle in the background!

1[71]

— Among mortals so far morality has been regarded as the most serious thing there is: this has been good for the moralists, for whom among gods — and perhaps also among human beings — no small laughter is waiting: in the long run one never bears the dignity of an instructor unpunished. To "instruct" humans, to "improve" humans — the presumption of such an undertaking

1[72]

That the cat human being always lands on its four feet, I meant to say on its single leg "ego," is only a symptom of its *psychological* "unity," better "union": no reason to believe in a "psychic unity."

1[73]

— Morality is a part of the theory of affects: how far do the affects reach into the heart of existence?

1[74]

If there were an "in itself" at all, what then would be the "In itself" of a *thought*?

1[75]

Thoughts are the *signs* of a game and struggle of affects: they are always connected to their hidden roots

1[76]

Whoever measures the value of an action according to the intention from which it occurs, does so meaning *the conscious intention*: but in all actions there is much unconscious intentionality; and what appears in the foreground as "will" and "purpose" is *manifoldly* explicable and in itself only a symptom. "A pronounced, pronounceable intention" is an explication, an interpretation that can be *false*; moreover an arbitrary simplification and falsification etc

1[77]

The *calculation of pleasure* as a possible consequence of an action and the pleasure associated with an action itself, as the triggering of a pent-up and stored-up force: what sort of effort has it already cost to keep these two pleasures separated! It is laughable! Just as the amenity of life — and *bliss* are confused for moral drunkenness and self-adoration.

1[78]

With human knowledge morality too has refined itself

a) instead of sin as a transgression against God "injustice toward myself"
b) instead of praying and the longing for wondrous help —
c) instead of the interpretation of experience as reward and punishment —
d) instead of hostility toward every kind of plight and unrest and strife —
e) instead of the obtrusive equalizing love of humanity of the Christian —

1[79]

The greatest sincerity and conviction about the value of one's own *work* achieves nothing: likewise my doubting underestimation cannot touch its value. *This is how it is with all actions*: however moral I may seem to myself with an intention, in itself here (nothing) is decided about the value of the intention and even less about the value of the action. *The entire descent of an* action would have to be known, and not only the little piece of it that falls into consciousness (the so-called intention) But this would be like demanding absolute knowledge —

1[80]

To what extent an overcoming of the moral human being is possible:

we no longer measure the value of an action by its consequences

we also no longer measure it by its intention

1[81]

As little as we still pray and raise up our hands will we someday need *slander and defamation* in order to treat certain drives in us as *enemies*; and likewise our power, that forces us to destroy humans and institutions, can do this someday without our personally having to succumb to emotions of outrage and disgust: to destroy with a divine eye and unperturbedly! Beginning with the annihilation of human beings *who feel themselves to be good*! *experimentum crucis.*[38]

1[82][39]

Beyond Good and Evil

Attempt
at an Overcoming of Morality.

By
Friedrich Nietzsche.

1[83]

The religious *interpretation* overcome.

Morality belongs in the theory of affects (only a means for their taming, whereas others should be cultivated.

1[84][40]

The Overcoming of Morality.

So far the human being has preserved itself meagerly, in that it has maliciously treated and slandered the drives that are most dangerous to it and likewise in a servile manner has flattered those that preserve it.

The gaining of new powers and lands

a) the will to untruth
b) the will to cruelty
c) the will to lust
d) the will to power

1[85]

aimed at the *understanding of the external world* and communicating to it, the intellect and senses must *be superficial.*

Complete emptiness of logic —

1[86]

"Division of labor, memory, exercise, habit, instinct, heredity, faculty, force" — all words with which we explain nothing, but certainly describe and indicate.

1[87][41]

The "ego" (which is *not* one with the unified governing of our nature!) is after all only a conceptual synthesis — therefore there is absolutely no acting from "egoism"

1[88]

— that some conscious or unconscious *calculation of pleasure* that one has as a result of acting (whether *in* the action or later), is really the *cause* of the action, is a hypothesis!!!

1[89]

We belong to the character of the world, there is no doubt! We have no access to it other than through us: everything that is lofty and lowly in us must be understood as necessarily belonging to its nature!

1[90]

NB. We want to honestly admit to ourselves our inclinations and disinclinations and resist decorating them from moral paint pots. Thus certainly we will no longer interpret our plight as our "struggle with God and the devil"! Let us be naturalistic and concede a good right even to that which we must fight, in ourselves and outside ourselves!

1[91]

Through the division of labor the senses are nearly detached from thinking and judging: whereas earlier this lay *in* them, undifferentiated. Still earlier the desires and the senses must have been *one*.

1[92]

All struggle — all events are a struggle — *needs* **duration**. What we call "cause" and "effect" leaves out the struggle and consequently does not correspond to the events. It is consistent to deny time in causes a⟨nd⟩ effects.[42]

1[93][43]

Let us free ourselves from a bit of the superstition that so far has been routine with respect to philosophers.

1[94][44]

The New Enlightenment.

Prelude to a Philosophy of the Future.

By
Friedrich Nietzsche.

1[95][45]

Free Spirits and Other Philosophers.
Beyond Good and Evil.

1[96][46]

Moralist Morality.

1[97]

On the confusion of cause and symptom

Desire and aversion are the oldest symptoms of all *value judgments*: but *not* causes of value judgments!

Therefore: desire and aversion belong like the moral and aesthetic judgments under *one category*.

1[98]

Words remain: people believe, even the concepts referred to by them!

1[99]

We are lacking many concepts for expressing relationships: how quickly we are ready with "master and servant" "father and child" etc.!

1[100]

Basic misunderstanding: one person interprets every other according to himself; therefore misunderstanding of many virtues and affects that correspond to a higher kind. Even the same person understands himself falsely when in lower moments he looks back on his high festive times. "Self-debasement" "humility"

1[101]

Oh, do you know the mute tenderness with which the evil and terrible human being dwells on that moment when he once — or still — was "different"! No one sees virtue so seductively, so much woman and child.

1[102]

In the purest spring a single drop of dirt is enough —

1[103]

The hand that wanted to reach out for a prayer, the mouth prepared to sigh — here the free spirit has his overcoming, but also his damming up. One day the dam will be overrun by wild waters —

1[104]

Many of the more refined want *calm*, peace from their *affects* — they strive for *objectivity*, neutrality, they are satisfied to be left over as *spectators* — and as critical spectators with a curious and bold superiority.

Others want calm on the *outside*, undangerousness of life — they would like not to be envied and not attacked — and prefer to give "everyone his right" — call it "*righteousness*" and love of humanity etc.

For the chapter: "Virtues as Disguise."

1[105]

The loss in all specializations: the synthetic nature is the *higher*. Now all organic life is already a specialization; the *inorganic world* that stands behind it is the *greatest synthesis of forces* and therefore the highest and most venerable. — Error, perspectival limitation are lacking there.

1[106]

Artists: inspired, sensual, childish, now overly suspicious, now overly trusting

1[107]

— Are you someone who *as thinker* is loyal to his proposition, not like a pettifogger, but like a soldier to his orders? There is disloyalty not only against persons.

1[108]

— Compassion in someone who has happiness and courage enough to be able even to stand aside and *look* aside, like an Epicurean god.

1[109][47]

The Mirror.

Philosophy of Forbidden Knowledge.

By
Friedrich Nietzsche.

1[110][48]

God has been refuted, not the devil. For clear-sighted and suspicious eyes that know how to gaze deeply enough into the backgrounds the spectacle of events is proof neither of truthfulness nor fatherly concern or superior reasonableness; neither something noble nor something pure and trustworthy.

1[111]

Northern unnaturalness: everything coated with silvery mists, one can only arrive at feeling good artificially,[49] art there is a kind of avoidance of oneself. Oh, this pale pleasure, this October light on all pleasures!

Northern artificiality

1[112]

The Tempter.

By
Friedrich Nietzsche.

1[113]

Harmlessness of our critical philosophers, who do not notice that skepticism — — — : they believe, if one first tests the tool before applying it, namely the capacity for knowledge — — — . This is even worse than wanting to test a match before one wants to use it. It is the match that wants to test itself to see if it burns

1[114]

The absolute necessity of all events contains nothing of a compulsion: whoever has thoroughly acknowledged and empathized this stands high in knowledge. From his belief no forgiving and pardoning results — I cross out a sentence that does not turn out well, just as I acknowledge the necessity by virtue of which I failed at it, for the noise of a wagon disturbed me — thus we cross out actions, and in some cases human beings, because they did not turn out well. "To comprehend everything"[50] — that would mean suspending all perspectival relations, that would mean comprehending nothing, misjudging the nature of knowing.

1[115][51]

The interpretive character of all events.

There is no event in itself. What happens is a group of appearances *selected* and summarized by an interpreting being.

1[116]

Fear has been further developed into the *sense of honor*, *envy* into *fairness* ("to each his own" and even "equal rights") obtrusiveness of the isolated and endangered into loyalty — — —

1[117]

the melancholy of the spirit that stays in place wherever it happens to end up, the indolence that does not want to learn anew, the good-natured subservience to a power and joy in serving, the moist-warm brooding over thoughts, desires — all German — origin of *loyalty* and *faith*.

1[118][52]

The splitting of a protoplasm in 2 occurs when its power no longer suffices to control the appropriated possession: reproduction is the result of an impotence.[53]

Where the males search for females out of hunger and are absorbed by them, reproduction is the result of a hunger.[54]

1[119]

The absolutely identical process, but the higher interpretation of the process!! The mechanistic sameness[55] of force, but the increase of the feeling of power! "The second time" —but there is no "second time."

The absolute *lack of effect* of the inner feeling of power as causality — — —

1[120][56]

The same text allows innumerable interpretations: there is no "correct" interpretation.

1[121][57]

Gai saber.
Prelude to a Philosophy of the Future.

1. *Free Spirits and other Philosophers.*
2. *World-Interpretation, not World-Explanation.*
3. *Beyond Good and Evil.*
4. *The Mirror.* An Opportunity for Self-Mirroring for Europeans.
5. *The Philosophy of the Future.*

1[122][58]

Overcoming of Affects? No, if it is supposed to mean their weakening and annihilation. *Rather taking them into service*: to which may belong tyrannizing them for a long time (not only as individuals, but as community, race etc.) Finally one restores to them ever more confidently their freedom: they love us like good servants and go willingly wherever our best wants to go.

1[123][59]

Happiness and self-contentedness of the Lazzaroni[60] or "bliss" in "beautiful souls" a⟨nd⟩ consumptive bodies a⟨nd⟩ Herrnhuter Pietists[61] prove nothing with respect to the *order of rank* of human beings. As a greater educator, one would have to mercilessly flog a race of such "blessed humans" into misfortune: the danger of diminution, of relaxation is immediately there: *against* Spinozistic or Epicurean happiness and against all relaxation in contemplative states. But if virtue is the means to such happiness, well, then *one must also become master over virtue*

1[124]

How do the perspective sphere and error emerge? Insofar as, by virtue of an organic being, not a being as such, *but instead struggle itself wants to preserve itself, wants to grow and wants to be conscious of itself.*

That which we call "consciousness" and "spirit" is only a means and tool by virtue ⟨of which⟩ not a subject, but *a struggle wants to preserve itself.*

The human being is proof of what enormous forces can be set in motion by a small being of manifold content (or by a perennial struggle concentrated on many small beings)

Beings that play with stars

1[125][62]

— To transform the belief "it is thus and such" into the will "*thus and ⟨such⟩ it shall be.*"

1[126][63]

— *The Paths to the Saint.* Conclusion of
"The Will to Power."

1[127][64]

— there must be those who sanctify all their actions, not only eating and drinking: and not only in memory of them, or in becoming one with them, *but always anew and in a new manner* this world should be transfigured.

1[128]

— what is essential about an organic being is a *new interpretation of events,* the perspectival inner multiplicity, which itself is an event.

1[129][65]

— the saints as the *strongest humans* (through self-overcoming, freedom, loyalty etc.

1[130][66]

— to *deny* merit, but to do that which is above all praise, indeed above all understanding

1[131][67]

The Will to Power.

1[132]

— a great human being who feels a right to sacrifice humans as a general sacrifices humans; not in the service of an "idea" but because he wants to rule.

1[133]

— less and less physical strength is necessary: with cleverness one lets machines work, the human being becomes *more powerful and more spiritual.*

1[134]

— why it is necessary today occasionally to speak crudely and act crudely. Something subtle and kept secret is no longer understood, not even by those who are related to us. That of which one does not *speak loudly* or shout, *that does not exist*: pain, privation, task, the long duty and the great overcoming — No one sees and smells anything of this. Cheerfulness is construed as a sign of lack of profundity: that it can be the bliss after all too severe tension, who knows that? — One goes around with actors and tries very hard to respect even there. But no one understands to what extent it is hard and painful for me to go around with actors. Or with a phlegmatic sensualist who has enough spirit to —

1[135]

— I have charged the Germans with philistinism and being comfortable: but this *letting-oneself-go* is European and "contemporary," not only in morality and art.

1[136]

— not to allow oneself that a virtue is made of curiosity and of the zeal of research, a "will to truth." The scholars of Port

Royal knew this and took this more rigorously. But we have allowed all our inclinations to go to seed and afterwards we also want to have the beautiful name of virtues for them. *But virtue belongs to the productions of stronger and more evil ages*: it is a privilege of aristocrats.

1[137]

I wonder about the most acknowledged things of morality — and other philosophers, like Schopenhauer, have only paused before the "wonders" in morality.

1[138][68]

Discords and dialogues

1[139]

Artists begin to value and overvalue their works when they cease to have respect for themselves. Their raging demand for fame often veils a sad secret.

The work does not belong to their rule, they feel it as their exception. —

Perhaps they also want that their works intercede for them as advocacy, perhaps that others deceive them about themselves. Finally: perhaps they want noise *in* themselves, in order no longer to "hear" themselves.

1[140]

"God wants my best when he visited sorrow upon me" — It is *your* responsibility to interpret this to your best: it meant no *more* even for religious people.

1[141]

Beyond Yes and No.

Questions and Question Marks
for Questionable Ones.

1[142]

We know better than we admit to ourselves that W⟨agner⟩ is poor, that a thought rarely comes to him, that he himself is most startled, delighted, bowled over by his appearance and for an overly long time has not tired of stroking and decorating these wonders of thought. He is too grateful and does not know the cold affability of the rich, even less their tender disgust, the weariness of those who do nothing but bestow — like Mozart, like Rossini: only the superabundant fountains leap and dance.

1[143][69]

"*We Lizards of Happiness.*"
Thoughts of a Grateful One.[70]

1[144][71]

The Last Virtue.
A Morality for Moralists

1[145][72]

— this last virtue, *our* virtue is called: honesty. In all other respects we are only the heirs and perhaps the squanderers of virtues that are not gathered and hoarded by us

1[146]

A moralist: by which I mean etc.

Question and objection: has there ever been a m⟨oralist⟩? — Perhaps no, perhaps yes; in any case from now on there should be only such m⟨oralists⟩.

1[147]

Let us flee, my friends, from what is boring, from the overcast sky, from the waddle-goose, from the honorable woman, from the spinsters who write and "lay" books — is life not too short to bore ourselves?

1[148]

"The World as Will and Representation" — translated back into the narrow and personal, into Schopenhauerian: "The world as sex-drive and contemplativeness."

1[149]

The German empire is distant to me, and there is no reason for me to be friend or foe with respect to a thing that lies so distant to me.

1[150]

So far we have been so well behaved toward women. Woe, the time will come when in order to interact with a woman one must first always hit her in the mouth.

1[151][73]

The Paths to the Saint.
What are Strong Spirits?
On Herd-Animal Morality

1[152]

New Dangers
and New Securities
A Book for Strong Spirits.

1[153][74]

NB. Against Aryan and Semitic.
Where races are mixed, the source of great culture.

1[154][75]

What is Noble?
Thoughts
on Order of Rank.

1]155]

What are we waiting for anyway? Is it not for a great herald- and trumpet-noise! What happiness lies in loud sounds! There is a silence that suffocates: we have been hearkening[76] too long already.

1[156]

Whoever has the greatest gifts to give, searches for those who understand how to take — he searches perhaps in vain? In the end he throws away his gift? That kind of thing belongs to the secret history and despair of the richest souls: it is perhaps the most misunderstood and melancholy of all misfortunes on earth.

1[157]

That moral judgment, insofar as it represents itself in concepts, looks narrow, clumsy, wretched, almost ridiculous measured against the subtlety of the same judgment insofar as it represents itself in actions, in selecting, rejecting, shuddering, loving, hesitating, doubting, in every touch of human to human.

1[158]

how the hearty mediocrity in Germany today feels good, namely feels related with the music of their Brahms — : how the fine and insecure greyhounds of the Parisian spirit today sniff around their Renan with a lusty flattery —

1[159]

The value of *monarchs* on the rise!

1[160][77]

How treacherous are all parties! — they bring to light something about their leaders that perhaps has been hidden by them under a bushel with great skill

1[161]

Perhaps everyone has his standard for what is regarded as "superficial" by him: well then, I have my own — a crude, simplistic standard for my use at home, as it fits my hand — may others have a right to more ticklish, fine-tongued instruments!

Whoever feels suffering to be an argument against life, I regard to be superficial, along with our pessimists; likewise whoever sees a goal in well-being.

1[162][78]

The orgiastic soul. —

I have seen him: his eyes at least — they are by turns deep still, then green and slippery honey-eyes
his halcyonic smiling
the sky looked on bloody and cruelly

the orgiastic soul of woman

I have seen him: his halcyonic smiling, his honey-eyes, in turn deep and veiled, then green, slippery, a trembling surface,

slippery, sleepy, trembling, tarrying,
the sea wells up in his eyes

1[163][79]

1. Caesar among pirates
2. On the bridge.
3. The wedding. — and suddenly, while the sky falls darkly
4. Ariadne.

1[164]

This music — Dionysian after all?
dance?
cheerfulness? the tempter?
the religious flood?
beneath Plato's pillow Ar⟨istophanes⟩?

1[165][80]

our street musicians and h⟨umans⟩ of a dishonest burial — they are the closest kin of witches, they have their Blocksbergs[81]

1[166]

the mystical nature, soiled by vices and foaming

1[167][82]

the goodly and pure spring that is never again able to get over a drop of garbage that fell into it, until in the end it is yellow and poisoned through and through: — the corrupted angels

1[168]

"*We Immoralists.*"

1[169]

"Hail to thee, if you know what you do; but if you do not know it, then you are under the law and under the law's curse"
Jesus of Nazareth.

1[170]

Industriousness, as a mark of an *ignoble* kind of human (which, as is self-evident, therefore is still an estimable and indispensable kind of human — explanatory note for asses!) in our age would like — — —

1[171]

compared to Rabelais and that exuberant power of the senses whose characteristic he is, — — —

1[172]

Raphael without hands[83]
the monasteries and hermitages of culture
this music is not sincere
"As little state as possible"[84] — the anti-national powers
For someone for whom "objectivity" "contemplativeness" is already the highest state, like Schopenhauer — he does not know enough
the fortune of finding[85] an unbroken naïve egoism
the tartuffery of the Germans! the old woman represented as the emanation of their sense of duty — I heard it with my own ears.

The screaming and scribbling of ugly girls — the decreasing influence of woman.

the new Melusine[86]

As much militaristics as possible, the kings who are fired upon — the sacrificing of the bivouac, without door and window the loaded revolver

"the cause of every action an act of consciousness," a *knowing*! Consequently the bad actions only errors etc.

The famous words "forgive them[87] their" the universalization "*tout comprendre*"[88] — *superficial* words

"the great ambiguous one and tempter"

1[173]

a cold reluctant lake, on which no delight ripples

1[174][89]

not yet one hour among my kind, with everything I do and try the secret worm "you have other things to do!" tortured by children geese and dwarves, nightmare

— only such types are around him, against whom he can neither retaliate nor give instruction — — —

1[175]

pampered consciences

1[176]

the little sorrow

1[177]

Of a great human being.

His descendants say of him: "since then things climbed higher and higher." — But they understand nothing of this ordeal of climbing; a great human being is pushed, pressed, crowded, tortured-up into *his* height.

1[178][90]

This is a problem of race as I understand it: for as concerns that clumsy drivel about Aryan — — —

1[179]

The Jesuitism of mediocrity that seeks to break or weaken the extraordinary and tense human being like a bow that is dangerous to it, with compassion and comfortable out-stretched hands as well as with poisoning of his necessary solitude and with secretive pollution of his faith — : which has its triumph when it can say "*that one* has finally become like one of us": this domineering Jesuitism that is the driving force in the entire democratic movement will, everywhere, quite removed from politics and the questions of nourishment a⟨nd⟩ — — —

1[180]

Mozart the flower of the German baroque —

1[181]

Inspiration. —

1[182]

It is difficult to be understood. He should have heartfelt gratitude for even the good will to a bit of *subtlety* of interpretation: on good days one demands nothing more at all. One should concede to one's friends an abundant space[91] for misunderstandings. It seems to me better to be misunderstood than not understood: there is something insulting in being understood. To be understood? You really know what that means? — *Comprendre c'est égaler.*[92]

It flatters more to be misunderstood than not understood: one remains cold toward the incomprehensible, and coldness offends.

1[183]

Alas, this is the sea: and this bird is supposed to build its nest here?

On those days when the sea becomes still and — — —

1[184]

On the *greed of the spirit*: where, as with avarice, the means become the end. Insatiability.

Today one loves everything that is fatalistically tremendous: so too the spirit.

1[185][93]

The Discipline of the Spirit.

Thoughts
on the Intellectual Conscience.

The avarice and insatiability of the spirit: — its tremendous, fatalistic, nocturnally roaming, pitiless, predatory and cunning qualities.

1[186][94]

The Scholar.
What is Truth?
On the Spirit's Lack of Discipline.
The Demagogic in our Arts.
Master and Slave Morality.
Morality and Physiology.
Piety.
On the History of the Free Spirit.
We Immoralists.
The Noble Soul.
The Mask.

1[187][95]

1. What is Truth?
2. On the Natural History of the Scholar.
3. The Mask
4. On the Noble Soul.
5. We Immoralists.
6. Herd Morality.
7. On the Demagoguery of the Arts.
8. Piety.
9. The Good Europeans.
10. The Philosophers of the Future. Skeptics. Free Spirits. Strong Spirits. Tempter. Dionysus.

1[188][96]

First Part:
our courage

Second part:
our compassion

Third Part:
our insight

Fourth part:
our solitude

1[189][97]

1. *Morality and Knowledge.*
2. *Morality and Religion*
3. *Morality and Art.*
4. *"We Europeans."*
5. *What is Noble?*
   Inspiration

1[190]

Among those who have freed themselves of religion I find human beings of many kinds and ranks. There are the intemperate, who have allowed themselves to be persuaded by their senses (because their senses no longer tolerated the compulsion and accusation of the religious ideal) — and who like to avail themselves of reason a⟨nd⟩ of taste as their advocates, as if they could no longer tolerate the unreasonable, the distasteful aspects of religion: — what suits this kind of human being is antireligious hatred, malice and sardonic laughter, but likewise in well-concealed moments a yearning shame, an inner subservience to the valuations of the renounced ideal. Alienated from the Church by sensuality, when they return to it they venerate the ideal of desensualization, as *the* religious "ideal in itself": — a source of many and difficult errors.

There are the more spiritual, less feeling, drier, also more conscientious human beings who from the ground up are incapable of believing in an ideal at all, and who know how to find their greatest strength and self-respect only in subtle nay-saying and critical disintegrating: they are freed because there is nothing in them that could have firmly bound; they free because — — —

phases —

loss, desolation, including in the feeling of disloyalty a⟨nd⟩ ingratitude, breaking free, all outweighed by an irrefutable bitter certainty

the feeling of respectful consideration and a shy earnestness (with great kindness toward the *h⟨omines⟩ religiosi*[98])

the feeling of superior a⟨nd⟩ kindly cheerfulness toward all religions mixed with a slight disdain for the impurity of the intellectual conscience, which still allows many to be religious, or a scarcely concealed amazement that it is possible to "believe"

1[191]

NB. Ultimately the *whole* of a Greek city was indeed more *valuable* than an individual! it is still preserved for us! — as certainly as the body is more valuable than some organ. Learning to obey, 1000 times in the body the highest sacrifice!

1[192]

more cleanly washed and more cleanly clothed skillful gymnasts with a lock on their "loose snouts," training themselves for silence, also for a dignified self-control *in Venere*[99] (and not, as so often, debauched and botched from boyhood on): may we soon see them "Europeanized" in this direction

1[193]

I love the magnificent frolicsomeness of a young predator that gracefully plays, and in playing tears to pieces

1[194][100]

Modern pessimism is an expression of the uselessness of the *modern* world — not of the world and of existence.

1[195]

It seems more and more to me that we are not superficial and not good-natured enough to help with this Junker fatherland-mania of the Brandenburg March[101] and to sing along with its hatred-snorting stupefaction-slogan "Deutschland Deutschland über Alles."[102]

1[196][103]

— one has to sink down to the old Wagner and his *Bayreuther Blätter* to encounter a similar swamp of presumption, obscurity and Teutonomania as are the *Addresses to the G⟨erman⟩ N⟨ation⟩*.[104]

1[197]

The old Romantics fall down and one day, one knows not how, they are stretched out on the ground before the cross: that also happened to Richard Wagner. To be one of those witnessing the degeneration of such a human being belongs to the most painful things I have experienced: — that one did *not* perceive it as painful in G⟨ermany⟩ was a strong impulse for me to mistrust even more that spirit that now rules in G⟨ermany⟩.

1[198][105]

Buatschleli batscheli
  bim bim bim
Buatscheli batscheli
  bim![106]

1[199]

To seize happiness and strangle, suffocate, choke it with one's embrace: — the melancholy of such experiences — otherwise it would flee and slip away?

1[200]

How much someone withstands of truth:

How much someone takes upon himself to answer for:

How much someone takes upon himself to provide and to protect:

Simplicity — and what the colorful taste of artists reveals:

1[201]

Middle Class Morality.

1[202]

There is something ineducable at bottom: a granite of *factum*,[107] of predetermined decision in measure and proportion to us and likewise a right to certain problems, a branded stamping of them on our names.

The attempt to conform, the agony of solitude, the longing for a community: this can express itself in a thinker in such a way that he subtracts precisely the most personal and valuable from his individual case and, by generalizing, also *coarsens*.[108] In this manner it is possible that the entire articulated philosophy of a remarkable human being is not really his philosophy, but precisely that of his environment, from which he *deviates* as a human being, paratypically. The extent to which modesty, a lack of courageous "I am" becomes fateful in a thinker. "The type is more interesting than the individual and exceptional case": in this way the scientism of taste can bring someone not to have the requisite sympathy and caution for himself. And finally: style, literature, the toss and fall of words — how all this falsifies and ruins what is personal! Mistrust of writing, tyranny of the vanity of writing *well*: which is formal dress anyway and also conceals us. Taste is inimical to the original! an old story.

Style that communicates: and style that is only a sign, "in memoriam." Dead style a masquerade; in others lively style. Depersonalization.

1[203]

Against an enemy there is no better antidote than a second enemy: for a single enemy — — —

1[204][109]

All too much upon myself, since when? almost from childhood on. My philology was only an eagerly seized-on escape: I cannot deceive myself about it, the Leipzig diaries spoke too plainly. — And no companion! — Careless in trusting? But a hermit always has too much supply of that stored up, likewise of course also of mistrust.

1[205]

The deepest misunderstanding of religion, "evil human beings have no religion."

1[206][110]

Russian music: how is it that — — —

1[207]

The extreme purity of the atmosphere into which I placed him, and which allows me things — — —

1[208]

I have become less capable of resisting phys⟨ical⟩ pain: and now when days come with the old attacks, then the pain immediately transforms into a psychic torture with which I can compare nothing

1[209]

The loftiness and goodness of one's nature are also given away to one's work: afterwards drought or mud. —

1[210]

How good conscience and well-being free us from deep problems!

1[211][111]

Beyond good and evil: that takes effort. I translate as if *into* a foreign language, I am not always certain of having found the meaning. Everything a bit too crude for my liking.

1[212]

On brown, yellow, green purple carpets comes

1[213]

We early risers, who for the — — —

1[214]

Opposite, there are truths that make one vomit, *materia peccans*,[112] that one wants to be rid of at any cost: one gets rid of them by communicating them

1[215][113]

To look upon the plight of the masses with ironic melancholy: they want something that *we* are capable of — oh!

1[216]

I have never profaned the holy name of love.

1[217]

well-rested forces

1[218]

if genuine in his objectivity, in his cheerful totality, he is false and deliberate in his affects, artificial and cunning in grasping the details, even in the senses

1[219]

NB How during the decrease of life force one *sinks down* to contemplativeness and to objectivity: a poet can feel it (Sainte-Beuve[114])

1[220]

The tremendous enjoying of human beings and of society in the age of L⟨ouis⟩ XIV had the effect that people were bored in nature and felt desolated. Desolate nature was the most painful, the high mountains.

The *Précieuses*[115] wanted to bring spirit, at least *esprit* into love. Symptom of a tremendous enjoyment in the *spirit* (in the bright, distinguishing one, as in the time of the Persian wars)

The most artificial forms (Ronsard, even the Scandinavians) cause the greatest joy in very juicy and forceful sensual natures: it is their self-overcoming. Also the most artificial morality.

Our human beings want to be hard, fatalistic, destroyers of illusions — desire of weak and tender human beings who relish[116] the formless, barbaric, form-destroying (e.g., "endless" melody — *Raffinement*[117] of German composers) Pessimism and brutality as stimuli of our precious ones.[118]

1[221]

Cataline — a romantic next to Caesar, *modo celer modo lentus ingressus*[119]

1[222]

Freedom of conscience is only useful and possible during great despotism — a symptom of *atomization*

1[223][120]

NB *The last virtue.*

We are the squanderers of the virtues that our forefathers gathered and, thanks to them, with respect to their long austerity and thriftiness, it may be a good long time that we ⟨behave⟩ like the rich and exuberant heirs.

1[224]

gloomy or frolicsome, a spirit who in everything he imagines took revenge for something that he had done (or for *not* having done something) — who did not understand happiness without cruelty.

1[225]

Here, where the peninsula runs into the sea

1[226][121]

Whoever does not enjoy watching oafs dance should not read German books. I just watched a German oaf dance: Eugen Dühring, to the tune of the anarchist motto "*ni dieu, ni maître*."[122]

1[227]

With most people even today their *prudence* is still the most genuine thing they have: and only those rare ones who know, who feel how they have grown up in the twilight of an aging culture — — —

1[228]

I do not understand what the lay-people see in R⟨ichard⟩ W⟨agner⟩: perhaps he arouses their romantic feelings and all the shudder and tickle of the infinite and of romantic mysticism — we musicians are enchanted and seduced

1[229][123]

Halcyon speeches. — Caesar among pirates —
The hour when the sun is down —
To love humanity for the sake of God —
For those whose laughter is golden.
Grateful for being misunderstood —
At the golden grill.
We lizards of happiness —[124]
Among children and dwarves.
On the bridge.
On the old fort.
The spa.
The greatest event —
Always disguised.
otium
Poverty, sickness — and the noble human being
the slow eye
"One's equals" — against intimacy
Being able to keep silent
Slow to reconcile, slow to anger
To take all formality under protection.
Women. — Dance, folly, little jewelry boxes
the tempter.
On bloodlines.
The mask.

1[230][125]

Halcyon Songs.

1[231][126]

Ariadne.

1[232][127]

The Problem of Order of Rank.

Provisional Thoughts and
Dashes[128]

by
Friedrich Nietzsche.

1[233]

NB. Harm makes us *prudent*, says the rabble: — To the extent it makes us prudent, it also makes us bad. But how often harm makes us stupid!

1[234]

The extent to which a craft physically and spiritually deforms: likewise scientism in itself, likewise earning money, likewise every art: — the *specialist* is necessary, but belongs in the *class of tools*.

1[235]

It is very interesting for once to see humans without reins and limits: nearly all superior humans (like artists) fall back into some kind of subordination, be it Christianity or fatherlandishness.

1[236][129]

If this is not an age of decline and of diminishing vitality with much melancholy, then at least it is one of thoughtless, arbitrary experimentation: — and it is probable that from its superabundance of *failed* experiments an overall impression of something like decline will arise: and perhaps the thing itself, *actual* decline.

1[237][130]

The problem of order of rank.

The problem of discipline and cultivation.

NB. {
The discipline of the will.
The discipline of obeying.
The discipline of commanding.
The subtlety of differentiation.
Education that excludes specialization.

1[238][131]

The deep necessity of the task that reigns over all individual destinies of every human being, in that a task becomes embodied and "comes into the world" — at the midpoint of life I comprehend what the *problem of order of rank* required by way of preparations, in order to finally rise up within me: — how I had to experience the most manifold states of happiness and distress in soul and in body, losing nothing, tasting everything and testing it to the bottom, purifying and sifting out everything accidental.

1[239]

Every morality that dominated anywhere was always the discipline and cultivation of a specific type of human being, assuming that the outcome would be primarily this type, indeed exclusively: in sum, always assuming a type. Every morality believes that *with intention* and compulsion one can change ("improve") much in human beings: — it takes the growing resemblance to the standard type as "improvement" (it has absolutely no other concept of it —).

1[240][132]

On naïveté. Reflection can still be a sign of n⟨aïveté⟩.
"Naïve egoism."

1[241]

the well-being of one's "neighbor" is more worthy of striving for 1) if well-being is *worth* striving for 2) if the kind of well-being is clearly established, because there are those that contradict and impede themselves as goals, 3) if already a value of persons is firmly established and it is clear that "the neighbor" has higher value than I . — The pleasant enthusiastic *sentiments*[133] of devotion etc. must be mercilessly criticized; in themselves they still contain, by virtue of the drop of pleasantness and enthusiasm in them, no argument *for*, but only a *seduction* to it.

1[242]

Knowledge of human beings: it depends on what one grasps, feels as "experience"; most need a clumsy particularity of the event and hundredfold repetition, and a few require blows with a club in order to get to the bottom of an experience and notice it

1[243]

The barbarization of Christianity by the Germans

1[244]

Science as a mean to education. Practiced for itself just another barbarism, a barbarizing skill

1[245][134]

Iti vuttakam[135]
(Thus spoke (the saint)

1[246]

do not cheat
do not compromise
despise such *obscurity* as Bismarck and W⟨agner⟩

1[247]

How human beings were sick from God and alienated themselves from *the* human being.

[2 = W I 8. Autumn 1885–Autumn 1886]

2[1][1]

There is a noble and dangerous carelessness that provides a deep inference and insight: the carelessness of the superabundant soul that has never *bothered* with friends but knows only hospitality, only ever exercises and knows how to exercise hospitality — heart and house open to everyone who wants to step inside, be they beggars or cripples or kings. This is genuine affability: whoever has it has a hundred "friends," but probably no friend.

2[2]

This magnificent spirit, now self-sufficient and well defended and closed off against attacks: — you are angered by his fortress and secrecy and yet peek curiously through the golden latticework with which he has fenced off his kingdom? — curious and seduced: for an unknown indistinct fragrance blows upon you maliciously and speaks vaguely of secluded gardens and delights.

2[3][2]

We are in the midst of the dangerous carnival of nationality-madness, where all finer reason has slunk to the side and the vanity of the scruffiest nook-peoples cries out for the rights of special existence and self-glorification — how ⟨can⟩ one today begrudge the Poles, the noblest variety of the Slavic world, entertaining hopes and — — —

they tell me that G⟨ermany⟩ has the great word to say in this regard.[3]

2[4][4]

Halcyon Interruptions.

For Recovering from "Thus Spoke Zarathustra"
Dedicated to his Friends

by
Friedrich Nietzsche

2[5]

The exclusive interest that is lavished today in Germany on questions of power, trade and commerce and — last but not least — on "living well," the rise of parliamentary nonsense, of newspaper reading and of the literati-like chiming in of everyone about everything, the admiration for a statesman who knows and cares just as much about philosophy as a peasant or a fraternity student and thinks he is making his bold ruthless politics of the moment "more acceptable" to German taste (or conscience —) through an antiquated glossing over with royalism and Christianity — : all of this has its origin in the uncanny and multiply alluring year 1815.[5] At that time suddenly night descended on the German spirit that up till then had experienced a long cheerful day: the "fatherland," the border, the soil, the ancestor — all kinds of narrow-mindedness suddenly began to assert their rights. Back then reaction and anxiety, fear of the German spirit awakened in the upper classes, and consequently in the lower classes liberalism and revolutionism and the whole political fever — one understands this "consequently." Since then — since it began to politicize — Germany lost its spiritual leadership of Europe: and now mediocre Engl⟨ishmen⟩ succeed in {making} the G⟨ermans⟩ — — —

2[6]

The last two centuries. —

It was not until the 17th and 18th centuries that Germany brought its most authentic art, music, to the peak: one may forgive an occasionally melancholy observer if he is capable of recognizing German music of the nineteenth century as only a gleaming manifold and scholarly form of decline. Likewise in the plastic arts it has shown in the same oft-maligned century a wasteful joy and strength: German baroque style in churches and palaces belongs as the closest relative to our music — a⟨nd⟩ in the sphere of the visual it builds the same genre of bewitchments and seductions that our music is for a different sense. Between Leibniz and Schopenhauer (born 1788) Germany thought through its entire circle of original thoughts, therefore likewise within those centuries: — and even this philosophy, with its powdered wig and conceptual cobweb, its suppleness, its melancholy, its mysterious infinity and mysticism belongs to our music and is a kind of baroque in the sphere of philosophy.

2[7]

The spirit[6] that we comprehend — we do not *resemble* it: we are superior to it!

2[8][7]

What is still young and stands on weak legs always lets out the loudest cry: for it still falls down too often. For example "patriotism" in today's Europe, "love of the fatherland," which is only a child: — one should not take the little crybaby too seriously!

2[9][8]

To my friends.

This book, which knew how to find its readers in a broad expanse of countries and peoples and must know some kind of art through which even coy and obstinate ears can be seduced:

precisely this book has remained most incomprehensible to my closer friends: — when it appeared, it was to them a shock and a question mark and it laid down a long alienation between them and me. In fact, the state from which it arose had enough of the enigmatic and the contradictory to it: at the time I was simultaneously *very* happy and *very* suffering — thanks to a great *victory* over myself that I had come away with, one of those dangerous victories by which one usually is destroyed. One day — it was in summer 1876 — a sudden contempt and insight came to me: and from then on I went mercilessly beyond all the beautiful wishful things on which my youth had bestowed its heart

2[10][9]

Nationalities-madness and fatherland-buffoonery are without magic for me: "Deutschland, Deutschland über Alles"[10] is painful to my ears, at bottom because I want and wish more from the Germans than — . Their first statesman, in whose mind a solid foundation of royalism and Christianity coexists with a ruthless politics of the moment, who is no more touched by philosophy than a peasant or a fraternity student, piques my ironic curiosity. It even seems useful to me that there are a few Germans who have remained indifferent toward the G⟨erman⟩ E⟨mpire⟩: not even as spectators but as those who look away. *Where* then do they look? There are more important things, compared to which these questions are only foreground questions: e.g., the growing ascendancy of the democratic man and the consequent stultification of Europe and *diminution* of the European human being.

2[11][11]

The Intellectual Conscience.

Attempt at a Critique of More Spiritual Human Beings.

The philosopher. The free spirit. The artist. The religious human being. The scholar. The noble human being. Dionysus.

2[12][12]

Inter pares:[13] a phrase that intoxicates — it includes so much happiness and unhappiness for the one who was alone his whole life; who met no one who belonged to him, though he searched in many ways; who in relations with others always had to be the man of benevolent and cheerful disguise, of the sought-after and often found resemblance, and who knows from all too long experience that ability to grin and bear it that people call "affability" — occasionally to be sure also those dangerous heart-rending outbreaks of all suppressed misfortune, all unsuffocated desires, all pent-up torrents of love grown wild — the sudden madness of that hour when the lonely one embraces someone or other and treats him as a friend and a godsend[14] and a precious gift, only to push him away with disgust an hour later — henceforth disgusted with himself, as if sullied, as if debased, as if estranged from himself, as if sick from his own company — .

2[13][15]

This is my suspicion that returns again and again, my worry that never goes to sleep in me, my question that no one hears or wants to hear, my sphinx, next to which there is not only *one* abyss: — I believe we are deceiving ourselves today about the things we Europeans love most, and a cruel (or not even cruel, only indifferent and childish) goblin is playing with our heart and its enthusiasm, just as perhaps he has already played with everything else that lived and loved — : I believe that what we are accustomed to honoring in Europe today as "humaneness," "morality," "humanity," "sympathy," "justice" may indeed have their foreground-value as a weakening and mitigation of certain dangerous and powerful basic drives, but in the long run they are nevertheless nothing more than the diminution of the entire type "human being" — its conclusive *mediocritization*, if one will permit me a desperate word in a desperate situation; I believe the *commedia umana*[16] for an

Epicurean spectator-god would have to consist in the fact that humans, by virtue of their growing morality, fancy that they elevate themselves in all innocence and vanity above animals to the rank of "gods" and to extraterrestrial destinies, but in truth they are *sinking*, that is, through the cultivation of all the virtues on the basis of which a herd thrives, and through suppression of those other and opposite virtues, which provide the origin for a new higher stronger *masterful* species, they are developing only the herd animal in humans and perhaps thereby *determining* the animal "human being" — for so far the human being was the as yet "undetermined animal" —; I believe that the great forward-driving and relentless *democratic* movement of Europe — that which calls itself "progress" — and likewise even its preparation and moral prefiguration, Christianity — at bottom signifies only the tremendous instinctive overall conspiracy of the herd against all that is shepherd, beast of prey, hermit and Caesar, in favor of the preservation and raising up of all the weak, oppressed, underprivileged, mediocre, semi-misfits, as a protracted slave rebellion against every kind of master, secretive at first then increasingly more self-conscious, ultimately against even the concept "master," as a life and death war against every morality that springs from the womb and consciousness of a higher stronger masterful kind of human being, as mentioned above — such a one that requires slavery in some form and under some name as its foundation and condition; I believe, finally, that every enhancement so far in the type human being was the work of an aristocratic society that believed in a long ladder of order of rank and value-difference between one person and another and required slavery: indeed without the *pathos of distance* as it grows out of the ingrained difference between classes, out of the constant looking at and looking down of the ruling caste on subordinates and instruments and out of its likewise constant exercise of commanding, of keeping down and keeping apart, neither could that other more mysterious pathos emerge at all, that craving in the soul for every new expansion of distance, the development of ever higher, rarer, more remote, more widespread and comprehensive states, in brief, the "self-overcoming of humanity," to use a moral formula in a supra-moral sense. One question comes to me again and again, a tempting and wicked question perhaps: let it be whispered in the ears of those who have a right to such questionable questions, the strongest souls of today who also have themselves best under control: would it not be time, the more the type "herd-animal" is now being developed in Europe, to attempt a fundamental artificial and conscious *cultivation* of the opposing type and its virtues? And would it not be a kind of goal, redemption and justification for the democratic movement itself if someone came along who *used* it — by finally adding to its new and sublime configuration of slavery, which one day will represent the culmination of European democracy, that higher order of masterful and Caesarian spirits that now also — *requires* this new slavery? For new vistas heretofore impossible, for *their own* vistas? For *their own* tasks?[17]

2[14]

Our four cardinal virtues: courage, sympathy, insight and solitude — they would be unbearable to one another if they were not fraternized with a cheerful and mischievous vice called "courtesy." —

2[15]

Cruelty can be the alleviation of tense and proud souls, of those who are accustomed to constantly practicing hardships on themselves; it has become a celebration for them to finally do harm for once, to see suffering — all warlike races are cruel; cruelty can, conversely, also be a kind of saturnalia of oppressed and weak-willed beings, of slaves, of women of the harem, a small tickle of power — there is a cruelty of evil and also a cruelty of bad and negligible souls.

2[16][18]

What is noble?

Belief in order of rank.
Work (about artists, scholars etc.)
Cheerfulness (symptom of turning out well).[19]
Master morality and herd morality.

2[17]

The writings in question, painstakingly and patiently interrogated, may be used as a means to perhaps gain access to an understanding of a still higher and more difficult type than is even ⟨the⟩ type of the free spirit: — no other way leads to the understanding of — — —

* * *

Writings from the youth of the same author.
The Birth of Tragedy. 1st edition 1872. 2nd ed.
Unfashionable Observations 1873–76.

2[18]

A god of love could one day say, bored by his virtue: "let's have a try for once at devilishness!" — and behold, a new origin of evil! From boredom and virtue! — —

2[19][20]

"Paradise is under the shadow of swords" — also a *symbolon*[21] and motto by which souls of noble and warlike lineage reveal and divine one another. —

2[20][22]

"*Eagles pounce straight-on.*" The nobility of the soul is not least recognized by the magnificent and proud stupidity with which it *attacks* — "straight-on."

2[21]

There is also a squandering of our passions and desires, namely in the modest and petit bourgeois way in which we satisfy them: — which ruins our taste, but even more our respect and fear of ourselves. Temporary asceticism is the means to *dam* them — to give them dangerousness and grand style — —

2[22]

With respect to what fruitful spirits require uppermost and undermost, in order to not suffer from the worms of their conscience — namely "lay eggs, cackle, brood eggs" and so forth with or without grace — they may justifiably, as Stendhal and Balzac have done — prescribe a diet of abstinence. And at least one must not doubt that the nuptial bed can be more disastrous for precisely the "genius" than concubinage and libertinage. — Also in many other respects —for example, as concerns "descendants" — one must occasionally take counsel with oneself and resolve: *aut liberi aut libri*.[23]

2[23]

Reflected long about that point of origin of religious genius and consequently also of "metaphysical need," the "religious neurosis" — reluctantly mindful of that expression famous and even proverbial in France, that reveals so much about the "health" of the French mind: "*le génie est une neurose*."[24] —

2[24][25]

— And to say it again: the beast in us wants to be *lied* to — morality is a white lie.

2[25][26]

"You seem to be up to something wicked," I once said to the god Dionysus: "namely driving human beings to ruin?" — "Perhaps," replied the god, "but in such a way that I get something out of it for myself." — "What then?" I asked, curious. — "*Who* then? you should be asking." Thus spoke Dionysus and he grew silent, in the way that is his own, namely seductively. — You should have seen him then! It was spring, and all the trees were in their early sap.

2[26][27]

Beyond Good and Evil.

Prelude
to a Philosophy of the Future.

By
Friedrich Nietzsche.

2[27][28]

Beyond Good and Evil.

All Sorts of Things to Ponder
for Halcyon Spirits.

By
Friedrich Nietzsche.

2[28][29]

My tolerably radical question mark for all your penal legislation is this: given that the punishments are supposed to hurt in proportion to the magnitude of the crime — and that's how you all want it at bottom! well, then they would have to be measured for each criminal proportionate to his sensitivity for pain — that is, there should be a *pre-existing* determination of punishment for an offense, a penal code ought *not to exist at all*? But, considering that it would not be easy to determine the scale of pleasure and displeasure in a criminal, then *in praxi*[30] one would surely have to dispense with punishing? What a loss! Right? Consequently — —

2[29]

Music does *not* reveal the essence of the world and its "will," as Schopenhauer claimed (who deceived himself about music as he did about compassion, and for the same reason — he knew them both too little from experience —): music reveals only the esteemed musicians! And they themselves do not know it! — And how good, perhaps, that they do not know it! —

2[30][31]

Our Virtues.

All Sorts of Questions and Questionable Matters
for Subtler Consciences.

By
Friedrich Nietzsche.

2[31][32]

Our Virtues.

Hints for a Morality of the Future.
By
Friedrich Nietzsche.

On the Strength of the Soul.
On Honesty.
On Cheerfulness.
On the Will to Solitude.
"What is Noble?"

2[32][33]

The Philosophers of the Future.
A Speech.

1.

Is such a greatness possible today? —

2.

But perhaps tomorrow, perhaps the day after tomorrow. — I see new ph⟨ilosophers⟩ coming up etc.

2[33]

There is a misunderstanding of cheerfulness that cannot be put to rest: but whoever shares it may ultimately be satisfied with it as it is. — We who *flee* to happiness — : we who need every kind of south and unruly fullness of sun and position ourselves at that point on the street where life, like a drunken parade of grotesque masks — like something that makes us lose our minds — tumbles past; we who demand of happiness precisely *that* it makes us "lose our minds": does it not seem that we have a knowledge that we *fear*? With which we do not want to be alone? A knowledge before whose pressure we tremble, before whose whispering we blanch? This stiff-necked turning away from sad spectacles, this plugging and hardening of our ears to all suffering, this brave, mocking superficiality, this willful Epicureanism of the heart that wants to have nothing warm and whole and worships the *mask* as its final divinity and redemptress: this scorn against the melancholic of taste, in whom we always detect a lack of profundity — is not all of this only hatred of life? It seems we know ourselves as all too brittle, perhaps even as shattered and incurable; it seems we fear this hand of life, that it must shatter us, and we flee into its appearance, into its falseness, its surface and colorful deceptiveness; it seems we are cheerful because we are tremendously sad. We are serious, we know the abyss: *that is why* we resist all that is serious.

— — — we smile to ourselves about the melancholics of taste — oh we even envy them, as we mock them! — for we are not happy enough to be able to allow ourselves their delicate sadness. We must flee even the shadow of sadness: our hell and darkness is always too near to us. We have a knowledge that we fear, with which we do not want to be alone; we have a belief before whose pressure we tremble, before whose whispering we blanch — the nonbelievers seem blessed to us. We turn away from the sad spectacles, we plug our ears against whatever suffers, compassion would immediately shatter us if we did know how ⟨to⟩ harden ourselves. Stay boldly at our side, mocking recklessness: cool us, wind, that has sped over glaciers: we want to take nothing more to heart, we want to pray to the *mask*

There is something in us that easily shatters: we fear the shattering childish hands? we avoid chance and rescue ourselves — — —

2[34]

I loved and honored Richard Wagner more than anyone else; and if in the end he had not had the bad taste — or the sad need — to make common cause with a quality of "spirits" that were impossible to me, with his followers, the Wagnerians, then I would have had no reason to bid him farewell already in his lifetime: him, the deepest and boldest, also the most misunderstood of all who are hard to understand today, whose acquaintance has advanced my knowledge more than any other acquaintance I have made. Let me say at the beginning what belongs at the beginning, that his cause and my cause did not want to be confused, and that it took a good bit of self-overcoming before I adequately learned to separate "his" and "mine" in the proper measure. That I came to my senses about the extraordinary problem of the actor — a problem that probably is more distant from me than any other, for a reason that is hard to articulate — that I discovered and recognized the actor at the bottom of every artist, that which is typically artistic, for that I needed to come into contact with that ⟨man⟩ — and it seems to me that I think more highly a⟨nd⟩ more lowly of both than an earlier philos⟨opher⟩.[34] — The improvement of the theater concerns me little, its "churchification" even less; the actual Wagnerian music does not sufficiently belong to me — I would be able to dispense with them for my happiness and for my health (*quod erat demonstrandum et demonstratum*[35]). What was most foreign to me in him, the Teutonomania and semi-churchiness of his last years — — —

2[35]

A new way of thinking — which is always a new way of measuring and presupposes the presence of a new standard, a new sensation-scale — feels itself to be in contradiction with old ways of thinking and constantly says, while resisting them, "that is false." Examined more closely such a "that is false" really only means "I do not feel anything of myself in that," "it's of no interest to me," "I do not comprehend how you are not able to feel as I do"

2[36]

On detachment.
On hardening.
On the mask.
On the order of rank.
European and super-European.

2[37]

One always has something more necessary to do than to get married: Heavens, this is what's always happened to me!

2[38][36]

Beyond Good and Evil.
Hints at a Morality of the Strongest.

2[39]

Mask and Communication.

2[40]

The philosophers of the future.
On the natural history of the free spirit.
Our virtues.
Peoples and fatherlands.
Defeminization.
homo religiosus.[37]

2[41][38]

On the Natural History of the Superior Human.

Thoughts of an Educator.

1. The philosophers of yore.
2. Artists and poets.
3. The religious genius.
4. We virtuous ones.
5. Woman.
6. Scholars.
7. The "tempters."
8. Peoples and fatherlands.
9. Wisdom of the mask.
10. Moral Psychology.
    Proverbs and dashes.[39]
    What is noble?

Appendix. Songs of Prince Vogelfrei.

2[42][40]

Beyond Good and Evil.

Prelude
to a Philosophy of the Future.

With an appendix: Songs and Arrows of Prince Vogelfrei.

By
Friedrich Nietzsche.

2[43][41]

On the Natural History of the Superior Human.

Dashes[42] of a Psychologist.

1. The philosopher.
2. The free spirit.
3. The religious genius.
4. On moral psychology
5. What is noble?

6. Peoples and fatherlands.
7. Woman in herself.
8. Scholars.
9. We virtuous ones.
10. Wisdom and mask.
11. The coming ones.
12. Proverbs of a laconic one.

Appendix: Songs and Arrows of Prince Vogelfrei.

2[44]

Preface.

1. What was the philosopher?
2. On the natural history of the free spirit.
3. Monologue of a psychologist.
4. Woman in herself.
5. The religious genius.
6. We scholars.
7. We virtuous ones.
8. What is noble?
9. Peoples and fatherlands.
10. The masks.
11. The tempters. Dionysus.

Appendix: — — —

Table of contents.

2[45]

Nothing of the advocate:[43] no man of the party; suspicious of that which is called "conviction"; unbelieving toward unbelief; — — —

2[46][44]

On the Natural History of the Superior Human.

Thoughts of an Idler.

By
Friedrich Nietzsche.

2[47][45]

Beyond Good and Evil.

Monologues
of a
Psychologist.

With an appendix: Songs and Arrows of Prince Vogelfrei.

By
Friedrich Nietzsche.

Appendix:
Songs and Arrows
of
Prince Vogelfrei.

1. To the mistral.
2. To Goethe.
3. To certain eulogists.
4. Sils-Maria.
5. Hermit's noon.
6. Toward new seas.
7. "The Pigeons of San Marco"
8. Inscription above the house door.
9. The genuine German.
10. Parsifal music.
11. To Spinoza.
12. *Rimus remedium.*[46]
13. Fool in despair.
14. Aftersong.

2[48]

Woman is so little satisfied with herself that she would rather permit herself to be beaten than —

2[49]

In most loves there is someone who plays and someone who lets himself be played with: Amor is above all a little theatre director.

2[50][47]

Contents:

Preface.
1. On the prejudices of philosophers.
2. The free spirit.
3. The religious genius. The religious character.
4. Woman in herself. Proverbs and Interludes.
5. On the natural history of morality.
6. We scholars.
7. Our virtues.
8. Peoples and fatherlands
9. Masks.
10. What is noble?
Appendix: Songs and Arrows of Prince Vogelfrei.

"*Carcasse, tu trembles? Tu tremblerais bien davantage, si tu savais, où je te mène.*"
Turenne[48]

2[51][49]

Monologues
of a Psychologist

By
Friedrich Nietzsche

On the Natural history of the superior human.[50]

What is noble?[51]

2[52][52]

Proverbs and Monologues.
With a Rhymed Addition.

By
Friedrich Nietzsche.

2[53][53]

Beyond Good and Evil

Prelude
to a Philosophy of the Future.

Introduction.	
First Book:	on the prejudices of philosophers.
Second Book:	hints of a moral-psycholo⟨gist⟩
Third Book:	we Europeans. An opportunity for self-mirroring.

2[54][54]

Beyond Good and Evil.

By
Friedrich Nietzsche.

2[55][55]

Penultimate chapter

Alcuin the Anglo-Saxon, who characterized the royal profession of the philosopher thus:

prava corrigere, et recta corroborare, et sancta sublimare.[56]

2[56]

Corruption of the strong natural human being in the compulsion of the civilized cities (— ends up in the leprous parts, learns bad conscience there)

2[57][57]

From now on there will be favorable preconditions for more comprehensive ruling structures, the like of which have never existed. And this is not even the most important thing; the emergence of international racial federations has been made possible, which set themselves the task of cultivating a ruler-race, the future "rulers of the earth"; — a new, tremendous aristocracy built upon the harshest self-legislation, in which the will of philosophical brutes and artist-tyrants will be given millennia of longevity: — a superior kind of human being that thanks to its preponderance of willing, knowing, wealth and influence, makes use of democratic Europe as its most pliable and flexible tool for taking the destinies of the earth in hand, for shaping "the human being" itself as an artist would. Enough, the time is coming when people will relearn what politics is.

2[58]

I believe we are lacking political passion: we would endure with honors under a demo⟨cratic⟩ sky just as well as under an abs⟨olutist⟩ sky.

2[59]

For 1

But finally: why must one speak of what *will* come so loudly and with such wrath! Let us look at it more coolly, distantly, cleverly, from on high, let us say it as it is allowed to be said among us, so secretively that everyone misses it — that everyone misses *us* . . . Let it be called a continuation.[58]

2[60]

What? Drama is the end, music is always only the means? That may be W⟨agner⟩'s theory: his practice was opposed to it: the (dramatic) *attitude*[59] is the end, the music always only a means to an attitude (to its elucidation, strengthening, internalization —)

2[61][60]

The development of the mechanistic-atomistic way of thinking is still not aware of its necessary goal even today; — this is my impression, after scrutinizing its followers for a long time. It will conclude with the creation of a system of signs: it will dispense with explanations, it will give up the concept "cause and effect."

2[62][61]

Not to want to deceive — and not to want to be deceived: this is something fundamentally different as inclination and will, but one tendency like the other is accustomed to using the word "philosophy," be it as ornament or concealment or out of misunderstanding.

2[63][62]

The physiologists should stop and think before positing the drive for self-preservation as the cardinal drive of an organic being: something that lives wants above all to *discharge* its strength: "preservation" is only one of the consequences of this. — Beware of *superfluous* teleological principles! And that is where the whole concept of "self-preservation" belongs.

2[64][63]

Every Philoctetes knows that without his bow and his arrows Troy will not be conquered.

2[65][64]

In media vita.[65]
Monologues of a Psychologist.

By
Friedrich Nietzsche.

2[66][66]

— *For the preface.* — Perhaps a continuation: the *artist*-philosopher (hitherto scientism, position on religion and politics mentioned): higher concept of *art.* Whether a human being can position himself so far from other human beings that he is capable of *shaping them*? (Practice exercises: 1) the one who shapes himself, the hermit 2) the artist so far, as the small completer, on a material[67] (no!⟨)⟩ — to this belongs the *series of rank* of the superior humans, which must be represented.

— *One Chapter: Music.* — On the theory of "intoxication" (itemization, e.g., worship of *petits faits*[68])
— German and French and Italian music. (Our politically lowest periods the *most fruitful*: —)
the Slavs?
— the cultural-historical ballet: — has conquered the opera.
— an error, that what was created by W⟨agner⟩ is a form — it is a formlessness. The possibility of a *dramatic* structure has yet to be found. Actor-music and musician-music
— The rhythmic. Expression at any cost.
— in praise of "Carmen"
— in praise of H. Schütz (and "Liszt-Verein"[69] —)
— whorish instrumentation
— in praise of *Mendelssohn*: an element of Goethe in him, and nowhere else! just as another element of Goethe came to perfection in Rahel![70] a third in H. Heine[71]

For the chapter "*free spirit*." — 1) I do not want to "glorify" him: a word in favor of the bound spirits.
2) the depravity of the intellect: the proof from *pleasure* ("it makes me happy, therefore it is true") Here the vanity of the "me" to be underscored.

For the chapter "*our virtues*": 3) new form of morality: *loyalty-oaths* in federations regarding what one wants to do and not do, quite *specific* renunciation of many things. Tests, to determine whether *ripe* for this.[72] —

For the chapter "*religious genius*." 1) mystery, the exemplary history of a soul ("Drama" — means?)
2) the interpretability of events, belief in "meaning" is maintained thanks to religion —
3) to what extent the higher soul grows and flourishes at the expense of the lower?
4) what has been refuted is the *morality* of Christianity as essential in the destinies of the world-soul: — yet the will to introduce it and to make it dominant has not yet been abolished. — In the end the latter could only be a

don-quixoticism anyway: — but *this* would be no reason to think dismissively of it!
5) to what extent religious genius is a **degeneration** of the artistic: — the *shaping* force.
6) to what extent only the *artist*-conscience provides freedom from "true" and "untrue." Unconditional "faith" to be transformed into unconditional *will* — —
7) religious literature, the concept "sacred book."

for "*our virtues*." Whatever we can unleash our scientism upon, we no longer take hard and seriously: a kind of immorality.

For the *chapter "natural history of morality." Corruption*, what is that? E.g., of the natur⟨al⟩ strong human being who comes into the cities. E.g., of the Fr⟨ench⟩ aristocrats, before the French Revolution.

For the chapter "*Man and Woman*."
The *triumph* of man over woman wherever culture begins.
NB: *magister liberalium artium et hilaritatum*.[73]
NB. I have grabbed something by the horns — only I doubt whether it was a steer —[74]

2[67]

"I" "subject" as horizon-line. Reversal of the perspectival gaze.

2[68][75]

Using *the body as a guide*. The self-dividing protoplasma. ½ + ½ *not* = 1, but = 2. ⟨Therewith⟩ the belief in soul monads is invalidated.

Self preservation only as one of the consequences of self-expansion. of one's "self"?

2[69][76]

Mechanical force is known to us only as a *sensation of resistance*: and the latter is only sensually *interpreted* with *pressure* and *thrust*, not *explained*.

What kind of compulsion is it that a stronger soul exerts on a weaker? — And it would be possible that the apparent "disobedience" toward the higher soul was based on not understanding its will. e.g., a boulder does not let itself be commanded. But what is needed is precisely a slow differentiation of degree and rank: *only* the most closely related can understand one another and consequently there can be obedience here.

Whether possible to comprehend all motions as signs of a psychic event? Natural science as a symptomatology —

It is perhaps wrong, because the life-forms are very small (cells e.g.,), now to seek even smaller units, "force-points" etc.?

The *pre-stage of ruling structures*

Devotion to the **person** (father, forefather, prince, priest, God) as *alleviation* of morality.

2[70][77]

Beyond Good and Evil

— Problem of the lawgiver.
Using the body as a guide. Mechanism and life.
The will to power.
— Interpretation, not knowledge. On doctrine of method.
The eternal recurrence.
— The artist. Culture and its substructure.
— We godless ones.
— Music and culture.
— On great and small politics.
"Mystery."
The good and the just.
The vow-makers.
— On the history of pessimism.
— Education.

2[71][78]
On "Zarathustra"

Calina:[79] brownish red, everything too sharp from close up. Highest summer. Ghostly

Sipo Matador.[80]

And who says that we do not want this? What music and seduction! There is nothing there that did not poison, lure, corrode, overthrow, revalue!

I The *decisive* moment:

The order of rank. 1) Smash the good and just!
2)
The eternal recurrence.

Noon and Eternity.
Book of the Prophet.

2[72][81]

Noon and Eternity.
By
F. N.

I The festival of the dead. Zarathustra discovers a tremendous festival:

II The new order of rank:

III On the rulers of the earth.

IV On the ring of recurrence.

2[73]
The titles of 10 new books: (spring 1886.)

Thoughts concerning the Ancient Greeks.[82]
By
Friedrich Nietzsche.

How in becoming everything *degenerates* and becomes *unnatural.* The degeneration of the Renaissance — of philology
Example of the *immoral* basic conditions of a higher culture, of an elevation of the human being.

The Will to Power.
Attempt at a
New World-Interpretation.[83]

The Artists.
Ulterior Motives of a Psychologist
By
Friedrich Nietzsche.

We Godless Ones
By
Friedrich Nietzsche

Noon and Eternity.[84]
By
Friedrich Nietzsche

Beyond Good and Evil.
Prelude to a Philosophy of the Future.[85]
By
Friedrich Nietzsche.

Gai Saber.
Songs of Prince Vogelfrei.[86]
By Friedrich Nietzsche.

Music.
By Friedrich Nietzsche

Experiences of a Literary Scribe.[87]
By
Friedrich Nietzsche.

On the History of Modern Dimming.[88]
By
Friedrich Nietzsche.

2[74][89]

The Will to Power.
1. Physiology of Order of Rank.
2. The Great Noon.
3. Discipline and Cultivation.
4. The Eternal Recurrence.

2[75][90]

The Eternal Recurrence. Book of new festivals and prophecies.

The Eternal Recurrence.
Sacred dances and vows.

Noon and Eternity.
Sacred dances of the recurrers.

2[76][91]

(28)

On the Order of Rank:
For I. *On the Physiology of Power.*

Aristocracy in the body, the majority of the rulers (struggle of the tissues?

Slavery and the division of labor: the higher type only possible through the *suppression* of a lower type to a mere function

Pleasure and pain not opposite. The feeling of power.

Nourishment only a consequence of insatiable appropriation, of the will to power.

Reproduction, decay setting in with the impotence of the ruling cells to organize what has been appropriated.[92]

It is the *shaping* force that always wants to have a new supply of "material" (still more "force"). The masterpiece of the construction of an organism from the egg.

"Mechanistic conception": wants nothing but quantities: but force lies in quality: mechanistics therefore can only describe, not explain processes.

"Purpose." One should proceed from the "sagacity" of plants.

Concept of "perfection": *not* only greater complexity, but greater *power* (— need not be only greater mass —)

Conclusion regarding the development of humanity: perfection consists in the production of the most powerful individuals, who wield the greatest masses as their tool (and indeed as the most intelligent and flexible tool)[93]

Artists as the small shapers. The pedantry of "educators" by comparison

Punishment: the up-holding[94] of a higher type.

Isolation.

Wrong lessons from history. *Because* something high did not turn out well or was abused (like the aristocracy) does not mean it is refuted!

2[77][95]

The appearance of the empty and the full, of the firm and the loose, of the resting and the moved and of the equal and the unequal.

(absolute space the *oldest* appearance has been made into *metaphysics*.

(substance)

— : the human-animalistic *security*-value standards are in there.

Our *concepts* are inspired by our *neediness.*

The positing of opposites corresponds with indolence (one differentiation that *suffices* for nourishment, security etc. is regarded as "*true*")

— *simplex veritas*![96] — Thought from indolence.

Our values are *interpreted into* things.

So is there a *meaning* in the in-itself??

Is not meaning necessarily but relational-meaning and perspective?

All meaning is will to power (all relational-meanings can be dissolved in it.)[97]

A thing = its properties = but these like everything that *concerns us* about this thing: a unity, under which we summarize those relations that *come into question* for us. At bottom the changes that we *have perceived* in ourselves (— except those that we do not perceive e.g., its electricity). In sum: Object is the sum of experienced *inhibitions* of which we have become *aware.* A property therefore always expresses something of "useful" or "harmful" for us. Colors e.g., — each one corresponds to a degree of pleasure or displeasure and each degree of pleasure and displeasure is the result of valuations about "useful" and "not useful." — Disgust.

2[78][98]

Themata.

Interpretation, *not* explanation.

Reduction of *logical* value judgments to moral and political (value of security, of peace, of laziness ("least energy") etc.

The problem of the artist, his morality (lies, shamelessness, inventiveness for what he lacks).

The slandering of immoral drives: regarded in consequence a *denial* of life.

The absolute and where the ideal features come from that are attributed to it.

Punishment as a means of cultivating.

Gravitation interpretable in many ways: like everything allegedly "factual."

The predicate expresses an effect that is produced upon us (or could be) *not* the effect in itself; the sum of predicates is summarized into a single word. Error, that the subject is supposed to be *causa*. — Mythology of the subject-concept. ("lightning" flashes — doubling — the effect *objectifies*.

Mythology of the causality-concept. Separation of "effecting" and "agent" *fundamentally wrong*. The appearance of what remains unchanged, now as before — —

Our European culture — toward what does it *hurry*, as opposed to the Buddhistic *dissolution* in Asia?

Religion, essentially doctrine of *order of rank*, even attempt at a *cosmic* order of rank and power.

weakness
lies, dissimulation
stupidity
lust to rule } to what extent *idealizing*?
curiosity
greed
cruelty

2[79]

My writings are very well defended: whoever reaches for them and ends up over-reaching as someone who has no right to such books — he immediately makes himself ridiculous — a little fit of rage drives him to pour out his innermost and his most ridiculous: and who wouldn't know what kinds of things always come out here! Little literary women as they tend to be, with pathological sexual organs and with ink stains on their fingers —

The inability to see the new and the original: the clumsy fingers that do not know how to grasp a nuance, the stiff earnestness that stumbles over a word and falls down: the shortsightedness that intensifies to blindness before the tremendous realm of distant landscapes

Have I ever complained about my fate, about being read too little and understood so poorly? But for how many may something extraordinary be created anyway! — Do you think that God created the world for the sake of humans?

2[80][99]

For the introduction.

The gloomy solitude and dreariness of the *campagna Romana*,[100] patience in uncertainty

Every book as a conquest, good decision — *tempo lento*[101] — — until the end dramatically coiled, ultimately *catastrophe* and sudden *redemption*.

2[81][102,103]

(15)

It is only a matter of strength: have all the pathological features of the century, but balance them in a superabundant plastic restorative force. *The strong human being*: description

2[82][104]

Beyond Good and Evil.

Second and Final Part

Preface.

Interpretation, *not* explanation. There are no factual findings, everything is fluid, ungraspable, retreating; what is most durable is still our opinions. Attaching meaning — in most cases a new interpretation over an old interpretation that has become incomprehensible, that itself is now only sign.[105]

On the physiology of power. A consideration according to which the human being feels his strongest drives and his ideals (and his good conscience) as identical.

We godless ones.

What are artists?

Justice and lawgiving.

On the history of modern dimming.

Acting.
On the good and the just.
Rank and order of rank.
To the mistral. A dance song.
Beyond good and evil as brightening for a few as deepest dimming for many.

On the history of modern dimming.
Psychology of the artist.
On acting.
The problem of the lawgiver.
Danger in music.
Interpretation, *not* knowledge.
The good and the just.
On great and small politics.
We godless ones.
To the Mistral. Dance Song.

In 30 pages.
2 folios.

(Preface: what my writings have in common)
Interpretation, *not* explanation.
On the physiology of power.
On acting
On the history of modern dimming
We godless ones.
The good and the just.
On order of rank.
Justice and lawgiving.
Artists

2[83][106]

(7)

The human being regards himself as cause, as doer —
everything that happens relates predicatively to some subject
In every judgment resides the entire full profound belief in subject and predicate or in cause and effect; and this latter

belief (namely as the claim that every effect is activity and that every activity presupposes an actor)[107] is even only an individual case of the former, so that what remains is the belief as basic belief: subjects exist.

I observe something and look for a *reason* for it: originally this means: I am looking for an *intention* in it and above all for one that has intentions, for a subject, a doer: — formerly one saw purposes in *all* events, all events were a doing. This is our oldest habit. Do animals have it too? Are they not, as living beings, also dependent on interpretation according to *themselves*? — The question "*why*?" is always a question about the *causa finalis*,[108] about a "what for?" We have nothing of a "meaning of the *causa efficiens*":[109] here *Hume* is right, habit (but *not* only that of the individual!) leads us to expect that a certain frequently observed process follows on another: nothing more! What gives us our extraordinary firmness in the belief in causality is *not* the great habit of succession of events, but our *inability* to *interpret* an event as anything but an event from *intentions*. It is the *belief* in what lives and thinks as uniquely *effective* — in the will, intention — that all events are a doing, that all doing presupposes a doer, it is the belief in the "subject." Shouldn't this belief in the subject- and predicate-concept be a big s⟨tupidity⟩?

Question: is intention the cause of an event? Or is that illusion too? Is it not *the* event itself?[110]

"Attracting" and "repelling" in a purely mechanical sense is a complete fiction: a word. Without an intention we cannot conceive an attracting: i.e., without an *intention*. — The will to master a thing or to resist its power and push it back — *that* "we understand": that would be an interpretation that we could use.

Briefly: the psychological necessity for a belief in causality lies in the *inconceivability of an event without intentions*: which naturally says nothing about truth or untruth (justification of such a belief). The belief in *causae*[111] falls with the belief in τέλη[112] (against Spinoza and his causalism).[113]

2[84][114,115]

(30)

Judging is our oldest belief, our most habituated holding-true or holding-untrue of something.

In judgment is found our oldest belief, in all judging there is a holding-true or a holding-untrue, an affirming or denying, a certainty that something is so and not otherwise, a belief that we have really "known" something here — *what* is believed as true in all judging?

What are *predicates*? — We have taken changes in ourselves *not* as such, but as an "in itself" that is foreign to us, that we only "perceive": and we have posited them *not* as an event, but as a being, as "property" — and we have added the invention to which they stick. *i.e.*, we have posited *effect* as *effecting* and the *effecting* as *being*. But even in this formulation the concept "effect" is arbitrary: for of those changes that occur in us and of which we believe ourselves definitely *not* to be the cause, we infer only that they must be effects: according to the conclusion: "to every change belongs an author;" — But this conclusion is already mythology: it *separates* the effecting *and* the effect. When I say "the lightning flashes," then I have posited the flashing once as activity and the other time as subject: hence I have supposed a being beneath the event, which is not one with the event, but on the contrary *remains, is*, and does not "*become*." — *To posit the event as effect*: and the *effect as being*: this is the *double* error, or *interpretation*, of which we make ourselves guilty. Therefore e.g., "the lightning flashes" — : "flashing" is a state in us: but we do not take it as effect on us, and say: "something flashing" as an "in itself" and seek an author for it, the "lightning."

2[85][116,117]

(32)

The properties of a thing are effects on other "things": if one thinks away other "things," then a thing has no properties i.e., *there is no thing without other things* i.e., there is no "thing in itself."

2[86][118,119]

(30)

Only what can *knowledge* be? — "Interpretation," *not* "explanation."

2[87][120]

(32)

All unity is *only* unity as *organization and interplay*: no different than a human community is a unity: therefore *opposite* of atomistic *anarchy*; hence a *ruling-structure* that *signifies* One, but *is* not one.[121]

One would have to *know* what being *is*, in order to *decide* whether this and that is real (e.g., "the facts of consciousness"); likewise what *certainty* is, what *knowledge* is and so forth. — But since we do *not* know this, then a critique of the faculty of knowledge is nonsensical: how is the tool supposed to be able to critique itself, if it can use only *itself* for critiquing? It cannot even define itself![122]

If all unity is unity only as organization? but the "thing" in which we believe is only *added as an invention* to different predicates as ferment. When a thing "effects," then this means: we comprehend as cause *all remaining* properties that otherwise are still present here and are momentarily latent, so that now a single property appears: i.e., *we take the sum of its properties — x* as **cause** *of the property x*: which is *entirely* stupid and crazy![123]

"The subject" or the "thing"

2[88][124]

(33)

A force that we cannot imagine (like the so-called purely mechanical force of attraction and repulsion) is an empty word and should not have any rights of citizenship in *science*: which *wants to make the world imaginable* to us, nothing more![125]

All events from intentions are reducible to the *intention of increase of power*.[126]

2[89][127]

Illusion that something *is known* where we have a mathematical formula for events: it has only been *characterized, described*: nothing more!

2[90][128,129]

(31)

Equality and similarity. 1) the cruder organ sees much apparent equality
2) the mind *wants* equality i.e., to subsume a sensory impression under an existing series: just as it *assimilates* the inorganic to itself.

On the understanding of *logic* : : : *the will to equality is the will to power.*
— the *belief* that something is so and so, the essence of *judgment*, is the consequence of a will that it *shall* be as much as possible equal.

2[91][130,131]

(30)

If our "ego" is for us the sole *being* according to which we make or understand all *being*: very good! then the doubt is very well justified whether here a perspectival *illusion* does not exist — the apparent unity in which everything closes together as in a line of a horizon. Using the body as a guide reveals a tremendous *multiplicity*; it is methodologically permissible to use the better-studiable *richer* phenomenon as a guide for understanding the poorer. Finally: supposing everything is becoming, then *knowledge is only possible on the basis of the belief in being.*

2[92][132]

Sense perceptions projected "outward": "inward" and "outward" — there the *body* commands — ?

— the same equalizing and ordering force that reigns in germ plasm also reigns in the incorporating of the external world: our sense perceptions are already the *result* of this *assimilation* and *equating* with respect to the *whole* past in us; they do not follow immediately upon the "impression" —

2[93][133,134]

(34)

To what extent dialectic and faith in reason still rest on moral prejudices. With Plato we are as erstwhile inhabitants of an intelligible world of the good still in possession of a legacy of that period: divine dialectic, as deriving from the good, leads to all things good. (— therefore "leads back" as it were —) Even Descartes had a concept of how in a Christian-moral fundamental way of thinking, which believes in a *good* God as creator of things, only the truthfulness of God *vouches* for our sensory judgments. Aside from a religious sanction and vouching for our senses and rationality — where are we supposed to have gotten our right to trust existence! That thinking is supposed to be a measure of the real — that what cannot be thought *is* not — is a clumsy *non plus ultra*[135] of a moralistic blind confidence (in an essential truth-principle at the basis of things), in itself an insane assertion that is contradicted in every moment by our experience. We can actually think nothing at all, insofar as it *is* . . .

2[94]

We are bad enough at observing the emergence of a judgment of quality

Reduction of qualities to value judgments.

2[95][136]

Our perceptions as we understand them: i.e., the sum of all *those* perceptions whose *realization* was useful and essential to us and to the entire organic process before us: therefore not all perceptions generally (e.g., not the electrical) This means: we have *senses* only for a selection of perceptions — those that must have been of consequence to us for our survival. *Consciousness exists to the extent that consciousness is useful.* There is no doubt that all sensory perceptions are completely permeated with *value judgments* (useful harmful — consequently pleasant or unpleasant) The individual color simultaneously expresses a value for us (although we seldom admit this to ourselves, or only after long exclusive exposure to the same color (e.g., prisoners in prison or insane people)) This is why insects react differently to different colors: some love them e.g., ants.

2[96][137]

Irony toward those who believe Christianity has been *overcome* by the modern natural sciences. The Christian value judgments are absolutely *not* overcome by them. "Christ on the cross" is the most sublime symbol — still. —

2[97][138]

Health and sickliness: one should be cautious! The standard remains the efflorescence of the body, the pouncing force, courage and merriness of the spirit — but, naturally also, *how much sickliness* it *can take upon itself a⟨nd⟩ overcome — make* healthy again. That which would ruin more delicate human beings belongs to the stimulants of *great* health.

2[98][139,140]

(35)

Poverty, humility and *chastity* — dangerous and slanderous ideals, but, like poisons, in the case of certain illnesses, useful remedies e.g., in the Roman imperial age.

All ideals are dangerous because they debase and stigmatize the actual, all are poisons, but as occasional remedies indispensable

2[99][141]

How has the entire organic process behaved *toward* the rest of nature? — There its *basic will* reveals itself.

2[100][142]

The Will to Power.

Attempt
at a Revaluation of all Values.

In four Books.

First Book: the danger of dangers (description of nihilism) (as the *necessary consequence of previous valuations*)

Second Book: critique of values (of logic etc.

Third Book: the problem of the lawgiver (including the history of solitude) *How* must human beings be constituted who make inverse valuations? — Human beings who have *all* the properties of the modern soul but are strong enough to transform them into sheer health.[143]

Fourth Book: the hammer
their means to their task. —[144]

Sils-Maria, summer 1886

Tremendous powers are unleashed: but contradicting themselves
the *unleashed* forces are mutually *annihilating* themselves
the unleashed forces are to be newly bound, so that they do not mutually annihilate each other and
our eyes have to be opened to the real *increase* in power!

Everywhere highlight the disharmony between the ideal and its individual conditions (e.g., honesty among Christians, who are constantly compelled to lying)

For Book 2.

In democratic communities, where everyone is a specialist, what is lacking is the What for? For whom? the class in which all the thousandfold atrophying of all individuals (to functions) acquires *meaning.*

The development of	sensuality cruelty revenge folly greed lust to rule etc.	to the sum of *culture.*

On
The danger in all previous ideals

Critique of Indian and Chinese way of thinking, likewise Christian (as preparations for a *nihilistic* one —)
The danger of dangers: Everything has no meaning.

(2)

The hammer: a teaching that achieves a *selection* of those *fittest for life* through *unleashing* of the most death-crazed pessimism

2[101]

The inference from the work to the creator: the terrible question of whether fullness or renunciation, the madness of renouncing pushes to creation: the sudden eye for the fact that every romantic ideal is a self-escape, a self-contempt and self-condemnation of the one who invents it.

Ultimately it is a matter of strength: this entire romantic art could be rechanneled entirely into the antiromantic by a super-rich and mighty-willed artist or — to use my formula — into the *Dionysian*, just as in the hands of the strongest every kind of pessimism and nihilism becomes only one more hammer and tool with which one mounts a new pair of wings on oneself.

I recognized with a single glance that Wagner had reached his goal, to be sure, but only as Napoleon had reached his Moscow — at every stage so much had been lost, irretrievably lost, that precisely at the end of the whole march and apparently in the moment of triumph, his fate was already decided. Fateful the verses of Brün⟨n⟩hilde — thus Napoleon came to Moscow (R. Wagner to Bayreuth —)

To not ally oneself with any sickly powers who are conquered from the start —

If I had trusted myself more: the Wagner⟨ian⟩ inability to *walk* (even more to *dance* —and without dance there is for me no recreation and bliss) was always difficult for me.

The demand *for* complete passions is revealing: whoever is capable of them demands the magic of the opposite i.e., of *skepticism*. Those who are believers through and through have their occasional benefit and recreation in skepticism.

Wagner speaking about the delights that he knew how to coax from the Christian Holy Communion: this was decisive for me, I regarded him as *conquered*. — Add to this that a suspicion arose in me, whether he did not consider it useful for the purpose of his repatriation to Germany, to play the role somewhat of Christian and neoconvert: this suspicion damaged him with me even more than my annoyance at having placed my hopes on an aging romantic whose knees were already weary enough to fall down before the cross.

2[102][145]

Belief in the *body* is more fundamental than belief in the soul: the latter has emerged from the aporias of unscientific observation of the body (something that leaves it. Belief in the *truth* of *dreams* —)

2[103]

Mistrust of self-observation. That a thought is the cause of a thought cannot be determined. On the table of our consciousness a sequence of thoughts appears, as if one thought were the cause of the following. In fact we do not see the struggle that plays out beneath the table. — —

2[104][146]

With Plato as with someone of super-irritable sensuality and fanaticism the charm of concepts was so great that he involuntarily honored and deified concepts as an ideal form. *Dialectic-drunkenness*, as the awareness of exerting a mastery over oneself by using it — as a tool of the power will.

2[105][147]

Pressure and stress something unspeakably late, derivative, unoriginal. They already presuppose something that *holds together* and is *able* to pressure and stress! But from where would it hold together?

2[106]

The significance of German philosophy (Hegel): to think up a *pantheism* in which evil, error and suffering are *not* perceived as arguments against divinity. *This grandiose initiative* has been misused by the existing powers (state etc.), as if the rationality of whatever happened to rule at the time was thereby sanctioned.

Schopenhauer by contrast appears as the obstinate moral human being who finally becomes a *world-denier* in order to be right about his moral⟨istic⟩ estimation. Finally becomes a "mystic."

I myself have attempted an aesthetic justification: how is the ugliness of the world possible? — I took the will to beauty, to persisting in the *same* forms, as a temporary means of preservation and healing: but fundamentally the eternally creative as *that which must eternally destroy* seemed to me bound to pain. The ugly is the form of observation of things under the will to posit a meaning, a *new* meaning into what has become meaningless: the accumulated force that compels the creator to feel previous things as untenable, misshapen, worthy of renunciation, as ugly? —[148]

The deception of *Apollo*: the *eternity* of the beautiful form; the aristocratic law-giving "*thus it shall always* be!"

Dionysus: sensuality and cruelty. Transitoriness could be interpreted as enjoyment of the begetting and destroying force, as constant creation.[149]

2[107][150]

NB. Religions perish from the belief in morality: the Christian-moral God is not sustainable: consequently "atheism" — as if there could be no other kind of gods.

Likewise culture perishes from the belief in morality: for when the necessary conditions from which it alone grows are discovered, then one no longer *wants* it: Buddhism.

2[108][151]

That the *value of the world* lies in our interpretation (— that perhaps somewhere yet other interpretations than merely human ones are possible —) that the interpretations so far are perspectival valuations by virtue of which we sustain ourselves in life, that is in the will to power, for the growth of power, that every *elevation of human beings* brings with it the overcoming of narrower interpretations, that every achieved strengthening and expansion of power opens up new perspectives and means believing in new horizons — this runs through my writings. The world that *concerns us* is false i.e., is not a fact, but a fiction and a rounding based on a meager sum of observations; it is "in flux," as something becoming, as a falseness that is ever-shifting, that never approaches truth: for — there is no "truth."

2[109][152]

The "meaninglessness of events": belief in it is the result of an insight into the falseness of interpretations so far, a generalization of discouragement and weakness — not a *necessary* belief.

Immodesty of human beings: where they do not see meaning, they *deny* it!

2[110][153]

On "The Birth of Tragedy."

"Being" as the invention of the one who suffers from becoming.

A book constructed exclusively from experiences about aesthetic pleasure and displeasure, with an artistic metaphysics in the background. At the same time a confession of a romantic, finally a work of youth full of youthful courage and melancholy. The one who suffers most longs most profoundly for beauty — he *begets* it.

Psychological basic experiences: with the name "Apollonian" is designated that enchanted tarrying before an invented and dreamed world, before the world of *beautiful appearance* as a redemption from *becoming*: baptized with the name of Dionysus, on the other hand, is becoming apprehended actively, subjectively empathized, out of raging lust of the creator who simultaneously knows the wrath of the destroyer. Antagonism of these two experiences and the *desires* on which they are based: the former wants appearance *eternally*, before it the human being becomes still, wishless, smooth as the sea, healed, in agreement with himself and all existence: the second desire pushes toward becoming, to the lust of making becoming i.e., of creating and annihilating.

Becoming, perceived and interpreted from the inside, would be the incessant creating of an insatiable, super-rich, infinitely tensed and pressured being, of a god who conquers the agony of being only through constant transformation and change: — appearance as his temporary redemption, achieved in every moment; the world as the resulting sequence of divine visions and redemptions in appearance. — This artistic metaphysics faces up to the one-sided observation of Schopenhauer, which knows how to appreciate art only from the standpoint of the receiver, not from the standpoint of the artist: because it brings with it liberation and redemption in the enjoyment of the not-real, as opposed to reality (the experience of someone who suffers from and despairs over himself and his reality) — redemption in *form* and its eternity (as Plato may have also experienced it: except that concepts already permitted him to enjoy the triumph of his all too irritable and suffering sensibility) This is set against the second fact, art from the experience of the artist, above all the musician: the *torture* of having to create, as *Dionysian drive*.

Tragic art, rich in both experiences, is characterized as the reconciliation of Apollo and Dionysus: appearance is granted the deepest significance, through Dionysus: and yet this appearance is denied and denied with pleasure. This is aimed at Schopenhauer's teaching of *resignation* as tragic worldview.

Against Wagner's theory that music is the means and drama is the end.

A longing for tragic myth (for "religion" and indeed pessimistic religion) (as for an isolating cloche in which growing thrives)

Mistrust of science: even though its momentary alleviating optimism is strongly perceived. "Cheerfulness of the theoretical human being.

Profound aversion to Christianity: why? The degeneration of the German character is imputed to it.

Only aesthetically is there a justification of the world. Thorough suspicion of morality (it belongs in the world of appearance).

Happiness in existence is only possible as happiness in *appearance*

Happiness in becoming is only possible in the *annihilation* of the real of "existence," of beautiful appearance, in the pessimistic destruction of illusion.

in the annihilation of even the most beautiful appearance Dionysian happiness reaches its pinnacle.

2[111]

The problem of the meaning of art: *why* art?
How did the most vitally robust and best-formed human beings the *Greeks* relate to art?
Fact: tragedy belongs to their richest period of strength — why?
Second fact: the need for beauty; likewise for logicizing the world belong to their decadence
Interpretation of both facts: — — —
Erroneous practical application to the present: I interpreted pessimism as the *consequence* of higher strength and fullness of life, which can allow itself the luxury of the tragic. Likewise I interpreted German music as the expression of a Dionysian superabundance and originality i.e.,

1) I overestimated the German character
2) I did not understand the sources of modern dimming
3) I lacked the cultural-historical understanding of the origin of modern music and its *essential romanticism*.

Aside from this erroneous practical application the problem persists: *how would a music be*, if it were *not* of romantic origin — but of a *Dionysian* instead?

2[112][154]

a romantic is an artist who is made creative by the great displeasure in himself — who looks away and looks back from himself and his contemporaries

2[113][155]

I began with a metaphysical hypothesis about the meaning of music: but what underlay it was a *psychological experience* to which I was not yet able to impute a sufficiently *historical* explanation. The transference of music into the metaphysical was an act of reverence and gratitude; at bottom all religious persons so far have done this with their experience. — Then came the other side: the undeniably *harmful* and destructive effect of precisely this venerated music on me — and therewith also the end of its religious veneration. Here too my eyes were opened to the modern need *for* music (which appears simultaneously in history with the increasing need for narcotics) Even the "Artwork of the Future" seemed to me like a *raffinement*[156] of the need for stimulation and narcotization whereby all the senses want to settle their account at the same time, including the idealistic, religious, hypermoral nonsense — as an overall-excitation of the entire nervous machinery. The nature of Romanticism dawned on me: the *lack* of a fruitful kind of human being has become reproductive here. At the same time the thespianism of means, the fakeness and borrowedness of all individual elements, the lack of probity of artistic education, the abysmal *falseness* of this most modern art: which essentially must be theater-art. The psychological impossibility of these alleged hero- and god-souls, which are simultaneously nervous, brutal and refined like the most modern of Parisian painters and poets. — Enough, I relegated this art to modern "barbarism." — All this says nothing about the *Dionysian*. In the period of greatest fullness and health tragedy appears, but also in the period of nervous exhaustion and overstimulation. Contrasting interpretation. — With Wagner it is characteristic that he already gave the Ring of the Nibelung a nihilistic (calm- and end-craving) conclusion.

2[114][157]

The artwork where it appears *without artist* e.g., as body, as organization (Prussian officer corps, Jesuit order). To what extent the artist is only a pre-stage.[158] What is the meaning of "subject" — ?

The world as an artwork that gives birth to itself — —[159]

Is art a consequence of our *dissatisfaction with reality*? Or an expression of *gratitude about savored happiness*? In the first case *Romanticism*, in the second halo and dithyramb (in brief *apotheosis*-art): Raphael belongs here too, only he had the falseness of deifying the *appearance* of the Christian world interpretation. He was grateful for existence where it did *not* manifest itself as specifically Christian.

With the moral⟨istic⟩ interpretation the world is unbearable. Christianity was the attempt to "overcome" the world with it: that is to negate it. — *In praxi*[160] such an attack of insanity — of an insane arrogance of human beings in the face of the world — led ⟨to⟩ dimming, shrinking, impoverishing of the human being: only the most mediocre and innocuous type, the herd-type of human being, profited from this, was *advanced* by this, if you will . . .

Homer as apotheosis-artist; Rubens too. Music has not yet had one.

The idealization of the *great desecrater* (the sense for his *greatness*) is Greek; the deprecating, slandering, rendering despicable of the sinner is Jewish a⟨nd⟩ Christian.[161]

2[115]

"God is dead." Danger in the worship of God according to Judeo-Christian scheme.

2[116]

That self-knowledge that is modesty — for we are not our own work — but that is also gratitude to the same exact extent — for we "turned out well" —

2[117]

Psychology of the scientific need.

Art from gratitude or dissatisfaction.

The moral world-interpretation ends in world negation (critique of Christianity).

Antagonism between "improvement" and strengthening of the type human being.

Infinite interpretability of the world: every interpretation a symptom of growth or of decline.[162]

The previous attempts to overcome the *moral* God (pantheism Hegel etc.)

Unity (monism) a need of inertia; the plurality of interpretation a sign of strength. *Not to want to dispute* the world's unsettling and enigmatic character![163]

2[118]

1. (I. Nihilism in all its signs is at the door.
   II. Unavoidable, in the event that one does not understand its prerequisites.
   These are the valuations (*not* the social facts: which all act alternatingly pessimistic and optimistic only through a specific *interpretation*)

2. III. Genesis of valuations, as critique of the same.
3. IV. The inverse ones. Their psychology.
4. V. The hammer: as the teaching that leads to *decision*.

1. The danger of dangers.
2. Critique of morality.
3. We inverse ones.
4. The hammer.

2[119]

"How far does art reach into the inside of the world? And are there still artistic forces aside from the 'artist'?" This question was, as one knows, my *point of departure*: and I said yes to the second question; and to the first "the world itself is nothing but art." The absolute will to knowledge, to truth and wisdom seemed to me in such a world of appearance to be a sacrilege against ⟨the⟩ metaphysical basic will, as anti-nature: and in fairness ⟨the⟩ sharp point of "wisdom" turns itself *against* the wise man. The anti-naturalness of wisdom reveals itself in its hostility to art: wanting to know where appearance is precisely redemption — what a reversal, what an instinct for nothingness!

2[120]

All cults establish a *unique* experience, the coming together with a god, an "act of salvation" in some sense; and they repeatedly reproduce it. The legend of place as the origin of a drama: where poetry plays the god.

2[121][164,165]

(38)

Histrionics

The colorful motleyness of the modern human being and its allure.
Essentially hiding place and satiety.
The literary man.
The politician (in the "nationalist swindle")
Histrionics in the arts
lack of probity in preparatory training and schooling (Fromentin)
the romantics (lack of philosophy and science and excess of literature)
the novelists (Walter Scott, but also the Nibelung-monstrosities with their most nervous music)
the lyricists
"Scientism"
Virtuosos (Jews)
the populist ideals as overcome but not yet *visible to the people*:
the saint, the wise man, the prophet

2[122][166,167]

(37)

On the history of modern dimming.

The state-nomads (officials etc.): without "homeland" —
The decline of the family.

"The good human being" as symptom of exhaustion.
Justice as will to power (cultivation)
Lasciviousness and neurosis.
Black music; — whither invigorating music?
The anarchist.
Misanthropy. Disgust.
Deepest distinction: whether hunger or superabundance becomes *creative*? The former begets the *ideals of romanticism*.
northern unnaturalness.
the need for alcoholic beverages in the "plight" of workers
philosophical nihilism.

2[123]

Christians must believe in the *truthfulness of God*: here unfortunately they also get the belief in the Bible and in its "natural science" in the bargain; they absolutely *may* not admit to any relative truth (or said more plainly,). Christianity will shatter from the *absolute* character of its morality. — Science has awakened doubt in the truthfulness of the Christian God: from this *doubt Christianity will die* (Pascal's *deus absconditus*[168]).

2[124][169]

1. Birth of Tragedy.	Artists metaphysics.
2. Unfashionable Observations.	The cultural philistine. Disgust.[170] Life and history — basic problem. The philosophical hermit. "Education." The artist-hermit. *What* is to be learned in W⟨agner⟩.
3. Human, All Too Human.	The free spirit.
4. Mixed Opinions and Maxims.	The pessimist of the intellect.

(7)

Causality. "Why am *I* thus and such? The senseless thought of thinking oneself free to choose one's existence, even one's being thus and such. Background: the demand that there *must* be a being that would have *prevented* a self-despising creature such as I am from emerging. To *feel* oneself as the counter-argument to God —

5. Wanderer and Shadow.	Solitude, as problem.
6. Dawn.	Morality as a sum of prejudices
7. Joyful Science.	Scorn of European moralistics. Outlook toward an overcoming of morality. How would a human have to be constituted, who lived beyond?
	Z⟨arathustra⟩ — — —

Seven Prefaces.
An Addendum
to Seven Publications.

2[125][171]
On the history of pessimism.
Modern dimming.
Histrionics.

2[126][172]
For 2) Critique of the highest values.
On the history of *slandering*.
How *ideals* are made.
Culture (and "humanization": antagonistic)
Morality as instinct of shame, as disguise, mask, fundamentally benevolent interpretation

(37)

Mix in judgments about the *pessimists*!
The Indians
Pessimism (as instinct) and the will *to* pessimism: major contrast

The pessimist of the intellect. { the former tracking the illogical,
The pessimist of sensibility { the latter the painful.

all these standards are only such for *moral* reasons
or, like Plato, ἡδονή[173] also feared as value-revaluator
and seductress

A. What is truth?
B. Justice.
C. On the history of empathy.
D. The "good human."
E. The "superior human."
F. The artist.

(36)

What is truth? (inertia, the hypothesis with which satisfaction emerges, least use of intellectual strength etc.)[174]

2[127][175,176]

(2)

Nihilism is at the door: where does this most uncanny of guests come from? —

I. 1. Point of departure: it is an *error* to point to "social distress" or "physiological degenerations" or even to corruption as *cause* of nihilism. These still permit quite different interpretations. Rather, nihilism lies in a *quite specific interpretation*: in the Christian-moral⟨istic⟩. It is the most honest, most empathetic period. Distress, psychic, physical, intellectual distress is in itself not capable in the least of producing nihilism, i.e., the radical rejection of value, meaning, desirability

2. The destruction of Christianity — from its morality (which cannot be superseded —) which turns against the Christian God (the sense of truthfulness, highly developed by Christianity, gets *nausea* from the falseness and mendaciousness of all Christian interpretation of the world and history. Backlash from "God is the truth" to the fanatical belief "all is false." Buddhism of *deed* . . .

3. Skepticism of morality is decisive. The destruction of the *moral⟨istic⟩* interpretation of the world that no longer has any *sanction* after it tried to flee into a beyond: ends in nihilism, "everything has no meaning" (the unfeasibility of a single interpretation of the world to which tremendous energy has been dedicated — arouses suspicion as to whether *all* interpretations of the world are not false —) Buddhistic trait, longing for nothingness. (Indian Buddhism does *not* have a fundamental moral development to it, therefore in its case nihilism is only unconquered morality: existence as punishment, existence equated with error, hence error as punishment — a moral valuation) The philosophical attempts to overcome the "moral God" (Hegel, pantheism). Overcoming of the populist ideals: the wise man. The saint. The poet. Antagonism of "true" and "beautiful" and "good" — —
4. Against "meaninglessness" on the one hand, against moral value judgments on the other hand: to what extent all science and philosophy so far have stood under moral judgments? and whether we do not incur the hostility of science in the bargain? Or anti-scientism? Critique of Spinozism. Christian value judgments residual everywhere in the socialist and positivist systems. A *critique of Christian morality* is lacking.
5. the nihilistic consequences of contemporary natural science (alongside its attempts to escape into the beyond). Ultimately a self-disintegration *results* from its activity, a turning against *itself*, an anti-scientism. — Since Copernicus human beings have been rolling out of the center into the x
6. The nihilistic consequences of the political and national-economic way of thinking where all "principles" eventually turn into histrionics: the whiff of mediocrity, wretchedness, insincerity etc. Nationalism, anarchism etc. Punishment. The *redeeming* class and human being are lacking, the justifier —
7. the nihilistic consequences of history and of the "*practical* historians" i.e., the romantics. The position of art: absolute

*un*originality of its position in the modern world. Its dimming. Goethe's alleged Olympian status.

8. Art and the preparation of nihilism: Romanticism (Wagner's Nibelungen *conclusion*.)

2[128][177,178]

I. Fundamental contradiction in civilization and the elevation of the human being. It is the time of the *great noon, of the most terrible* **brightening: my** *kind of pessimism*: — great point of departure.

II. Moral⟨istic⟩ valuations as a history of lying and the art of slander in the service of a will to power (of the *herd*-will) that revolts against the stronger human beings

III. The conditions of all elevations of culture (of the enabling of a *selection* at the expense of a crowd) are the conditions of all growth.

IV. The *ambiguity* of the world as question of *strength*, which observes all things under the *perspective of its growth*. The *moral Christian* value judgments as slave-revolt and slave-mendacity (against the aristocratic values of the *ancient* world)

How far does *art* reach down into the nature of *strength*?

2[129][179]

The
Eternal Recurrence.

Zarathustran Dances and
Processions.
Part One: God's Death Festival.

By
Friedrich Nietzsche.

1. God's death festival.
2. At the great noon.
3. "Where is the hand for this hammer?"
4. We Oath-Takers.

I.

The plague city. He is warned, he is not afraid and goes inside, disguised. All kinds of pessimism parade by. The prophet *interprets* every parade. The mania for the different, the mania for No, finally the mania for nothingness follow one another.

In the end Zarathustra gives the *explanation*: God is dead, this is the *cause* of the greatest danger? what? it could also be the cause of the greatest courage!

II.

The appearance of the friends.

The enjoyment of *the perfect* by those who are going under: People departing.

The accounting of friends.

Processions. The decisive time, the great noon.

The great gratitude- and death-sacrifice to the dead God.

III.

The new task.
The means to the task.
The friends abandon him.

The death of God, for the prophet the most terrible event, is the happiest and most hopeful event for Zarathustra.

Zarathustra dies.

IV. We oath-takers

2[130][180]

The phenomenon "artist" is still the most easily *transparent*: — from there look to the *basic instincts of power*, of nature etc.! Also of religion and morality!

"play," the useless, as the ideal of the one who is bristling with strength, as "childish." The "childishness" of God, παῖς παίζων[181]

2[131][182]

Plan of the first book.

What is dawning is the contrast between the world that we venerate, and the world that we live, that we — are. What remains is to do away either with our venerations or with ourselves. The latter is nihilism.

Preponderance of the north over the south.[183]

1. The nihilism that is approaching, theoretical and practical. Erroneous derivation of the same.
   (Pessimism, its types: preludes of nihilism, even though not necessary.)
2. Christianity perishing from its morality. "God is truth." "God is love" "the just God." — The greatest event — "God is dead" — only dully felt. The German attempt to transform Chr⟨istianity⟩ into a gnosis has broken out into deepest mistrust: what is "untruthful" in it is perceived most strongly (against Schelling e.g.)
3. Morality, henceforth without sanction, does not know how to maintain itself anymore. One finally lets the moral interpretation *drop* — (Emotions everywhere still full of after-notes of the Christian value judgment —)
4. But *value* so far rested on moral judgments, above all the value of philosophy! ("of the will to truth" —)
   the populist ideals "the wise man" "the prophet"[184] "the saint" have lapsed
5. *Nihilistic* trait in the natural sciences. ("meaninglessness" —) Causalism, mechanism. "Conformity to law" an interlude, a residue.
6. Likewise in politics: what is lacking is belief in *one's* rights, innocence, what reigns is telling lies, pandering to the moment
7. Likewise in the national economy: the abolition of slavery: lack of a redeeming class, of a *justifier* — Rise of anarchism. "Education?"
8. Likewise in history: fatalism, Darwinism, the last attempts to interpolate interpretations of reason and divinity fail. Sentimentality for the past; one should not bear biography! — (phenomenalism here too: character as mask, there are no facts)

9. Likewise in art: romanticism and its *backlash* (aversion to romantic ideals and lies) the pure "artists" (indifferent toward content) The latter, moral, as the sense of greater truthfulness, but pessimistic (Father-confessor-psychology and puritan-psychology, two forms of psychological romanticism: but also its backlash, the attempt to position oneself purely artistically in relation to "human beings" — even here the *inverse* valuation is not yet *dared*!)[185]
10. The entire European system of human striving *feels itself* partly "meaningless," partly "immoral." Probability of a new Buddhism. The highest danger. "How do truthfulness, love, justice relate to the *real* world?" Not at all! —

The signs
European nihilism.
Its cause: the devaluation of previous values.

The obscure word "pessimism": people who find themselves to be badly off and people who find themselves to be too well off — both have been p⟨essimists⟩.

Relationship between nihilism, romanticism and positivism (latter a backlash against romanticism, the work of disappointed romantics)

"return to nature": its stations: background of Christian blind confidence (roughly Spinoza already "*deus sive natura*"![186])
Rousseau, science according to romantic idealism

Spinozism extremely influential: 1) Attempt to be satisfied with the world *as it is*

2) happiness and knowledge naïvely posited as *interdependent* (is expression of a will *to* optimism that betrays someone who suffers deeply —)
3) attempt to *get rid of* the moral world order, *in order* to preserve "God," *a world existing prior to* **reason** . . .

"When human beings cease to regard themselves as evil, they cease to be evil —" Good and evil are only interpretations, and by no means facts, no in-itself. One can figure out the origin of this kind of interpretation; one can then make an attempt to slowly free oneself from the ingrained necessity of interpreting morally.

For the second book.

Emergence and *critique* of moral value estimations. The two do *not* coincide, as one casually believes (this belief is already the *result* of a moral valuation "something emerging thus and such is of little value as unmoral in origin")

Standard *according to which* the value of moral value estimations is to be determined: critique of words "improvement, perfection, elevation."

The *overlooked* fundamental fact: contradiction between "becoming more moral" and the elevation and strengthening of the type human being

Homo natura.[187] The "will to power."[188]

For the third book.

The will to power.

How those human beings must be constituted who take this revaluation upon themselves.

Order of rank as power order: war and danger the prerequisite that a rank maintains its conditions. The grandiose model: the human being in nature, the weakest smartest being making itself the master, subjugating the more stupid forces[189]

For the fourth book.

The *greatest* struggle: for it a new *weapon* is needed.

The hammer: to conjure up a terrible decision, to make Europe face the *consequence* of whether its will to destruction "wills"

Staving off mediocritization. Destruction preferable![190]

2[132][191]

(36)

The assumption that at the ground of things moral conditions apply to such an extent that human reason is proved correct — is an ingenuousness and bourgeois assumption, the aftereffect of the belief in divine truthfulness — God thought of as creator of things. — Concepts an inheritance from a pre-existence beyond — —[192]

A tool cannot *critique* its own usefulness: the intellect cannot determine its own borders, nor its having turned out well or turned out badly. —

"Knowing" is a *referring back*: according to its nature a *regressus in infinitum*.[193] What comes to a halt (at an alleged *causa prima*,[194] at an absolute etc.) is *laziness*, exhaustion — —[195]

As well as one may have understood the conditions under which a thing *emerges*, still *therefore* one does not understand at all a thing itself: — this whispered into the ears of our illustrious historians.

2[133][196]

Against wanting to reconcile and peaceableness. This is also where every attempt at monism belongs.

2[134][197]

(39)

The popular and mass effect on the part of artists: Balzac V. Hugo, R. Wagner

2[135]

— *Error veritate simplicior*[198] —

2[136]

— One of those *striking* arguments that strikes the one who applies it —

2[137][199]

Signpost for Thoughts.
Aids
to a Serious Study
of my Writings.

Fundamentals. On the theory of the feeling of power.
On psychological optics.

On the critique of religions
On the *disciplina intellectus.*[200]
What is questionable in the virtues.
In honor of evil.
The problem of the artist.
Politika.[201]

To the logicians.
Against the idealists.
Against the reality-believers.
Of music.
Enlightenment concerning genius.
From the secrets of solitude.
What is Greek?

On the art of living. Modern dimming. Woman and love. Books and human beings. Peoples and "common people."[202]

2[138][203]

Beyond Good and Evil.

Prelude
to a Philosophy of the future.

By
Friedrich Nietzsche

New more comprehensible edition.
Second volume.
With an appendix: *Signpost for Thoughts.*[204]
An Aid to the Serious Study of my Writings.

2[139]

(7)

On "Causalism."

It is plain as day that *neither* can things in themselves stand in a relation of cause and effect to one another, *nor* appearance with appearance: from which arises that the concept "cause and effect" within a philosophy that believes in things in themselves and in appearances is *not applicable*. The errors of Kant — . . . In fact the concept "cause and effect," recalculated psychologically, stems only from a way of thinking that only and everywhere believes will to be acting upon will — that believes only in the living thing and at bottom only in "souls" (and *not* in things). Within the mechanistic worldview (which is logic and its application to space and time) that concept reduces itself to a mathematical formula — with which, as one must underscore again and again, nothing is ever comprehended, but something is indeed represented, *misrepresented*.[205,206]

The immutable sequence of certain phenomena does not prove a "law," but instead a power relationship between 2 or more forces. To say: "but precisely this relationship stays the same!" means nothing other than: "one and the same force cannot also be another force." —What is at stake is not a *succession* — but an *interpenetration*, a process in which the individual successive moments do *not* condition one another as causes and effects . . .

The separation of the "doing" from the "doer," the event from a ⟨something⟩ that *makes* the event, the process from a something that is not process but enduring, substance, thing, body, soul etc. — the attempt to comprehend events as a kind of shifting and place-changing of "what is," of what remains: this old mythology established the belief in "cause and effect" after it had found a solid form in ling⟨uistic⟩ grammat⟨ical⟩ functions. —[207]

2[140][208]

Against the two claims "the same can only be known by the same" and "the same can only be known by the unsame" — about which already in antiquity there had been a centuries-long battle — today we can object, from the point of view of a more rigorous and more cautious concept of knowing: *there can be no knowing at all* — and this precisely because the same cannot know the same, just as little as the same can be known by the unsame. —

2[141]

These divisions of doing and doer, of doing and suffering, of being and becoming, of cause and of effect

even the belief in changes posits in advance the belief in *something that* "is changed."

Reason is the philosophy of *appearance*

2[142][209,210]

(30)

the "regularity" of succession is only a symbolic expression, *as if* here a rule were being followed: no fact. Likewise "conformity to law." We find a formula in order to express an ever-recurring kind of result: in doing so we have *not discovered a "law,"* still less a force that is the cause of the recurrence of results. That something *always* happens thus and ⟨such⟩ is interpreted here as if a being always acted thus and such as a result of obedience to a law or a law giver: whereas, aside from the "law," it would have the freedom to act differently. But precisely that thus-and-not-otherwise could stem from the being itself, that did *not* behave thus and such only with regard to a law, but as constituted thus and such. This means only: something cannot also be something else, cannot do now this now that, is neither free nor unfree, but precisely thus and such. *The error lies in the fictional insertion of a subject*

2[143][211]

Supposing the world possessed a single quantum of force, then it is plain that every power-shift in any place would condition the whole system — therefore along with the causality *succeeding one another* would be a dependence *next to and with one another.*

2[144][212,213]

(40)

Supposing even that a counter-proof to the Christian faith could not be produced, Pascal considered it prudent in the highest sense to be a Christian given the *fearful* possibility that it could nevertheless be true. Today as a sign of how much Christianity has lost in terms of fearfulness, one finds those othe⟨r⟩ attempts at its justification, namely that even if it were an error one would still have the great advantage and pleasure of this error one's whole life long: it seems therefore that this faith should be maintained precisely for the sake of its *calming* effects — hence not out of fear of a threatening possibility, but rather out of fear of a life that loses its charm. This hedonistic turn, proof derived from *pleasure*, is a symptom of decline: it replaces proof derived from *strength*, from that which is devastating in the Christian idea, from *fear*. In fact in this reinterpretation Christianity approaches exhaustion: one makes do with an *opiatic* Christianity, because one has neither the strength to want to search, to fight, to dare, to stand alone nor for Pascalism, for dee⟨p⟩ brooding self-contempt, for faith in human unworthiness, for the anxiety of the "possibly-damned." But a Christianity that above all is supposed to calm sick nerves has *no need* at all of that fearful solution of a "God on the cross": which is why everywhere in Europe Buddhism is silently making progress.

2[145][214]

The interpretation of an event as *either* doing *or* suffering — therefore every doing a suffering — says: every single change, a becoming different presupposes an author and someone *on whom* "change" is made.

2[146]

A perfect analogy can be drawn between the simplifying and compressing of countless experiences to general principles *and* the becoming of the sperm cell that bears within it the entire abbreviated past: and likewise in the artistic forming from fertile basic thoughts up to a "system" *and* the becoming of an organism as a thinking-out and thinking-forth, as a *remembering-back* of an entire previous life, of realizing-back, incorporation.

In brief: *visible* organic life and *invisible* creative psychic controlling and thinking contain a parallelism: in the "art-work" one can demonstrate these two sides most clearly as parallel. — The extent to which thinking, inferring and everything logical can be seen as *exterior*: as symptom of much more inward and more basic events?

2[147][215,216]

(30)

"end" and "means"	as interpretation	(*not* as facts)
"cause and effect"	as interpretation	all in the sense of a
"subject and object"	as interpretation	will to power
"doing and suffering"		

("thing in itself" and "appearance") as interpretation and to what extent perhaps *necessary* interpretations? (as "preserving")

2[148][217]

The will to power *interprets*: *in the formation of an organ interpretation is at stake*; it demarcates, determines degrees, power differentials. Mere power differentials could not perceive themselves as such: a growth-willing something must be there, that interprets every other growth-willing something in terms of its value. *In this* similar — — In truth *interpretation is a means itself of becoming master over something.* (*The organic process presupposes constant* **interpreting**.

2[149][218]

A "thing in itself" just as wrong as a "meaning in itself," "a significance in itself." There are no "facts in themselves," *rather a meaning must always be inserted first, so that there can be "facts"*

The "what is that?" is a *positing-of-meaning* from the point of view of something else. "*Essence*," "*essentiality*" is something perspectival and already presupposes a multiplicity. What underlies here is always "what is that for *me*?" (for us, for everything that lives etc.)

A thing would be described only when all beings had asked and received an answer to their "what is that?" about it. Suppose a single being with its own relations and perspectives to all things were missing: and the thing would still not be "defined."

2[150][219]

In brief, the essence of a thing is also only an *opinion* of the "thing." Or rather: the concept "*that counts as*" is the real "*that is*," the only "that is."

2[151][220]

One is not allowed to ask "then *who* is interpreting?" rather interpretation itself, as a form of the will to power, has existence (but not as a "being," but instead as a *process*, a *becoming*) as an affect.

2[152][221]

The emergence of "things" is entirely the work of the representing, thinking, willing, inventing ones. The concept "thing" itself just as well as all properties. — Even "the subject" is such a creation, a "thing," like all others: a simplification in order to describe the *force* that posits, invents, thinks as such, in contrast to all individual positing, inventing, thinking itself. Therefore the *capacity* described in contrast to all that is individual: at bottom activity summarized with respect to all expected activity (activity and the probability of similar activity)

2[153][222]

NB. From the world known to us the humanitarian God cannot be *proven*: today you can be compelled and driven this far — but what conclusion do you draw from this? Either he is not provable to *us*: skepticism of knowledge. But all of you *fear* the conclusion: "from the world known to us an entirely different god would be *provable*, one who at least is *not* humanitarian" — — and, that means, i.e., you hold on tightly to your God and invent for him a world that is *not known to us*.

2[154][223]

(36)

Against the scientific prejudice. —

The greatest fable is the one about knowledge. One wants to know how the *things in themselves* are constituted: but behold, there are no things in themselves! But supposing even that there were an in-itself, an unconditioned, then precisely for that reason it *could not be known*! Something unconditioned cannot be known: otherwise it would precisely *not* be unconditioned! But knowing is always "positing-oneself-in-condition-to-something" — — ; such a "knowing one" desires that what he wants to know does not concern him; and that this same thing should not concern anyone at all; whereby first a contradiction occurs, in *wanting*-to-know and in the demand that it should not concern him (why then know at all!) and second, because something that does not concern anyone does not at all *exist*, therefore also cannot be known. — Knowing means "to posit oneself in condition to something": to feel oneself conditioned by something and between us — — it is therefore in any case a *determining describing making conscious of conditions* (**not** a *fathoming* of essences, things, "in-themselves") [224]

2[155][225,226]

Deep aversion to resting once and for all in some overall-view of the world; magic of the opposing ways of thinking; not letting oneself be deprived of the charm of the enigmatic character.

2[156]

For the chapter "*artists*" (as molders, value-assigners, appropriators)

Our languages as after-notes of the *oldest appropriations of things*, by rulers and thinkers alike — — : running alongside every coined word was the command "thus *shall* the thing be named from now on!"

2[157][227]

Shouldn't all *quantities* be signs of *qualities*? The greater power corresponds to a different consciousness, feeling, desire, to a different perspectival gaze; growth itself is a desire *to be more*; out of a *quale*[228] grows a desire for a more of quantum; in a purely quantitative world everything would be dead, rigid, unmoved. — The reduction of all qualities to quantities is nonsense: what results is that one and the other stand together, an analogy —

2[158][229]

Psychological history of the concept "subject." The body, the thing, the "whole" constructed by the eye trigger the differentiation of a doing from a doer; the doer, the cause of the doing, ever more subtly comprehended, in the end left the "subject" behind.

2[159][230]

Has a force ever been demonstrated? No, instead effects, translated into a completely foreign language. But the regularity of succession has spoiled us so much that we *are not surprised by its oddness*[231]

2[160]

Today, when what matters is to give this book, which lies open, but nevertheless demands its key, an entrance a preface, it should be the first to say why I *feared* a preface back then.

2[161][232,233]

(41)

For the *Preface*.

Deeply mistrustful of epistemological dogmas, ⟨I⟩ loved to look out of now this, now that window, I was wary of committing ⟨myself⟩ to them, regarded them as harmful — and ultimately: is it probable that a tool *can* criticize its own suitability?? — What I paid attention to instead was that never has an epistemological skepticism or dogma arisen without ulterior motives — that it has a second rank value as soon as one considers *what* at bottom *forced* one to this position: even the very will to certainty, when it is not the will "I only want to live" — — — Basic insight: Kant as well as Hegel as well as Schopenhauer — the skeptical-epochal position as well as the historical and the pessimistic are *of moral* origin. I saw no one who would have dared a *critique of moral value feelings*: and I soon turned my back on the meager attempts to arrive at a history of the emergence of these feelings (as among the English and German Darwinists). — How does one explain Spinoza's position, his renunciation and rejection of moral value judgments? (Was it *one* consequence of a theodicy?)

2[162][234]

One notices in my earlier writings a good will to unlocked horizons, a certain prudent caution before convictions, a mistrust of the enchantments and dupings of conscience that accompany every strong belief; one might see in this in part the wariness of the burned child, of the deceived idealist — more essential to me seems the Epicurean instinct (of a friend of riddles —) who does not want to permit himself to take cheaply the enigmatic character of things, most essential finally an aesthetic aversion toward the big virtuous unconditional words, a taste that defends itself against all quadrangular opposites, *desires* a good portion of uncertainty in things and takes away the opposites: — as a friend of intermediary colors, shadows, afternoon lights and infinite seas.

2[163]

Customary errors of moral-historians:

1. they show that among different peoples there are different moral valuations and conclude from this that they are non-binding generally. — Or they assert some arbitrary consensus of peoples, at least of the civilized, in certain matters of morality and conclude from it that it is binding for us! Both are equally naïve.

2. they criticize the opinions of a people concerning its morality (concerning the morality's descent, sanction, reasonableness etc.) and believe they have criticized a morality itself, which has been overgrown with the weeds of this unreason.

3. they themselves stand under the rule of a morality without knowing it and at bottom do nothing more than assure the triumph of their belief in it: — their grounds only prove their own will that this and that be believed, that this and that should be absolutely true.

There isn't much to the moral-historians so far: they themselves usually stand under the command of a morality and at bottom do nothing more than generate its propaganda. Their usual error is that they criticize the foolish opinions of a people concerning its morality (also concerning its descent, sanction, reasonableness) and believe that precisely in doing so they have criticized the morality itself, which has been overgrown with the weeds of this unreason. But the value of a rule "thou shalt" is independent of the opinion people have of it, just as certainly as the value of a medication is independent of whether I think scientifically or like an old woman about medicine

Or on the other hand they assert some arbitrary consensus of peoples, at least of the tamed peoples concerning certain matters of morality and conclude from this its absolute binding nature, even for you and me: which are both equally big naïvetés —

2[164][235]

A spirit strengthened by wars and victories, for whom conquest, adventure, danger, pain have even become a requirement; a habit of sharp high air, of winter wanderings, of ice and mountains in every sense; a kind of sublime malice and final mischief of revenge, for there is revenge in it, revenge on life itself when someone who suffers greatly takes life under his protection. This book, which might need not only one preface, is difficult to understand for many reasons, not due to a lack of skill of its author, even less due to his bad will, but ⟨due to⟩ the final mischief of someone who suffers greatly, who constantly makes fun of an ideal believed in by the people, whom he perhaps has reached in this condition.

— And perhaps I have a right to have my say about these conditions, because I have not merely watched them.

I have no doubt: at that time what I lived beyond, with an ironic self-superiority, was the condition of the *wise man* as the people imagine him: the gentle infertility and self-satisfaction of the wise man as the people imagine him, the remoteness and beyond of the "pure-knowing one," the whole sublime onanism of a spirit who has lost the good will to deeds, to begetting, to creating in every sense. Who shares with me in feeling the wondrous happiness of that period in which this book emerged! The sublime malice of a soul who — — —

My taste of today takes pleasure in something else: the human being of great love and of great contempt, who is driven out of all "remoteness" and "beyond" straight into the world by his overflowing strength, who is forced by solitude to create beings for himself who are like him — a human being with the will to a terrible responsibility, forged to his problem

What is perhaps most difficult to understand in this difficult to understand book, which needs not only one preface, is the irony of the contrast between its theme, a disintegration and unwinding of moral values — and its tone, that of the highest mildest wisest serenity, in which the greatly suffering one, the one who turns away from life delights as in his final mischief.

2[165][236]

(41)

For the *Preface* of "*Dawn*"

An attempt to think about morality without standing under its spell, mistrustful of being duped by its beautiful gestures and glances

A world that we can revere, that corresponds to our worshipping drive — that continuously *proves* itself — through guidance of the particular and the universal — : this the Christian viewpoint from which we all stem.

Through a growth in acuity, mistrust, scientism (also through a more highly cultivated instinct of truthfulness, therefore again under Christian influences) *this* interpretation has become increasingly *disallowed* to us.

Most subtle way out: Kantian criticism. The intellect disputed its own right to interpretation in this sense as well as to *rejection* of interpretation in this sense. One satisfied oneself with filling the gap with a *more* of trust and faith, with a sacrificing of all verifiability of one's faith, with an incomprehensible and superior "ideal" (God).

The Hegelian way out, following Plato, a piece of Romanticism and reaction, simultaneously the symptom of the historical sense, of a new *force*: the "spirit" itself is the self-disclosing and self-realizing ideal, in "process," in "becoming" an ever more of this ideal reveals itself, in which we believe — therefore the ideal realizes itself, faith directs itself toward the *future*, in which it can worship according to its noble requirements. In brief,

1) God is unknowable and unverifiable to *us* — deeper meaning of the epistemological movement

2) God is verifiable, but as something becoming, and we belong to it, precisely with our push for what is ideal — deeper meaning of the historicizing movement

But the same historical sense, transferring over to natural history, has — — —

It is obvious: the critique is *never* shifted to the ideal itself, but only to the problem where its opposition comes from, why it has not yet been reached or why it is not verifiable in matters small and great.

The ideal of the *wise man* to what extent fundamentally moralistic so far? — — —

It makes the biggest difference: whether one feels this distress as distress as a result of passion, as a result of craving or whether one barely reaches it as problem using the pinnacle of thought and a certain strength of historical imagination . . .

Apart from religious-philosophical observation we find the same phenomenon: utilitarianism (socialism, democratism) criticizes the descent of moral valuations, *but it believes in them*, just like the Christian. (Naïveté, as if morality would remain if the sanctioning *God* were missing. The "beyond" absolutely essential if the belief in morality is to be maintained.)

Basic problem: where does this omnipotence of *faith* come from? *Of faith in morality*?

(— which also betrays itself in the fact that even the basic conditions of life are falsely interpreted in favor of morality: despite knowledge of the animal world and the plant world.

"self-preservation," Darwinistic perspective on reconciliation of altruistic and egoistic principles.[237]

(critique of egoism, e.g., Larochefoucauld)

My attempt to understand moral judgments as symptoms and sign languages in which processes of physiological flourishing or failing, likewise the consciousness of preservation- and growth-conditions are betrayed: a manner of interpretation with the value of astrology. Prejudices prompted by instincts (of races, communities, of different stages like youth or dotage etc.)

Applied to the specifically Christian-European morality: our moral judgments are signs of decline, of unbelief in *life*, a preparation of pessimism.

What does it mean that we have interpreted a *contradiction* into existence? — Decisive importance: behind all other valuations those moral valuations stand commanding. Supposing they fall away, by what do we measure then? And then what is the value of knowledge etc. etc.???

My main proposition: there are no moral phenomena, but only a moral⟨istic⟩ interpretation of these phenomena. This interpretation itself is of extra-moral origin.[238]

2[166][239]

Preface to the "Joyful Science"

A diversion before a great undertaking for which one now finally feels strength returning to himself: as Buddha devoted himself for 10 days to world⟨ly⟩ pleasures when he had found his main proposition.

General mockery of all moralizing of today. Preparation for *Zarathustra's naïve-ironic position on all holy things* (naïve *form of superiority*: **playing** *with the holy*)

(42)

Concerning the misunderstanding of "cheerfulness." Temporary redemption from protracted tension, the exuberance, the saturnalia of a spirit who consecrates and prepares himself for protracted and terrible resolutions. *The "fool" in the form of "science."*[240]

This book requires perhaps not only one preface: people have understood nothing at all about its "joyful science." Even about the title — — —

People have understood nothing at all about this "joyful science"; not even its title, about whose Provençal meaning at least many scholars — — —

The triumphant condition from which this book emerged is hard to comprehend — but I myself had emerged from a condition.

the consciousness of aversion to everything that lay behind me, paired with a sublime will to gratitude even for my "behind me," which was not too distant from the feeling of the right to a long revenge

a piece of gray ice-cold senility switched on at the most unjust point of life, the tyranny of pain outdone by the tyranny of pride that rejects the *consequences* of pain, solitude as self-defense against a pathologically clairvoyant misanthropy and therefore still loved and enjoyed as redemption, on the other hand a longing for what is most bitter sour and harmful in knowledge

It belongs to the things that I will not forget that people congratulated me on this book more honestly than on any other, they even let me know how healthy such a way of thinking was

Nothing offends as deeply as letting people notice the height and severity of one's own demands on oneself.

Nothing offends as deeply, nothing sets people apart so thoroughly as letting people notice something of the height a⟨nd⟩ severity with which one treats oneself: oh how accommodating and lovely everyone shows themselves to be toward us as soon as we do as everyone does and "let ourselves go" as everyone does!

It belongs to the things that I will not forget that people expressed more congratulations to me for this book of the "*gai saber*" than for all the others put together: suddenly they were reconciled with me, they showed themselves to be accommodating and lovely once more, everyone saw in it a recovery, return, homecoming, soul-searching — namely as a return to "everyone."

Aside from a few scholars whose vanity took offense at the word "science" (— they let me know, Perhaps this is "joyful" but certainly not "science" —) everyone took this book as a return to "everyone" and for its sake showed themselves to be accommodating and lovely toward me: and I figured out after the fact how nothing offends most deeply, and most thoroughly against us — — —

NB Perhaps we could also lend an ear in conclusion to a few exuberant songs in which a poet makes fun of the poets and their beautiful lyrical feelings.
NB!! Zarathustra, who in a holy manner counters all holy things with courage and mockery and goes his way with innocence to the most forbidden, evil things — — —

2[167]

Denial of causality. In order not to make everything responsible for anything and to hold *short* the thread on which something hangs. "Chance" really exists.

2[168][241]

Tendency of moral evolution. Everyone desires that no other theory and estimation of things should gain validity except for the one from which he himself benefits. *Basic tendency consequently of the weak and the mediocre of all times to make the strong weaker, to pull them down: chief means the* **moral judgment**. The behavior of the stronger toward the weaker is stigmatized; the higher conditions of the strong get bad labels.

The struggle of the many against the few, of the ordinary against the rare, of the weak against the strong

— one of its most subtle interruptions is that the chosen refined more demanding presented themselves as the weak and rejected the cruder means of power —

2[169][242,243]

(34)

It could appear as if I had evaded the question of certainty. The opposite is true: but while I asked about the criterion of certainty I tested to determine in the first place according to which scales things have been weighed so far — and whether the question of certainty itself were not already a *dependent* question, a question of the *second* rank.

2[170][244,245]

(44)

What is lacking is the knowledge and consciousness of which turn-arounds moral judgment has already gone through, and how actually several times already in the most fundamental sense "evil" has been rebaptized "good." To one of these shifts I have with the antithesis "morality of customs" and — — —

Conscience has also switched spheres: there used to be a sting of conscience of the herd

To what extent even our conscience, with its apparent personal responsibility is in fact still herd-conscience.

2[171][246]

(43)

The *sting of conscience* like all *ressentiments* is missing in a great fullness of strength. (Mirabeau, B. Cellini, Cardanus).

2[172][247]

"Being" — we have no other idea of it than "*living*." — Therefore how can something dead "be"?

2[173]

On *l'art pour l'art* cf. Doudan *Penseés*[248] p. 10 how the cult of colors depraves

Scherer VIII[249] p. 292.

2[174][250]

One rediscovers in things nothing other than what one previously oneself put into them: this childish game, of which I do not wish to think poorly, calls itself "science"? On the contrary: let us continue with both, both require our good cheer — some of us to rediscover, the others — *we* others! — to put things in!

— ultimately a human being rediscovers in things nothing other than what he himself put into them: rediscovery calls itself science, putting things in — art, religion, love, pride. In both, even if they should be childish games, — — —

2[175][251,252,253]

(45)

NB. *Against* the theory of the influence of *milieu* and of external causes: the inner force is infinitely *superior*; much that looks like influence from without is only its adaptation from the inside out. The very same *milieu*'s can be oppositely interpreted and exploited: there are no facts. — A genius is *not* explained from such conditions of origin —

2[176]

What constitutes the *strong* human being of the 20th century: —

2[177][254]

(46)

Populist ideals e.g., Francis of Assisi: denial of the soul hierarchy, before God all equal.

2[178][255]

It does good to take "right" and "wrong" etc. in a certain narrow bourgeois sense, like "do right and fear no one": i.e., to do one's duty according to a certain crude scheme within which a community exists.

2[179][256]

Preface

Proceeding from an idea of life (that is not a wanting-to-preserve-oneself but a wanting-*to-grow*) I took a glance at the basic instinct of our political intellectual social movement of Europe.

On what have I possibly contributed ideas?

1) that behind the most fundamental differences of philosophies stands a certain equality of confession: the unconscious guidance by *moral ulterior intentions*, better: *by popular ideals*; — that consequently the moral problem is more radical than the epistemological

2) that at some time a reversed look is necessary in order to bring into the light the *prejudice of morality* and of all popular ideals: for which every kind of "free spirit" — i.e., immoral ones — can be used.

3) that Christianity, as a plebian ideal, aims with its morality at damaging the stronger more highly constituted manly types and favors a herdlike human being: that its morality is a precursor of the democratic way of thinking

4) that science goes forward in league with the equality movement, is democracy, that all virtues of the scholar reject *order of rank*

5) that democratic Europe is heading only for a sublime cultivation of slavery, that must be commanded by a strong race in order to tolerate itself

6) that an aristocracy only emerges under harsh prolonged pressure (mastery over the earth)

2[180][257]

Perhaps there are a couple of human beings in Europe, even in Germany, who are able to reach the problem of this book, and not only with their curiosity, not only with the feelers of a pampered intellect, of their divining power of imagination and imitation, even of their "historical sense," but instead with the passion of the abstinent: whose soul has enough elevation to understand my conception of the "free spirit" as a means of expression, as a subtlety, if you will, as a modesty: they will not complain about my obscurity.

There are many things against which I have not found it necessary to speak out: it goes without saying that the "literary man" is repugnant to me, that all political parties of today are repugnant to me, that a socialist is treated not only with pity by me. The two noblest forms of human being whom I encountered in the flesh ⟨were⟩ the perfect Christian — I count it an honor to stem from a family that took its Christianity seriously in every sense — and the perfect artist of the romantic ideal, which I found to be deep below the Christian level: it is plain as day that when one has turned his back on *these* forms, because they do not satisfy, then one does not easily find satisfaction in another kind of human being of today — to this extent I am condemned to solitude, even though I can very well imagine a kind of human being in whom I would have pleasure. My patient and lenient disgust with the self-sufficiency of our metropolises, which adorn themselves with culture, of our scholars — — —

2[181][258]

(42)

The irony of Plato, with which an overly large tenderness of feelings and of the senses, a vulnerability of the heart knew how to protect itself, at least to conceal itself, that Olympian nature of Goethe, who composed verses about his sufferings in order to be rid of them, likewise Stendhal, Mérimée[259] —

2[182][260,261]

(10)

In order for something to last that is longer than the individual, therefore in order for a *work* to last that perhaps an individual has created: for this all possible kinds of limitation, of onesidedness etc. must be imposed on the individual. By what means? Love honor gratitude toward the person who created the work are a help: or that our forefathers fought for it: or that my descendants are only guaranteed if I guarantee that *work* (e.g., the πόλις[262]). *Morality* is essentially the means to bring something to duration over and beyond individuals, or rather by an *enslavement* of individuals. It is self-evident that the perspective from below to above will yield entirely different expressions than the one from above to below.

A power-complex: how is it *preserved*? By the fact that many generations sacrifice themselves to it, i.e., — — —

2[183][263]

For the *Introduction*

For anyone who has lived together with a big question mark as if with his destiny and whose days and nights were consumed by purely solitary dialogues and decisions, the opinions of strangers about the same problem are a kind of noise against which he defends himself and covers his ears: moreover, something obtrusive inappropriate and shameless so to speak, on the part of those who, as he believes, have no right to such a problem: because they did not find it. They are the hours of mistrust toward himself, of mistrust toward his own right and prerogative where the hermit-like loving one — for that is a philosopher — demands to hear everything that is said and not said about his problem; perhaps in doing so he divines that the world is full of jealous loving ones like him, and that everything loud, clamorous, public, the whole foreground of politics, routine, annual fair, "time" seems to be invented only so that everything that is hermit and philosopher in us today can hide behind it — as in *its* ownmost solitude; all occupied with one thing, in love with one thing, jealous of one thing, precisely of *his* problem. "There is nothing else at all being thought today where thinking even gets done" — he finally says to himself; "everything turns on this question mark; what seemed reserved for me is being wooed by the entire age: at bottom nothing else is happening at all; I myself — but what do I matter!"

2[184][264]

(47)

I come late to the awareness of how far moralistic skepticism has gone: how do I recognize myself?

Determinism: we are not responsible for our natures

Phenomenalism: we know nothing about a "thing in itself"

My problem: What damage so far has humankind had from morals as well as from its morality? Damage to the spirit etc.[265]

my disgust with the wise man as a spectator

my higher concept "artist"

2[185][266]

(47)

"*We Immoralists*"

real critique of the moral ideal

— of the good human being, of the saint, of the wise man
— of the slandering of so-called *evil* properties
— what meaning do the different moral interpretations have?
— what is the danger of the interpretation that is dominant in Europe now?
— what is the standard according to which measuring can be done? ("will to power")

2[186]

Do not believe that I will challenge you to the same risk! Or even to the same solitude. For whoever goes his own way encounters no one: "one's own ways" are like that. No one comes to "help" him in this, and he must deal himself with everything that buffets him by way of danger, chance, malice and bad weather. He happens to have his way *for himself*, and also his occasional annoyance with his harsh inexorable "for himself": to which it belongs for instance that even his good friends do not always see and know where he really goes, where he really wants to go — and at times ask themselves: what? is he going at all? does he have — a *way*? . . .

— Insofar as I am here making an attempt to give a hint about the way I have come to those who so far have remained sympathetic to me — despite everything — it behooves me to reveal first the paths on which people have occasionally searched and even believed to have found me. People have a tendency to mistake me: I admit it; likewise that it would be of great service to me if someone else were to defend and define me against these mistakings. But, as I said, I must come to my own aid: why does one go "one's own way"?

antimetaphysical, antiromantic, artistic, pessimistic, skeptical, historical

An artistic world view an antimetaphysical — yes, but an artistic one —[267]
a pessimistic-Buddhistic —
a skeptical —
a scientific — *not* posit⟨ivistic⟩

2[187]

— *placatumque nitet diffuso lumine coelum*[268] —

2[188][269]

that the history ⟨of⟩ all ph⟨enomena⟩ of morality could be simplified to the extent that Schopenhauer believed — namely such that compassion is to be discovered as the root of every moral⟨alistic⟩ impulse so far — this degree of absurdity and naïveté could be achieved only by a thinker who was bereft of all historical instinct and had eluded in the most astonishing manner even that strong schooling in history that the Germans from Herder to Hegel had undergone.

2[189][270]

The inquiry into the descent of our valuations and tablets of good does not in the least coincide with their criticism, as is so often believed: even though the insight into some *pudenda origo*[271] brings with it for our emotions a decline in value of whatever thing originated thus and prepares a critical mood and attitude toward the same.

2[190][272,273]

(47)

what are our valuations and even our moral tablets worth? *What comes out of their rule*? For whom? With respect to what? — Answer: for life. But *what is life*? Here then a new more definite version of the concept "life" is needed: my formula for it is: life is will to power.

what does valuating mean in itself? does it point back or down to another metaphysical world? As Kant still believed (who is prior to the great historical movement) In sum: *where did it emerge*? Or did it not "emerge"? Answer: moral valuating is an *interpretation*,[274] a way of interpreting.[275] The interpretation itself is a *symptom* of certain physiological conditions, likewise of a certain spiritual level of ruling judgments. *Who interprets*? — Our affects.

2[191]

My assertion: that one must subject moral valuations themselves to a critique. That one must call a halt to the moral emotional impulse with the question: why? That this demand for a "Why?", for a critique or morals, is precisely our *current form of morality itself*, as a sublime sense of honesty. That our honesty, our will not to deceive *ourselves* must prove itself: "why *not*?" — In what forum? The will not ⟨to⟩ allow oneself to be deceived is of different origin, a caution against being overpowered, exploitation, a self-defense instinct of life.

These are *my* demands of you — they may sound harsh enough to your ears —: that you should subject moral valuations themselves to a critique. That you should call a halt to the moral emotional impulse that here demands submission and *not* criticism with the question: "why submission?" That you should regard this demand for a "Why?", for a critique of morality, precisely as your *current* form of morality itself, as the most sublime kind of righteousness, which does honor to you and your age.[276]

2[192]

the feeling: thou shalt!, one's disquiet in being violated — question: "who is giving orders here? Whose disfavor do we fear here?"

2[193][277,278]

(7)

Our bad habit of taking a mnemonic device, an abbreviating formula as essence, finally as *cause* e.g., to say of lightning: "it flashes." Or even the little word "I." To posit a kind of perspective in seeing again as the *cause of seeing itself*: that was the trick in the invention of the 'subject," of the "I"!

2[194][279,280]

Stendhal: "*Combien de lieues ne ferais-je pas à pied, et à combien de jours de prison ne me soumettrais-je pas pour entendre* Don Juan *ou le Matrimonio segreto: et je ne sais pour quelle autre chose je ferais cet effort.*"[281] At the time he was 56 years old.

2[195][282,283]

(41)

Hegel: his popular side the theory of war and of great men. Right is with the victor: he represents the progress of humankind.

Attempt to prove the rule of morality using history.

Kant: detached from us, invisible, real, a realm of moral values

Hegel: a verifiable development, the becoming-visible of the moral realm

We do not want to be deceived either in the Kantian or the Hegelian manner: — we no longer *believe*, like them, in morality, and consequently nor do we have any philosophies to found *so that* morality remains justified. Criticism as well as historicism do not have their charm for us *in this* — well, what charm then do they have?

2[196]

We homeless ones — yes! But we want to exploit the *advantages* of our situation and, far from perishing of it, let ourselves benefit from the open air and powerful fullness of light.

2[197]

Nonbelievers and godless ones, yes! — but without that bitterness and passion of one who tears himself away and fabricates a faith, a purpose, often a martyrdom from his non-faith: we have simmered and grown cold in the realization that in the world things are absolutely not divine, indeed they are not even compatible with a rational, merciful, humane standard; we know it, the world in which we live is immoral, undivine, inhuman — for far too long we have interpreted it in the sense of our reverence. The world is not worth that which we have believed: and the last thread of solace that was spun by Schopenhauer we have ourselves torn: that precisely this is the meaning of the whole of history, that it figures out its own meaninglessness and grows sick of itself. This growing-sick-of-existence, this will to no-longer-willing, this shattering of our personal will, our personal well-being, self⟨lessness⟩ (as an expression of this inverted willing) — this and nothing else Schopenhauer wanted to see honored with the higher honors: he called it morality, he decreed that all selfless action — — — he believed he ensured the value even of art by interpreting the indifferent states that it creates as preparations for that total detachment and satiety of disgust.

— but would we really be *pessimists* with respect to the sight of an immoral world? No, because we do not believe in morality — — we believe that mercy, right, compassion a⟨nd⟩ lawfulness are by far *overvalued*, that their opposite has been slandered, that in both, in exaggeration and slander, in the entire application of the *moral*⟨istic⟩ *ideal* and standard there has been a tremendous danger for humans. Nor should we forget the good byproduct: the *raffinement*[284] of *interpretation*, of moral⟨istic⟩ vivisection, the sting of conscience has elevated the *falseness* of humans in the extreme and made them intelligent.

In itself a religion has nothing to do with morality: but the two descendants of the Jewish r⟨eligion⟩ are both *essentially* moral religions, those that issue precepts about how people *should* live and create an audience for their demands by means of reward and punishments.[285]

2[198]

the era of Bismarck (the era of German dumbing-down)

in such swampy terrain thrive, as is only fair, also the genuine swamp plants, e.g., the a⟨nti-Semite⟩

2[199]

— to be nationalistic in the sense and to the degree that is now demanded by public opinion, would seem to me, to us more spiritual humans, to be not only a matter of bad taste: but a dishonesty, an arbitrary anesthetizing of our better science and conscience

2[200]

Likewise we are no longer Christians: we have grown apart from Christianity, not because we lived too distant from it, but because we lived too close to it, even more because we grew *out* of it — it is our stricter and more pampered piety itself that *forbids* us today from still being Christians —

2[201]

When I once wrote the word "unfashionable" on my books, how much youth, inexperience, isolation expresses itself in this word! Today I comprehend that with this kind of lament enthusiasm and dissatisfaction I actually belonged to the most modern of moderns.

2[202][286]

Kant: the mere idea of a possible science that one seeks to nourish in many different ways, up to the point where the single footpath, quite overgrown with sensuality, is removed" —

2[203][287]

And even today the philosophers unknowingly give the strongest evidence for how far this authority of morality reaches. With all their will to independence, with their habits or principles of doubt, even with their vice of contradiction, of innovation at any cost, of haughtiness of every height — what becomes of them as soon as they reflect on "thou shalt" and "thou shalt not"? Immediately there is nothing more modest on earth: the Circe morality just breathed on them and enchanted them! All these proud and solitary wanderers! — Now all at once they are lambs, now they want to be the herd. At first the whole lot of them wants to have their "thou shalt" and "thou shalt not" in common with everyone — first sign of abandoned independence. And what is their criterion of a moral precept? They are all of one mind: their universal validity, their focus away from the person. This I call "herd." Thereupon, of course, they part ways: for each one wants to be of service to m⟨orality⟩ with *his* best energy. Most of them resort to "grounding morality," as they say, namely wedding and uniting it to reason, if possible to the point of unity; the more subtle ones on the contrary find the token and prerogative of their rank, their rank that is superior to reason, in the ungroundability of morality; others will want to deduce it historically (perhaps with the Darwinists, who invented the home remedy for bad historians, "first utility and compulsion, then habit, finally instinct, even pleasure"), still others refute these deductions and deny in general any historical deductability of morality, and this likewise to the honor of their rank, their high species and calling: but all are of one mind in the main thing "morality is here, morality is given!", they all believe, honestly, unconsciously, unfailingly in the value of that which they call morality, that is, they stand under its authority. Yes! The *value* of morality! Is it permissible that here someone speaks up who has doubts about precisely this value? And is also concerned only in this respect about its deduction, deductability, psychological possibility and impossibility?

2[204][288]

Book Five. We Contrarians.

Our new "freedom"
Against the popular ideal human beings
How far do art and falsity go into the essence of being?
Why we are no longer Christians.
Why we are antinationalistic.
Pessimism and Dionysianism.
Our mistrust of logic
l'art pour l'art[289]
The limitedness of all teleology.
Against the causality-fatalism.
Against the theory of milieu: mask and character. On the concept "phenomenalism."
Against romanticism.
Concept of slavery i.e., of making into tools
Misunderstanding of cheerfulness.[290]
What the order of rank does.
Critique of modern philosophy: erroneous point of departure, as if "facts of consciousness" existed — and no phenomenalism in introspection[291]

2[205][292]

There is no egoism at all that stays within itself and does not overreach — consequently that "permissible," "morally indifferent" e⟨goism⟩ of which you speak does not exist at all.

One promotes one's ego constantly at "the expense of another"; life always lives at the expense of other life. — Whoever does not comprehend this has not yet taken the first personal step toward honesty.

2[206][293,294]

(48)

What a feeling of freedom there is in perceiving as we freed spirits perceive, that we are *not* harnessed into a system of "purposes"! Likewise that the concepts "reward" and "punishment" do not reside in the essence of existence! Likewise, that the good and the evil deed are called good and evil not in themselves, but only under the perspective of the preservation tendencies of certain kinds of human communities! Likewise that our accounts of pleasure and pain have no cosmic, let alone a metaphysical meaning! — That pessimism that opts to put the pleasure and displeasure of existence itself on the scales, with its arbitrary imprisonment in the pre-Copernican prison and field of vision, would ⟨be⟩ something backwards and back-sliding, if it were not merely a bad joke of a Berliner (the p⟨essimism⟩ of E⟨duard⟩ von Hartmann

2[207][295,296]

Beginning

Conclusion.

To what extent this self-annihilation of morality is still a part of its own force. We Europeans have in us the blood of those who have died for their faith; we have taken morality as terrible and serious and there is nothing that we have not at some time sacrificed to it. On the other hand: our spiritual subtlety has been achieved essentially through conscience-vivisection. We do not yet know the Where to? toward which we are driven, now that we have detached ourselves in this manner from our old soil. But this very soil cultivated in us the strength that now drives us out into the distance, into adventure ⟨by which we⟩ are thrust out into the boundless, unexplored, undiscovered — we have no choice, we must be conquerors once we no longer have a country where we are at home, where we could "subsist." No, you know this better, my friends! The hidden Yes in you is stronger than all the No's and Maybe's from which you and your times are sick and addicted; and if you must ship out, you emigrants, then a *faith* compels you to do so — —

2[208]

the not-finishing with Christianity

2[209]

It is a point of honor for my friends to be active on behalf of my name, reputation and worldly security and to build me a fortress where I am preserved from being crudely misjudged: I personally do not want to lift a finger for this anymore

2[210]

The perfect functional certainty of the regulating instincts

[3 = W I 7b. W I 3b. Mp XVI 2b. Mp XVI 1b. Beginning 1886–Spring 1886]

3[1][1]

On the Natural History of the Free
Spirit.

3[2]

On the
Natural History of the Free Spirit.
Thoughts and Dashes
by
Friedrich Nietzsche.

3[3]

Dedication and Final Verse.[2]

"To him who makes all heavens bright
And causes all the seas to roar — "

3[4][3]

The Will to Power.
Omen
of a Philosophy of the Future.
By
Friedrich Nietzsche.

3[5]

Misunderstanding of the lust to rule.
Cheerfulness as redemption.

Dance.

Mockery of "divine" — symptom of convalescence.

The demand for "solid facts" — epistemology how much pessimism there is in it![4]

Creating Z⟨arathustra⟩ as one's *opponent*

3[6][5]

Love of the fatherland is something young in Europe and it still stands on weak legs: it falls down easily! One should not let oneself be deceived by the clamor it makes: little children scream the loudest.

3[7]

"Stupid to the point of holiness" they say in Russia.[6]

3[8][7]

Toward New Seas.

All Sorts of Questions and Questionable Matters.
for Good Europeans.

By
Friedrich Nietzsche.

3[9][8]

Beyond Good and Evil.
Prelude
to a Philosophy of the Future.

First Book: Morality and Knowledge.
Second Book: Morality and Religion.
Third Book: Morality and Art.
Fourth Book: Our Virtues.
Fifth Book: On the Order of Rank.

3[10][9]

Our Virtues.

All Manner of Questions for the Questionable.

By
Friedrich Nietzsche.

3[11][10]

Human, All Too Human.

A Book for Free Spirits.
New Sequel.

And if this book is a mirror and consequently an opportunity for self-mirroring: well, you good Europeans, what do you think of our vanity? Does it like to see itself — "in the mirror"? —

3[12]

From the natural history of the free spirit.[11]
The philosophy of the future.
Scientific laborers.
Artists.
On the philosophy of the superior human.
On the dimming of Europe.[12]

3[13]

It is this solitude that we *guard* when we speak of the religious organization of humankind: — and perhaps nothing distinguishes us so distinctly from the herd animals and equality apostles mistakenly called "free spirits": — all of whom *could* not bear solitude. Religion conceived as the continuation and deepening of fundamental political theory, which is always the theory of unequal rights, of the necessity of a social structure with High and Low, with commanders and obeyers: to us religion means the theory of the difference in rank of souls, of the cultivation and possibility of higher souls at the expense of the lower.

3[14]

The world is not worth *that* which we have believed: we have figured it out. The pessimist even lets us know that precisely this is the remaining value that it holds for us, namely *that* we can figure it out — and that it is not worth *that* which we believed. In this manner the world would be a means of spoiling the world for oneself, of "deworlding" oneself in the best possible manner; an absurdity that is finally starting to comprehend itself after mis⟨er⟩able detours, a somewhat long-winded comedy of errors that shamefully loses itself in nothingness

3[15]

There remains enough to object to in a long invalidism; I am least inclined to agree with a Christian moralist that it improves a h⟨uman⟩, namely if he is afflicted with protracted pains that one ⟨observes⟩ with cold presence of mind — neither that Oriental mute deaf self-dissolving, self-surrendering nor that over-exciting of the power of will and of bravery that {displays} pride, scorn to such an enemy as is pain — — —

In the midst of long agonies, burned as it were with green wood and without the benefit that fever, faintings — — —

3[16]

Manzoni
Stifter
(G. Keller)

3[17][13]

"*Maledetto colui —*
che contrista un spirto immortal!"[14]
Manzoni (Act II of *Conte di Carmagnola*)

3[18][15]

gangasrotogati "flowing like the current of the Ganges"	= *presto*[16]
kurmagati "moving like the tortoise"	= *lento*[17]
mandeikagati "moving like the frog"	= *staccato*[18,19]

3[19]

We philosophers of the beyond — of beyond good and evil, if I may!, who in truth are shrewd interpreters and diviners — we whose fate it was as spectators of European things to be placed before a mysterious and *unread* text: which reveals itself to us more and more — what a chore we have in remaining silent and keeping our mouths shut, while ever more and rarer things crowd up in us and pile up in us and yearn for light, air, freedom, *words*!

But the word — — —

[4 = D 18. Mp XV 2c. Mp XVII 3a. Mp XVI 1b. Beginning 1886–Spring 1886]

4[1]

A philosopher: what a modest creature if he really stays true to his *name*! — which does not characterize a "friend of wisdom," forgive an old philologist! but only "someone who likes wise men." Therefore if you want there to be philosophers in the Greek sense and meaning of the word, first bring on your "wise men"! — But it seems to me, my friends, that *we* ultimately love the unwise men more than the wise, supposing even there were any wise men —? And perhaps there, right there lies more wisdom? What? Should even the wise themselves — seen from up close, perhaps — not be "philosophers"? But "philasophers"?[1] Friends of folly, good company for itinerant musicians and foolish folk? And not for — themselves? —

4[2]

On the problem of the mask. "*Une croyance presque instinctive chez moi, c'est que tout homme puissant ment, quand il parle, et à plus forte raison, quand il écrit.*"[2] Stendhal, *Vie de Napoléon*, Préface p. XV.

4[3]

"*Je sais, quel est le pouvoir des hommes,*" said Napoleon on St. Helena; "*les plus grands ne peuvent exiger d'être aimés.*"[3] — Let us immediately add what can be suspected for all too good reasons: they do not even demand it of themselves — and they also do not love themselves!

4[4][4]

"You seem to be up to something wicked, one could believe you wanted to drive human beings to ruin?" — I once said to the god Dionysus. "Perhaps," replied the god, "but in such a way that they get something out of it for themselves." — "What then?" I asked, curious. — "*Who* then? you should be asking." Thus spoke Dionysus and he grew silent, in the way that is his own, namely seductively. — You should have seen him then! It was spring, and all the trees were in their early sap.

4[5]

There is a part of the night of which a hermit will say: "listen, now time is stopping!" In all night watches, especially if one finds oneself on unusual nocturnal travels and wanderings, one has with respect to this part of night (I mean the hours from one to three) an odd astonished feeling, a kind of "much too short!" or "much too long!", in sum, the impression of a time-anomaly. Could it be that in those hours, as people who are awake for a change, we have to do penance for the fact that we usually find ourselves in the time-chaos of the dream world at that time? Enough, at night from one to three we "have no clock in our heads." To me it seems that this is precisely what the ancients expressed with "*intempestiva nocte*" and "ἐν ἀωρονυκτί"[5] (Aeschylus), thus "there in the night where time does not exist"; and I also etymologically use this thought to explain to myself an obscure word of Homer for describing the deepest stillest part of the night, even if the translators believe they have reproduced it with "time of the night milking": — where in the whole wide world were people ever stupid enough to milk the cows at night between one and three! — But to whom do you tell your night thoughts anyway? —

4[6][6]

⟨In⟩ marriages in the *bourgeois* sense of the word, mind you in the most respectable sense of the word "marriage," it is not at all a matter of love, just as little as it is a matter of money — no institution can be made out of love —: rather, it is a matter of the social permission granted to two persons for their mutual sexual gratification, under conditions, as is self-evident, but those that have the *interest of society* in mind. It is plain as day that among the prerequisites that will belong to such a contract are a degree of pleasure on the part of the participants and very much good will — will to patience, compatibility, caring for one another; but one should not misuse the word love for this! For two lovers in the complete and strong sense of the word sexual gratification is simply not essential and really only a symbol, for one party, as mentioned, a symbol of unconditional submission, for the other a symbol of consent to it, a sign of taking possession. — In a marriage in the aristocratic, old-aristocratic sense of the word it is a matter of the *breeding* of a race (does aristocracy still exist today? *Quaeritur*[7]) — thus of maintaining a fixed, specific type of ruling human being: man and woman were sacrificed to this point of view. It is self-evident that for this love was *not* the first requirement, on the contrary! and not even that measure of good will for one another that conditions the good bourgeois marriage. The interest of a family was primarily decisive, and beyond it — the class. We would shiver a bit at the coldness, severity and calculating clarity of such a noble concept of marriage as reigned in every healthy aristocracy, in ancient Athens as still in the Europe of the eighteenth century, we warm-blooded animals with our delicate hearts, we "moderns"! This is precisely why love as passion, according to the broad understanding of the word, was *invented* for the aristocratic world and in it — there, where precisely the compulsion, the privation were greatest . . .

4[7][8]

— "Illness makes people better": this famous assertion that one encounters throughout all centuries, indeed from the mouths of the wise just as from the mouths and maws of the people, gives us something to think about. One is tempted to ask for once, with respect to its validity: is there perhaps a causal bond between morality and illness generally? The "improvement of human beings" regarded on the whole, for example the undeniable softening humanizing good-naturing of the European within the last millennium — is it perhaps the consequence of a long mysterious-uncanny[9] suffering and failing, privation, atrophy? Has "illness" "made" the European "better"? Or asked differently: is our morality — our modern tender morality in Europe — which one may compare with the morality of the Chinese — the expression of a physiological *regression*? . . . For one would not be able to deny that every place in history where "the human being" has shown himself in the special magnificence and power of his type immediately assumes a sudden, dangerous, eruptive character in which humanity was badly off; and perhaps in those cases *where it seems to be otherwise* there was simply a lack of courage or subtlety to practice psychology to the depths and to extract the universal principle there as well: "the healthier, stronger, richer, more fruitful, more enterprising a human being feels, the more 'immoral' ⟨he⟩ also becomes." A painful thought! on which one should absolutely not dwell! But supposing one were to run forward with it for a brief little moment, how astonishedly one gazes into the future there! Then what would have been purchased more dearly than precisely that which we are promoting with all our strength — the humanization, the "improvement," the growing "civilization"[10] of the human being? Nothing would be more costly than virtue: for in the end it would have the earth as hospital: and "everyone the nurse of everyone" would be wisdom's last verdict.[11] To be sure: then one would also have that long sought-after "peace on earth"! But also so little "delight in one another"![12] So little beauty, exuberance, daring, danger! So few "works," for whose sake it would still be worth it to live on earth! Oh! and no "deeds" at all anymore! All *great* works and deeds that have remained standing and were not washed away by the waves of time — were they not all in the deepest sense of the word great immoralities? . . .

4[8]

That the mere strength of a belief guarantees nothing at all with respect to its truth, indeed is even capable of slowly, slowly spinning forth a fat stupidity from the most reasonable of things: this is our genuine European insight — in it, if in anything, we have become experienced, burned, shrewd, *wise*, through much damage, as it seems . . . "Belief makes blessed": good! Sometimes at least! But under all circumstances belief makes *stupid*, even in the rarer case when it *is* not, when from the start it is a clever belief. Every long-held belief finally *becomes* stupid, that means, expressed with the clarity of our modern psychologists, its reasons sink "into the unconscious," they disappear in it — henceforth it no longer rests on reasons, but on affects (that is in the event that it needs help, it lets the affects fight for it and *no longer* the reasons). Assuming one could ascertain what is the best-believed, longest-held, least controversial, most honest belief there is among human beings, one would be permitted to speculate with a high degree of probability that it was at the same time also the profoundest, most stupid, "most unconscious" belief, best defended against reasons, and abandoned by reasons for the longest time. —

Admittedly; but what is this belief? — Oh you curious ones! But now that I have let myself open for riddle-solving I want to be humane and quickly provide you with an answer and a solution — they won't be easily anticipated from me.

The human being is above all a *judging* animal; but in judgment lies our oldest and most constant belief, in all judging there is a fundamental holding-true of things and an asserting, a certainty that something is so and not otherwise, that here the human being has really "known": *what* is it that in every judgment is unconsciously believed to be true? — That we have a right to *differentiate* between subject and predicate, between cause and effect — that is our strongest belief; indeed at bottom even the belief in cause and effect, in *conditio* and *conditionatum*[13] is only an individual case of the first and universal belief, our primal belief in subject and predicate (namely as the claim that every effect is an action and that every conditioned thing presupposes a conditioner, every action a doer, in sum, a subject) Should this belief in the subject- and predicate-concept not ⟨be a big stupidity?⟩

4[9][14]

Afterlude.

— But here you interrupt me, you free spirits. "Enough! Enough!" I hear you shouting and laughing, "we cannot take it anymore! Oh this horrific tempter and disturber of the conscience's peace! Do you want to ruin our reputation throughout the world? Blacken our good name? Saddle us with nicknames that eat their way into not only our skin? — And why, on a bright sunny day, these gloomy ghosts, these moral gurgling noises, this whole tragic raven-black music? If you speak truths: there are no feet that could *dance* to such truths, therefore not by a long shot are they truths for *us*! *Ecce nostrum veritatis sigillum*![15] And here there is lawn and soft ground: what would be better than to swiftly chase away your mopey thoughts and make ourselves a good day after your night? It is finally time that a rainbow stretched itself again over this land, and that someone gave us gentle crazy songs to hear and milk to drink: — we all are thirsty again for a pious, heartfelt-silly and milky way of thinking." — My friends, I see that you are losing my patience — and who is telling you that I have not already waited a long time *for that*? But I am at your disposal; and I also have what you need. Do you not see there my herds leaping, all my tender sunny sheltered thought-lambs and thought-rams? And here standing waiting for you already is a whole pail full of milk; but once you have drunk — for you are all thirsting for *virtue*, I see it — then there will be no lack of songs as you wish them! To start with a dancing song for the merriest legs and hearts: and truly, whoever sings it does honor to One who deserves honor, one of the freest of free spirits, who makes all heavens bright again and causes all the seas to roar. —

Reference Matter

Notes

The following symbols are used throughout the text and notes:

[ ]	Deletion by Nietzsche
| |	Addition by Nietzsche
{ }	Addition by the translators
⟨ ⟩	Addition by the editors (Colli and Montinari)
———	Unfinished or incomplete sentence or thought
Italics	Underlined once by Nietzsche
Bold	Underlined twice or more by Nietzsche
NL	Books in Nietzsche's personal library

Variants and editions of Nietzsche's works are referred to by the following abbreviations:

CW	*The Complete Works of Friedrich Nietzsche*
KGB	*Briefwechsel: Kritische Gesamtausgabe*
KGW	*Werke: Kritische Gesamtausgabe*
KSA	*Werke: Kritische Studienausgabe*
Le	Twenty-volume 1894 Leipzig edition of Nietzsche's works (*Großoktav-Ausgabe*)
Pd	Preliminary draft
Pm	Printer's manuscript (clean final copy of handwritten MS)

Sd	Second draft
Se	Subsequent emendation

Titles of Nietzsche's works are referred to by the following abbreviations:

AC	*The Antichrist*
BGE	*Beyond Good and Evil*
BT	*The Birth of Tragedy*
D	*Dawn*
DD	*Dionysus Dithyrambs*
DS	*David Strauss the Confessor and the Writer*
EH	*Ecce Homo*
GM	*On the Genealogy of Morality*
HAH	*Human, All Too Human*
HL	*On the Utility and Liability of History for Life*
JS	*The Joyful Science*
MM	*Mixed Opinions and Maxims*
NCW	*Nietzsche Contra Wagner*
SE	*Schopenhauer as Educator*
TI	*Twilight of the Idols*
UO	*Unfashionable Observations*
WA	*The Wagner Case*
WB	*Richard Wagner in Bayreuth*
WP	*The Will to Power*
WS	*The Wanderer and His Shadow*
Z	*Thus Spoke Zarathustra*

Editorial Note to Volume 16

Unless another volume in the *CW* is cited, all cross-references to fragments in the notes are references to fragments in this volume. In cases where a cross-reference to a fragment is followed by a number (e.g., 41[2] 1), this indicates that the reference is to the sentence or paragraph numbered 1 in fragment 41[2].

In cases where the format of a fragment in this volume differs significantly from the format of the fragment as it appears in *KSA*, we have chosen to follow as closely as possible the format of the fragment as it appears in Nietzsche's handwritten notebooks.

ALAN D. SCHRIFT

[34 = N VII 1.]

1. Cf. 34[213]; 35[84]; 36[6].

2. *Gai saber.]* "Gay science." {The Old Provençal term for the art of the troubadours.}

3. {Cf. *CW* 15, 26[426] and the corresponding note.}

4. Cf. 41[2] 1; 41[9].

5. On *BT*.

6. {Cf. Stendhal, *Correspondance inédites: Précedée d'une introduction par Prosper Mérimée* ("Unpublished correspondence: Preceded with an introduction by Prosper Mérimée") (Paris: Michel Lévy Frères, 1855), I: 167; cf. Hippolyte Taine, *Geschichte der englischen Literatur* ("History of English literature"), German edition by L. Katscher und G. Gerth, vol. 3: *Die Neuzeit der englischen Literatur* ("The modern age of English literature") (Leipzig: Ernst Julius Günther Nachf., 1880), 136.}

7. Cf. 34[1].

8. *niaiserie]* "silliness"

9. *"femininisme"]* "feminism" {N here uses his French neologism *femininisme* to render his own German neologism *femininismus*, which he preferred to the more standard *feminismus*.}

10. {Cf. Blaise Pascal, *Pascal's Gedanken, Fragmente und Briefe* ("Pascal's thoughts, fragments, and letters"), German trans. by C. F. Schwartz (Leipzig: Wigand, 1865), 1:193, *NL*: "*Lustravit lampade terras.* Das Wetter und meine Stimmung haben wenig Berührungspunkte. Meine Stimmung hängt ganz und gar nicht von der Witterung ab. Ich habe meine Nebel und mein schönes Wetter in meinem Innern." ("He has illumined the earth with a lamp. The weather and my mood have little connection. My mood does not depend entirely on the weather. I have my foggy and my fine weather within me.")}

11. *milieu]* {Taine's use of the expression *race, milieu et moment* was familiar to N, who corresponded with Taine and spoke highly of him (cf. *BGE* 254; *GM* III 19).}

12. {Cf. *BGE* 247.}

13. *WP* 133 adds in the text the following supplement, provided by Peter Gast, to Galiani's quote: "La prévoyance est la cause des guerres actuelles de l'Europe. {Gast omits the following line from Galiani's quote: "Parce qu'on prévoit que la maison d'Autriche s'agrandira; que les Américains, dans quelques siècles d'ici, que les Anglais, les Français, les Espagnols, dans cent ans, feront ou ne feront pas certaines choses, on commence par s'égorger à l'instant."} Si l'on voulait se donner la peine de rien prévoir, tout le monde serait tranquille, et je ne crois pas qu'on serait plus malheureux parce qu'on ne ferait pas la guerre." {"Foresight is the cause of Europe's present wars. Because we predict that the House of Austria will expand; that the Americans, in a few centuries hence, the English, the French, the Spanish, in a hundred years, will or will not do certain things, we begin by immediately cutting each other's throats. If one would take pains to foresee nothing, the whole world would be tranquil, and I do not believe that one would be worse off for not waging war."} {Ferdinando Galiani, *Lettres de l'Abbé Galiani à Madame d'Épinay, Voltaire, Diderot, Grimm, le Baron d'Holbach, Morellet, Suart, D'Alembert, Marmontel, la Vicomtesse de Belsunce, etc.*, vol. 2 (Paris: G. Charpentier, 1881), 323.}

14. {Cf. *WP* 133.} Cf. *CW* 15, 32[12]; *CW* 18, 13[5].

15. {Cf. *BGE* 254.}

16. *Beyle]* {Marie-Henri Beyle, pseudonym of Stendhal.}

17. Allusion to Gustave Flaubert {author of *Salammbô* (1862), which N here misspells, and *The Temptation of Saint Anthony* (1874)}.

18. *pro pudor!]* "for shame!"

19. Cf. *CW* 15, 26[467].

20. *the being] das Seiende*

21. Cf. 34[201, 207].

22. *acedia]* {a state of restlessness and inability either to work or to pray}

23. {Cf. Lefebvre Saint-Ogan, *Essai sur l'influence française: Deuxième édition* ("Essay on the influence of the French: Second edition") (Paris: Cerf, 1885), 18–19. *NL*.}

24. {Cf. ibid., 49.}

25. *"they . . . do."]* Cf. Luke 23:34.

26. *façon]* "manner"

27. *Plaire]* "to please"{Underlined by N.}

28. {Cf. Saint-Ogan, 178.}

29. *High Mass]* {Also known as the Mass in B minor.}

30. {Cf. *WP* 60. Cf. Saint-Ogan, 248–50.}

31. Cf. ibid., 248. Goethe's judgment in *Dichtung und Wahrheit*, pt. 3, bk. 11. {Cf. *Goethes Werke*, bd. IX, ed. Erich Trunz (Hamburg: Christian Wegner Verlag, 1955), 487.}

32. *Galiani]* Cf. Saint-Ogan, 194.

33. Cf. 38[6]; Baudelaire's judgment about Victor Hugo in Charles-Augustin Saint-Beuve, *Les Cahiers suivis de quelques pages de literature antique* ("The notebooks followed by some pages of ancient literature") (Paris{: Alphonse Lemerre,} 1876), 36, *NL*.

34. *causa finalis . . . causa efficiens]* "final cause . . . efficient cause"

35. {*WP* 413.}

36. Cf. *BGE* 11; 38[7]. {Cf. Kant's introduction to the 2nd ed. of *Critique of Pure Reason*, trans. Allen Wood (Cambridge: Cambridge University Press, 1998), 146.}

37. *good science] Wissenschaftlichkeit*

38. *ulterior motives . . . to ruin.]* {"Ulterior motives" = *Hintergedanken*; "dashes" = *Gedankenstriche*; "freedom of thought" = *Freiheit des Gedankens*; "thinkers" = *Denker*. N uses combinations of nouns based on *denken*, "to think."}

39. *ironice]* "ironically" {Underlined by N.}

40. *back parts and foregrounds] Hintertheilen und Vordergründen*

41. Cf. *BGE* 208.

42. Cf. 37[14].

43. *Kant's words]* Cf. *Kritik der reinen Vernunft*, Ak.-Ausgabe III:105, 496 {*Critique of Pure Reason*, 225, 654}.

44. {Cf. Maximilian Drossbach, *Ueber die scheinbaren und die wirklichen Ursachen des Geschehens in der Welt* ("On the Apparent and real causes of events in the world") (Halle: Pfeffer, 1884), 2. *NL*.}

45. *contradictio in adjecto]* "contradiction in terms"

46. {*WP* 973.}

47. *the plant "human being"]* {Cf. note to 34[146].}

48. Cf. 34[145].

49. Cf. *BGE* 11; 38[7].

50. {Kant says this in the preface to *Prolegomena to Any Future Metaphysics*; cf. Friedrich Albert Lange, *Geschichte des Materialismus und Kritik seiner Bedeutung in der Gegenwart* ("History of materialism and critique of its significance in the present") (Iserlohn: Baedeker, 1882), 396. *NL*.}

51. *delicatesse]* "delicacy," "tact" {Underlined by N.}

52. *nihil humani]* "nothing of the human" {Cf. Terence, "Homo sum, humani nihil a me alienum puto" ("I am human, and think nothing of the human is alien to me"), which appears in his play *Heauton Timorumenos* (*The Self-Tormentor*; 163 BCE).}

53. Cf. *BGE* 11; 38[7].

54. {Cf. Galiani, *Lettres de l'Abbé Galiani à Madame d'Épinay*, 279.}

55. {Cf. Drossbach, 8–9.}

56. *Tübingen Seminary]* {Seminary in Tübingen attended by Hegel, Hölderlin, Schelling.}

57. *ἀνάμνησις]* "anamnesis"

58. {Cf. Francis Galton, *Inquiries into Human Faculty and Its Development* (London: Macmillan, 1883), 73–74.}

59. *esprit]* "spirit"

60. *civis romanus . . . imperium romanum]* "citizen of Rome . . . Roman empire"

61. Cf. *BGE* 268.

62. *amor]* "love" {Underlined by N.}

63. *"Nibelungs"]* {Richard Wagner's cycle of four operas, collectively called *Der Ring des Nibelungen* (*The Ring of the Nibelung*), consisting of *Das Rheingold* (*The Rhine Gold*), *Die Walküre* (*The Valkyrie*), *Siegfried*, and *Götterdämmerung* (*Twilight of the Gods*). These operas premiered as a cycle at the first Bayreuth Festival of 1876 and are often referred to as *The Ring*, less often as *The Nibelungs*.}

64. *The Germans . . . press.]* {Cf. *BGE* preface.}

65. *aeternae]* "eternal"

66. *"féminisme"]* "feminism" {Cf. note 9 above.}

67. *WP* 955.

68. *absorption] Bindung*; *WP* 955 erroneously printed this as *Bildung* {"education," "cultivation"}.

69. Cf. *CW* 18, 15[34].

70. {*WP* 962.}

71. *The astonishment . . . poet!]* Cf. *BGE* 209.

72. N is quoting from Lange, *Geschichte des Materialismus*, {820}.

73. *let the . . . but the men"]* {"Let the little children come to Me"; Matthew 19:14.}

74. Cf. *BGE* 28 and 247.

75. *allegro]* "lively"

76. *presto]* "rapid"

77. *il principe]* {Machiavelli's *The Prince*}

78. Cf. 35[80], 36[55]; for this planned book: 34[104–6, 114–15, 138, 145, 154, 157, 221, 227–28].

79. To 34[103].

80. To 34[103].

81. To 34[103]; cf. 34[102, 97].

82. *Epicureisme]* "Epicureanism"

83. *homines novi]* "new men" {In ancient Rome, the first man in a family to serve in the senate.}

84. To 34[103]; cf. 36[45].

85. {*WP* 900.}

86. To 34[103], in the manuscript attached to *Pd* for *BGE* 244.

87. To 34[103] {cf. 36[46–47]; 40[70]; 41[16]; 42[1–3, 6]}.

88. *The "Mind."] Das "Gemüth."* {Cf. Johann Wolfgang von Goethe, *Maximen und Reflexionen*, in *Goethe's sämmtliche Werke in vierzig Bänden* ("Goethe's collected works in forty volumes"), vol. 3 (Stuttgart: J. G. Cotta, 1853), 196. *NL*.}

89. *niaiserie allemande]* "German silliness" {Cf. Prosper Mérimée, *Lettres à une inconnue* ("Letters to an Unknown [Jenny Dacquin]"), vol. 1 (Paris: Michel Lévy Frères, 1874), 328, where Mérimée uses this phrase in a reference to Goethe. Schopenhauer uses the phrase "*Deutscher* [German] *Niaiserie*" in reference to Hegel's philosophy in *Die Welt als Wille und Vorstellung*, vol. 1 (Leipzig: Brockhaus, 1873), 508; translated by Judith Norman, Alistair Welchman, and

Christopher Janaway as *The World as Will and Representation* (Cambridge: Cambridge University Press, 2010), 456.}

90. {Cf. Gustav Teichmüller, *Die wirkliche und die scheinbare Welt: Neue Grundlegung der Metaphysik* {"The real and the apparent world: New groundwork of metaphysic"} (Breslau: Koebner, 1882), 139.}

91. *discordia]* "discord," "chaos"

92. *facta]* "facts"

93. {Cf. Drossbach, *Ueber die scheinbaren und die wirklichen Ursachen des Geschehens in der Welt*, 10.}

94. {Cf. *BGE* 43.}

95. *origin] Entstehung* {Here and elsewhere in this fragment.}

96. *commanders] Dienenden* {N actually wrote "the servants in some sense must also be obeyers," but clearly it was his intention to juxtapose servants with commanders, not servants with obeyers, since the latter are the same. The ones who exchange roles are commanders and obeyers.}

97. *"individual"] "Individuum"*

98. Cf. Heinrich von Kleist to Wilhelmine and Ulrike {Wilhemine von Zenge (1780–1852) was Kleist's fiancée, Ulrike (1774–1849) his half-sister}, 22–23 March 1801, quoted by N in *SE* 2 {*CW* 2, 188}.

99. *unknowability]* {Heinrich von Kleist was distressed throughout his brief and tumultuous career by his understanding of the Kantian treatment of knowledge; his characters (prose, drama) frequently function on the basis of desperate faith in the absence of knowledge.}

100. Cf. 34[188].

101. *Intelligence] Geistigkeit*

102. {Cf. Drossbach, *Ueber die scheinbaren und die wirklichen Ursachen des Geschehens in der Welt*, 10.}

103. *"perceiving"] wahrnehmen* {"to perceive," consisting of *wahr* (true) and *nehmen* (to take)}

104. New *Zarathustra* plan; cf. 35[71–75].

105. *perished] untergieng*

106. Cf. 34[78]; 35[39–41, 71–75]; 34[191].

107. Cf. *BGE* 44.

108. *plant "human being"]* According to Vittorio Alfieri's statement: "La pianta uomo nasce più robusta qui che altrove" {"The

plant human being is born more robust here [in Italy] than anywhere else"}, quoted in Stendhal, *Rome, Naples et Florence* (Paris{: Michel Lévy Frères,} 1854), 383, *NL*; the quote is underlined by N.

109. Cf. *BGE* 45.

110. Cf. *CW* 18, 11[296], 18[3]{; *BGE* 254}.

111. *blue flower]* {The blue flower (*die blaue Blume*) is symbolic of Romanticism and is featured as the object of the mysterious quest of Heinrich von Ofterdingen, the titular hero of Novalis's (Friedrich von Hardenberg) Romantic novel.}

112. *The Parisians]* {Heinrich Heine lived in exile in Paris, supported by a stipend from the French government. His writings and those of other "Young Germans" were banned in Germany. Cf. Edmond and Jules de Goncourt, *Idées et sensations* (Paris: Charpentier, 1877), 219: "L'esprit le plus parisien qu'ait eu la France est l'esprit français des étrangers: de Galiani, du prince de Ligne, d'Henri Heine." ("The most Parisian spirit in France has been the French spirit of foreigners: Galiani, the Prince of Ligne, Heinrich Heine.") *NL*.}

113. Cf. 34[159–60].

114. To 34[155].

115. Cf. *BGE* 209.

116. *homines religiosi]* "religious men"

117. {Cf. *BGE* 15.}

118. *reductio ad absurdum]* "reduction to absurdity"

119. Cf. 34[155].

120. *The . . . Prerogatives.] Das Recht der Vorrechte.*

121. {Cf. *WP* 75.}

122. *virtù]* "strength" {from Latin *vir*, "man"}

123. {Cf. *WP* 75.}

124. *someone presented himself] trat man selber auf* {from *auftreten* "to appear," to "present itself"}

125. *kick!] Tritt*! {"kick," derived from *treten*, "to kick," and by wordplay from *vertreten*, "to represent"}

126. *The two . . . democracy.]* {Cf. *BGE* preface.}

127. {*WP* 762.}

128. Cf. 35[78]; 42[1].

129. *peintre-poète]* "painter-poet"

130. *Coriolan overture]* {The Coriolan Overture was composed by Ludwig van Beethoven in 1807 for Heinrich Joseph von Collin's 1804 tragedy *Coriolan*.}

131. *The expression expression] Die Ausdruck expression* {N underlines "*Ausdruck*"; the second mention is French in the original.}

132. *liberum "nego"]* "I freely 'deny'"; perhaps based on *liberum veto*, "I freely forbid" or "free veto." {The *liberum veto* was a parliamentary device in the Polish-Lithuanian Commonwealth (1648–1764) that gave any member of the legislature the right to call an end to the session and nullify any legislation that had been passed during the session.}

133. {Cf. Drossbach, *Ueber die scheinbaren und die wirklichen Ursachen des Geschehens in der Welt*, 9. Cf. *BGE* 4.}

134. *Nux et Crux]* "nut and cross"

135. *the "people"] das "Volk"*

136. *bonhomie]* "good-naturedness"

137. {Cf. Galton, *Inquiries into Human Faculty and Its Development*, 72ff.}

138. *Moralities . . . customs.]* {*WP* 144.}

139. *the plant human being]* Cf. note 108 above.

140. *kind] Art*, "kind," or possibly "species"

141. {WP 753.}

142. {WP 961.}

143. Cf. *BGE* 295; 4[4].

144. *nakedness]* {Cf. Genesis 3:7.}

145. Cf. 34[181, 213].

146. Cf. Matthew 7:14.

147. *how are live children . . . slumber]* {N here and in the remainder of this fragment parodies Kant by invoking the *Critique of Pure Reason* ("How are synthetic judgments a priori possible?") and the *Prolegomena to Any Future Metaphysics* (where he credits David Hume for interrupting his "dogmatic slumber").}

148. *the god]* On the "*Philosophy of Dionysus*," cf. 34[181].

149. Cf. *BGE* 11; 34[79].

150. *"random willing"] Willelei*

151. {Cf. Friedrich Schiller, "Die Künstler" ("The Artists"), in *Sämmtliche Werke: Erstes Bändchen* (Stuttgart: J. G. Cotta, 1822), 179. *NL*.}

152. Cf. 34[129].

153. *comme une neurose]* "like a neurosis"

154. *bonté]* "kindness"

155. Cf. 34[188, 129].

156. *Science and Conscience.] Wissen und Gewissen.*

157. To 34[191].

158. *Knowing] das Wissen*

159. *Felix Fallax.]* "Happy Deceiver."

160. {Cf. *WP* 409.}

161. *contradictio in adjecto]* "contradiction in terms"

162. *satis . . . nullus.]* "Few suffice for me, one suffices for me, none at all suffices for me." {Seneca, *Epistulae morales ad Lucilium*, bk. 1, letter 7.}

163. *μέμνησ' ἀπιστεῖν]* "remember not to trust" {Part of a line from the Greek comic playwright Epicharmus, quoted by Polybius and by Cicero in his Letters to Atticus (1.19); also attributed to Epicharmus in Lucian's *Hermotimus*; cf. Kaibel fragment 250.}

164. To 34[145].

165. *the children . . . come.]* {Cf. the conclusion of *Z*, where Zarathustra has signs that "his children" are near.}

166. *the swarm comes]* {Cf. the conclusion of *Z*, where a swarm of doves, along with the lion, symbolize the imminent arrival of Zarathustra's children.}

167. Cf. 34[33, 191, 207].

168. To 34[201]; cf. 35[72].

169. *da capo]* "play it again," "encore"

170. Cf. 35[49].

171. *little treatise]* = *WB*

172. *Bayreuther Blätter]* {Journal of the Wagner society and festival established in Bayreuth. See p. 433, note 11.}

173. Cf. 34[212, 209].

174. *Century of fairs] Jahrmarkts-Jahrhundert*

175. Cf. 34[33, 201].

176. Cf. 34[206, 212].

177. *fairgrounds-taste] Jahrmarkts-Geschmack*

178. *in the age of fairs]* Cf. 34[206, 209].

179. Cf. 34[1, 182]; 35[84]; 36[1, 6]; 34[194]; *CW* 15, 30[11]; 34[202, 201].

180. *Reich-foolishness] Reichs-Narrheit* {folly or foolishness concerning the (Second) Reich}

181. *e.g., . . . case]* {Cf. William Henry Rolph, *Biologische Probleme: Zugleich als Versuch zur Entwicklung einer rationellen Ethik* ("Biological problems: At the same time an attempt at a rational ethics") (Leipzig: Engelmann, 1884), 148: "Ich selbst fasse die Parthenogenese ⟨ . . . ⟩ als eine ganz allgemeine Erscheinung auf, dagegen aber eigentlich die sexuelle Fortpflanzung als eine exceptionelle." ("I myself interpret parthenogenesis . . . as an entirely general phenomenon, conversely, however, sexual reproduction actually as an exceptional one.") *NL.*}

182. *that at bottom . . . female]* {Cf. Rolph, *Biologische Probleme*, 159: "Aus meiner Auffassung geht also hervor, dass ich die Männchen theoretisch als eine durch mindere Ernährung hervorgebrachte Form von Weibchen betrachte" ("Hence it follows from my interpretation that I regard the males theoretically as a form of females produced by insufficient nourishment").}

183. *origin . . . origin] Entstehung . . . Entstehung*

184. *that all organs . . . what is there.]* {Cf. Karl Semper, *Die natürlichen Existenzbedingungen der Thiere* ("Animals' natural conditions of existence") (Leipzig: Brockhaus, 1880), vol. 1, esp. 18–19. *NL.*}

185. {Cf. *BGE* 264.}

186. Cf. *BGE* 209; 35[43].

187. {*WP* 109.}

188. *master]* {Wagner liked to be called "Meister."}

189. {*WP* 540.}

190. Cf. 34[181]; *BGE* 295.

191. *"stupid to the point of sanctity"]* {Cf. Ivan Turgenev, "Sonderlinge," trans. Wilhelm Lange, in *Vom fels zum Meer: Spemanns's Illustrierte Zeitschrift für das Deutsche Haus*, vol. 1, October 1881 through March 1882 (Stuttgart: Spemann, 1881), 235.}

192. Cf. *BGE* 228.

193. *neminem . . . juva]* "Harm no one, rather help everyone to the extent that you can" (cf. *BGE* 186; the Latin phrase is from Arthur Schopenhauer, *The Two Fundamental Problems of Ethics*, trans. and ed. Christopher Janaway (Cambridge: Cambridge University Press, 2009), 140.}

194. *"prithee"] "Bitte"* {*Bitte* means a request but is also the word used to say "please"; *beten* = to pray; *Gebet* = prayer; *bitten* = to request.}

195. *"sent"] Schicksal* = "fate"; *geschickt* = "sent"

196. *right and righteousness] Recht und Gerechtigkeit*

197. *causae efficientes]* "efficient causes"

198. *causae finales]* "final causes"

199. *"Cognition"] "Erkennen"*

200. *know] wissen*

201. *Tarpeian Rock"]* {The Tarpeian Rock is a cliff on the Capitoline Hill of Rome, from which criminals were hurled to their death.}

202. {Cf. Honoré Gabriel Riquetti, comte de Mirabeau, *Oeuvres de Mirabeau*, vol. 8: *Discours et opinions*, bk. 2 (Paris: Brissot-Thivars, 1825), 186: "Je n'avais pas besoin de cette leçon pour savoir qu'il est peu de distance du Capitole à la roche Tarpéienne" ("I did not need this lesson to know that it is a short distance from the Capitol to the Tarpeian Rock").}

203. *"discern" . . . know] "erkennen" . . . wissen*

204. *made-up] erdichteten*, i.e., fictionalized, made up

205. *Our . . . error]* {Cf. Drossbach, *Ueber die scheinbaren und die wirklichen Ursachen des Geschehens in der Welt*, 10.}

206. Cf. 34[182].

207. *acting] wirkende*

208. {Cf. WP 493.}

209. Fragment about Richard Wagner.

210. Thoughts on *BT, UO, HAH, Z.*

211. {This and the following two fragments were written by N on a letter he received from Paul Lanzky, dated 1 June 1885, *KGB* III:4, 28.}

212. Cf. 34[256].

213. {In the Nachbericht to *KGW* VII, 4/2, 70–73, thirteen additional fragments (34[260–272]) are added to Notebook 34 that do not appear in *KSA*. Parts of two of these, 34[260] and 34[264], were included in *WP*.}

214. *the two . . . ideals]* {*WP* 1061.}

215. *contradictio ⟨in adjecto⟩]* "contradiction in terms"

216. *By morality . . . being]* {*WP* 256.}
217. *The criterion . . . power]* {*WP* 534.}
218. *niaiserie allemande]* "German silliness" {Cf. note 89 above.}

[35 = W I 3a.]

1. Cf. *BGE* 224.
2. {Cf. *BGE* 229.}
3. *knowing] Wissen*
4. *Thoughts and Dashes] Gedanken und Gedankenstriche*] {Literally, "thoughts and thought dashes" — N's favorite punctuation mark is the dash, used to break off a thought for aposiopetic effect, similar to his use of ellipsis. Cf. the conclusion of 35[7] above.}
5. {*WP* 132.}
6. *"Socialism"]* N's English.
7. *disciplina voluntatis]* "discipline of the will"
8. {*WP* 956; cf. *BGE* 200.}
9. Cf. 35[8, 9].
10. *1. organic . . . assimilating etc.]* {Cf. *WP* 658.}
11. {Cf. *WP* 967.} Numbered according to *CW* 17, 5[50].
12. Cf. *BGE* 205.
13. {Cf. *BGE* 212.}
14. *indifferentism]* N's English.
15. Cf. 34[182]; *CW* 14, 24[248].
16. {Cf. *WP* 899.}
17. {Cf. *WP* 899.}
18. {*WP* 263.}
19. {Cf. *WP* 424.}
20. *arrangement]* N's French.
21. {Cf. *WP* 424.}
22. Numbered according to *CW* 17, 5[50].
23. *"equal rights" . . . equal demands"]* {Cf. William Henry Rolph, *Biologische Probleme: Zugleich als Versuch einer rationellen Ethik*, 2nd ed. ("Biological problems: At the same time an attempt at a rational ethics") (Leipzig: Engelmann, 1884), 27: "Diese Ansicht aber ist eine Irrlehre, denn statt des Satzes: Gleiches

Recht für Alle, substituirt sie jenen anderen: Gleichen Anspruch für Alle." ("But this view is a false doctrine, for instead of the proposition: Equal rights for all, it substitutes that other: Equal demands for all." This sentence underlined by N. *NL*.}

24. *cant]* N's English.

25. *comfort]* N's English.

26. *fashion]* N's English.

27. N refers here to Eduard von Hartmann, *Phänomenologie des sittlichen Bewusstseins: Prolegomena zu jeder zukünftigen Ethik* ("Phenomenology of ethical consciousness: Prolegomena to any future ethics") (Berlin: C. Duncker, 1879). *NL*.

28. Added according to Peter Gast: *Über den Ursprung der moralischen Empfindungen* (Chemnitz: Schmeitzner, 1877). *NL*. {Paul Rée, *The Origin of the Moral Sensations*, trans. and ed. by Robin Small in Paul Rée, *Basic Writings* (Urbana: University of Illinois Press, 2003.)}

29. {Cf. Stendhal, *Correspondance inédite: Précedée d'une introduction par Prosper Mérimée* ("Unpublished correspondence: Preceded with an introduction by Prosper Mérimée") (Paris: Michel Lévy Frères, 1855), 2:87: "Pour être bon philosophe, il faut être sec, clair, sans illusion." ("To be a good philosopher, one must be dry, clear, without illusion.")

30. Cf. Jean-Marie Guyau, *Esquisse d'une morale sans obligation ni sanction* ("Outline of a morality without obligation or penalty") (Paris{: Alcan,} 1885). *NL*.

31. *"petits faits"]* "little facts"

32. *"positivisme"]* "positivism"

33. *"shuddering . . . of humanity"]* Cf. Goethe, *Faust* II:6272. {Goethe writes "der Menschheit bestes Teil" ("the best portion of humanity"), not "der Menschheit *schönster* [underlined by N] Teil," as N misquotes.}

34. *bêtise]* "stupidity"

35. {Cf. note 23 above. In N's library was a heavily annotated copy of the 1884 second edition.}

36. *⟨tremble . . . immodesty⟩]* {About this lengthy editorial insertion, the editors in the Nachbericht to *KGW* VII (p. 384) write that "the restored text derives from the fragmentary second

draft in folder XVI 1,11, which begins: ⟨following a gap in the text⟩est, like that fine fellow Guyau, tremble; this enabled the correction of the text reproduced above."}

37. Cf. *BGE* preface; 38[3].

38. {Cf. *BGE* 4.}

39. *persuaded us.]* {Cf. Goethe, *Faust* II:6215–306, which describes his visit to The Mothers.}

40. Cf. 38[5].

41. Cf. 34[145, 191].

42. Cf. 34[145].

43. Cf. 34[145].

44. Cf. Thucydides 2.41.4. {Cf. Thucydides, *Geschichte des Peloponnesischen Kriegs* ("History of the Peloponnesian War"), trans. Dr. Adolf Wahrmund (Stuttgart: Krais & Hoffmann, 1866), 128. *NL.*}

45. Cf. 34[221].

46. *enlarges . . . great] vergrößert . . . groß*

47. {Cf. *WP* 422.}

48. *Those who . . . their emergence.]* {*WP* 463.}

49. *Paete, non dolet!]* "Paete, it does not hurt!" {Under Emperor Claudius, Arria, wife of Paetus, speaks these words to him as she stabs herself with his dagger when he is unable to commit suicide as commanded by the emperor. Cf. *WS* 75 and note 202 in *CW* 4, p. 499.}

50. *that the . . . "desolation"]* {*WP* 603.}

51. *§ Basic . . . "chance")]* {*WP* 979.}

52. *§ The new . . . for this]* {*WP* 978.}

53. On Richard Wagner, cf. 41[2].

54. Cf. 34[205]; 41[2].

55. *in partibus infidelium]* "in the land of the unbelievers"

56. {Cf. *WP* 1064.}

57. {Cf. *WP* 1064.}

58. N quotes from Afrikan Spir, *Denken und Wirklichkeit*{*: Versuch einer Erneuerung der kritischen Philosophie*. Bd. 1. *Das Unbedingte*. Bd. 2. *Die Welt der Erfahrung* ("Thought and reality: Attempt to renew critical philosophy, vol. 1: The unconditional; vol. 2: The world of experience")} (Leipzig{: Findel,} 1877). *NL*.

59. {Cf. Spir, *Denken und Wirklichkeit*, vol. 2, bk. 2, chap. 5: "Das Urtheil."}

60. Cf. note 58 above.

61. *sujet]* "subject"

62. Crossed out by N himself in the manuscript.

63. Cf. 35[73].

64. Cf. 34[202].

65. Cf. 35[71]; 39[3]; 34[144–45].

66. Cf. 34[144–45]; 39[3].

67. Cf. 34[144–45]; 39[3].

68. {Cf. *WP* 943.} Numbered according to *CW* 17, 5[50]; written on 22 July 1885, cf. N to Peter Gast, 23 July 1885 {*KGB* III:3, 68–69}.

69. *comprendre c'est égaler]* "to understand is to equalize" {Cf. Bourget, *Essais*, 148; 1[182].}

70. *inter pares]* "among equals"

71. *otium]* "idleness," "leisure"

72. Cf. 35[78].

73. To 35[77]; cf. 34[165]; 42[1].

74. Cf. 34[103]; 36[55].

75. *A pessimistic . . . die out.]* {*WP* 1055.}

76. Cf. 34[1, 213]; 36[1].

77. *To the Mistral.]* Cf. *JS* preface.

78. *Among Friends: An Aftersong.]* Cf. the concluding poem of *HAH*.

[36 = W I 4.]

1. Cf. 34[1]; 36[6]; 34[213]; 35[84].

2. {*WP* 792.}

3. *homines bonae voluntatis]* "men of good will"; cf. Luke 2:14.

4. *causer, . . . poser, . . . oser]* "chat . . . sit . . . dare"

5. *Rahel]* Rahel Levin (1771–1833), in 1814 married to Karl August Varnhagen von Ense (1785–1858), was a well-known admirer of Goethe whose literary salon in Berlin included many leading figures of German Romanticism.

6. Cf. 34[1, 213]; 35[84]; 36[1].

7. {*WP* 367.}

8. *with . . . here.] mit dem ich da litte.* {N is using "passion" and "compassion" in the obsolete sense of English, whereby passion means suffering and compassion means suffering along with someone.}

9. Categorized in view of the revision of *HAH* (summer 1885).

10. *Moralia]* "ethics"

11. Cf. note 9 above.

12. {Cf. Maximilian Drossbach, *Ueber die scheinbaren und die wirklichen Ursachen des Geschehens in der Welt* ("On the apparent and real causes of events in the world") (Halle: Pfeffer, 1884), 2.}

13. In summer 1883 N planned a work with the title "The Innocence of Becoming."

14. *jurisdictio]* "jurisdiction"

15. {*WP* 443.}

16. Cf. note 9 above.

17. *qui range aux souverains]* "who ranks as sovereign"

18. Cf. note 9 above.

19. On Wagner, cf. 41[2].

20. *poser-humans]* {N uses *Attitüden-Menschen*, in which *Attitüden* indicates the kind of performative individuals who suggest posing and dancing.}

21. {*WP* 1062.}

22. *deus sive natura]* "God or nature"

23. *contradictio in adjecto]* "contradiction in terms"

24. *But we . . . deceive ourselves.]* {*WP* 988.}

25. {*WP* 630.}

26. {*WP* 494.}

27. {*WP* 637.}

28. {*WP* 655.}

29. *"beings"] "Wesen"*

30. {*WP* 642.}

31. {*WP* 520.}

32. {*WP* 545.}

33. {Cf. Drossbach, *Ueber die scheinbaren und die wirklichen Ursachen des Geschehens in der Welt*, iii–iv.}

34. *post hoc]* "after this"

35. *propter hoc]* "because of this" {*Post hoc ergo propter hoc* is a logical fallacy.}

36. *"Subject" "object" . . . a quality.]* {*WP* 549.}

37. {*WP* 645.}

38. *causae finalis]* "final cause"

39. *causae efficientes]* "efficient cause"

40. {*WP* 646.}

41. {*WP* 619.}

42. {Cf. Drossbach, *Ueber die scheinbaren und die wirklichen Ursachen des Geschehens in der Welt*, 93–94.}

43. {Cf. Otto Liebmann, *Gedanken und Thatsachen: Philosophische Abhandlungen, Aphorismen und Studien*. Heft 1: *Die Arten der Nothwendigkeit. — Die mechanische Naturerklärung. — Idee und Entelechie* ("Thoughts and facts: Philosophical essays, aphorisms, and studies, vol. 1: The types of necessity — The mechanical explanation of nature — Idea and entelechy") (Strasbourg: Trübner, 1882), 66.}

44. Cf. 36[38–53, 55].

45. {*WP* 618.}

46. *rock bottom]* {The idiom *aus dem letzten Loch pfeifen* means to be on one's last legs, here "rock bottom."}

47. *actio in distans]* "action at a distance"

48. *dynamis]* "force"

49. {Cf. *WP* 659.}

50. {Cf. *WP* 659.}

51. For the revision of *HAH*.

52. {Cf. *BGE* 244. August Friedrich Wilhelm von Kotzebue (1761–1819) was a prolific writer whose career was filled with controversy. He was assassinated by Karl Ludwig Sand (1795–1820), a theology student, an event used by the conservative Metternich regime to impose strict sanctions on writers and on freedom of speech in central Europe in the form of the Carlsbad Decrees (1819).}

53. {Cf. Theognis, lines 215–16: "Adopt the disposition of the octopus, crafty in its convolutions, which takes on / the appearance of whatever rock it has dealings with." Andrew M. Miller, ed. and trans., *Greek Lyric: An Anthology in Translation* (Indianapolis: Hackett, 1996), 85–86.}

54. *mesquinen]* "shabby"

55. Cf. 34[111].

56. *imperium romanum]* "Roman Empire"

57. *spiritual enlightenment . . . "progress"!]* {*WP* 129.}

58. {*WP* 91. The sentence "I do *not* count . . . 'pleasant literatures' — — — etc." was omitted from most editions of *WP*.}

59. {Cf. Ferdinando Galiani, *Lettres de l'Abbé Galiani à Madame d'Épinay, Voltaire, Diderot, Grimm, le Baron d'Holbach, Morellet, Suart, D'Alembert, Marmontel, la Vicomtesse de Belsunce, etc.*, vol. 2 (Paris: G. Charpentier, 1882), 332: "Le raisonner tristement s'accrédite; Ah! croyez moi, l'erreur a son mérite." ("Reasoning sadly accredits itself; Oh! believe me, error has its merit.") *NL*.}

60. {*WP* 108.}

61. Cf. 34[103]; 35[80]; 36[38–53]; 40[70].

62. *Questions and Dashes.] Fragen und Gedankenstriche.* {Literally, "Questions and Thought-Dashes."}

63. {Cf. *WP* 959.}

[37 = W I 6a.]

1. For revision of *HAH*.

2. Cf. *CW* 15, 26[467].

3. *Satis . . . nullus.]* "A few are enough for me, one is enough for me, even no one at all is enough for me." {Seneca, *Epistles*, 7, 11. Cf. *CW* 15, 26[467, 139, 241, 297, 325]}

4. {*WP* 990.}

5. *thoughts . . . matters] Gedanken, Bedenken und Bedenkliches*

6. {Cf. *BGE* 289.}

7. {*WP* 980.}

8. {*WP* 957.}

9. {Cf. *BGE* 256.}

10. *broker role] Makler-Rolle* {A reference to Bismarck, who offered himself as an "honest broker" (*ehrlicher Makler*) to negotiate peace between Russia and Turkey in 1878.}

11. *homines novi]* "new people"

12. Cf. *BGE* 244.

13. *la niaiserie allemande]* "German silliness" {Cf. note to 34[115].}

14. {Cf. Johann Wolfgang von Goethe, *Maximen und Reflexionen*, in *Goethe's sämmtliche Werke in vierzig Bänden* ("Goethe's collected works in forty volumes"), vol. 3 (Stuttgart: J. G. Cotta, 1853), 196. *NL*. Cf. also 34[115]; *CW* 15, 25[476].}

15. *I had . . . Strauss.]* {Cf. *DS*.}

16. {Cf. Gottfried Wilhelm Leibniz, *Leibnizens Gesammelte Werke*, ed. Georg Heinrich Pertz, Erste Folge, Geschichte, Vierter Band: *Leibnizens Geschichtliche Aufsätze und Gedichte* ("Leibniz's collected works, ed. Georg Heinrich Pertz, 1st ser., History, vol. 4: Leibniz's historical essays and poems") (Hanover: Hahn, 1847), 269.}

17. {Cf. *WP* 125.}

18. *demonstratio ad absurdum]* "demonstration to absurdity"

19. *marasmus femininus]* "feminine marasmus"

20. *In the main matter . . . transfigure himself.]* {*WP* 820.}

21. *I have named . . . today!]* {*WP* 464.} Cf. 34[68].

22. Cf. 41[2].

23. *romantisme]* "Romanticism"

24. *find and invent] fanden und erfanden*

25. *lento]* "slowly" {musical notation}

26. *"two . . . breast"]* {Cf. Johann Wolfgang von Goethe, *Faust: Ein Tragödie*, I:1112, in *Goethe's sämmtliche Werke in vierzig Bänden*, vol. 11 (Stuttgart: J. G. Cotta, 1854), 47. *NL*. Cf. Johann Wolfgang von Goethe, *Faust: A Tragedy*, ed. Cyrus Hamlin, trans. Walter Arndt (New York: W. W. Norton, 2001): "Two souls, alas, are dwelling in my breast, / And either would be severed from its brother"; lines 1112–13.}

27. {Cf. *BGE* 232.}

[38 = Mp XVI 1a. Mp XVI 2a. Mp XV 2b.]

1. *presto]* "quickly, rapidly" {musical notation}
2. *nervus sympathicus]* "sympathetic nerve"
3. *sensorium commune]* "sensory nerve center"
4. {*WP* 483.} Cf. 35[35]{; *BGE* 17}.
5. {*WP* 535.}
6. Cf. 35[38]{; *BGE* 254}.
7. *in artibus et litteris]* "in arts and letters"

8. *petits faits]* "little facts"

9. *grand fait]* "great fact"

10. *Gemüt]* {Modernized spelling of N's *Gemüth*: mind, soul, disposition, attitude, spirit, style, or way. *Gemütlich* and *Gemütlichkeit* celebrate good feeling, conviviality, and sentimentality; archaic *Gemüt* usually refers to mind or soul. Cf. *BGE* 244 and 244n19 (*CW* 8, p. 394).}

11. *caterwauling] Katzenjammer* {Both caterwauling literally and figuratively "hangover."}

12. Cf. 34[45] and note 33.

13. *esprit]* "spirit"

14. *justice is . . . him]* {Cf. Paul Bourget, *Essais de Psychologie Contemporaine* (Paris: Lemerre, 1883), 224.}

15. Cf. *BGE* 11; 34[185]; 34[79, 62, 82].

16. *"this . . . metaphysics"]* {Cf. Friedrich Albert Lange, *Geschichte des Materialismus und Kritik seiner Bedeutung in der Gegenwart* ("History of materialism and critique of its present importance") (Iserlohn: Baedeker, 1882), 396.}

17. {Cf. *BGE* 19.}

18. *mobile]* "motive power"

19. {*WP* 985.}

20. {*WP* 1067.} Cf. *BGE* 36.

21. *a ring . . . nothing else] Pd*: it is a ring of good will to rotate always around one's own old axis and only around oneself: this my world — who is bright enough to behold it without wishing blindness on oneself? Strong enough to hold his soul up to this mirror? His own mirror to the Dionysus-mirror? To hold up his own solution to the Dionysus-riddle? And whoever is capable of this, would he not then have to do *more*? Betroth *himself* to the "ring of rings"? With the oath of his own *recurrence*? With the ring of the eternal self-blessing, self-affirmation? With the will to willing-again-and-one-more-time? To the wanting-back of all things that have ever been? To the wanting-out of everything that must ever be? Do you know now what *the world* is to me? And what *I* will when I will — *this* world? — —

22. {Cf. *WP* 972.}

23. *Dutchman]* F. W. van Eeden to N, 20 February 1885 {*KGB* III:4, 8–9}.

24. *in . . . philosophicis]* "in music and philosophy"
25. *Rée]* Cf. note 22 to *CW* 14, 7[17].
26. Cf. *GM* preface 3; *CW* 12, 28[7].

[39 = N VII 2a. Z I 2b.]

1. First *WP*-plan; cf. 40[2], to which belong fragments 39[12–15].
2. Collection of expressions and metaphors.
3. Cf. 34[144–45]; 35[71–75]; 39[10, 22].
4. *Rialto]* {The commercial section of Venice whose iconic bridge spans the Grand Canal.}
5. *pointe]* "point," "purpose"
6. For Heinrich von Stein, cf. "Chronology" {*CW* 19}.
7. *matador fig]* {A parasitic fig variety that strangles and kills its host in order to survive; called by the Brazilians *cipó-matador*; cf. Hermann Burmeister, *Geologische Bilder zur Geschichte der Erde und ihrer Bewohner* ("Geological images for a history of the earth and its inhabitants"), vol. 2 (Leipzig: Wigand, 1855), 238–40.}
8. *The sublime . . . generations.]* {*WP* 996.}
9. {Cf. *WP* 959.}
10. Cf. 39[3] and note 3 above.
11. To 39[1].
12. To 39[1].
13. *Palazzo Pitti]* {Pitti Palace, Renaissance palace in Florence.}
14. *de omnibus dubitare]* "everything is to be doubted" {Cf. Descartes, *Principia Philosophiae* I, §39.}
15. To 39[1].
16. To 39[1].
17. *pleasure and pain] Lust und Unlust*
18. {Cf. Goethe, *Faust* I:4406.}
19. For Siegfried Lipiner, cf. "Chronology" {*CW* 19}.
20. Cf. 39[10].
21. *For the . . . easy life]* {Cf. *WP* 764.}

[40 = W I 7a.]

1. Cf. 39[1]; to this belong fragments 40[3, 50, 61]; 43[1, 2]; 44[1].
2. To 40[2].

3. *prompted] soufflirt* {From French *souffler*, to prompt as on the stage.}

4. *"many mortal souls"]* {Cf. *MM* 17 (*CW* 4, 18): "someone . . . who, in contrast to the metaphysicians, is happy to shelter within himself not '*one* immortal soul,' but *many mortal souls*."}

5. *Teichmüller p. 25]* Cf. Gustav Teichmüller, *Die wirkliche und die scheinbare Welt*{*: Neue Grundlegung der Metaphysik* ("The real and the apparent world: New groundwork of metaphysics") (Breslau: Koebner,} 1882), 25.

6. *terminus medius]* "middle term"

7. *terminus major]* "major proposition"

8. *Spir I p. 76]* Cf. Afrikan Spir, *Denken und Wirklichkeit*{: *Versuch einer Erneuerung der kritischen Philosophie*. Bd. 1. *Das Unbedingte* ("Thought and reality: Attempt to renew critical philosophy, vol. 1: The Unconditional")} (Leipzig{: Findel,} 1877), 76. *NL*.

9. {*WP* 512.}

10. {*WP* 532.}

11. {Cf. Paul Heinrich Widemann, *Erkennen und Sein: Lösung des Problems des Idealen und Realen, zugleich eine Erörterung des richtigen Ausgangspunktes und der Principien der Philosophie* ("Knowledge and being: Solution of the problem of the ideal and the real, together with a discussion of the right starting point and the principles of philosophy") (Karlsruhe: Reuther, 1885), 5. *NL*.}

12. *aut libri aut liberi]* "either children or books"

13. {Cf. *BGE* 34.}

14. *veritas aeterna]* "eternal truth"

15. {Cf. Widemann, *Erkennen und Sein*, 5. Cf. also Eugen Dühring, *Der Werth des Lebens: Eine philosophische Betrachtung* ("The value of life: A philosophical examination") (Breslau: Trewendt, 1865), 170–71.}

16. *de omnibus dubitare]* "everything is to be doubted"

17. *In summa]* "In sum"

18. {*WP* 492.}

19. *Cogito]* "I think"

20. *ergo sum]* "therefore I am"

21. *direct] unmittelbar* {also "unmediated"}
22. *cogitatur]* "there is thinking"
23. *cogitat]* "he/she/it thinks"
24. *contradictio in adjecto]* "contradiction in terms"
25. For Teichmüller and Spir, see notes 5 and 8 above.
26. *fit]* "it is done" {Latin *facere*}
27. {*WP* 783.}
28. *inter pares]* "among equals"
29. *pulchrum est paucorum hominum]* "beauty is for the few"
30. *comprehensibility of the concept] Begreifbarkeit im Begriff*
31. {*WP* 502.}
32. *what is experienced] das Erlebte*
33. For Teichmüller, see note 5 above.
34. *valeurs]* "values"
35. *regressus]* "return"
36. {Cf. John Locke's critique of innate ideas in book 1 of *An Essay Concerning Human Understanding* (1689). In the next sentence, N puns on the link between "birth" (*Geburt*) and "innate" (*angeboren*)}
37. {Cf. Goethe, *Faust* I:1112–13.}
38. *"activum and passivum"]* "active and passive"
39. *Quaeritur]* "The question is asked"
40. For Spir, see note 8 above.
41. {*WP* 490.}
42. *pares]* "equals"
43. {*WP* 278.}
44. Cf. 40[48].
45. *Discipline and Cultivation] Zucht und Züchtung* {Depending on context, *Züchtung* could be translated "selection," "breeding," or "cultivation." It should also be noted that the German translation of Darwin's "natural selection" was *natürliche Züchtung.*}
46. Cf. 40[45].
47. To 40[2].
48. *Appearance] Schein* {In 40[52], N uses *Erscheinungen*; here he uses *Schein*. Both words possess a range of meanings, but when used opposite "reality," they both connote appearance.}

49. For revisions of *HAH* in summer 1885; cf. 4[9].

50. {Cf. Montaigne, *Essais*, 1:26 ("De l'institution des enfants" ["On the education of children"]): "L'ame qui loge la philosophie, doit par sa santé rendre sain encores le corps. ("The soul that harbors philosophy should, by its own health, make the body healthy also.") *NL*.}

51. *Vogelfrei"]* "outlaw" or "free as a bird"

52. *Ecce . . . sigillum!]* "Behold our symbol of the truth!"

53. *Incipit]* "Here begins"

54. *It is . . . together — — —]* Cf. *HAH* concluding poem.

55. *vanitatum vanitas]* "vanity of vanities" {Cf. Ecclesiastes 1:2.}

56. To 40[2].

57. For revisions of *HAH* in summer 1885.

58. *otium]* "leisure"

59. Cf. 41[2].

60. Cf. 41[9].

61. {Cf. *HAH* 34 (*CW* 3, 42).}

62. *"It is not . . . lap"]* {Cf. *HAH* 29 (*CW* 3, 38).}

63. {Cf. *HAH* 20 (*CW* 3, 31).}

64. For revisions of *HAH* in summer 1885.

65. *mistaken] Verwechslung*

66. *scabies anarchistica]* "anarchistic scabies"

67. For revisions of *HAH* in summer 1885.

68. *facta]* "facts"

69. For revisions of *HAH* in summer 1885.

70. Cf. 34[103]; 35[80]; 36[38–53, 55]; 41[16].

71. *Questions and Dashes] Fragen und Gedankenstriche*

72. *Voilà un homme.]* "Behold a man!" {Napoleon's words on meeting Goethe in 1808.}

[41 = W I 5.]

1. *Exultabit . . . lilium.]* "The desert shall rejoice and blossom as the lily." {Cf. Isaiah 35:1–2 (in St. Jerome's Latin Vulgate translation).}

2. Cf. 40[64]; 37[15]; 36[14]; 35[48–49]; *BGE* 31.

3. *al fresco]* "open air"; a technique of mural painting.

4. *"Richard Wagner and No End"]* {N here alludes to Goethe's 1813 essay "Shakespeare und kein Ende."}

5. *exist for the "chamber"!] für die "camera" da sein*!

6. *"Redemption to the Redeemer!"]* {Cf. *WA* postscript: "At Wagner's burial, the first Wagner Association in Germany, founded in Munich, laid a wreath at his grave with an *inscription* that immediately became famous. 'Redemption to the Redeemer!'" These are the final words of Wagner's *Parsifal*.}

7. *pulchrum . . . hominum]* "beauty is for the few"

8. *"Music . . . drama."]* {Cf. Richard Wagner, introduction to *Oper und Drama* ("Opera and drama"), in *Gesammelte Schriften und Dichtungen* ("Complete works and poetry"), vol. 3 (Leipzig: Fritzsch, 1872), 282. *NL*. Cf. *WA* §10.}

9. *gesture] Attitüde*

10. *"wagnetized"] "wagnetisirt"* {A play on *magnetisirt* ("magnetized").}

11. *Bayreuther Blätter]* {The journal of the Bayreuth Wagner Society. The Bayreuth Festival was established in 1876 as a venue for performing Wagner's works. Nietzsche was highly critical of the Bayreuth phenomenon and the people associated with it, and his experiences there contributed to the break with Wagner. See *EH* "Books" HAH2 for his scathing account of the Bayreuth milieu.}

12. *belief and superstition] Glauben und Aberglauben*

13. {*WP* 942.}

14. *the Gothaische Kalender]* {The equivalent of England's *Royal Calendar* and France's *Almanach Royal*, *Der Gothaische Kalender* (generally known in English as the *Almanach de Gotha*) was an annual directory of government and court officials, with a comprehensive listing of the nobility.}

15. {*WP* 419.}

16. *graecofying] gräcisirende*

17. {Cf. *WP* 1051.}

18. {Cf. *WP* 1051.}

19. *the Greek] das Griechische*; the Greek culture and character overall, i.e., what is Greek, as opposed to the Greek individual or the Greeks as a people.

20. Cf. 41[15]; N is referring to *DS*.
21. For revisions of *HAH* in summer 1885; cf. 40[65].
22. *secret . . . uncanny]* *vieles Heimliche, und manches Unheimliche*
23. *Perhaps I will once . . . more humane.]* {Cf. *BGE* 295; *CW* 8, 195–96.}
24. Variants of 41[9]; cf. 40[65].
25. {*WP* 499.}
26. For revisions of *HAH* in summer 1885.
27. Cf. *BGE* 251.
28. {*WP* 791.}
29. Cf. 41[8] and note 20 above.
30. *virum optime meritum]* "a man of the highest merit"
31. Cf. 40[70].

[42 = Mp XVII 2a.]

1. Cf. 34[165]; 35[78].
2. *The genuinely . . . sublimare.]* {*WP* 977; cf. 2[55].}
3. *prava . . . sublimare]* "To correct what is wrong, and strengthen the right, and elevate the holy" {See Alcuin, *Abbatis et Caroli Magni Imperatoris Magistri Opera Omnia, Tomus Primus* ("Abbot and teacher of Emperor Charlemagne, complete works, 1st vol."), ed. J.-P. Migne (Paris: 1863), "Operum Pars Prima. — Epistolæ" ("Works pt. 1 — Letters"), Epistola 43, 207. Cf. 2[55].}
4. {42[3] lists fragments Nietzsche has already written, using the first line of the fragment; these are apparently intended for additions to *Human, All Too Human* that he later abandoned, as he famously abandoned the so-called "Will to Power."}
5. For revisions of *HAH* in summer 1885.
6. *{}]* {The empty curly brackets indicate that in the German there is a verb implied.}
7. *homines]* "humans"
8. For revisions of *HAH* in summer 1885.
9. *Beyond what is good and evil]* {*Jenseits des Guten und Bösen* versus *Jenseits von Gut und Böse* = Beyond Good and Evil.}
10. For revisions of *HAH* in summer 1885.
11. For revisions of *HAH* in summer 1885.
12. For revisions of *HAH* in summer 1885.

13. {*WP* 744. In the ongoing revisions to the Colli-Montinari edition, it has been discovered that this fragment is a duplication of fragment 8[13] in *CW* 10.}

[43 = Z I 2c.]

1. To 40[2].
2. To 40[2].
3. *actio in distans]* "action at a distance"
4. *argute loqui]* "adroitness of speech"
5. *"two . . . breast]* {Allusion to Goethe's *Faust* I:1112: "Two souls, alas, are dwelling in my breast." Cf. 37[16], note 26 above.}

[44 = Mp XVII 2b.]

1. To 40[2].
2. *What is this . . . crucify them. —]* {*WP* 228.}
3. Written February 1886.

[45 = W I 6b.]

1. Cf. *JS* preface; 45[4].
2. Cf. 3[3].
3. *Closing Refrain] Abgesang* {The third and final strophe of a minnesinger's song.}
4. Cf. *JS* preface; 45[2].
5. Das Unglück holt den Flüchtigen ein — und sei's

Als goldner Kummer der verarmten Hand,
Als Traurigkeit des ewig-Schenkenden:
Das Unglück fieng den Flüchtigen ein — und sei's
Sorglos und selber uneingedenk
Warf er die Perlen weg

Das den Besiegten nieder zwingt
Das jeden Stolz zu Thränen kehrt:
Unehrlich Gebild,
Warfst du die Perlen in den Sand —
Das Meer schlang sie in seinen Schlund!
Was dankt das Leben dem Verschwendenden

6. Der Tag klingt ab, es gilbt sich Glück und Licht,
Mittag ist ferne.
Wie lange noch? Da kommen Mond und Sterne
Und Wind und Reif: nun säum' ich lange nicht,
Der Frucht gleich, die ein Hauch vom Baume bricht

[1 = N VII 2b.]

1. Cf. N to Overbeck, October 1885 (from Leipzig) {*KGB* III:3, 96–99, 101–3} and December 1885 (from Nice) {*KGB* III:3, 119–23}.

2. For the Dance Poem "To the Mistral."

3. "The Mirror" as title surfaces repeatedly in N's manuscripts from the year 1885; cf. here: 1[109, 121]; 3[11].

4. *Gleba] La servitù della gleba* ("servitude of the turf") is the standard Italian term for "serfdom."

5. *the most powerful . . . politicians]* {*WP* 869.}

6. *To be demonstrated . . . regressed).]* {*WP* 1042.}

7. Cf. 1[10]; *BGE* 257; *GM* I 2, III 14.

8. For the planned revision of *HAH*, cf. "Chronology" {*CW* 19}.

9. Cf. 1[7].

10. *publisher]* Ernst Schmeitzner

11. *"intellectual intuition"] "intellektuelle Anschauung"* {Concept of post-Kantian philosophy, especially in Schelling, against which Schopenhauer was already strongly polemicizing.}

12. *pia fraus]* {"pious fraud"} Cf. Ovid, *Metamorphoses* 9.711.

13. *power] Gewalt* {versus *Macht* / power}

14. *esse]* "being"

15. {Cf. *WP* 355.}

16. Peter Gast in his letter to N of 26 August 1881 {*KGB* III:2, 182} had included a conversation, translated by Carl von Gersdorff, that took place between Sir Samuel White Baker and the Latuka (a tribe of the Nile delta region) chief Commoro {N misspells Commoro's name as "Comorro"}; the conversation is found in Baker's book *The Albert Nyanza, Great Basin of the Nile, and Explorations of the Nile Sources* (London{: Macmillan,} 1866), {169: "*Commoro.* — 'Most people are bad; if they are strong they take from the weak. The good people are all weak; they are good because they are not strong enough to be bad.'"}

17. According to J. Wellhausen?

18. *spiritus]* "spirit" or "breathing"

19. {Cf. *WP* 355.}

20. {Cf. Fyodor Dostoyevsky, *L'esprit souterrain* (*Notes from Underground*), adapted and translated into French by Ely Halpérine and Charles Morice (Paris: Plon-Nourrit, 1886), 120: "Il n'y a pas des malheurs pour les cœurs faibles." Examining the French edition that N translates in this fragment into German reveals a problem with the dating of this fragment: a note that precedes the title page indicates that the French text was published in November 1886, while this notebook is supposed to include N's notes from fall 1885–spring 1886.}

21. {Cf. Otto Liebmann, *Gedanken und Thatsachen: Philosophische Abhandlungen, Aphorismen und Studien. Heft 1: Die Arten der Nothwendigkeit. — Die mechanische Naturerklärung. — Idee und Entelechie* ("Thoughts and facts: Philosophical essays, aphorisms and studies, vol. 1: The types of necessity — The mechanical explanation of nature — Idea and entelechy") (Strasbourg: Trübner, 1882), 66–67, 85–86. *NL*.}

22. {Cf. ibid.}

23. *mobile]* {Nietzsche uses the French or Italian *mobile* as a noun, lowercase.}

24. {Cf. Liebmann, *Gedanken und Thatsachen*, 109–10.}

25. {*WP* 720.}

26. This first title of "The Will to Power" can already be found in the notebooks W I 7a {see above, 40[2]} and N VII 2a {39[1]} originating in summer 1885. Further titles for *WP* in this volume: 1[131]; 2[73, 74, 100]; 3[4]; *CW* 17, 5[75], 7[64].

27. {Cf. Friedrich von Hellwald, *Kulturgeschichte in ihrer natürlichen Entwicklung bis zur Gegenwart* ("Cultural history in its natural development to the present") (Augsburg: Lampart, 1883), 1:25.}

28. *tout comprendre c'est tout pardonner]* "to understand everything is to forgive everything." This proverb, often quoted by N, is of uncertain origin; according to {Georg} Büchmann, it goes back to the statement "tout comprendre rend très indulgent" {("understanding everything makes us very lenient")}, found in Madame de Staël's *Corinne, ou l'Italie* (*Corinne, or Italy*), (bk. 18, chap. 5), published 1807.

29. *Sapienta victrix]* "Wisdom is the conqueror"

30. The subtitle, *Prelude to a Philosophy of the Future*, recurs frequently in N's notes and ultimately became the subtitle of *BGE*; cf. also 1[94].

31. *eternal-feminine]* {See the conclusion of Goethe's *Faust II*: "Das Ewig-Weibliche / Zieht uns hinan" ("The Eternal-Feminine / Lifts us up").}

32. {*WP* 975.}

33. {Cf. Liebmann, *Gedanken und Thatsachen*, 85–86.}

34. *reification] Verdinglichung*

35. Supposedly for *WP*, plan 1[35].

36. *self-contained] Selbst-in-sich-Ruhenden*

37. In spring 1885 N read Augustine's *Confessiones*, about which he wrote to Overbeck: "Moreover in this book one sees right into the belly of Christianity: I stand there with the curiosity of a radical physician and physiologist" (31 March 1885 {*KGB* III:3, 34}).

38. *experimentum crucis]* "crucial experiment"

39. Cf. 1[95, 121]; 2[26–27, 38, 42, 47, 53–54, 70, 73]; 3[9].

40. Cf. subtitle in 1[82].

41. {*WP* 371.}

42. {Cf. Maximilian Drossbach, *Ueber die scheinbaren und die wirklichen Ursachen des Geschehens in der Welt* ("On the apparent and real causes of events in the world") (Halle: Pfeffer, 1884), 22. *NL*.}

43. {*WP* 406.}

44. The main title, *The New Enlightenment*, originates in the year 1884. For the subtitle, cf. 1[45].

45. Cf. 1[82] and the corresponding note.

46. N was planning *A Morality for Moralists* in summer 1883. Cf. 1[144] as well as the note to *CW* 14, 7[1].

47. Cf. 1[3] and the corresponding note.

48. Cf. 1[4] at the conclusion.

49. *artificially] künstlich* {from *Kunst*, "art"}

50. *"To comprehend everything"] Alles begreifen*. Cf. 1[42].

51. For *WP*, plan 1[35].

52. {*WP* 654.}

53. *The splitting . . . impotence.]* {Cf. William H. Rolph, *Biologische Probleme, zugleich als Versuch zur Entwicklung einer rationellen Ethik* ("Biological problems, at the same time as an attempt

at the development of a rational ethics") (Leipzig: Engelmann, 1884), 122–29. *NL*.}

54. *Where the males . . . hunger.]* {Cf. ibid., 136–37.}

55. *sameness] Einerleiheit* {also "inconsequentiality"}

56. For *WP*, plan 1[35].

57. The main title, *Gai Saber*, occurs very frequently in N from 1884 to 1885; for the chapter headings of this plan, cf. 1[35, 82, 3]. For the subtitle, cf. 1[45]. Cf. also 2[73].

58. {*WP* 384.}

59. {*WP* 911.}

60. *Lazzaroni]* {Large and relatively coherent underclass of Naples, loyal to chieftains or gangs; beggars.}

61. *Herrnhuter Pietists]* {Herrnhut is a town in Saxony where Moravians (= *Herrnhuter*) were given asylum in the eighteenth century to practice their brand of Christianity.}

62. {*WP* 593.}

63. Cf. 1[151]. For *WP*, plan 1[35]. Cf. also 1[129].

64. {*WP* 1044.}

65. Cf. 1[126].

66. {*WP* 913.}

67. Cf. 1[35] and the corresponding note.

68. Probably thought of as a heading.

69. Cf. N to Overbeck: " . . . when after noon, nearly day by day, I sit or lie on my lonely seaside cliffs, sunning myself like a lizard, my thoughts embarking on adventures of the spirit . . . " (8 January 1881, from Genoa {*KGB* III:1, 57}). Cf. 1[229].

70. *Thoughts of a Grateful One.] Gedanken eines Dankbaren.*

71. Cf. 1[96, 223].

72. Cf. 1[223] and *CW* 13, 6[457, 459, 461].

73. Cf. 1[126].

74. Cf. *CW* 17, 7[67].

75. Cf. 35[76]; *BGE* title of part 9. Cf. 1[232, 237]; 2[16].

76. *hearkening] horchen* {As opposed to *hören* (hearing) or *lauschen* (listening); *horchen* is the stem of *gehorchen*, to obey.}

77. {*WP* 756.}

78. Fragment of a poem?

79. Headings of a poem? Cf., e.g., *CW* 18, 11[52] and the plans for collections of poetry from autumn 1884; cf. 1[129].

80. Cf. 35[79].

81. *Blocksbergs]* {Plural. The *Blocksberg* or *der Brocken* is the gathering place of witches on Walpurgis Night; the highest peak in the Harz Mountains, it is the location of the Walpurgis Night scene in Goethe's *Faust*.}

82. Cf. 1[102].

83. *Raphael without hands]* Cf. *BGE* 274. This popular quotation is from Lessing's *Emilia Galotti* I:4: "Or do you think, Prince, that Raphael would not have been the greatest artistic genius if unfortunately he had been born without hands?" *NL*.

84. *As little state as possible]* Quote from *D* 179.

85. *fortune . . . finding]* Cf. N to Malwida von Meysenbug (about Lou von Salomé): "Actually I had never encountered such a purely natural egoism, lively in every detail, unbroken by consciousness, such an animalistic egoism: and that is why I spoke of 'naiveté'" ({1 January} 1883 {*KGB* III:1, 315}).

86. *the new Melusine]* Cf. Goethe, *Wilhelm Meisters Wanderjahre*, bk. 3, chap. 6. *NL*.

87. *"forgive them]* Cf. Luke 23:34.

88. *"tout comprendre"]* Cf. note 28 above.

89. Cf. 1[204]; 2[12].

90. Cf. 1[153].

91. *space] Spielraum* {literally, room for play}

92. *Comprendre c'est égaler.]* "To understand is to be equal to."

93. Cf. 2[11].

94. Plan for the arrangement of the fragments originating since summer 1885; cf. also 1[187–89].

95. Cf. 1[186].

96. Cf. 1[186].

97. Cf. 1[186].

98. *h⟨omines⟩ religiosi]* "religious people"

99. *in Venere]* "in sexual love"

100. {*WP* 34.}

101. *Junker . . . March] märkischen Junker-Vaterländerei* {Junkers were the landed aristocracy of the march (*Mark*) Brandenburg, which is now the state of Brandenburg; its capital, Potsdam, was the seat of the Prussian kingdom. Nietzsche reminds us here that Germany was united under the leadership of Prussia; the

song "Deutschland Deutschland über Alles" was Germany's national anthem through the Third Reich.}

102. *"Deutschland Deutschland über Alles"]* {German national anthem refrain based on Hoffmann von Fallersleben's poem "Das Lied der Deutschen" ("The Song of the Germans"; 1841).}

103. Aimed at Paul de Lagarde.

104. *Addresses . . . N⟨ation⟩.]* {Johann Gottlieb Fichte, *Reden an die deutsche Nation*, speeches circulated in Napoleon-occupied Berlin in 1810, appealing to Germans to rise up and evict the occupiers. Fichte's *Addresses* contain some of the most chauvinistic expressions of German superiority based on race, language, morality, etc.}

105. Cf. N to Elisabeth and Bernhard Förster: "Then your beast drank three really big glasses of a sweet country wine and was nearly a bit drunk; anyway afterwards I said 'cluck! cluck! cluck!' to the waves when they washed up too violently, as if they were chickens (shortly after Christmas 1885 {*KGB* III:3, 128–29}).

106. *Buatschleli . . . bim!]* {*Butsch* is how Germans refer to the cluck of a chicken; *bimbam* is how Germans say ding-dong. Nietzsche appears to be using nonsensical dactyls for their musical effect (first syllable stressed followed by two unstressed), perhaps in the context of bad taste, nonsense, and Teutonomania.}

107. *factum]* "fact"

108. *coarsens] vergemeinert*

109. Cf. 1[174]; 2[12].

110. Cf. *CW* 18, 18[9].

111. Probably refers to the *Sd* for *BGE* stemming from winter 1885/86.

112. *materia peccans]* "material cause or origin of a sickness"

113. {*WP* 761.}

114. For Sainte-Beuve, cf. *CW* 18, 11[9]; *TI* "Forays" 3.

115. *Précieuses] Prezieusen* ("precious ones") {The seventeenth-century women's literary salon that gathered at the Hôtel de Rambouillet, the Paris residence of Catherine de Vivonne (1588–1665).}

116. *relish] goutieren*

117. *Raffinement]* "refinement"

118. *precious ones] Preziösen* {N here uses a more Germanized spelling for what appears to be a sarcastic reference to a German equivalent of the Précieuses. Cf. note 115 above.}

119. *modo celer . . . ingressus]* {This is a paraphrase of part of a sentence from Sallust's *The War with Catiline* (43–42 BCE), where in chapter 15 Sallust describes the character and some physical features of Catiline. N may be quoting from memory, as he doesn't remember the words exactly, which are "citus modo, modo tardus incessus" (Cataline's "gait was now quick, now slow").}

120. Cf. 1[144–45].

121. Probably refers to Eugen Dühring's autobiography: *Sache, Leben und Feinde* ("Things, life and enemies") (Karlsruhe{: H. Reuther,} 1882), *NL*; cf. N to Peter Gast, 24 November 1887 {*KGB* III:5, 203}.

122. *"ni dieu, ni maître"]* "neither God nor master" {Title of a journal founded in 1880 by French revolutionary socialist Auguste Blanqui (1805–81); cf. *BGE* 22, 202.}

123. For collection of poems? Cf. 1[163] and the corresponding note.

124. *We . . . happiness —]* Cf. 1[143].

125. Title for 1[229]? Cf. 2[4].

126. Title for 1[229]?

127. Cf. 1[154, 237]; 2[16].

128. *Dashes] Gedankenstriche*

129. {*WP* 58.}

130. Cf. 1[154, 232]; 2[16].

131. Cf. *HAH* preface §7.

132. Cf. 1[172].

133. *sentiments]* {N uses the French term here.}

134. Edited by Ernst Windisch, a friend of N's.

135. *Iti vuttakam]* {The *Itivuttaka* is a collection of the sayings of Buddha; N's friend Ernst Windisch published an edition under this title in 1889. N appears to have been aware of the work in progress.}

[2 = W I 8.]

1. {*WP* 939.}

2. Cf. 2[10].

3. *they tell me . . . regard]* {According to *KGW* IX, placement of this line is uncertain.}

4. Cf. 1[230].

5. *1815]* {In this year the Congress of Vienna decided the fate of post-Napoleonic Europe. It is also the year of Napoleon's second and final abdication.}

6. *The spirit]* {In Goethe's *Faust,* lines 511–13, Faust claims kinship with the Earth Spirit, but it spurns him: "You resemble the spirit you comprehend / Not me!"}

7. Cf. 3[6].

8. Refers to *HAH* (as its preface).

9. Cf. 2[3].

10. {Cf. 1[195], note 101. }

11. Cf. 1[185].

12. Cf. 1[174, 204].

13. *Inter pares]* "among equals"

14. *godsend] Zuwurf des Himmels*

15. Cf. *BGE* 242, 257.

16. *commedia umana]* "human comedy" {The Italian suggests an ironic reference to Dante's *Divina Commedia* (*Divine Comedy*) rather than to Balzac's *Comédie humaine* (*Human Comedy*).}

17. *One question comes . . . tasks?]* {*WP* 954.}

18. Cf. 1[154, 232, 237].

19. Cf. 2[166, 31, 33].

20. {*WP* 952.} Cf. *CW* 15, 25[3].

21. *symbolon]* "symbol"

22. {*WP* 950.} Cf. *CW* 15, 25[4].

23. *aut liberi aut libri]* "either children or books"

24. *"le . . . neurose"]* "genius is a neurosis." Cf. *Journal des Goncourt* (Paris{: Charpentier}, 1887), 2:279. *NL.* (The same expression is found in *Idées et sensations* (Paris{: Charpentier}, 1877). *NL.*)

25. Cf. *HAH* 40.

26. Cf. 4[4].

27. Cf. 1[82] and the corresponding note.

28. Cf. 1[82] and the corresponding note.

29. {*WP* 743.}

30. *in praxi]* "in practice"

31. Cf. 2[31]; as chapter heading in 2[66, 40]; 3[9]. Cf. 3[10].

32. Cf. 2[30] and note 31 above.

33. Cf. 2[40] (as chapter heading).

34. *philos⟨opher⟩.]* {Presumably Schopenhauer.}

35. *quod erat demonstradum et demonstratum]* "which was to be proved and has been proved"

36. Cf. 1[82] and the corresponding note.

37. *homo religiosus]* "the religious human being"

38. Cf. 2[43, 44, 46]; as chapter heading in 2[51].

39. *dashes] Gedanken-Striche*

40. Cf. 1[82] and the corresponding note.

41. Cf. 2[41, 44, 46]; as chapter heading in 2[51].

42. *Dashes] Gedankenstriche*

43. *advocate] Advokat* {also "lawyer"}

44. Cf. 2[41, 43, 44]; as chapter heading in 2[51]].

45. Cf. 1[82] and the corresponding note.

46. *Rimus remedium]* "rhyme as remedy"

47. Plan for *BGE*. The motto was later used by N for the fifth book of *JS*.

48. *Carcasse . . .Turenne]* {N used this quote by Henri de La Tour d'Auvergne Turenne (1611–75), French general, as the dedication to the fifth book of *JS*: "Carcass, you tremble? You would tremble even more if you knew where I am taking you." Cf. Ximénès Doudan, *Mélanges et lettres: Avec une introduction par M. le comte d'Haussonville et de notices par MM. de Sacy, Cuvillier-Fleury* ("Concoctions and letters: With an introduction by the Count of Haussonville and notes by Mr. de Sacy and Mr. Cuvillier-Fleury"), vol. 3 (Paris: Calmann Lévy, 1879), 31.}

49. Cf. subtitle of 2[47] and 2[65]. {The format of this fragment has been corrected to match the format in W I 8, p. 159.}

50. Cf. 2[41, 43, 44, 46].

51. Cf. 1[154] and the corresponding note.

52. Cf. 2[51].

53. Cf. 1[82] and the corresponding note.

54. Cf. 1[82] and the corresponding note.

55. {*WP* 977; cf. 42[1].}

56. *prava . . . sublimare.]* "To correct what is wrong, and strengthen the right, and elevate the holy." {See Alcuin, *Abbatis et Caroli Magni Imperatoris Magistri Opera Omnia, Tomus Primus* ("Abbot and teacher of Emperor Charlemagne, complete works, 1st vol."), ed. J.-P. Migne (Paris: 1863), "Operum Pars Prima. — Epis-

tolæ" ("Works pt. 1 — Letters"), Epistola 43, 207. Cf. 42[1] and note 3. Cf. 42[1]. Cf. also Leopold von Ranke, *Weltgeschichte. Fünfter Theil: Die arabische Weltherrschaft und das Reich Karls des Großen* ("World history. Fifth part: Arab world domination and the empire of Charlemagne") (Leipzig: Duncker und Humblot, 1884), 2:169–70.}

57. {*WP* 960.}

58. *continuation]* uncertain reading

59. *attitude] Attitüde*

60. {Cf. Carl Wilhelm von Nägeli, *Mechanisch-physiologische Theorie der Abstammungslehre: Mit einem Anhang: 1. Die Schranken der naturwissenschaftlichen Erkenntniss. 2. Kräfte und Gestaltungen im molecularen Gebiet* ("Mechanical-physiological theory of the doctrine of descent, with an appendix: 1. The limits of scientific knowledge. 2. Forces and formations in the molecular domain") (Munich: Oldenbourg, 1884). *NL*. For other references to Nägeli in this notebook and elsewhere in *CW* 12, see Andrea Orsucci, "Nachweise aus Johann Carl Friedrich Zöllner, Wilhelm Roux, Friedrich Albert Lange, Ernst Haeckel, Carl von Nägeli und Karl Semper," *Nietzsche-Studien* 22 (Berlin: Walter de Gruyter, 1993), 379–83.}

61. {Cf. *JS* 344.}

62. {*WP* 650.}

63. Cf. N to H. von Stein, 18 September 1884 {*KGB* III:1, 533} (and H. von Stein to N, 1 December 1884 {*KGB* III:2, 485}).

64. Cf. *CW* 18, 24[2] (title draft for *EH*).

65. *In media vita.]* "In the middle of life."

66. In *Le* (*WP*^{2} and XIV) fragmented. Plan of a continuation of *BGE*?

67. *the artist-philosopher . . . material]* {Cf. *WP* 795.}

68. *petits faits]* "small facts"

69. *"Liszt-Verein"]* {The Franz Liszt Association (*Verein*) was founded in Leipzig in 1885.}

70. *Rahel]* {Rahel Varnhagen, German-Jewish writer and salon hostess (1771–1833).}

71. *One chapter . . . Heine]* {Cf. *WP* 835.}

72. *new form . . . this]* {*WP* 914.}

73. *magister liberalium artium et hilaritatum]* "master of liberal arts and hilarity"

74. *NB. I have . . . steer —]* Cf. N to Peter Gast: "I feel as though I had grabbed something 'by the horns': quite certainly it is no 'bull'" (21 April 1886 {*KGB* III:3, 181–82}; after completion of the work on *BGE*).

75. {Cf. William H. Rolph, *Biologische Probleme*, 122–29. NL.}

76. {Cf. Liebmann, *Gedanken und Thatsachen*, 66–67, 85–86.}

77. Cf. 1[82] and the corresponding note. For the continuation of *BGE*?

78. Plan for a Zarathustra work; cf. 2[72, 73, 75, 129].

79. *Calina]* "heat haze," "haze"

80. {Cf. *BGE* 258.}

81. Cf. 2[71] and note 78 above.

82. *Thoughts . . . Greeks.]* Cf. *CW* 17, 5[96].

83. *The Will . . . World-Interpretation.]* Cf. 1[35] and the corresponding note.

84. *Noon and Eternity.]* Cf. 2[71] and note 78 above.

85. *Beyond . . . Future.]* Cf. 1[82] and the corresponding note.

86. *Gai . . . Vogelfrei.]* Cf. 1[121] and the corresponding note; here, however, intended as a collection of poems.

87. *Scribe] Schriftgelehrter* {Luther's biblical word for "scribe"; cf. Matthew 23.}

88. *On . . . Dimming.]* Cf. 2[122, 125]; 3[12] (as chapter heading).

89. Cf. 1[135] and the corresponding note.

90. Cf. 2[71] and note 78 above.

91. For plan 2[74]. The number (28) refers to *CW* 17, 5[50]; this text fragmented in *Le*.

92. *Nourishment only . . . been appropriated.]* {Cf. Rolph, *Biologische Probleme*, 60–68, 122–29.}

93. *Aristocracy . . . tool)]* {*WP* 660.}

94. *up-holding] Aufrecht-Erhaltung*

95. For plan 2[74]. In *Le* fragmented.

96. *simplex veritas!]* "simple truth!" Allusion to Schopenhauer's motto: *simplex sigillum veri* ("simplicity is the seal of the true").

97. *Our values . . . in it.)]* {*WP* 590.}

98. Thematics for *WP*. In *Le* fragmented.

99. For *WP*.

100. *campagna romana]* {Roman campagna, the low-lying area surrounding Rome, widely depicted in landscape paintings of the eighteenth and nineteenth centuries.}

101. *tempo lento]* "slowly" (musical time); *lento* underlined by N.
102. {*WP* 1014.}
103. The number (15) refers to *CW* 17, 5[50].
104. Plan of a continuation of *BGE*; cf. 2[138] and *CW* 17, 6[2].
105. *Interpretation, not . . . sign.]* {*WP* 604.}
106. The number (7) refers to *CW* 17, 5[50].
107. *activity presupposes an actor] Thätigkeit einen Täter voraussetze*
108. *causa finalis]* "final cause"; the goal or end of a thing.
109. *causa efficiens]* "efficient cause"; that which actually produces the effect.
110. *In every judgment . . . event itself?]* {*WP* 550.}
111. *causae]* "causes"
112. *τέλη]* "goals" or "ends"
113. *"Attracting" . . . causalism).]* {*WP* 627.}
114. {Cf. *WP* 531.}
115. {The number} (30) refers to *CW* 17, 5[50].
116. {*WP* 557.}
117. {The number} (32) refers to *CW* 17, 5[50].
118. {Cf. *WP* 604.}
119. {The number} (30) refers to *CW* 17, 5[50].
120. {The number} (32) refers to *CW* 17, 5[50].
121. *All unity . . . not one.]* {Cf. *WP* 561.}
122. *One would . . . itself!]* {*WP* 486.}
123. *If all . . . crazy!]* {Cf. *WP* 561.}
124. {The number} (33) refers to *CW* 17, 5[50].
125. *A force . . . more!]* {*WP* 621.}
126. *All events . . . power.]* {*WP* 663.}
127. {*WP* 628.}
128. {*WP* 511.}
129. {The number} (31) refers to *CW* 17, 5[50].
130. {*WP* 518.}
131. {The number} (30) refers to *CW* 17, 5[50].
132. {*WP* 500; cf. Nägeli, *Mechanisch-physiologische Theorie der Abstammungslehre*, 34, 101, 129, 222.}
133. {*WP* 436.}
134. {The number} (34) refers to *CW* 17, 5[50].
135. *non plus ultra]* "uttermost point"; "the highest expression of something"

136. {*WP* 505; cf. Nägeli, *Mechanisch-physiologische Theorie der Abstammungslehre*, 567–68.}
137. {*WP* 219.}
138. {*WP* 1013.}
139. {*WP* 223.}
140. {The number} (35) refers to *CW* 17, 5[50].
141. {*WP* 691.}
142. Draft for *WP* with a new and final subtitle (until 1888). This important fragment is fragmented in *Le*.
143. *How must . . . health.]* {Cf. *WP* 905.}
144. *the hammer . . . task. —]* {Cf. *WP* 905.}
145. {*WP* 491.}
146. {Cf. *WP* 431.}
147. {*WP* 622.}
148. *The significance . . . ugly? —]* {*WP* 416.}
149. *The deception . . . creation.]* {*WP* 1049.}
150. {*WP* 151.}
151. {*WP* 616.}
152. {*WP* 599.}
153. Thoughts for a new preface, "Attempt at a Self-Critique," to *BT*; cf. 2[113].
154. {*WP* 844.}
155. Cf. 2[110] and note 153 above.
156. *raffinement]* "refinement"
157. Cf. 2[110] and note 153 above.
158. *The artwork . . . pre-stage.]* {Cf. *WP* 796.}
159. *The world . . . itself — —]* {Cf. *WP* 796.}
160. *In praxi]* "in practice"
161. *Is art . . . Christian.]* {*WP* 845.}
162. *Infinite interpretability . . . decline.]* {Cf. *WP* 600.}
163. *Unity . . . character!]* {Cf. *WP* 600.}
164. {*WP* 78.}
165. Cf. 2[125] (as chapter heading); the number (38) refers to *CW* 17, 5[50].
166. {*WP* 59.}
167. Cf. 2[73, 125]; 3[12]; the number (37) refers to *CW* 17, 5[50].
168. *deus absconditus]* "hidden god"

169. Overall plan for the new prefaces of the earlier writings. Cf. *CW* 17, 6[3].

170. {*KSA*/*KGW* omit the bracket; cf. W I 8, p. 99.}

171. Cf. 2[73, 122]; 3[12]; 2[121].

172. Plan for book 2 in 2[100]. The numbers (37) and (36) refer to *CW* 17, 5[50]. This text also fragmented in *Le*.

173. *ἡδονή]* "pleasure," "delight"

174. *What is . . . etc.)]* {*WP* 537.}

175. {Cf. *WP* 1.}

176. Draft for book 1 in 2[100]. The number (2) refers to *CW* 17, 5[50].

177. {Cf. *WP* 134.}

178. Cf. the four-part arrangement 2[100].

179. Advertised on the cover of *BGE*; draft; cf. also 2[71] and 2[75].

180. {*WP* 797.}

181. *παῖς παίζων]* "a child playing"

182. Draft for the four books in 2[100].

183. *Preponderance . . . south.]* {Looking at the manuscript (W I 8, p. 87), this line appears above number 1, as part of the unnumbered first paragraph. *KSA* places it at the conclusion of paragraph number 1.}

184. *"the prophet"]* {Here N uses *Prophet*; he much more frequently uses *Wahrsager*.}

185. *5. Nihilistic . . . dared!)]* {Cf. *WP* 69.}

186. *"deus sive natura"]* "God or nature"

187. *Homo natura]* "the natural human being"

188. *Standard according . . . power."]* {*WP* 391.}

189. *The will to power . . . stupid forces]* {*WP* 856.}

190. *The greatest . . . preferable!]* {*WP* 1054.}

191. The number (36) refers to *CW* 17, 5[50].

192. *The assumption . . . beyond — —]* {*WP* 471.}

193. *regressus in infinitum]* "infinite regress"

194. *causa prima]* "first cause"

195. *"Knowing" . . . exhaustion — —]* {*WP* 575.}

196. {*WP* 601.}

197. {The number} (39) refers to *CW* 17, 5[50].

198. *Error veritate simplicior]* "Error is simpler than truth"; against Schopenhauer's motto "Simplex sigillum veri" {"Simplicity is the seal of the true"}; cf. 2[77].

199. Cf. *CW* 17, 6[6].

200. *disciplina intellectus]* "intellectual discipline"

201. *Politika]* "politics," "political matters" {plural of *Politikum*}

202. *Peoples and "common people."] Völker und "Volk."*

203. Cf. 2[82]; *CW* 17, 6[2].

204. Cf. 2[137].

205. *represented, misrepresented] bezeichnet, verzeichnet*

206. *"On Causalism." . . . misrepresented.]* {*WP* 554.}

207. *The immutable . . . functions. —]* {*WP* 631.}

208. The number (30) refers to *CW* 17, 5[50].

209. {*WP* 632.}

210. {The number} (30) refers to *CW* 17, 5[50].

211. {*WP* 638.}

212. {*WP* 240.}

213. {The number} (40) refers to *CW* 17, 5[50].

214. {*WP* 546.}

215. {*WP* 589.}

216. {The number} (30) refers to *CW* 17, 5[50].

217. {*WP* 643.}

218. {Cf. *WP* 556.}

219. {Cf. *WP* 556.}

220. {Cf. *WP* 556.}

221. {Cf. *WP* 556.}

222. {*WP* 1036.}

223. {The number} (36) refers to *CW* 17, 5[50].

224. *The greatest fable . . . "in-themselves")]* {*WP* 555.}

225. {*WP* 470.}

226. Cf. 2[162].

227. {*WP* 564.}

228. *quale]* "how constituted?" "what quality?"

229. {*WP* 547.}

230. {*WP* 620.}

231. *are not surprised at its oddness] über das Wunderliche daran nicht wundern* {*wunderlich* "odd" and *sich wundern* "to be surprised"}

232. {*WP* 410.}

233. The number (41) refers to *CW* 17, 5[50]. For *D*?; cf. 2[165].

234. Cf. 2[155].

235. For *D* 1; cf. 2[165].

236. Cf. 2[161, 164]. The number (41) refers to *CW* 17, 5[50].

237. *An attempt to think . . . principles.]* {Cf. *WP* 253.}

238. *My attempt . . . origin.]* {Cf. *WP* 258.}

239. Discarded beginning for the preface of *JS*; the number (42) refers to *CW* 17, 5[50]. Cf. 2[16, 31, 33].

240. *Concerning . . . "science."]* {*WP* 991.}

241. {*WP* 345.}

242. {*WP* 587.}

243. The number (34) refers to *CW* 17, 5[50].

244. {*WP* 265.}

245. {The number} (44) refers to *CW* 17, 5[50].

246. {The number} (43) refers to *CW* 17, 5[50].

247. {*WP* 582.}

248. *Doudan pensées]* Cf. Ximénès Doudan, *Pensées et fragments suivis des révolutions du goût* ("Thoughts and fragments followed by the revolution of taste") (Paris {: Calmann Lévy,} 1881), 10. *NL*.

249. *Scherer VIII]* Edmond Scherer, *Études sur la littérature contemporaine* ("Studies on contemporary literature"), vol. 8 (Paris{: Calmann Lévy,} 1885), 292. *NL*. {N's library had only this one volume of Scherer's ten-volume work.}

250. {Cf. *WP* 606, where the two paragraphs are in inverse order and edited to appear as a single, grammatically correct paragraph.}

251. {*WP* 70.}

252. The number (45) refers to *CW* 17, 5[50].

253. {Cf. Nägeli, Mechanisch-physiologische *Theorie der Abstammungslehre*, 134–37, 177, 181, 294.}

254. {The number} (46) refers to *CW* 17, 5[50].

255. {Cf. *WP* 267.}

256. For *WP*? In any case not for *BGE* (as claimed by *Le*).

257. For *D*?; cf. also 2[183, 161, 165, 164].

258. The number (42) refers to *CW* 17, 5[50].

259. *Mérimée]* {N omits the accent on the first *e*.}

260. {*WP* 730.}

261. {The number} (10) refers to *CW* 17, 5[50].

262. *πόλις]* "ancient Greek city-state"

263. Cf. 2[181] and note 258 above.

264. The number (47) refers to *CW* 17, 5[50].

265. *My problem: . . . etc.]* {*WP* 301.}

266. Cf. 1[168]. The number (47) refers to *CW* 17, 5[50].

267. *An artistic . . . one —]* {Cf. *WP* 1048.}

268. *placatumque . . . coelum]* Lucretius, *De rerum natura* 1.9: "the peaceful heaven shines on high with scattered light" {underlined by N}.

269. {*WP* 366.}

270. {Cf. *WP* 254.}

271. *pudenda origo]* "shameful origins"

272. {Cf. *WP* 254.}

273. The number (47) refers to *CW* 17, 5[50].

274. *an interpretation] eine Auslegung*

275. *interpreting] interpretiren*

276. *That our honesty . . . and your age.]* {Cf. *WP* 399, where the order of the paragraphs is reversed and the first paragraph truncated.}

277. {*WP* 548.}

278. {The number} (7) refers to *CW* 17, 5[50].

279. {Cf. *WP* 105.}

280. Cf. *CW* 17, 7[7]. The number (23) refers to *CW* 17, 5[50].

281. *"Combien de lieues . . . cet effort."]* ("How many leagues would I not go on foot, and how many days of prison would I not subject myself to in order to hear {Mozart's opera} *Don Giovanni* or {Cimarosa's opera} *Il matrimonio segreto*: and I don't know of any other thing for which I would make such an effort.") {Stendhal's remark is cited by Charles-Augustin Sainte-Beuve in *Causeries du lundi*, vol. 9 (Paris: Garnier Frères, 1854), 307.}

282. {*WP* 415.}

283. The number (41) refers to *CW* 17, 5[50].

284. *raffinement]* "refinement"

285. *In itself . . . punishments.]* {*WP* 146.}

286. {The quote from Kant is from the *Critique of Pure Reason*, A838/B866. Cf. Heinrich Romundt, *Grundlegung zur Reform der Philosophie: Vereinfachte und erweiterte Darstellung von Immanuel Kants Kritik der reinen Vernunft* ("Laying the foundation for reforming philosophy: Simplified and expanded representation

of Immanuel Kant's *Critique of Pure Reason*") (Berlin: Stricker, 1885), 16. *NL.*}

287. Cf. preface to *D* §3.

288. Plan for the continuation (fifth book) of *JS*.

289. *l'art pour l'art]* "art for art's sake"

290. *Misunderstanding of cheerfulness.]* Cf. 2[166, 33].

291. *Critique . . . introspection]* {*WP* 475.}

292. {*WP* 369.}

293. {Cf. *WP* 789.}

294. The number (48) refers to *CW* 17, 5[50].

295. {Cf. *WP* 405.}

296. Cf. *JS* 377.

[3 = W I 7b. W I 3b. Mp XVI 2b. Mp XVI 1b.]

1. Cf. 3[2, 12] (chapter heading).

2. *Final Verse] Abgesang* {The concluding section of the bar in *Minnesang*, medieval German lyric and epic poetry (12th–14th centuries) based on courtly love (*Minne*); Gottfried von Strassburg (d. 1210), for example, wrote and sang *Tristan und Isolde*, which became the basis of Wagner's opera of 1859.}

3. Cf. 1[35] and the corresponding note.

4. *The demand . . . it!]* {*WP* 591.}

5. Cf. 2[8].

6. {Cf. Ivan Turgenev, *Sonderlinge*, translated into German by Wilhelm Lange, in *Vom Fels zum Meer: Spemanns's Illustrierte Zeitschrift für das Deutsche Haus*, vol. 1 (October 1881) (Stuttgart: Spemann, 1881): 235: "Melanie Pawlowna war, wie man zu sagen pflegt, dumm bis zur Heiligkeit" {English translation: "Old Portraits," in *A Desperate Character and Other Stories*, trans. Constance Garnett (New York: Macmillan, 1899), 193: ("Malania Pavlovna was foolish to the point of 'holy innocence,' as it is called; . . . ").}

7. Cf. the poem by the same name in *JS*.

8. Cf. 1[82] and the corresponding note.

9. Cf. 3[9] (chapter heading); 2[30, 31]; 2[40] (chapter heading).

10. For the mirror, cf. 1[3] and the corresponding note.

11. *From the . . . free spirit.]* Cf. 3[1].

12. *On the dimming of Europe.]* Cf. 2[73] and the corresponding note.

13. {*WP* 986.}

14. *"Maledetto . . . immortal!"]* "Damned be the one — who saddens an immortal spirit!" {Cf. F. von Sarburg, "Alessandro Manzoni," *Deutsche Rundschau* 39 (April–June 1884): 400.}

15. Cf. *BGE* 27.

16. *presto]* in music, a rapid tempo

17. *lento]* in music, a slow tempo

18. *staccato]* in musical performance, abruptly disconnected notes

19. {Cf. Julius Jolly, "Eine Reise nach Ostindien: IV. Calcutta," *Deutsche Rundschau* 40 (July–September, 1884): 121.}

[4 = D 18. Mp XV 2c. Mp XVII 3a. Mp XVI 1b.]

1. *"philasophers"]* {Greek ἀσοφία means "folly," "stupidity," so N is mischievously inventing the neologism φιλἀσοφία — *philasophy*.}

2. *"Une croyance . . . écrit."]* "An almost instinctive belief of mine is that every powerful man lies when he speaks and all the more so when he writes." {Stendhal, *Vie de Napoléon: Fragments* ("Life of Napoleon: Fragments") (Paris: Calmann-Lévy, 1876), xv.}

3. *"Je sais, . . . aimés."]* "I know what is the power of human beings; the greater ones cannot demand to be loved." {Cf. Eugène Loudon (pen name of Eugène Balleyguier), "Souvenirs d'Italie," *Revue du monde catholique* 79 (Paris: Sociéte Générale de Librairie Catholique, 1884): 898–99.}

4. Cf. 2[25].

5. *"intempestiva nocte" . . . "ἐν ἀωρονυκτί"]* "untimely night"

6. {*WP* 732.}

7. *Quaeritur]* "One asks"

8. {*WP* 395.}

9. *mysterious-uncanny] heimlich-unheimlichen*

10. *"civilization"] "Civilisierung"*

11. *wisdom's last verdict]* Cf. Goethe, *Faust* II:11574.

12. *"delight in one another!"]* Cf. Luke 2:14.

13. *conditio . . . conditionatum]* "condition" . . . "conditioned"

14. Cf. 40[59].

15. *Ecce . . . sigillum!]* "Behold the seal of our truth!"

Afterword to the Unpublished Fragments from {Spring 1885} to Autumn 1885 (Group {34}–40)

Giorgio Colli[1]

The later fragments from the period of spring to autumn 1885 (34–40) offer a different picture {than do the earlier fragments in groups 28–33}; they transition step by step from the poetic to the abstract sphere. The dithyrambic state of excitement has faded; it now transforms into a ripe, melancholy meditating. As Nietzsche again concentrates on himself and his own past, he considers a revision of his earlier works.

Zarathustra allowed him to surpass philosophy. Suddenly he is no longer interested in everything that was regarded as philosophy according to tradition. Not only is written text incapable of mediating inner exceptional states; even the word is unable to achieve this. "In order to understand one another," we must "also use the same words for the same species of inner experience." The connection is cut off as soon as access to the soul is lacking: "This is said to explain why it is difficult to understand writings like mine: the inner experiences, valuations and needs are different in me" (34[86]). This mistrust of communication leads Nietzsche to the past: "Someone for whom nearly all books have become superficial, who still has the belief about a few people of the past that they possessed

1. {Giorgio Colli's "Afterword" in KSA 11 was written to cover N's unpublished notebooks from autumn 1884 through autumn 1885, that is, notebooks 28–40. We include here only his discussion of the notebooks translated in this volume. His discussion of the other notebooks can be found in the afterword to *CW* 15.}

enough profundity to — not write what they knew" (34[147]). Greece once again forces itself into his mind, where the highest wisdom was dependent neither on writing nor on the word. Incidentally, Nietzsche is only returning here to something he had already indicated earlier; his concept of the "Dionysian" already referred to this wisdom: "For this **ac***cess* to antiquity is what has been buried best [. . .] It seems the Greek world is a hundred times more hidden and foreign than the obtrusive manner of today's scholars would wish. If there is ever to be any recognizing here, then certainly only the same by the same" (34[4]). In accord with his intuition of the agonizing isolation of the soul, with his conviction of the incommunicability of wisdom, his vision of Greece takes on different, more mysterious and concealed features. Double meaning dominates the image: "I believe this was the magic of Socrates: he had a soul and behind it another and behind it another" (34[66]). The contrast consists in the fact that Dionysus is the immediacy of life, whereas our philosophy is text and word: "When the Greek body and Greek soul 'blossomed,' and not to be sure in conditions of pathological effusion and madness, that mysterious symbol emerged of the highest world-affirmation and transfiguration of existence attained so far on earth." Therefore, in Nietzsche's eyes the concept of "Dionysian" has deepened; its core no longer consists of the orgiastic, exalted element: "Here a *standard* is given according to which everything that has grown since is found to be too brief, too poor, too narrow: — merely pronounce the word 'Dionysus' before the best modern names and things, before Goethe, perhaps, or before Beethoven, or before Shakespeare, or before Raphael: and all at once we feel our best things and moments *judged*. Dionysus is a *judge*! — Have I been understood?" What Nietzsche means is not direct, pure, and simple life without qualities — rather, life as the conquest of knowledge, as the pinnacle of humanity: "There is no doubt that the Greeks attempted to interpret the ultimate mysteries 'of the fate of the soul' and everything they knew about the education and purification, above all about the unbudgeable rank order and value-inequality from human to human, from their Dionysian experiences: here for all things Greek is the great depth, the great silence — *one does not know the Greeks* as long as the hidden underground entrance still lies here blocked by rubble" (41[7]). Hence it is the Greeks' experience of the mysteries that is placed at the midpoint of this puzzle. The "underground entrance" leads to a mystical view. For the rest, Nietzsche had already claimed earlier that the Greek faith in mysteries had consisted in an intuition of the eternal return.

To this reorientation of his thinking in spring 1885 Nietzsche gives the name "philosophy of Dionysus." He finds support for this new philosophy even in more recent times: pessimism with its condemnation of the present, artists like Byron who believe in a rank order of human beings, and finally the scholars of antiquity. "Is the 'philosopher' today still *possible*?" The field of knowledge is too great, so that someone who attempts to be a philosopher very probably "will never achieve an *overview* [. . .] Or *too late*, when his best time has passed? Or damaged [. . .], so that his *value judgment* means nothing anymore?" And what counts most, he is lacking the immediacy of experience: "Must he not have experimented with his life in 100 ways in order to be able to speak of its value?" (35[24]). The philosopher is now detached from life: "There are complaints about how bad philosophers have had it so far: the truth is that at all times the conditions for the education of a powerful crafty daring implacable spirit were more favorable than today" (34[68]). Parallel to this the valuation of the concept of truth is completely turned around. The rejection of philosophy (and science) is a rejection of truth: When a great human being "is not talking to himself he has his mask. He would rather lie than tell the truth: it requires more spirit and *will*" (34[96]). And if philosophy and science have always been the search for truth, then now the "philosophy of Dionysus" is supposed to be the search for deception: "Supposing the world were false, [. . .] Could the exhortation not be precisely: '*be* a deceiver'? [. . .] The very great and powerful *were* deceivers so far: their task demanded it of them." But the world is quite definitely false, and the philosophers as seekers of truth contradict the meaning of life: "If life and the *value* of life rest on well-believed errors, then precisely the truth-teller, the truth-willer could be the harmful one" (40[44]). And life itself coincides with error and death with truth: "supposing we live as a result of error, what then can the 'will to truth' be? Would it not have to be a 'will to death'?" (40[39]).

At this point in time Nietzsche was ripe for the silence of the mysteries. But the destroyer of philosophy was still a philosopher, and above all his kind of loneliness could not dispense with the comfort of the word. Thus he sets about designing a philosophy of error, of fraud, and of deception. The most broadly propagated, concrete, and fraudulent deception is the world of the beings that surround us, the principle of individuation: "That a human being is a multiplicity of forces that stand in an order of rank"; the individual consists of many living beings, "and he who otherwise commands must obey for once. The concept 'individual' is false. These beings do not exist at all in isolation" (34[123]). From his disappointment over the individual results an even greater disappointment over consciousness, the intellect: "Just as a general does not want to hear about many things and must not hear about them, in order not to lose his total overview: so too in our conscious intellect *above all* there must be an *excluding* drive that *scares thing away*, a selecting one, which only permits *certain facta* to present themselves. Consciousness is the hand with which the organism reaches about itself most widely: [. . .] A concept is an invention that does not correspond *entirely* to anything; but to many things a little bit." The path to abstraction even strengthens the deceptive: "But with this invented rigid world of concepts and numbers humans gain a means to master tremendous quantities of facts as if with signs [. . .] *This intellectual world, this sign-world is pure 'illusion and deception'*" (34[131]).

And precisely the dissolution of reality into error and deception awakens the need for a firm foundation, for a background from which the deceptive can stand out. This is the first development of the teaching of the will to power: "To comprehend the 'person' as *deception* [. . .] — a will to power cuts through persons, it requires the *diminution* of perspective, '*egoism*,' as an *occasional condition of existence* [. . .] The diminution of the effective principle to a 'person,' to the individual" (35[68]). Individuation is the deception in which the will to power conceals itself.

Thus the possibility took shape for Nietzsche to develop a constructive teaching. But the thread of these epistemological speculations had been broken at the time of *Thus Spoke Zarathustra*. Now Nietzsche takes it up again, but finds himself faced with a concept that no longer seems to him adequate. In these unpublished fragments of summer 1885, one experiences an interesting moment in Nietzsche's development: the emergence of the theory of will to power proceeds from the language of his so-called positivistic period, from the mechanistic formulations, and from the scientific concept of "force": "that it is the will to power that also guides the inorganic world [. . .] The 'effect at a distance' cannot be set aside: *something pulls something else to itself, something feels itself pulled*. This is the fundamental fact: on the other hand the mechanistic notion of pressure and thrust is only a hypothesis on the basis of *appearance* and the *sense of touch*" (34[247]). As is clear, Nietzsche is attempting as always to stay on positivistic terrain: "The triumphant concept 'force' with which our physicists have ousted God from the world requires one more enhancement: an internal world must be attributed to it, to which I refer as 'will to power,' i.e., as an insatiable demand for displaying power." And here comes the metaphysical transition. An inner world is attributed to force, an inside, a substratum; something not physical, not capable of being experienced, a demand, a Spinozist or Schopenhauerian *conatus*: "There is no helping it: one must grasp all motion, all 'appearances,' all 'laws' only as symptoms of an internal event and use to the limit the analogy of the human being" (36[31]). Science is betrayed: one knows how analogism is maligned in science, and besides — with an eye toward a rigorous judgment on cosmic events — such an anthropomorphic confession seems naïve.

The inner structure of this will to power is seen in an Empedoclean manner, as a play of attraction and repulsion: "The weaker presses itself upon the stronger [. . .] The stronger on the contrary fends things off [. . .] The greater the pressure for unity, the more one can infer weakness; the greater the pressure for variety, difference, internal dissolution, the more strength is there." Here a logical intuition of the highest order surfaces — that the separation is still a bond: "The drive to approach — and the drive to repel something are the bond in the inorganic and well as the organic world. The whole separation is a prejudice. The will to power in every combination of forces, *fending off the stronger, pouncing on the weaker* is *more correct*" (36[21]). If in the structure of the individual the urge to exclude, to chase things away, is determinative for the expansion of consciousness, then this is also valid for the structure of the will to power, whose deceitful projection is the individual: "The connection between the inorganic and the organic must lie in the repelling force that every atom of force exerts. Life would be defined as an enduring form of the *process* of *force determinations* [. . .] The extent to which a resistance lies even in obeying; one's individual power is by no means surrendered. Likewise in commanding there is a concession that the absolute power of the opponent is not vanquished, not incorporated, dissolved. 'Obeying' like 'commanding' are forms of jousting." (36[22]). This last formulation even allows us to conceive of a substitute for the "will to power" as principle through the "struggle for power": "a struggle, assuming that one understands this word broadly and deeply enough still to understand the relationship of the ruler to the ruled as one of wrestling, and the relationship of the obeyer to the ruler as one of resisting" (40[55]). The same thing is said once again in more "physical" and positivistic language: "Battle of the atoms [. . .] The atom fights for its duration, but other atoms attack it in order to increase their strength. *Both* processes: that of disintegration and that of compression to be understood *as effects* of the will to power" (43[2]).

In order to bolster this conception, the perspective of the "inside" has to be broadened, its universal and objective validity postulated; that is, the metaphysical operation has to be completed: "the question is [. . .] whether we acknowledge the will really as *effecting*? If we do this, then naturally it can only have effect on something that is *of its kind*: and not on 'materials.' *Either* one must interpret all effect as illusion [. . .] and then nothing at all is comprehensible: *or* one must attempt to think all effects as being of the same kind, like acts of will, hence make the hypothesis as to whether all mechanical events, insofar as there is a force in them, are not simply force of will" (40[37]).

One can summarize as follows: Spirit, emotions, and sensations in us stand in the service of our valuations. But the latter reveal something about our life conditions, for the most part about the conditions that make life possible at all (40[69]). These conditions of existence in turn can be traced back to the will to power. This formulation is not unequivocal, and in fact Nietzsche also adds: "The will to power is the last factum to which we are able to get down" (40[61]). But in order to prove that the will to power is *no* fact, everything that has been said and quoted so far suffices. The positivistic prejudice does not die so easily, and even when Nietzsche allows metaphysical abstractions to arise, he still believes he has "facts" in hand. Nietzsche is more skilled in defending against another attack that could be directed at the will to power — in case one were to interpret it too substantially, almost in opposition to what is illusory in the world from which the investigation had proceeded: "*Appearance* [*Schein*] as I understand it is the actual and single reality of things [. . .] A specific name for this reality would be 'the will to power,' namely described from the inside and not from the standpoint of its incomprehensible fluid protean nature" (40[53]).

Translator's Afterword

Adrian Del Caro

The *Nachlass* or literary remains that concern us here, often referred to as Nietzsche's unpublished or posthumous notes or fragments, make up a considerable portion of his total output as a writer. When used in the fullest, most extensive sense, the *Nachlass*, as Alan Schrift explains, would also include several late titles that Nietzsche never saw through to publication because of his descent into madness, as well as early essays and lectures that he completed but did not intend for publication. Schrift further describes the unpublished notes and notebooks portion of the *Nachlass* in the following terms: "[I]n the thirteen volumes of Nietzsche's writings that comprise the *Kritische Studienausgabe* (*KSA*), edited by Giorgio Colli and Mazzino Montinari, Nietzsche's unpublished notes and notebooks make up 4,869 of the total 7,945 pages."[1] On the sheer volume that it represents, Nietzsche's *Nachlass* cannot be ignored, but another factor that elevates its significance is the controversy surrounding the so-called *Will to Power*, that "non-book" as Schrift calls it, because Nietzsche's famous "non-book" was pieced together by his sister and her editors from unpublished notes and drafts from the *Nachlass* of the years 1885–88. Schrift gives a comprehensive treatment of the *Nachlass* of the last three years of Nietzsche's sanity, providing a reliable and coherent picture of

1. Alan D. Schrift, "Nietzsche's *Nachlass*," in *A Companion to Friedrich Nietzsche: Life and Works*, ed. Paul Bishop (Rochester, NY: Camden House, 2012), 405.

how the non-book was constructed, editorial evidence that Nietzsche abandoned the writing of a major work under the title *The Will to Power*, information regarding the contents of the *Nachlass* 1885–88, and finally, commentary on the significance of these three volumes of the *Kritische Studienausgabe* for Nietzsche scholarship generally.[2] My intentions in this Afterword are more modest, inasmuch as I focus on the unpublished notes from the period during which Nietzsche was working on *Beyond Good and Evil* and *On the Genealogy of Morality*, namely, April 1885 until summer 1886. Before I analyze the value and content of these notes subsuming 460 pages of *KSA* volumes 11 and 12, it is necessary to give a sense of their scope and physical presence, their "footprint" if you will, within the *Nachlass* generally and within the controversy surrounding the *Nachlass* of the 1880s.

Walter Kaufmann's edition of *The Will to Power*, based on the 1911 edition of *Der Wille zur Macht* that appeared as volumes 15 and 16 of the *Grossoktav-Ausgabe*, contains 1,067 entries, ranging from fragments consisting of one or two lines all the way up to multipage entries that resemble the longer "aphorisms" of *Beyond Good and Evil*; this collection of over one thousand fragments "offers a selection from Nietzsche's notebooks of the years 1883 through 1888."[3] By my count, 203 of the 1,067 entries were taken from the *Nachlass* that is translated in this volume, hence 19 percent of *The Will to Power* can be traced to these notes from the period of *BGE* and *GM*. For further context, the total number of entries in this volume is 1,062, roughly equal to the number of entries in *The Will to Power*. By and large, given the heavy reliance in the English-speaking world on *The Will to Power* by readers who did not consult the *Nachlass*, our understanding of Nietzsche's unpublished notes rests on a sliver of a corpus whose scope and content has yet to

2. Ibid.

3. Friedrich Nietzsche, *The Will to Power*, ed. Walter Kaufmann, trans. Walter Kaufmann and R. J. Hollingdale (New York: Vintage Books, 1968), "Editor's Introduction" xv.

be explored — and the same can be said of Nietzsche scholarship that is informed by readings in the original German insofar as those readers relied on *Der Wille zur Macht*. In Nietzsche scholarship we should allow ourselves to be guided by the principle that Nietzsche's preferred version of the various forms and iterations of his writing is reflected in the works he chose to publish; publications trump literary remains in the matter of establishing the authoritative text or what Germans call "die Ausgabe letzter Hand." But the *Nachlass* gains in importance to the overall writings of Nietzsche precisely because it is so large in relation to the published texts, and because it contains far more than discarded drafts. Here a word about how Nietzsche wrote may help to explain why the *Nachlass* is so vast and why it has yet to be mined.

The first thing we should bear in mind is that beginning with *Human, All Too Human* (1878–80), Nietzsche was no longer employed, having taken a medical retirement from the University of Basel in 1879. His entire activity from 1879 to January 1889 consisted of writing, and we find constant expressions of this independence throughout his writings — Nietzsche's unfettered, stateless existence (he gave up his Prussian citizenship in order to accept his position in Switzerland) was both a blessing and a curse. In his published writings, letters, and notes, we see him riding the highs of a life of reading, contemplation, and sovereign commentary, but we also witness the lows that included personal loneliness, social isolation, lack of recognition, and generally disappointments with his family (his sister and mother) and his publishers. It could be said that during these years Nietzsche lived in and for his writings, with writing serving as a lifeline and manifesting a bigger, more tumultuous and consequential life than the rather quiet, unremarkable one of a sickly pensioner. With the help of his friend Heinrich Köselitz (pseudonym Peter Gast), his former student turned composer, and sometimes with the help of his sister, Nietzsche would prepare manuscripts for publication; inevitably these manuscripts were the result of notes Nietzsche had penned into quarto- and octavo-sized volumes, notebooks, and loose-leaf paper. The *Nachlass* consisting of unpublished notes spans 106 notebook collections, as Schrift points out, whose chronological arrangement is rendered difficult by the fact that Nietzsche often recycled his paper and "wrote on the backs of pages, sometimes wrote from front to back and at other times from back to front."[4]

In the *Kommentar* volume of *KSA* we find detailed information regarding the physical circumstances under which Nietzsche wrote his various books, as well as the variants of his published manuscripts. With respect to *Human, All Too Human II* (published 1879), we learn that "between May and November 1878, N[ietzsche] wrote notes in ten small notebooks," the first five containing mainly autobiographical sketches and thoughts about Wagner, while the other five notebooks were devoted to the manifold themes of the first volume of *Human, All Too Human*.[5] The new volume of *Human, All Too Human* was published in March 1879 by the Schmeitzner publishing house. Montinari describes in detail the process that led to the second volume of *Human, All Too Human*, drawing on a letter from Nietzsche to Gast:

> In St. Moritz, between the end of June and the beginning of September 1879, N[ietzsche] filled six pocket notebooks (two of these no longer exist) with notes, which he then transferred as a clean copy into two larger notebooks and 22 loose sheets . . . [to Gast] "Except for a few lines, everything was conceived *while underway* and sketched by pen in 6 small notebooks: transcribing it made me ill almost every time. About 20 *longer* chains of ideas, unfortunately quite essential ones, I had to let slip, because I never found time enough to draw them out

4. Schrift, "Nietzsche's *Nachlass*," 419.

5. Mazzino Montinari, *Friedrich Nietzsche: Kommentar zu den Bänden 1–13*, in *Kritische Studienausgabe*, ed. Giorgio Colli and Mazzino Montinari (Berlin/Munich: Walter de Gruyter / Deutscher Taschenbuchverlag, 1967–1977 and 1988), 14:156; *CW* 4, 433.

> from the most awful ink scrawling: just as occurred for me already the preceding summer [as *MM* (*Mixed Opinions and Maxims*) emerged]. Afterward, I lose the connection of ideas from my memory" (5 October 1879, *KGB* II:5, 450). This passage from his letters is significant because it describes N[ietzsche]'s manner of working after *MM* and explains the origin of many remaining fragments — from *MM* on.[6]

This manner or style of writing is indeed significant, if for no other reason than to vividly demonstrate how Nietzsche's entire physical activity was at work on and affected by his writing — his writing was constant and torturous, and *from the start* his penmanship was difficult to decipher. Montinari tells us that this style was typical of Nietzsche beginning in 1878, so that the entire decade of productivity spanning his retirement from the University of Basel to his last work on the preparation of manuscripts in Turin in winter 1888–89 falls under the arduous procedures described above. It would be an understatement, then, to assert that Nietzsche took "great pains" to record his thoughts at every available opportunity and to preserve them against odds. Given his relatively short career as a writer (ca. 1870–88); the number of published books; the voluminous production of unpublished essays, lectures, notes, and fragments that itself outweighs the volume of the published material; and the primitive conditions under which his writings were produced, we would have to conclude that Nietzsche is one of the most dedicated and tenacious writers of the modern era, an individual who sacrificed most of his time and much of his health to committing his thoughts to paper.

When Karl Schlechta published his three-volume edition of Nietzsche's works (1954–57), he brought a new spirit to the enterprise and challenge of establishing a critical edition by virtue of his treatment of the *Nachlass*. Schlechta revealed in his "Philological Postscript" and his afterword to the third volume

6. Montinari, *Kommentar*, 157; *CW* 4, 433.

that previous editors had falsified Nietzsche's letters under instructions from Nietzsche's sister; he also presented his own unnumbered arrangement of the *Nachlass* of the 1880s, thereby departing from the prewar practice of maintaining a so-called *Will to Power* consisting of numbered entries designed to resemble all of Nietzsche's publications since *Human, All Too Human* (1878). While Schlechta's arrangement of the *Nachlass* is itself problematic in its chronology and selectivity, it did indeed throw open the prospect of delving into the editorial obfuscations and falsifications that had tainted Nietzsche editions since the 1890s, and shortly after Schlechta's efforts we have the comprehensive undertaking of Colli and Montinari for the first critical edition (first Italian volumes appearing in 1964). Schrift writes that "Karl Schlechta may overstate the case when he concluded that 'no *new* central thought is to be found'" in the posthumous notes,[7] and to this I would add that Schlechta oversimplified the *Nachlass* when he wrote: "Der Nachlass vergröbert" (the *Nachlass* coarsens).[8] Schlechta performed a service by pointing out the deficiencies and manipulations that characterized earlier Nietzsche editions, but he was too dismissive of the *Nachlass*, and we can only accept his "coarsens" verdict in a narrow and qualified sense. When it comes to comparing the *Nachlass* to the published writings straight up, where the *Nachlass* is defined as texts deliberately discarded by Nietzsche (early drafts), then one might conclude that the *Nachlass* gives a coarse or lesser version. But as I noted earlier, the *Nachlass* cannot reasonably be defined in this limited sense — it contains too much writing that Nietzsche did not merely discard or clearly revise in favor of published writings. My own view would be slightly closer to Karl Jasper's view, as it is explained by Schrift: Jaspers already in 1936 held that it was impossible to establish the primacy of

7. Schrift, "Nietzsche's *Nachlass*," 420.

8. Karl Schlechta, ed., *Friedrich Nietzsche: Werke in drei Bänden* (Munich: Carl Hanser Verlag, 1966), 3:1433.

either the published or unpublished works, and he argued that the entire *Nachlass* needs to be reproduced as faithfully as possible.[9] While I do indeed insist on the primacy of the published works, I would like to see more use of the *Nachlass* to inform and enhance scholarship on Nietzsche, and I agree that the *Nachlass* should be published in its entirety.

In a partial approach to making the *Nachlass* accessible in English, Rüdiger Bittner has edited a volume that includes yet another selection of notes under the title *Friedrich Nietzsche: Writings from the Late Notebooks*. Bittner begins his selection with the post-*Zarathustra* phase, just as I do here, but he makes his own selection from the years 1885–88, thereby creating yet another "alternative" text instead of translating and publishing the entire *Nachlass*. Moreover, Bittner is convinced that Nietzsche's notes after *Zarathustra* differ in a "radical" manner from previous notes, and he finds the explanation in a letter to Franz Overbeck in which Nietzsche comments that his philosophy is no longer communicable in print.[10] Taking this comment at face value, instead of assessing it more soberly as a typical Nietzschean commentary on the enormity of his philosophical task post-*Zarathustra* and as yet another sample of Nietzsche's hyperbole and hypochondria, Bittner extrapolates that "[t]he notebooks became the field where Nietzsche was still able if not to communicate, then at least to express, his ideas."[11] This is a baffling assertion when we consider that post-*Zarathustra* Nietzsche published and completed for publication the following books: *Beyond Good and Evil* (1886); *On the Genealogy of Morality* (1887); an expanded edition of *Joyful Science* (fifth part added, 1887); *The Case of Wagner* (1888); *Twilight*

9. Schrift, "Nietzsche's *Nachlass*," 420.

10. Friedrich Nietzsche, *Writings from the Late Notebooks*, ed. Rüdiger Bittner, trans. Kate Sturge (Cambridge: Cambridge University Press, 2003), x.

11. Ibid., x. See also p. xiii: "[A]nd as I have mentioned, it is the post-*Zarathustra* Nietzsche whose philosophical projects, no longer finding adequate expression in his published writings, have to be gathered from the notebooks."

of the Idols (finished and printed 1888, published 1889); *Nietzsche Contra Wagner* (finished 1888, published February 1889); *The Antichrist* (finished 1888, published 1895); *Ecce Homo* (finished 1888, published 1908); and *Dionysus Dithyrambs* (finished 1888, published 1898). The importance of the *Nachlass* must not be elevated at the expense of the published works, for clearly Nietzsche was in fact quite capable of expressing his philosophy in his publications in the years 1885–88, contrary to Bittner's hyperbolic claim. Another area in which I heartily disagree with Bittner regarding the nature of the *Nachlass* is his interpretation of "philosophical import" as it guided his selection of entries: "Following the criterion of philosophical import also meant entirely neglecting a number of themes to which Nietzsche devoted some attention in his writing, like that of men and women, or of 'peoples and fatherlands' . . . to the best of my understanding Nietzsche had nothing of interest to say on either of these matters — nothing of philosophical interest, that is."[12] Again, when an editor "selects" based on his understanding of what constitutes "philosophical interest," errors of omission are bound to occur. Much of Nietzsche's writings for the period 1885–88 feature serious discussions about women, peoples, the theme of Europe, nationalism, anti-Semitism, and so on — to relegate all of this to irrelevance and to exclude it from a selection of the *Nachlass* is another instance in the long history of editorial intervention and bias in the matter of "which Nietzsche" we should be allowed to read.

With respect to the value of the *Nachlass*, it is easy to exaggerate, as demonstrated historically by the fabrication and marketing of the so-called *Will to Power*, and the subsequent elevation of the *Nachlass* by Heidegger and Jaspers — two very different spirits, yet each inclined to overstate the significance of these copious unpublished writings. When Bittner in our time suggests that the *Nachlass* gives voice to Nietzsche's philosophical

12. Nietzsche, *Writings from the Late Notebooks*, xv.

projects whereas the published writings do not, we have a contemporary example of overexaggerating its value. Schrift summarizes the value of the *Nachlass* in five main points, which I will briefly paraphrase here before commenting on an emerging sixth point. First, we are given a view to Nietzsche's "workshop," to his thought experiments with all their twists and turns; in the case of the idea of the eternal recurrence, for instance, there are more "remnants" about it in the workshop notes than there are published explanations. Second, the *Nachlass* serves as a chronicle of Nietzsche's thought process; although his thoughts are not synonymous with his philosophical positions, they reveal his concerns and include frequent references to and sometimes transcriptions of the writings of other philosophers, scientists, novelists, and so on. Third, there is considerable philological value in the unpublished notes, insofar as they sometimes represent earlier versions of the published formulations; variants play a key role in Nietzsche's technique as a writer. A fourth indicator of the value of the *Nachlass* is the very extent to which it has been used until now to provide provocative interpretations, including those by Heidegger, Jaspers, Löwith, Bataille, Deleuze, Kofman, et al. Schrift's fifth point about the value of the *Nachlass* is that it presents "a great deal of philosophical material that never makes its way into the published texts."[13] It is this fifth point regarding the philosophical material that was never published by Nietzsche that prompts analysis in the direction of uncovering a sixth point.

Schrift asks, What are readers to make of this body of material that is philosophical in nature but not published by Nietzsche? He quotes Bernd Magnus, who divided Nietzsche commentators into two groups, lumpers and splitters; the former have no qualms about assigning an equal (or higher) value to Nietzsche's unpublished notes, the latter make sharp distinctions between the unpublished and the published writings.

13. Schrift, "Nietzsche's *Nachlass,*" 421–24.

> Since Magnus first drew this distinction, and since the Colli-Montinari edition has become the canonical edition, the number of scholars who simply lump all of Nietzsche's writings together, treating published and unpublished works in the same way, has dwindled to near zero, especially among English-speaking Nietzsche scholars. But the number of extreme splitters, who generate their interpretations of Nietzsche exclusively in terms of the published works, remains a small minority.[14]

The sixth point concerning the value of the *Nachlass*, then, is this: there is every positive motivation to explore and reasonably rely on the *Nachlass* now that it is no longer synonymous with the infamous so-called *Will to Power*. In other words, as long as the use of the *Nachlass* included and frequently was limited to citations from that non-book, at least among English-speakers, the rest of the *Nachlass* was ignored and remained suspect; both "lumpers" and "splitters" did not come to grips with the actual *Nachlass*. Now that the content of *The Will to Power* has returned to its home in the *Nachlass*, and the Colli-Montinari edition has taken hold, individuals are free to make independent evaluations of the *Nachlass* generally. On balance, the *Nachlass* simply represents *more Nietzsche, more Nietzsche material*, and readers should be provided with the unembellished, unstaged, unmediated, and full text.

Since the publication of Alan Schrift's "Nietzsche's Nachlass" in 2012, another important contribution has been published by Peter Poellner: "Nietzsche's Metaphysical Sketches: Causality and Will to Power."[15] Some of the "great deal of philosophical material" referenced by Schrift immediately above, which as he explains did not make its way into Nietzsche's published works, is given thorough treatment by Poellner; he acknowledges the importance of weighing the merits of the published works over

14. Ibid., 424.

15. In *The Oxford Handbook of Nietzsche*, ed. Ken Gemes and John Richardson (Oxford: Oxford University Press, 2013), 675–700.

and against the unpublished fragments, but his main concern is with the nature of the fragments themselves: "For these notebooks, as well as other notes from the same period but not included in *The Will to Power*, prominently contain many apparent positive claims and reflections on metaphysical issues, while such claims are very largely — some would even say entirely — absent from the writings published by Nietzsche himself during his 'mature' period."[16] Poellner's is not a new view, given that Nietzsche's earliest editors and others like Heidegger wanted a metaphysical Nietzsche for various purposes, and even used the metaphysical, that is, allegedly more "philosophical," writings of the so-called will-to-power notes as a demonstration that Nietzsche had done his best philosophical work under this banner. But Poellner is correct in identifying metaphysics as a chief concern of Nietzsche in his notes and fragments, and this same concern largely applies to the notes of this *Nachlass* volume.

The bulk of Poellner's essay is concerned with the content of Nietzsche's metaphysical fragments across four major areas: forces, willing, the psychology of the will to power, and the will to power in nature. A final section of his essay is closer to my efforts in this Afterword, namely, to assess the importance of the *Nachlass* for Nietzsche's work in its entirety. Poellner is not completely satisfied with the explanation of Maudemarie Clark that "we should interpret Nietzsche's apparently metaphysical exercises as performative illustrations of the futility of metaphysics," because Poellner sees Nietzsche investing too much detail and too much consistency in these notes.[17] He likewise considers but glosses over the suggestion of Ken Gemes (also made by Schrift) that the metaphysical notes represent thought experiments to which Nietzsche remained uncommitted.[18] In sizing up the place of metaphysics in Nietzsche's philosophy,

16. Poellner, "Nietzsche's Metaphysical Sketches," 675–76.
17. Ibid., 695–96.
18. Ibid., 696.

Poellner opts for the following hypothesis: "At the center of Nietzsche's indifferentism in (most of) the later published writings lies the idea that most metaphysical disputes are disputes about *purely theoretical* propositions, that is, about propositions which have no predictive consequences and cannot in principle be assessed by our techniques of empirical confirmation or disconfirmation."[19] This is easy enough to follow, given Nietzsche's early and sustained critique of metaphysics once he had gotten *The Birth of Tragedy* out of his system; his pursuit of the "closest things," beginning with *Human, All Too Human*, whereby the things closest to us are all in the here and now, all vital aspects of our quotidian lives, all properly of major concern to us because they are the substance of our existence, in my view represents one of the more compelling dismissals of metaphysics (read: the furthest things) in the history of philosophy.[20] But Poellner still does not have an explanation for why Nietzsche obviously invested much time and effort in sketching out details of metaphysical scenarios in these notes, so he concludes that Nietzsche must have had misgivings and unease about his own indifference to metaphysics: "The metaphysics of the will to power is an interpretation of reality which Nietzsche seems to have accepted at least some of the time, and which inscribes in the nature of the world at large that which he — again, some of the time — values above all: the conscious will to power."[21] Poellner may be right in ascribing this unease to Nietzsche, an unease about metaphysical explanations that suggests hedging one's bets, or keeping two sets of books — one for the official "public" record, another for himself and posterity. However, along the

19. Ibid.

20. See Adrian Del Caro, *Grounding the Nietzsche Rhetoric of Earth* (Berlin: Walter de Gruyter, 2004), 29–32; chap. 4, "Logic and Limit in the Eternal Recurrence of the Same"; and throughout, where I discuss "the closest things" as those with which the immanent life should be concerned.

21. Poellner, "Nietzsche's Metaphysical Sketches," 698.

axis represented by science on one end and metaphysics on the other, Nietzsche clearly embraced science, even while he critically observed that scientists themselves were still too beholden to metaphysics (*GM* III 23–24; *JS* 344, 373). Judged in terms of potentially divided loyalties, Nietzsche ends up championing scientific method above metaphysics at every turn, and this not only informs his philosophy overall but also helps to explain why he relegated his metaphysics and non-book *The Will to Power* to his notes, eventually deciding to abandon the whole project of a "will to power" main work. Too often readers forget that Nietzsche based his reputation as a "coming philosopher" and a new "Dionysian philosopher" on the quality and content of his very deliberately selected and meticulously edited nontraditional philosophical writing, which in turn owes much of its spirit and élan to the critique of metaphysics. The unpublished notes prove that Nietzsche was capable of doing old-school philosophy, but then we disrespect his *new philosophizing*, that is, the actual published works, by wondering so much about why he wrote these notes.

Nietzsche's State of Mind for the Period April 1885 to June 1886

This was a transitional time for the author of *Thus Spoke Zarathustra*, whose fourth and final part he published in April 1885, at his own expense in a tiny edition of forty copies, for distribution to his friends and acquaintances.[22] His latest work and masterpiece now behind him both chronologically and psychologically, Nietzsche began searching for his philosophical voice, the voice that would provide "a type of provisional glossarium in which the most important conceptual- and value-innovations" of *Zarathustra* could be unpacked.[23] That

22. Montinari, *Kommentar*, 282 (translation forthcoming in *CW* 7).
23. See Montinari's editorial introduction to *BGE* in *CW* 8, 355.

"glossarium" turned out to be *Beyond Good and Evil*, the book in which Nietzsche emerges for the first time as a philosopher.[24] Thus Nietzsche engaged in looking forward for the purpose of establishing his philosophical task, while simultaneously looking back to *Zarathustra* for the energy and fuel that would underlie the philosophical task. As usual, his physical health would play a major role, even a delimiting role, in shaping the outcome of his plans.

This inseparable linkage between his physical health and his daily production of writing is expressed by David Farrell Krell and Donald L. Bates in terms of mobility: "If his ill-health served as the barometer that sent him packing from one work site to another, the storm of thinking and writing was all he ever craved."[25] Earlier I alluded to Nietzsche's astonishing productivity as a writer, despite his relatively short career and his precarious, on-and-off health; the expression "storm of thinking and writing" appears to do it justice. The same authors also give us an idea of how dangerous it was for Nietzsche to move about Europe:

> Indeed, travel for him was always agony: one day's train journey would cost him at least three days' recuperation in bed. Nietzsche undertook his journeys against all the odds, and he seldom won for losing. He was clearly driven by the need to find the place that would be propitious for his *work*, even if the search and the discovery of new sites should menace his *life*.[26]

It is doubtful whether Nietzsche ever escaped from the vicious circle of establishing a place and a physical equilibrium suitable for working, only to suffer the consequences later on as his health became progressively worse. The extraordinary sense of

24. Adrian Del Caro, "Afterword," in *CW* 8, 432–33.

25. David Farrell Krell and Donald L. Bates, *The Good European: Nietzsche's Work Sites in Word and Image* (Chicago: University of Chicago Press, 1997), 3.

26. Ibid., 5.

mission, and what the biographer Curt Paul Janz has referred to as "demonic drivenness,"[27] compelled Nietzsche to exceed the boundaries of his own frailty.

Letters from the period are an excellent source of information regarding his health. On 31 March 1885 he writes to his friend Overbeck, complaining that his eyes are getting worse since last summer; he sees spots, has blurring, and his eyes are watery (*KGB* III:3, 33). In April he tells Overbeck that his eyes are worse than ever, and that he longs to be in Venice, "the darkest of all cities" (*KGB* III:3, 36–37), a wish that he reiterates in a letter to Gersdorff on the next day: "I long for the darkness of its little lanes" (*KGB* III:3, 8). But by the end of April his sojourn in Venice has not helped his eyes, and he complains once more in a letter about difficulty with reading, blurring, and constant tears (*KGB* III:3, 42). Nietzsche wrote even more detailed letters to his mother during this period, telling her at the end of May that his eyes get worse by the day, "and if no one comes to my aid, I will probably be blind by the end of the year" (*KGB* III:3, 55). A month later, he explains to his mother why he must move away from Sils-Maria: there is no shade; he needs a room with high ceilings, a comfortable armchair, and light without direct sunlight and without reflective light from white house walls. He informs his mother that Frau Roeder-Wiederhold from Zurich takes dictation from him for three hours a day (*KGB* III:3, 57).

In July Nietzsche writes to Overbeck that he has help now from a German woman from Meiningen who reads to him and takes notes; he describes a "sudden, abrupt disappearance of vision" like he had last summer: "I dictated every day for 2–3 hours, but my 'philosophy,' if I have the right to use that name for something that abuses me down to the roots of my being, is *no longer communicable*, at least not in print" (*KGB* III:3, 62). This is the passage interpreted by Bittner to mean that only in

27. Curt Paul Janz, *Friedrich Nietzsche: Biographie in drei Bänden*, vol. 2 (Munich: Carl Hanser Verlag, 1978), 425. See also Krell and Bates, *The Good European*, 138.

the notebooks could Nietzsche express his ideas (see Bittner, p. 479 above), whereas in the context of Nietzsche's physical health as he describes it in his letters, he certainly appears to be expressing alarm about the possibility of going blind and no longer being able to bring his ideas to publication. He follows up on this concern on 13 July, explaining to Overbeck that he is just now recovering from an attack that lasted almost the whole week: "To demand *such* things of oneself, as I do — and such *health as mine*!" He claims this will be his last summer in Sils: "My eyes give the orders here too, I can no longer tolerate things in the *light*" (*KGB* III:3, 66–67).

Among the things he complains about to his mother on 10 August 1885 is not light but its absence; he remarks now that he is ill every day when the sky is cloudy, though his diet of milk, rice, and meat seems to be working out well (*KGB* III:3, 79). In letters to Köselitz and Overbeck in September and October, respectively, he mentions improvements in Sils-Maria that will make it possible for him to stay on: new streets with more shade and new furnishings in his room are easier are on his eyes (*KGB* III:3, 94, 97–98). By December Nietzsche had moved to Nice, and he rejoices to his mother that for the first time he has found a room that meets all the demands of his health and taste, including just the right size, high ceilings, tall windows, dark-yellow wallpaper, dark rug, and a large bed (*KGB* III:3, 125). Three weeks later, in January 1886, he laments to his mother that he is having to spend his best years in barren wastelands, despite having been born for the richest and broadest achievements; a thinker such as himself, who cannot plant his best in books but only in people's souls, is "forced with half-blind painful eyes to 'make literature' — it's all so crazy! So hard!" (*KGB* III:3, 136). Ultimately Nietzsche spent most of his year in Sils-Maria and Nice, with a brief interlude in Venice at the apartment of his friend Köselitz.

During the period in question, Nietzsche experienced considerable difficulties with the publisher of his previous books, and he was on the hook for publishing his future books. His first work, *The Birth of Tragedy*, had been published with E. W. Fritzsch, who was also Wagner's publisher. Nietzsche stayed with this publisher through *Unfashionable Observations* II (1874), then found a new publisher, Ernst Schmeitzner, who beginning in 1874 published the remaining two essays of *Unfashionable Observations*, *Human, All Too Human* volumes I and II, *Dawn*, *The Joyful Science*, and the first three parts of *Thus Spoke Zarathustra* (1883–84). The fourth and final part of *Zarathustra* was published by C. G. Naumann in 1885, at Nietzsche's own expense, so in effect he was seeking a new publisher for his post-Zarathustra works. Meanwhile, he had filed a lawsuit against Schmeitzner, from whom he wished to win back the rights to his previous books, and from whom he demanded a settlement that was finally paid to Nietzsche in 1885. As Paul Bishop explains, "[I]n September [1885], Nietzsche visited Leipzig for negotiations with his old publisher, Schmeitzner. Sales of Nietzsche's works had never been strong (in fact, he never sold many more than a hundred copies), so the new prefaces for the revised editions of his works were part of his efforts to establish a reputation for himself as a recognized philosopher."[28] Bishop explains in part why Nietzsche felt motivated to part company with Schmeitzner, but he leaves out two important details, namely, the lawsuit that cost Nietzsche much effort and aggravation, and the distaste Nietzsche had for Schmeitzner as a publisher with a reputation for anti-Semitism.

Nietzsche informed Overbeck on 7 May 1885 that Schmeitzner had changed his mind and now promised a settlement of 5,600 marks in June; one of the first things he planned for the money was to pay off the publication of *Zarathustra* IV (*KGB* III:3, 46). Two days later he shared the same news with Gersdorff, but added a request to keep silent about the publication of *Zarathustra* IV, a request he had also made to Overbeck and Köselitz (*KGB* III:3, 50–51). The settlement was not paid out in June, however, such that Nietzsche complained to his mother

28. Bishop, *A Companion to Friedrich Nietzsche*, 228.

on 10 August that he feared Schmeitzner would not pay up after all; he expressed concern about the debt he had already taken on with his new publisher, and to make matters worse, he had just learned that the University of Basel would reduce his pension by 1,000 francs annually (*KGB* III:3, 79). On 17 October he wrote again to Overbeck, describing how Schmeitzner's entire publishing house had been sealed off by court order; how he expected it would be auctioned off and then he would be able to offer his previous titles to Veit & Comp. Janz tells us that "[f]inally on the 23rd of October he can report to his mother: 'Schmeitzner's money is now safely in my hands.'"[29]

There is no doubt that Schmeitzner's payment was an enormous relief to Nietzsche at a stressful time financially, but it was only a partial victory. He did not succeed in liberating his books from Schmeitzner's publishing house, and this misfortune he shared with Overbeck, to whom he wrote early in December 1885: "[A]nd your writings like mine are lying totally *buried* and *unexcavatable* in this anti-Semitic hole. (This is *my* view of the matter; Schmeitzner himself thinks no differently about it.)" Meanwhile, Nietzsche continues, he had arranged with Veit & Comp. to publish a second edition of *Human, All Too Human*, investing a whole summer's efforts in it, but Schmeitzner blocked the move by demanding 2,500 marks for the destruction of the remaining first edition: "Schm⟨eitzner⟩ himself now considers my books lead (they are included everywhere among the 'anti-Semitic literature,' as the Leipzig book dealers confirm for me — and now the good Widemann plays a trick on me by praising me in the same breath with that dreadful anarchist and venomous big mouth Eugen Dühring!) Not even a hundred copies of Zarathustra have been sold (and these almost only to Wagnerians and anti-Semites!!)" (*KGB* III:3, 116–18). As Janz explains, Nietzsche had two main reasons for desiring to extricate his books from Schmeitzner's control: to regain the rights to his earlier works for the purpose of

29. Janz, *Friedrich Nietzsche*, 404.

adapting and incorporating them into his complete works, and to remove them from the "suspicious vicinity" of anti-Semitic propaganda of which Schmeitzner was a strong purveyor.[30]

Nietzsche's concern for his reputation had long been a factor in his break with Wagner, since the Wagnerians included anti-Semites who followed in the footsteps of their master. Nietzsche on 6 December sheds more light on the difficulty of extricating his books from Schmeitzner in a letter to Köselitz, to whom he explains that Widemann was recommended by Schmeitzner as someone who could help promote Nietzsche's books: "It's a misfortune that he is so close to this Schmeitzner: several times he interceded in the legal affair with Schmeitzner (his father was Schmeitzner's attorney) In the end I have never experienced such a disparagement as having the names 'Dühring' and 'Zarathustra' associated with one another: — I've had enough of this omen. Anti-Semitism annihilates any finer taste" (*KGB* III:3, 120). Köselitz apparently knew Widemann and gave Nietzsche assurances, such that on 24 January 1886, Nietzsche asked him what he thought about a second edition of *Human, All Too Human* now that he had spoken with Widemann: "As long as the book remains stuck in that anti-Semitic nook, not a single copy more will be sold: Schmeitzner himself knows this" (*KGB* III:3, 142). It is therefore puzzling and disappointing that Nietzsche did not make a point of including Wagner's anti-Semitism as one of the causes of his break with him, since he had opportunity to do this in the two new prefaces he wrote for *Human, All Too Human* in 1886. But perhaps he opted to forgo the opportunity because his new publisher for the "second edition" was none other than Fritzsch, both Nietzsche's and Wagner's publisher going back to the period of *The Birth of Tragedy*.

Ultimately Nietzsche solved the problem of issuing a second edition of *Human, All Too Human* without having to pay Schmeitzner for the destruction of the remaining first edition,

30. Ibid., 422.

by allowing Fritzsch to acquire the rights to those books published by Schmeitzner. Fritzsch then used the remaining copies (*Lagerbestände*), added a new preface and a concluding poem ("Among Friends"), and issued this old edition of volume I as the "New edition with an introductory preface."[31] The same procedure was followed for the two subsequent volumes of *Human, All Too Human*, namely, *Mixed Opinions and Maxims* and *The Wanderer and His Shadow*, except these two separately published volumes were bound together into one volume for what now appeared as volume II of *Human, All Too Human*, accompanied by a similar subtitle: "New edition with an introductory preface."[32] Nietzsche wrote of his disenchantment with Wagner in these two new prefaces, but he couched his criticism in terms of Wagner's incurable Romanticism, his German nationalism, and his succumbing to Christianity in his old age.[33] He had no such inhibitions by the time he wrote *Ecce Homo* (published 1908, completed winter 1888/89), because now Nietzsche had his new publisher C. G. Naumann, and he was free to speak of Wagner and his Bayreuth following as he wished: "In truth, a hair-raising company! . . . No monstrosity was missing among them, not even the anti-Semite" (*EH* III; *HAH*). Of course, once Nietzsche had engaged Naumann as his publisher for *Beyond Good and Evil* and *On the Genealogy of Morality*, he made overt references to Dühring, Wagner, and Wagner's anti-Semitic following in both works.[34]

Notwithstanding the creative recycling that enabled Fritzsch to publish "new" editions of Nietzsche's books, he was still quite beset by his record of low sales and now perhaps even more by his reputation as an author who took extreme measures against his publisher — these had to be factors in his continuing difficulties in engaging a new publisher. On 12 April 1886, he wrote

31. Montinari, *Kommentar*, 116; *CW* 3, 309–10.

32. Montinari, *Kommentar*, 157; *CW* 4, 435.

33. See the prefaces and the translators' afterwords to these two volumes, *CW* 3 and *CW* 4.

34. See *CW* 8, 156–57, 262, 345.

to the Carl Duncker's Verlag in Berlin, offering a new philosophical work titled *Beyond Good and Evil*; even though this publisher declined, Nietzsche wrote again on 20 April, sounding desperate by explaining that he was prepared to forgo an honorarium until six hundred copies had been sold (*KGB* III:3, 175, 180). The next day, he wrote to Köselitz and reported that he was still negotiating with Carl Duncker's, hopeful for a good outcome for his "terrifying book" (*KGB* III:3, 181). However, on the first of May he wrote to Overbeck that all his efforts to secure a publisher had failed; they claimed to want to publish his work, but they were not allowed to, he surmised, owing to public opinion (*KGB* III:3, 186). This meant that the temporary arrangement Nietzsche had used for publishing the fourth part of *Zarathustra*, namely, C. G. Naumann, was his only alternative; in his letter of 3 June 1886 to Naumann, Nietzsche urged him to print as rapidly as possible, so that he could have peace of mind for the summer for his next project (*KGB* III:3, 193). At this time Naumann was a printer more than a publisher, and Nietzsche once again paid with his own money for the publication of his book. As Krell and Bates observe, Naumann became an independent publisher by taking on *Beyond Good and Evil*. For his part, Nietzsche had been motivated not by commercial concerns but by the "need to reassess his task and yet seek continuity," such that the prefaces he wrote for the new edition now owned by Fritzsch were "among the most powerful pieces of writing in his oeuvre."[35] This is an important point: timing was everything for Nietzsche in the summer of 1886, inasmuch as he was redefining himself and his work after *Zarathustra*. *Beyond Good and Evil* would be the debut title for Nietzsche as a philosopher, but the previous works all had philosophical content and inclinations that Nietzsche needed to foreground as he made his passage. The continuity Nietzsche sought to maintain, along with a certain momentum of philosophical energy, was not limited to the

35. Krell and Bates, *The Good European*, 140.

pre-*Zarathustra* books, and we should recall that Nietzsche considered both *Beyond Good and Evil* and *On the Genealogy of Morality* as a kind of "glossarium" to *Thus Spoke Zarathustra*.[36]

When he wasn't pivoting between the two extremes of trying to shut down one publisher while trying to persuade a new one to accept his books, Nietzsche was spending time on maintaining familial relations. Having always been close to his mother and sister, Nietzsche developed a dependency on them, but the three of them were close enough in any case that, for example, Nietzsche did not have free rein in his affair with Lou Salomé in 1882 owing to meddling by his sister and mother. During the period under scrutiny here, Nietzsche's family continued to play an outsized role in his life, and I will sketch out only the most salient examples.

Claiming that "Nietzsche's strong ties to his father — and the severing of those ties — marked him for life," Krell and Bates go on to describe how, after being awarded seven thousand Swiss francs in his settlement against Schmeitzner, "the very first thing he bought after paying off his debts to bookstores was an engraved tombstone for his father." The co-authors also conclude that Nietzsche himself, "the budding antichrist," designed the stone and selected the verse from Paul that concluded the inscription: "Love never fails."[37] Janz finds this expenditure surprising, given Nietzsche's financial state and the fact that Overbeck had to intercede for him at the University of Basel for the continuation of his pension, which had originally been granted for a period of six years beginning in 1879.[38] Among the factors that probably inspired such a major commitment of resources, Janz speculates, were Nietzsche's guilt in

36. See note 23 above; and for a most detailed and intriguing analysis of the relationship between *Z* and Nietzsche's next two books, see Paul Loeb, *The Death of Nietzsche's Zarathustra* (Cambridge: Cambridge University Press, 2010), 208–9, 211, 213, 220–25, 232–34, 236–42.

37. Krell and Bates, *The Good European*, 15. The verse is found in 1 Corinthians 13:8 and is commonly used today in wedding vows.

38. Janz, *Friedrich Nietzsche*, 405.

straying so far off the path that his father, Pastor Nietzsche, had walked; reinforcement of the bond with his real father after the debacle with his ersatz father Richard Wagner; and perhaps most convincingly, his mother's wish to be buried beside her husband.[39]

The settlement from Schmeitzner allowed Nietzsche a rare opportunity to honor his parents as he clearly felt they deserved; the newly arisen matter of his brother-in-law would not be so readily dispatched. On 15 October 1885, Nietzsche celebrated his forty-first birthday in Naumburg with his family, and here for the first and only time he came face to face with Bernhard Förster (*KGB* III:3, 408). He had avoided meeting him, even to the point of not attending the wedding held on 22 May (Wagner's birthday) in 1885, despite the fact that he had the financial means to do so (*KGB* III:3, 386); given the closeness to his sister, we can safely conclude that Nietzsche objected to her marriage in the strongest terms. Förster was an outspoken anti-Semite who had immigrated to Paraguay, where he founded a colony of German Aryans. Nietzsche's sister was having difficulties tolerating the heat there, and Nietzsche himself had been approached by a local manufacturer who sought his endorsement of imports to Paraguay: "[W]hat a terrible winter!" he wrote to Overbeck in April 1886 (*KGB* III:3, 183).[40] Krell and Bates provide context for the anguish Nietzsche experienced as a result of his sister's marriage to Förster:

> An important aspect of *Beyond Good and Evil* was Nietzsche's intensified preoccupation with "nations and fatherlands." In part, that intensification had to do with his brother-in-law, Bernhard Foerster [*sic*], whose book *German Colonies in the Upper La Plata Region, with Special Attention to Paraguay*, Nietzsche had read in the fall of 1885. The chauvinism and imperialism of Foerster's [*sic*] colonial plans — which were completely in line with the militarism and anti-Semitism of

39. Ibid.

40. See Graham Parkes, "Nietzsche and the Family," in *The Oxford Handbook of Nietzsche*, 41–44.

> Adolf Stoecker, court chaplain in Berlin and head of the "Christian Socialist" party — stood for everything Nietzsche had come to despise . . . His final notes in 1888, on the verge of madness, called for the abolition of the House of Hohenzollern and the execution of Stoecker, Bismarck, and "all the anti-Semites."[41]

The preoccupation with nationalism that contributed to the chapter of *Beyond Good and Evil* called "Peoples and Fatherlands" is also evident in the *Nachlass*, where, as we will see, Nietzsche devoted much time to sketches regarding Germany and Europe more broadly. But it cannot escape our notice that at the same time Nietzsche began to extricate himself from his association with an anti-Semitic publisher, his previous close allegiance to Wagner, and by association to Wagner's circle, had returned to haunt him through his own sister, who remained a Wagnerian and had even married an ideological anti-Semite.

Hence, while Nietzsche attempted to appeal to "free spirits" and "good Europeans" with his new philosophy, his brother-in-law was more in step with the Zeitgeist that grew increasingly shrill about racial purity and the threat of the Jews; Janz describes Nietzsche's focus on a unified European culture, in juxtaposition to Förster's ambitions for Germany: "The ideas of his brother-in-law had to disappoint, indeed repulse him all the more, for the latter did not see the whole of a possible European culture, but instead proposed to colonize a nationally circumscribed culture defined as specifically 'German' in a South American country, and to culturally 'Germanize' this part of the world from the vantage point of this nucleus."[42] Janz also explains that Nietzsche was blind to the problem of colonialism, and ironically his only real contact with it came via his brother-in-law, who happened to be a vehement adherent of colonialist-racist ideology; for his part, Nietzsche was too concerned with the current state of culture in Europe

41. Krell and Bates, *The Good European*, 140.
42. Janz, *Friedrich Nietzsche*, 416.

itself, of which he was both critical and hopeful, to ever consider exporting that culture through colonization.[43]

On the Substance of the Various Groupings within the Nachlass

Nietzsche's preoccupation with peoples and fatherlands did not extend to his own case, or to phrase it differently, his own lack of citizenship and nationality concerned him all too little. As meticulous as he was about the physical environment in which he dwelled, down to the height of the ceiling, the amount of sunlight admitted by the windows, and the color of the neighbors' walls, he was nearly indifferent to his legal status as a European. We recall that Nietzsche was required to relinquish his Prussian citizenship when he acquired his professorship at Basel in 1869; ten years later, when he retired from the university, he was still without citizenship, having failed to acquire citizenship from Switzerland in the meantime. Now that he was no longer working in Switzerland, Nietzsche had been traveling and living in Switzerland, Germany, and Italy on the strength of a temporary pass that been granted in Basel on 29 September 1876, which was valid for one year. That same pass had last been extended in April 1883, again for one year. In December of 1885 Nietzsche visited the Swiss consulate in Nice, to obtain a Swiss pass whose validity was for a period of six months.[44] Under these rather fragile auspices, typical for the last several years of his productive, healthy life, Nietzsche penned and penciled his thoughts with little if any regard for

43. Ibid., 417. Janz offers revealing glimpses into the mentality of Förster, who even opposed German immigration to the United States because Germans risked becoming assimilated there (419). Adding to the injury Nietzsche must have felt, Förster became a collaborator on the *Bayreuther Blätter*, the official periodical of the Wagnerians, which Nietzsche had opposed since its inception (421).

44. Ibid., 422.

how he might be treated by the authorities of any of the three countries in which he routinely traveled. The 1880s were years in which Nietzsche functioned sovereignly, if naïvely, until his mental collapse in Turin in January 1889, when he was first ushered by train from Turin to Basel by his friend Overbeck, then ultimately repatriated to Germany a few days later and transferred to the psychiatric clinic at Jena.[45]

With *Zarathustra* and its prophetic discourse behind him, as Janz explains, Nietzsche began in 1885 to live the secluded, detached, and isolated lifestyle that he had attributed to his philosophical prophet in part IV.[46] He was determined, finally, to act on an idea that he had expressed already in 1871 when he applied for a professorship in philosophy at Basel, namely, his desire to dedicate himself to a problem in a unified, philosophical, and protracted manner, without outside disturbances. But as Janz correctly observes, his timing was off again, these fifteen years later, and his own Europeanism put him at odds with the nationalistic Zeitgeist and contributed to his isolation.[47] Janz describes Nietzsche's philosophical motivation as resting not on a principle, distillation, or point of departure that could lead to the construction of systems, but instead on musical variations: "In music there is the possibility of retrograde variations, of gradual unveiling of the theme: from an entire sequence of variations the theme in the end bursts forth. Thus from the thousands of variations and evaluations that Nietzsche entrusted to his notebooks, his 'philosophy' in the end had to burst forth." In my analysis of the *Nachlass* fragments of this volume, I have identified seven rough clusters or strands of meaning, each of which will be discussed below on the basis of samples. In selecting these samples, moreover, I

45. Sander L. Gilman, *Begegnungen mit Nietzsche*, 2nd ed. (Bonn: Bouvier Verlag Herbert Grundmann, 1985), 314. Gilman relies too much on testimonials and writings of Elisabeth Förster-Nietzsche, but Overbeck's recollections are reliable.

46. Janz, *Friedrich Nietzsche*, 387.

47. Ibid., 415.

have tried to include only those that have not been available already insofar as they were included in either *Beyond Good and Evil* or *On the Genealogy of Morality* (i.e., variants or drafts), or in the so-called *Will to Power*. In other words, I prefer here to emphasize those fragments and notes that have not yet circulated in English as publications in one form or another. My groupings are: drafts of titles for books; Nietzsche's retrospection; Europe (its soul, peoples, culture, literature); the feminine; philosophy proper (metaphysics, epistemology, history of philosophy, ethics, aesthetics, language); Germany; and finally, the Dionysian.

In the swirl of legal protocols, negotiations with publishers, plans and instructions for second editions of his pre-*Zarathustra* books, and keeping his distance from the specter of German cultural imperialism as personified in his brother-in-law,[48] Nietzsche still found time to write and to plan new works and continuations of some of his previous works. The numerous drafts of titles for books are a prominent and revealing feature of the *Nachlass*, and while I will comment on them specifically, I will first offer a very brief summary of the overall content of this particular volume.

As was the case with the aphorisms ultimately used for *Beyond Good and Evil*, the material that comprises the *Nachlass* dips back into the *Zarathustra* years (1882–85), and in its spectrum of ideas even further back, to *Human, All Too Human*, inasmuch as Nietzsche was planning a revision of this work for its second edition, despite its failure to generate sales the

48. A good source regarding the ubiquity of German nationalism and anti-Semitism in Nietzsche's day is Robert Holub, *Nietzsche's Jewish Problem: Between Anti-Semitism and Anti-Judaism* (Princeton, NJ: Princeton University Press, 2016). While Holub tries to prove definitively that Nietzsche was in fact an anti-Semite, his methods include far too much innuendo and far too much reliance on Elisabeth Förster-Nietzsche to inspire confidence in informed readers. Brian Leiter has provided an illuminating review titled "Nietzsche's Hatred of Jew Hatred": http://newramblerreview.com/book-reviews/philosophy/nietzsche-s-hatred-of-jew-hatred.

first time around.[49] Similarly, when he referred in his letters to a planned second volume of *Dawn*, this material was in fact the same as the planned continuation of *Unfashionable Observations*, and as Janz points out, this same material ultimately appeared as *Beyond Good and Evil*.[50] Nietzsche had an abundance, if not a superabundance, of material on hand, many more titles than he needed or could ever have used, in fact; so often the same set of material would sail under different flags until he finally settled on the title of his next book. The notebooks, as Janz explains, "offer a glimpse into the tremendous versatility of Nietzsche's working thought, which ceaselessly chases him back and forth from one end to the other of his philosophical landscape." In addition to displaying a rich catalogue of thematic entries, Janz describes another important feature of the notes: "Although Nietzsche's thoughts always revolve around more or less the same core issues . . . he scarcely stays with the same theme for more than two or three notes — from brief entries regarding the aphorism to small drafts of essays."[51] Krell and Bates speak of "notes of enormous range and power that did not dwindle until the spring or summer of 1888."[52] During this period Nietzsche also reads again, as his eyesight permits, and Janz reminds us that Nietzsche's philosophizing is generally dialogic. These notes contain not only quotes from a number of authors but also borrowings, such as the expressions "perspectivism" and "the real and the apparent world" which he adopted from Teichmüller's eponymous book

49. Janz, *Friedrich Nietzsche*, 392.

50. Ibid., 439. See also Krell and Bates, *The Good European*: "The notes that went into it, the bulk of them written during the labor-intensive period from 1884 to 1886, rejoined the themes first developed in Nietzsche's turning-point work, *Human, All-Too-Human*. For many months he called the projected new work the 'second volume' of *Daybreak*" (139). See also *CW* 8, 429 and 431, where both Colli and I discuss the continuity of the notes and materials used for *Beyond Good and Evil*.

51. Ibid., 425.

52. Krell and Bates, *The Good European*, 138.

of 1882.[53] Another book heavily annotated by Nietzsche during this period was Maximilian Drossbach's *Ueber die scheinbaren und die wirklichen Ursachen des Geschehens in der Welt* ("On the apparent and real causes of events").[54]

Regarding the drafts of titles themselves, Janz classifies them into three main categories: those dealing with Nietzsche's concept of the *order of rank* among humans, "in different formulations"; *beyond good and evil*; and *the will to power*.[55] By my own classification of the notes limited specifically to this volume, I agree with Janz regarding "beyond good and evil" and "the will to power" as recurring titles, but my third title is *gai saber*, "gay science," inasmuch as Nietzsche sketched just as many drafts of this title as he did for "will to power." I should also point out that I am referring only to main titles, not to the frequent subtitles; Nietzsche complicated matters by sometimes using the same main titles later as subtitles or as chapter titles. He was also fond of trying out his subtitles and chapters as main titles. Additional main titles that appear at least two or three times are as follows:

Dionysus (three mentions)
The Educator / Education (three mentions)
Zarathustra Part V / Noon and Eternity (eight mentions)
The Soul (European, German, Modern) (five mentions)
Philosophy / Philosophers / Lawgivers of the Future (three mentions)
The Mirror (two mentions)

53. Ibid., 598–99.

54. Maximilian Drossbach, *Ueber die scheinbaren und die wirklichen Ursachen des Geschehens in der Welt* (Halle: C. E. M. Pfeffer, 1884). Cf. Rüdiger W. Schmidt, "Nietzsche's Drossbach-Lektüre: Bemerkungen zum Ursprung des literarischen Projekts 'Der Wille zur Macht,'" *Nietzsche-Studien* 17 (1988): 465–77; and Helmut Heit, "Erkenntniskritik und Willen zur Macht? Kommentar zu Maximilian Drossbach: 'Ueber die scheinbaren und die wirklichen Ursachen des Geschehens in der Welt,' 1884," http://www.nietzschesource.org/SN/Heit-2019.

55. Janz, *Friedrich Nietzsche*, 426.

Our Virtues (two mentions; cf. title of part VII of *BGE*)
On the Natural History (of free spirit / of superior humans)
(two mentions; cf. titles of part V and part II of *BGE*)
Germans (two mentions).

Far more numerous are the individual titles that are not repeated, by my count thirty-three of them,[56] ranging from the suggestive "Halcyon Interruptions for Recovering from *Thus Spoke Zarathustra*," to "*In media vita: Monologues of a Psychologist.*" While I see only one main title for "The Order of Rank," it was frequently used as a chapter title, and clearly as a concept it was frequently discussed by Nietzsche in *Beyond Good and Evil* (six times) and *On the Genealogy of Morality* (twice). The title "The Tempter" had only one mention, but it alludes to Dionysus. Some of the single-mention titles are strongly reminiscent of themes Nietzsche had taken up already: "Skeptical Objections"; "Science and Conscience"; "The Problem of 'Human Being'"; "The Strong and the Weak"; "The Intellectual Conscience"; "Proverbs and Monologues"; "The Artists"; "We Godless Ones"; "Music"; "Attempt at a Revaluation of All Values";[57] "The Eternal Recurrence"; "We Immoralists"; "Rulers of the Earth." Two titles for books were actually taken from poems Nietzsche wrote: "To the Mistral" and "To New Seas." The titles that I would classify as obscure are "*Nux et crux*"; "Letters of Count — — —"; "The New Japan"; "Cultivation of the Heart"; "Thoughts of an Idler"; "Experiences of a Literary Scholar"; "On the History of Modern Dimming"; "Histrionics"; "Signposts for Thoughts"; "Arrows"; "The Right of Prerogatives."

56. It is difficult sometimes to ascertain whether N is referring to a book title where we find only one isolated line among unrelated fragments; suffice it to say that "by my count" strives to be accurate but could err by a few titles on either side.

57. N announced a future work titled *The Will to Power* with this as the subtitle in *GM* III 27 (*CW* 8:346), and he often considered this in later notebooks, first as a subtitle for *The Will to Power* and then as an alternative title for that work.

I regard the single-mention title "Experiences of a Literary Scholar" to be significant as a rare expression of Nietzsche's affinity to literature. At this stage he regarded himself not as a writer of literature but as a philosopher, and one finds several mentions of his ambivalence, if not disdain, for literature and literary men and women. He was of course capable of heaping praise on certain writers, and many are mentioned, quoted, and criticized in his notes and published works, but along the axis of fiction versus philosophy, Nietzsche performed as Zarathustra does in the chapter "On Poets" — adopting Plato's view that the poets, including Goethe, lie too much. Perhaps what Nietzsche meant in self-identifying with this odd title was something closer to his work as a classical philologist, in which he specialized in the ancient literary texts. Or perhaps he planned to use the word "literature" in the title ruefully, as he did in the letter to his mother on 5 January 1886, when he complained that a "thinker" like himself "is forced with his half-blind eyes to 'make literature'" (*KGB* III:3, 136). Finally, there is part VI of *Beyond Good and Evil*, titled "We Scholars," in which Nietzsche shows his respect for and to an extent solidarity with scholars, who are depicted as stepping stones to the philosophers and as laborers for the philosophers. As usual with the one-off titles, it is interesting to speculate, but some of them remain opaque.

One can see in the fragments how Nietzsche gradually settled on a title, and its subtitle, after testing it in a variety of settings. Usually he scrawled the title exactly as he wanted it to appear on the printed title page, each time inserting his byline with his complete name, sometimes using only his initials — it was important for him to visualize the title in its entirety. Given the fifteen main titles that have multiple mentions, plus the thirty-three single-mention titles, it is surprising that only very few made their way into the books of 1886 and 1887 as titles, subtitles, or chapter headings. Apparently he derived considerable pleasure from inscribing these titles and his name. At the very least the titles are significant indicators of the direction of his thoughts at a given point in time, and they also speak to the versatility and abundance of his creative process.

What I refer to as Nietzsche's retrospection is also a considerable dimension of the *Nachlass*, as it clearly must be, given the watershed period in question. On the biographical side, I think it is worth reflecting upon Janz's observation that at age forty-one, Nietzsche was highly motivated to "bring in the harvest." According to Janz: "Deeply rooted in antique thought, the conviction stamped itself upon him that he had therewith reached the acme of his life, indeed exceeded it."[58] Perhaps even more compelling as a motivation for Nietzsche to bring in the harvest was his miserable health, which left him worrying about how much eyesight he might retain for his reading and writing. There are numerous instances in these note and fragments when Nietzsche is looking back; sometimes he does this as if taking stock — he had after all transformed several times since his first book in 1872, and by 1885/86 he was well on his way to launching the final philosophical period. But the retrospection was needed because of the tasks that he had set out: finding a new publisher for his previous titles; finding a new publisher for his post-*Zarathustra* books; recasting the earlier works by means of new prefaces for the two volumes of *Human, All Too Human*, *The Birth of Tragedy*, and *Dawn*; and the addition of a fifth book to *The Joyful Science*. At the same time, and notwithstanding the new sense of purpose and strong sense of *task* (*Aufgabe*) that drove him, Nietzsche was intent upon demonstrating a continuity with his previous books, not only those beginning with *Human, All Too Human* but with *The Birth of Tragedy* and *Thus Spoke Zarathustra* in particular. In essence this retrospective writing was necessitated by Nietzsche's rapid metabolism as a writer — he was constantly reinventing himself and reevaluating his past. It is therefore not surprising that *Ecce Homo* is but his final and most systematic retrospective.

58. Janz, *Friedrich Nietzsche*, 435.

The fragment 34[256] concerning Richard Wagner is likely a remnant of either of the *Human, All Too Human* prefaces or the "Attempt at a Self-Critique" for the second edition of *The Birth of Tragedy*. Nietzsche reveals, as he does elsewhere, that his writings were "nets cast," with which he wanted to "catch human beings with deep rich and exuberant souls." The biblical foundation for this metaphor is Matthew 4:19, where Jesus, walking by the Sea of Galilee, encounters Peter and his brother casting their net: "Follow me, and I will make you fishers of men." In his typical irreverent and sometimes blasphemous manner, Nietzsche too is fishing for men, only Zarathustra's paradoxical need is not for followers but for those who follow themselves. He provides a serious treatment of this fishing metaphor in the first chapter of *Zarathustra* IV, "The Honey Sacrifice," in which Zarathustra, instead of going down the mountain, now attempts to lure human beings to come up to him. Fragment 34[256] is confessional in revealing that Nietzsche spent a lot of effort on "that manifold and mysterious human being" called Richard Wagner; he later considered "seducing" German virtue, and still later "I crafted a language for daring manly heads and manly hearts . . . I composed 'Thus Spoke Zarathustra.'" On the basis of this note, then, we see that Nietzsche engaged in a kind of recruitment throughout his career, but reversed himself in *Zarathustra* with the understanding that even the higher types, say the Richard Wagners, cannot be recruited and will ultimately go their own way. When we read this fragment in connection with "The Honey Sacrifice," moreover, we see that fishing and recruitment for Nietzsche must be transformed into giving: Zarathustra's superabundance (honey) may lure humans to his height, and he keeps an extremely hopeful, indeed euphoric tone in "The Honey Sacrifice," underscoring his vision of an unexplored and dawning humanity pointing to the superhuman.

Meanwhile the conclusion of this fragment is not so euphoric: "Shall I confess? So far I have found no one, but again and again some odd form of that 'raging stupidity' that even wants to be worshipped as *virtue*: my favorite name for it is 'the moral tartuffery,'[59] I honor it as the vice of our century and am prepared to accompany it with a hundred curses." This calling out of the "raging stupidity" is not in vain, and cursing out moral tartuffery should not be seen as futile, either; as Paul Loeb argues, "definitive answers to the traditional questions of philosophy" are often sought in the post-*Zarathustra* books, but "[i]f I am right, however, these works contain only Nietzsche's destructive critiques of the accounts of freedom accepted in his day (e.g., Schopenhauer's in *BGE* 19; Kant's in *GM* I:13)."[60] Loeb's point throughout his book is that *Zarathustra* contains the actual philosophical key to Nietzsche's thought, while the later works perform the task of clearing. Fragment 34[256] provides insight into how Nietzsche approached his Wagnerian experience, how he proposed to communicate his Dionysian-Zarathustran philosophy designed "for all and none," and how in looking back he still managed, simultaneously, to engage with his philosophy of the future.

Fragment 35[48] also adopts a retrospective tone, as it was designed to contribute to a preface for a planned expanded version of *Unfashionable Observations*, from its original four essays to include three more. Two of the original *Observations* were devoted to Schopenhauer and Wagner, of whom Nietzsche writes in this fragment: "It matters little to me today whether I was right or wrong with respect to R⟨ichard⟩ W⟨agner⟩ and Schopenhauer: if I erred, well, my error accrues to the dishonor neither of those mentioned nor myself." He elaborates on how these *Observations* seem to him now more like paintings than writings, and if he were to repaint them from the vantage point of his current midlife, the writings would not therefore become more true: "Each period of life understands 'truth' in its own way; and whoever steps up to

59. "Tartuffery," from Molière's *Tartuffe*, refers to hypocritical piety. This was a favorite word of Nietzsche's, used in *BGE* and *GM*; cf. *CW* 8, 326, 345, 359.

60. Loeb, *The Death of Nietzsche's Zarathustra*, 220.

that painting with youthful and stormy senses and great demands will find as much truth in it as he is capable of seeing." He suggests here that one's perspective is affected by age, or possibly that in matters of truth, there are truths that are age appropriate and commensurate with one's capacity or need for truth. The third paragraph of the fragment is highly reminiscent of 34[256]: "My first four *U⟨nfashionable⟩ O⟨bservations⟩*, to which I now add a fifth, sixth and seventh after ten years, were attempts to lure to myself the kind of humans who belong to me: thus fish hooks cast to hook 'my kind.' Back then I was young enough to go fishing in such a way with impatient hope. Today — after a hundred years if I may measure time according to my standard! — I am *still not old enough* to have lost all hope, all patience." This fragment is an effective illustration of the philosophical continuity Nietzsche was trying to coax out of his earlier work. The *Observations* were clearly products of his youth, just as Schopenhauer and Wagner had been profound influences on his youth, yet he revisits them now with an eye toward foregrounding the hope and patience that he still carries in his soul for a future humanity. Also revealing is the fact that he feels as though he has lived a hundred years since the original *Observations* (1873–76), yet apparently he is still invested in them. But one has to quibble with Nietzsche's insistence here that he was fishing back then for "his kind," because in fact he was still a Wagnerian then, and the *Observations*, like *The Birth of Tragedy*, were written for a German audience. At this point in the fragment, with the concluding sentence of the third paragraph, a most interesting transition takes place.

I do not know the precise Goethe quote regarding old age that Nietzsche wished to use here, but the juxtaposition of Wagner, Schopenhauer, and Goethe is not lost; Nietzsche considered the first two, mentors of his youth, to be Romantics, that is, all-too-modern types whose weariness with life, declining vitalism, and spiritual exhaustion characterized their art and philosophy, respectively. Goethe, on the other hand, considered himself a "classical" figure and Nietzsche eagerly adopted Goethe's equation of Romanticism with illness and classicism with health.[61] The final paragraph of 35[48] therefore pivots from the early Romantic mentors to a figure Nietzsche claimed to resemble more: "Thus speaks Goethe: could he be right? . . . And it would be fair like the Greeks to heed their judgment concerning old age: — they hated growing old more than death, and loved to die when they felt themselves becoming reasonable in that manner." We are reminded of Zarathustra's speech "On Freely-Chosen Death," just as we are reminded by Janz that Nietzsche took his arrival at midlife (forty-one) as the final stage of his life, in part based on his respect for the culture of antiquity. Finally, just as Nietzsche had ascribed a "seasonal" variety to truth in 34[256], here he offers that "youth, too, has its own kind of reason: a reason that believes in life, love and hope." Apparently, the operation of retrospection inspired Nietzsche to salvage what he could from his youthful writings by focusing now on the universality of his own striving.

Yet a third example of looking back is fragment 2[111], which I reproduce here in its entirety for the purpose of conducting close textual analysis:

> 2[111]
> The problem of the meaning of art: *why* art?
> How did the most vitally robust and best-formed human beings the *Greeks* relate to art?
> Fact: tragedy belongs to their richest period of strength — why?
> Second fact: the need for beauty; likewise for logicizing the world belong to their decadence
> *Interpretation* of both facts: — — —
> *Erroneous practical application to the present*: I interpreted pessimism as the *consequence* of higher strength and fullness of life, which can allow itself the luxury of the tragic.

61. Adrian Del Caro, "Nietzsche and Romanticism: Goethe, Hölderlin, and Wagner," in *The Oxford Handbook of Nietzsche*, 111–13.

> Likewise I interpreted German music as the expression of a Dionysian superabundance and originality i.e.,
> 1) I overestimated the German character
> 2) I did not understand the sources of modern dimming
> 3) I lacked the cultural-historical understanding of the origin of modern music and its *essential romanticism*.
> Aside from this erroneous practical application the problem persists: *how would a music be*, if it were *not* of romantic origin — but of a *Dionysian* instead?

What is striking about this fragment is how much substance, historically and culturally, Nietzsche is able to distill into barely half a page of notes, and how critical he is about himself in retrospect. For this fragment he obviously had *The Birth of Tragedy* on his mind, so this material was intended for the "Attempt at a Self-Critique," but it was not included there, at least not in these succinct formulations. Great care must be exercised in reading the "Attempt at a Self-Critique" because, as I have explained elsewhere, Nietzsche makes revisionist claims there about the Dionysian, with the objective of making the original *Birth of Tragedy* seem much more in line with his late thinking on the Dionysian that did not in fact manifest until and through *Zarathustra*.[62] First he provides a clear statement of the problem he was trying to illuminate: the Greeks' use of art elevates or distinguishes them above all others, yet tragedy represents their richest and most robust state (Dionysian), while the need for beauty and logic represents their decadence or decline (Socratic) — both of these facts he intends to interpret. On balance we would conclude that Nietzsche did indeed make a compelling case for why tragedy was their zenith in cultural terms, and why the need for (Apollonian) beauty and Socratic logicizing contributed to their decline (judged in aesthetic terms). But there is no doubt that

62. Del Caro, "The Birth of Tragedy," in *A Companion to Friedrich Nietzsche*, 73–75.

Nietzsche was much better at formulating and answering these questions later in his life, during and following the *Zarathustra* experience; once again his penchant for looking back persuades him of a philosophical continuity between the late work and the early work. In fairness to Nietzsche on this point, there is indeed a latent, perhaps theoretical Dionysian that erupts or becomes activated in *Zarathustra*, and I have discussed this in terms of the "justification of existence" argument.[63]

Now where he had gone wrong, according to this fragment, was in applying this ancient paradigm to present-day culture. In *The Birth of Tragedy* Nietzsche is able to demonstrate that pessimism was an existential threat to the ancient Greeks, who responded by transfiguring or sublimating their suffering into tragedy. Nietzsche's concept of pessimism in the present had been borrowed from Schopenhauer, whereas among the pre-Socratics pessimism was a collective, shared experience of the futility of mortality, so widespread that it occasioned collective artistic responses such as the Homeric epics, the numerous myths and cults, and later, tragedy. For Nietzsche to admit now that he erred in regarding Schopenhauer's pessimism as a consequence of higher strength and fullness of life is basically to recognize that modern pessimism is not an expression of strength but of weakness, basically synonymous with Romanticism. Similarly, he acknowledged that he erred in similar fashion when he ascribed Dionysian superabundance and originality to German music, an error that makes reading the final chapters of *The Birth of Tragedy* rather tedious because the otherwise compelling argument is superimposed onto Wagner's music, where it obviously does not fit. The three reasons Nietzsche provides for why he perpetrated this erroneous application of the Dionysian on the present time echo throughout his *Nachlass* and his published works: the overestimation of Germans, his misunderstanding of the source of

63. Ibid., 61–62.

modern dimming, and his lack of cultural-historical savvy for recognizing modern music's Romantic origin.

At this point Nietzsche scrolls forward again to the present, still admitting the erroneous application of his theory of the Dionysian, but persisting in his belief in the Dionysian and by extension in art. What would this genuine Dionysian music be? And by extrapolation, what would be the role of the genuine Dionysian in modernity? His original question from the beginning of the fragment comes back to mind: Why art? Fragment 2[111] summarizes Nietzsche's project of the post-*Zarathustra* years.

Europe is another major grouping that emerges from the fragments of this period: its culture, its religion, its art, and its future are central to everything Nietzsche writes beginning with *Beyond Good and Evil.* Fragment 34[110], with its discussion of the Slavs in terms of strength of will, at first reminds us of *BGE* 208, from the chapter "We Scholars," in which Nietzsche exposes the insidious damage of what he calls paralysis of the will. Here in this fragment, however, we see a different take. The Slavs have an accumulation and store of will, to be sure, but Nietzsche adds here: "[T]hanks to an absolutist regime: and a *Slavic* earth regime is not the most improbable of things." He observes prophetically in *BGE* 298 that the peoples of western Europe might be catalyzed into unification by the Russian threat, but lest we forget, the strength of the Slavs is based on an absolutist regime, which Nietzsche now juxtaposes with the leadership of western Europe represented by England. If the Slavs are characterized by an excess of will accumulated under an absolutist (regressive, archaic, patriarchal) form of governance, the English, when they are not glorifying themselves, increasingly rely on "new men," or first-generation politicians, and on women to lead in parliament — parliament of course representing the institutionalization of democratic ideology. So Nietzsche pits these two forces against each other, reactionary politics with its strong men versus progressive politics with its inclusion of new stakeholders and women in particular. Nietzsche appears to be suggesting the decline of England and the rise of a new aristocracy of sorts among the Slavs: "But practicing politics is ultimately also a matter of *heredity*: no one begins to become a man of tremendous horizon from a private man." In the three-page mini-essay that constitutes *BGE* 208, along with the very pro-Russian comment in *GM* II 15, where Russian fatalism is elevated above Europe's on the question of punishment, we have overt, published expressions of Nietzsche's growing admiration for and attention to the Slavs. In fragment 34[110] we have terse, succinct formulations highlighting the impending showdown between absolutist Russia and modernist Europe — a showdown, it will not escape notice, that continues into the present day along lines very reminiscent of Nietzsche's argument.

BGE 250 and 251 contain two formulations of the past and future roles of Jews in Europe, and of course Nietzsche also has much to say about ancient Judaism in *On the Genealogy of Morality*, in connection with the so-called slave revolt in morality and with *ressentiment*. Fragment 36[42] resembles the ones in *Beyond Good and Evil* but provides a different approach to Jewish motivations. While Holub belittles Nietzsche's philo-Semitic comments from the published works, rationalizing them as secret code that is familiar to anti-Semites in his day,[64] on balance I conclude that Nietzsche was as crude and politically incorrect in his discourse concerning Jews and their religion as he was in his discourse concerning all other peoples and their religion, especially Christianity. In this fragment, which is reminiscent of *BGE* 251 but contains nuance extending to several different European peoples, we have a good example of how a European thinker, as opposed to a German, approached the issue of European Jews.

In *BGE* 251 he claims, as he does in the fragment, that the Jews *could* come to power, based on certain superior traits, but in *Beyond Good and Evil* he concludes that they are not attempting to come to power, because they wish instead to be

64. Holub, *Nietzsche's Jewish Problem*, xvii, 70, 74, 86, 117.

assimilated among the European peoples. The fragment, however, uses a different explanation: "What excludes them from this is their inability to represent power: the Jews even in their fatherland have not been a *ruling* caste." From here, after claiming that they *would* have power in their hands on the strength of their intellect, industriousness, and capability, Nietzsche reverses himself and begins to describe the attributes that ultimately render the Prussian Jews incapable of ruling: their eyes (the gaze?), their speech, their lack of honest anger, their digestive frailty and intolerance of wine, their physical awkwardness — all these demonstrate "that the Jews have never been a *knightly* race." Some very typical Jewish stereotypes are assembled here, and no doubt many anti-Semites of the day held similar views, but Nietzsche is not yet finished. These apparently "unknightly" failings (and "knightly" or "courtly" is basically synonymous with "warlike") are not the fault of the Jews; Nietzsche explains that "the Jew of Prussia must be a diminished and atrophied kind of Jew; for in itself the Oriental understands representation incomparably better than, say, a north German." So in a side-by-side comparison of a non-Prussianized Jew (an "Oriental" or eastern Jew) and a north German, the Jew is superior in matters of representation (leadership). The degeneration must have occurred, according to Nietzsche, as a result of the wrong climate and having to be neighbors with "ugly and oppressed Slavs, Hungarians, and Germans." Observe that in this explanation, it is the Europeans who have a corrupting influence on the Jews, not vice versa. It is different "among the Portuguese and Moors," in whom "the higher race of Jews is preserved," and this idea is one that Nietzsche included in *BGE* 215, when, for example, he faulted the German "stomach" for not being able to "digest" (assimilate) Jews in the successful manner of other Europeans, that is, the Italians, French, and English. He concludes this fragment with high praise for the Old Testament Jews' solemnity and their sanctifying of passion, especially high praise from the instinct-celebrating Nietzsche, who even claims here that the ancient Jews were superior to the Greeks in this regard. With today's sensitivities, what does one come away with from this fragment?

An overly politically correct reading might focus on the Jewish stereotypes, concluding that anyone who speaks in such terms must be an anti-Semite. But this conclusion would lump Nietzsche in with real anti-Semites, who not only spoke of Jews using these stereotypes but used them to deduce the Jews' inferiority and the need to take action against them. Nietzsche, on the other hand, provides a rather philo-Semitic explanation of the perceived negative traits, one that positions northern and eastern Europeans quite negatively vis-à-vis the Jews, and he does this not to ratchet up the growing hysteria against Jews by making them out to be a threat but to argue for their assimilation into Europe. This is part of the European turn in Nietzsche's thinking — he is conscious of the anti-Semitism in his own people, the Germans, and he is clearly not immune to the ubiquitous stereotypes that circulate in his day; however, he addresses the Jewish problem by advocating for a future Europe that assimilates the Jews and benefits from their contributions — this he does in the fragments, letters, and published works.

The feminine rises in these fragments to the status of a major grouping based on Nietzsche's observation of the increasing feminization of Europe over a period of hundreds of years, as well as the rapidly changing social standing of women beginning in his day — we must not forget that one reason Lou Salomé came to western Europe from Russia was to attend the University of Zurich. Nietzsche included major commentaries on women in his works beginning with the first volume of *Human, All Too Human* (1878), with the frequency and nuance of the commentary intensifying over the years. Basically inept, chivalrous, and naïve in his dealings with women and hopelessly reliant on his mother and sister throughout his adult life, Nietzsche presents a fascinating case of a thinker whose insights on women remain controversial and influential but whose own experience proved time and again that he was dominated and bested by women at virtually every turn. As I and others have argued, often his position on women appears to be strident despite his better understanding of the problem of the social rise of women, just as much of his anti-Romantic rhetoric betrays the fact that in many ways Nietzsche had indeed been and remained in part a Romantic.

Fragment 34[38] leaves us with a concise summary of his untimely stand on the rise of women: "[P]recisely because I have a higher and deeper, also more scientific conception of woman than the emancipators and emancipatresses have of her, I resist emancipation: I know *better* where their strength is and say to them: 'they know not what they do.'[65] They are dissolving their instincts! with their strivings of today." His published comments repeat the point about women having superior instincts, sometimes expanding on that point to caution that women should not repeat the same stupidities as Europe's failing men. The two details of this brief fragment that I do not recall seeing in his published remarks are the insistence that his stand is informed by "a higher and deeper, also more scientific" conception and his use of the biblical allusion to Christ's words on the Cross. By invoking science to justify his position, Nietzsche is relegating the movement for women's emancipation to the zone of quackery, to sentimentality, idealism, and other forms of modernist decadence. He doesn't offer any scientific evidence here, or elsewhere for that matter, but he confidently claims to *know* this about women and hence the allusion to the catastrophic blunder of crucifying Christ — "Father, forgive them, for they know not what they do." This fragment throws open the question: Is the emancipation of women a world-historical blunder committed out of ignorance?

For a sample of what is at stake by adopting feminized or effeminate positions, fragment 34[141] serves to highlight Nietzsche's

65. Luke 23:34.

typically historical approach. Here he takes strong issue with *prayer* and *praying* because of their cumulative de-masculinizing and de-manning effect, claiming that the German nature has suffered damage from all this praying since the Reformation. His explanation for this damage is consistently Nietzschean: "It is a matter of bad taste under all circumstances to beg much instead of to give much." This is vintage Nietzschean blasphemy and championing of the dignity of human being before all gods; *Zarathustra* is brimming with rhetoric on the bestowing or gift-giving virtue, and Nietzsche is consistent in his conviction that humans should be great, not small. His historical concern here manifests again where he cautions that such practices as praying and humbling oneself do not go without consequence over time: "The praying interaction with G⟨od⟩ cultivates a demeaning mood and attitude that demands its right also in impious times, through heredity: it is well known that Germans were awestruck by princes or by party leaders or by the phrase 'as your most humble servant.' There should be an end to this." So the anti-feminism in Nietzsche has cultural-historical moorings, and if we were to agree with him regarding the servility and authority-worship of Germans in his day, we would also tend to agree with his premise that the de-masculinizing and "de-manning" values can be practiced to excess and with negative results. Could it be that when Nietzsche points to the "cultivating" and "heredity" of the demeaning moods and attitudes, he regards these as "scientific" evidence as invoked in 34[38]?

The single largest grouping of fragments concerns philosophical issues as they have been classified in the various branches of philosophy. As discussed above, Nietzsche's earliest editors and certainly his sister, who came into ownership of his literary estate, strived to present the metaphysical so-called *Will to Power* fragments and notes as Nietzsche's real philosophy. The first fragment I will discuss from this philosophy grouping, 34[150], is devoted to Schopenhauer and to the history of philosophy. Before we analyze what Nietzsche has to say about Schopenhauer in this unpublished fragment, it is helpful to remind ourselves that Nietzsche's genuine position on Schopenhauer is hard to pin down; in the preface to *On the Genealogy of Morality* (§5) he is alternatingly critical and complimentary of Schopenhauer, as he had been earlier throughout *Before Good and Evil*, but in *Genealogy* he uses the reverential expression "my great teacher Schopenhauer." The fragment hedges a bit on this "great teacher": Schopenhauer is a "thinker of integrity and likewise not a bad writer on philosophical issues, even though in himself no philosopher." In *Beyond Good and Evil* Nietzsche argued for Kant's being a mere philosophical laborer and critic, not a philosopher in his own right, and here the same ploy is used against Schopenhauer! What is good about Schopenhauer is that "he teaches *veneration* where he himself venerated, for the critical spirit of Kant, for Goethe, for the Greeks, for the free-spirited French." Schopenhauer is praised further as one of the best-educated Germans of his day, as someone with a European perspective and the additional vantage point of Eastern vision. Finally, Schopenhauer taught veneration for Indian antiquity and for Catholicism as ancient Christianity, which Nietzsche seems to prefer to Protestantism. In one short fragment we have a host of reasons for why Schopenhauer should be venerated — but the most important takeaway is that he is "in himself no philosopher."

An example of metaphysics is fragment 40[39], where Nietzsche makes one of his strongest cases for the sway of perspectivism in all matters of truth. What is perspectival is basically synonymous with the reach of human understanding; Nietzsche lists space, time, the soul, the subject, the object, the concepts of active versus passive, cause and effect — all of these "stand *and fall* together." But as usual, he is not condemning our "world of deception," because it is the only world we have and to cast aspersions on it for the sake of some idealized "truth" would be suicidal: "But supposing now that we are not so foolish as to value truth, in this case x, higher than appearance, supposing we have resolved to *live* — then we do not want to be dissatisfied with this seemingness of things and instead just firmly embrace that no one stops at any kind of ulterior motives in the representation of this *perspectivity*." The problem with philosophers of the past, he continues, is that they did love *their* truths and they did have ulterior motives, which leads Nietzsche to ask: "[S]upposing we live as a result of error, what then can the 'will to truth' be? Would it not have to be a 'will to death'?" — Would the striving of philosophers and scientific people perhaps be a symptom of degenerating dying-out life, a kind of life-weariness of life itself?" This puts the will to truth in a questionable light, on the side of forces that oppose error, deception, and perspectivism on principle, even when these are the very conditions of life. I don't see Nietzsche throwing the will to truth overboard, even if it tends in the direction of life-negation, because he has an overall positive reading of the European spirit and its built-up tension — surely the will to truth, along with "God" and other metaphysical concepts, has contributed to this tension (*BGE*, preface). Instead, I see him engaging in the same kind of genealogical probing that he displays in the second aphorism of the first book of *Beyond Good and Evil*, "On the Prejudices of the Philosophers," where he asks: "How *could* something originate from its opposite? For example, truth from error?" In any case, what Nietzsche presents here as the "problem of truthfulness" emerges in the context of one of his main concerns, promulgated already in *The Joyful Science*, namely, the primacy of the proper question: What is life-preserving?

A fragment on ancient religion's disposition toward sin, 1[46], sheds further light on the concept of sin as explored in *On the Genealogy of Morality* (III 20). For the longest time, he claims, religions existed without a morality because their main purpose was to provide redemption from the fear of distress. As the consequence of evil spirits, distress inflicted upon us is never deserved, but if we are the recipients of this distress, questions naturally arise about which spirits might be unfavorably disposed toward us. The individual then examines his behavior, "and if there are any means at all to render friendly certain spirits that he knows, then he will ask himself *whether* he has really done everything that he could have done in this regard. As a courtier examines his own behavior toward the ruler . . . he looks for some omission etc. 'Sin' is originally that whereby some spirit could be sorely offended." By tracing the origin of sin to the feeling that an individual may have offended a spirit by some omission that he must now "make good," Nietzsche has de-moralized sin — there is no moral failing on the part of the individual who feels he may have slighted the evil spirit, and the omission can and will be made whole through some gesture provided by the strictures of this primitive religion. The reason Nietzsche wishes to detach morality, and sin in particular, from early religion is because, as he argues in *GM* III 20, sin is perhaps the most powerful tool in the hands of priests, the palpable and permanent manifestation of bad conscience, which according to Nietzsche is "the most dangerous and fateful artifice of religious interpretation" (*CW* 8:329). By demonstrating that sin is a later moral construct invented and perpetuated by priests, Nietzsche is able to shed light on the genealogy of morality in a way that helps to liberate the modern psyche and restore it to health. This motivation is visible in the preface and the first two sections of *On the Genealogy of Morality*, where he is very critical of British moral psychologists for conducting misguided genealogies of morality that result in self-serving critiques and generalizations. I see more of this insight in fragment 2[163], where Nietzsche takes moral historians to task for spending too much effort on criticizing a people's opinions about their morality, believing "they have criticized a morality itself." In fact, he claims in this fragment, "the value of a rule 'thou shalt' is independent of the opinion people have of it, just as certainly as the value of a medication is independent of whether I think scientifically or like an old woman about medicine." In other words, what the people think or believe about their morality is not the point — the point is to determine the *effect* of a moral rule and lay out the implications for humanity when such moral rules hold sway over us throughout history.

Nietzsche started out writing for a German audience, only to learn that in that fateful inaugural decade of unified Germany's Second Reich, in the wake of the Franco-Prussian War that launched Germany to the status of the greatest power on the European continent, the "Germans" he was attempting to reach were increasingly nationalistic, anti-Catholic, anti-Semitic, and culturally chauvinistic. His exploration of the question "What is German?" preoccupied him his whole life, and whether we assign this strain in his writing to the category of cultural criticism, political philosophy, or cultural geography, the fact remains that Nietzsche's methods and motivations as a thinker are closely tied to his roots in German thought and his growing mistrust of Germans in his day. Fragment 36[3] is revealing of how Nietzsche sizes up a popular German philosopher, Eugen Dühring (1833–1921), with whom Nietzsche had at least an early intellectual affinity before he broke the staff over him and pronounced him an anarchist, an anti-Semite, and an apologist for *ressentiment*. Germany "is wealthy in talented and highly-educated scholars," he begins, reminiscent of his chapter "We Scholars" in *Beyond Good and Evil*, and his preferred mechanism for attacking an opponent is by damning him with faint praise. But what Germany lacks is great souls, powerful spirits, and so mediocre minds bring themselves to market where they pose as great men and reformers. Dühring is "a talented and well-educated scholar," but his writings reveal "that he harbors a petty soul and is crushed by narrow jealous feelings." Moreover, Dühring fails Nietzsche's test of a great soul, and therefore ends up a mere German as opposed to a European spirit who surmounts nationalism: "[H]e is not driven by a powerful, brimming, benevolently-squandering spirit — but by ambition! But to thirst for honors in this age is far unworthier of a philosopher than in any earlier age: today where the rabble rules, where the rabble bestows the honors!" (see 34[141] above, in which begging is juxtaposed with giving).

For those quick to relegate Nietzsche to the historical heap of anti-Semitism, an examination of another fragment, 43[3], should help to provide perspective on where he stood in the matter of Germans in relation to other peoples. After all, this most "anti" of modern thinkers proudly claimed to be *anti* many things, and though anti-Semitic was not among them, anti-anti-Semitic was. In a scathing two-page invective against the German spirit, or lack thereof, he starts by reminding us that not even Tacitus, the first to comment on the ancient Teutons, "was able to praise the spirit, or even only a pleasure in spirituality," in these early Germans. To make matters worse, the Germans themselves did everything within their power to make themselves stupid over the centuries, slamming the door on the arrival of the spirit; they sweat in overheated beds, crouch in narrow stuffy rooms, prefer indigestible dishes like dumplings and fatty broths, and "above all" they drink until they fall down, "so that going to sleep and being drunk were for a long time neighboring concepts of a German mind." Now if there is something approaching "German spirit," he polemicizes, "it was only made possible through de-Germanification, I mean through mixing with foreign blood. Who keeps a ledger of everything that the Slavs or the Celts or the Jews are owed for the spiritualization of Germany!" The mixing of blood for the Germans "has no equal in Europe and has made of the German an all-comprehending, all-sympathizing and accommodating people of the middle." So much for the "racial purity" of Aryan superiority that became the foundation of National Socialist ideology. Nietzsche goes on to describe the resulting hybrid German soul that led to "inwardly imbalanced, multifaceted, multifarious h⟨uman beings⟩" who were "outwardly weak, servile, comfortable, clumsy, inwardly a playground of spiritual temptations and struggles."

Into this tumult the character of Luther was thrown, what Nietzsche calls "a kind of stirring peasant-and preacher-spirit" that found its mark in waging "the peasant war of the spirit against the 'superior human beings' of the Renaissance." Observe that the first instance of spirit among Germans arrives in the form of a peasant revolt against the Renaissance. A couple of centuries later, the peasant-and preacher-spirit transforms into "the aggressive, cutting and biting citizen- and critic-spirit — Lessing . . . who waged a 'citizens' war' . . . against the aristocratic spirit of French culture." Observe that the second instance of German spirit is likewise a rebellion based on class warfare, this time the bourgeoisie against the aristocracy. The final manifestation of spirit among Germans occurs with "our last double-type of the ever-developing spirit, Goethe and Hegel," who manifest "the all-encompassing boa constrictor 'spirit in itself.'" At this point "all of Europe sank to its knees in admiration of it," despite this spirit's "complete lack of limits, of measure in the Greek sense, of any sense of 'style.'" At least, Nietzsche adds, this "last great European remarkable event," namely, the spirit represented by Goethe and Hegel, is far preferable to the current German spirit of empire: "Why in all the world a new empire if it does not rest on a new idea, or at least on a new stupidity?" Here Nietzsche concludes his history of the German spirit by enumerating the stupidities that preoccupy the Germans of his day: equal political rights, popular representation, parliamentarianism, newspapers, politicization: "[O]nce again the idiocy-producing European sickness of constant politicizing expanded to one *more* great people: what new things would a ph⟨ilosopher⟩ have to learn here — or even to despise! —" This fragment contains prominent Nietzschean insights into the German character, phrased in grand historical strokes ranging from the days of the barbarian Germans (Tacitus as historian) to the heyday of the German spirit in the first half of the nineteenth century. The German spirit's emergence, its progress if you will, depends each time on a rebellion against something noble, until in its third stage it manifests as "spirit in itself" (an allusion to Kant and post-Kantian thinkers) in such a way that Europe "sank to its knees." The problem that ensues, however, is that Germans cannot sustain this spirit; they lack measure, style, proportion, limits — exit the highest spirit, enter the same old copy-cat stupidities that Germans enlist for their Second Empire.

My seventh and final grouping of the fragments is the Dionysian. The universe of associations suggested by the name Dionysus when used by Nietzsche encompasses art (tragedy in particular, also music), the body, instinct, vitalism, life affirmation, the eternal recurrence,[66] the entire Zarathustra nexus of ideas, and the new "Dionysian philosophizing" of all of Nietzsche's post-*Zarathustra* books. Commentators have pointed out for years that the mention of Dionysus disappears in Nietzsche's published works between 1872 and 1886, with the exception of a minor mention in *HAH* 112. While he suppressed the Dionysian more or less successfully in his publications and his *Nachlass* for roughly thirteen years, no doubt in part owing to the unsavory memories associated with the critical savaging of his first book, the Dionysian begins to get prominent space once more in his notes beginning in 1885, and actually the return of Dionysus as a philosophical idea can be seen in the period of *The Joyful Science*, where we find the first expression of the doctrine of the eternal recurrence in that book dedicated to demonstrating gratitude and affirmation for life (*amor fati*). By and large, the Dionysian remains underexplored by philosophers, despite the fact that Nietzsche stresses its importance to his emergence as a new philosopher.

Fragment 34[204] starts out addressing "my friends" in a manner reminiscent of *BGE* 295, where Dionysus finally resurfaces in Nietzsche's writings. He speaks in the familiar first person as if divulging secrets. There is also early mention

66. In some notes, N refers to the concept as "eternal recurrence of the same," though not in the notes of this volume. See Del Caro, *Grounding the Nietzsche Rhetoric of Earth*, 245–55, for why I include "the same." The basic arguments against including "the same" are that N is highly critical of the notion of identity and that he affirms a state of becoming versus a state of being.

in this fragment of "an opposite ideal" that Nietzsche is seeking, one that expresses the highest affirmation; in *GM* III 23, Nietzsche is demanding the "counterideal" to the ascetic ideal (*CW* 8:335). His approach here in the fragment is to explain what has occupied him for many years, namely, his attempt to think through pessimism, "to free it from the half Christian, half German narrow-mindedness and simplicity" in which he first discovered the concept in Schopenhauer. In thinking through the highest expression of pessimism, he maintains, he "sought an opposite ideal — a way of thinking that is the most exuberant lively and world-affirming of all possible ways of thinking." This language is illustrative of the Dionysian, which connotes a state of superabundant life affirmation as well as constant, ceaseless self-annihilation and self-creation, as expressed in 38[12], which appears as the last fragment of the so-called *Will to Power*. Nietzsche claims, in 34[204], that he has thought mechanism, the view that the universe is the result of matter in motion, to its logical end: "[I]t truly takes the very best humor in the world to tolerate such a world of eternal recurrence as I have taught through my son Z⟨arathustra⟩ — hence we ourselves included in an eternal *da capo*." The eternal recurrence results from mechanism, according to Nietzsche, because infinite time is the background to the unfolding of all motion (this is the formulation he provides in *Zarathustra* "On the Vision and the Riddle"). "In the end I decided that for me the most world-denying of all possible ways of thinking is the one that denounces becoming, originating and passing as bad in themselves and that affirms only the unconditional, the one, the certain, being." Thus Nietzsche places the highest stress on becoming, on the dynamic, for which Dionysus is the personification and for which the eternal recurrence is the doctrine. This doctrine counters the concept of God, which Nietzsche finds "the most annihilating and life-inimical of all thoughts." He goes so far in this fragment to cynically praise Christianity and Buddhism for their nihilistic properties, claiming "and, in order to give the death-thrust to degenerating and dying-out races, e.g., the Indians, and the Europeans of today, I myself would defend the invention of an even stricter, genuinely nihilistic religion or philosophy." He concludes the fragment by reiterating, via implication, that the idea of "God" is hostile to life, and by citing the Eleatics (Parmenides' school) as the "best nihilists among the philosophers so far": "Their god is the best and most thorough portrayal of Buddhistic nirvana; being and nothing are identical here."

This fragment on the Dionysian does not actually mention Dionysus, but it is unmistakable as a Dionysian contribution for its tone of address and its argued value as a counter to existing religious nihilism. Wherever being is worshipped, from the Eleatics to modern-day Christians, there is need of the corrective Dionysian. And should anyone construe this fragment as dark, it could easily be contrasted with the much darker 38[12], in which the mechanism of the universe is spelled out in rather terrifying metaphors culminating in the will to power. The Dionysian was aestheticized early on in *The Birth of Tragedy*, but the late Nietzsche uses it to carry his least idealistic, most vividly and creatively nihilistic doctrine of the eternal recurrence — nihilistic not for the sake of wallowing in the consequences of the loss of meaning, but instead for embracing the absence of meaning in the act of affirming life and engaging the endless possibilities for creating meaning.

A fragment devoted to the Dionysian demonstrates how Nietzsche used his new Dionysian standard for judging different types of art and artists. Fragment 2[101] invites us to consider not just the work but its creator; is the creation a product of fullness, or is it "the madness of renouncing"? Wherever we find the Romantic ideal, he cautions, we are witnessing "a self-escape, a self-contempt and self-condemnation of the one who invents it." Here we have a formulation of Nietzsche's appropriation of classicism as strength, Romanticism as weakness, but with the nuance that now the Dionysian is associated with the classical: "Ultimately it is a matter of strength: this entire romantic art could be rechanneled entirely into the anti-romantic by a superrich and mighty-willed artist or — to use my formula — into the *Dionysian*, just as in the hands of the strongest every kind of pessimism and nihilism becomes only one more hammer and tool with which one mounts a new pair of wings on oneself." That Wagner was clearly not a Dionysian is argued in the remaining fragment, which contains several criticisms of Wagner that Nietzsche included in the prefaces of 1886 and later in *Ecce Homo*. Of interest to me here in the case of fragment 2[101] is the possibility that Nietzsche holds out for "rechanneling" Romantic art by means of the Dionysian: was his *Zarathustra* just such a rechanneling, after he cured himself of the illness of Romanticism? Certainly the Wagnerian problem is present in *Zarathustra*, and Rudolf Kreis has even argued that *Zarathustra* is Nietzsche's deliberate counter to Wagner's *Parsifal*.[67] One is also reminded of the tone in which Nietzsche glorifies *Zarathustra*, together with himself, in *Ecce Homo*, claiming, "My concept 'Dionysian' became here the *highest deed*" (*EH* III Z6).

I reserve the last pages of this Afterword for a brief analysis and commentary on how *The Complete Works of Friedrich Nietzsche* deals with errors that have been circulating in the published *Nachlass* versions because of the difficulty of deciphering Nietzsche's handwriting. The errors appeared first in the German version of the non-book, namely, *Der Wille zur Macht*, then spread to subsequent German editions before World War II (see Schrift 406–8); in the 1950s, Karl Schlechta's arrangement debunked the "will to power" structure but used the same material; then Kaufmann and Hollingdale's *The Will to Power* reinstated the "will to power" arrangement, followed later by partial English-language selections from the *Nachlass* such as Bittner's arrangement. My point here is that all previous

67. See Rudolf Kreis, *Nietzsche, Wagner und die Juden* (Würzburg: Königshausen & Neumann, 1995), 19–21, 40; see also Del Caro, "Nietzsche and Romanticism," 122–27; and Loeb, *The Death of Nietzsche's Zarathustra*, 157–67.

arrangements have included the errors that precede the publication of the *KGW* IX as well as *Nachbericht* volumes, whose corrections are now available digitally via subscription at Walter de Gruyter's Nietzsche-Online database and via open access at www.nietzschesource.org, which contains the up-to-date version of the *Nachlass* and shows approximately 6,600 philological corrections. Below I have arranged selected samples based on the fragment number, the word as it appears before correction, and the corrected word; these are given in both German and English, so that readers can see why it was so difficult to determine the correct text. Readers can draw their own conclusions on how much difference is made by the correct version.

34[55] *wie* (as if) to *rein* (purely)
34[83] *unphilosophischer* (unphilosophical) to *unphilologischer* (unphilological)
34[97] *eine zweite angebärt* (a second has begotten itself) to *eine zweite angebaut* (a second has built itself onto)
34[176] *heute* (today) to *Härte* (harshness); *beherrschende* (prevailing) to *bestehende* (existing); *überhaupt* (generally) to *unbewußt* (unconscious)
34[216] *Unwahrheit* (untruth) to *Unwissenheit* (ignorance)
34[221] *pathetisch* (pathetic) to *synthetisch* (synthetic)
34[236] *in Körper* (in body) to *in Küche* (kitchen)
35[21] *ich habe meine* (I have my) to *ich habe nie* (I have never)
35[22] *führt sie* (it displays) to *fühlt sie* (it feels)
35[36] *Enthaltsamkeit* (abstinence) to *Erhaltbarkeit* (preservability)
35[84] *käuflichen Künstler* (venal artists) to *kirchlichen Künstler* (ecclesiastical artists)
36[31] *mit dem unsere Physiker Gott und die Welt geschaffen* (with which our physicists created God and the world) to *mit dem unsere Physiker Gott aus der Welt geschaffen haben* (with which our physicists have ousted God from the world)
36[36] *Tätigkeit im Dämmern* (twilight activity) to *Tätigkeit von Dämonen* (demonic activity)

37[1] *Zwiegespräch zu Einem* (dialogue with myself) to *Zweikampf zu Einem* (dueling with myself)
37[15] *erotischen Gerüchen* (erotic smells) to *exotischen Gerüchen* (exotic smells)
40[26] *Los* (fate) to *Lob* (praise)
43[2] *Zustand* (state, condition) to *Bestand* (duration)
45[5] *Unheimlich* (uncanny) to *Unehrlich* (dishonest)
1[123] *Liebe* (love) to *Leibern* (bodies)
1[192] *einiger* (a bit, some) to *würdiger* (dignified)
2[28] *neueren* (recent) to *euren* (your)
2[33] *eine Leidenschaft* (a passion) to *nur Lebenshaß* (only hatred of life)
2[163] *sagen* (say) to *zeigen* (show); *der christlichen* (of Christian) to *der civilisirten* (of civilized)

When the entire *Nachlass* is finally published in *The Complete Works of Friedrich Nietzsche*, it will be exponentially more valuable for general readers and scholars in the English-speaking world than the existing English versions. Some corrections and recalibrations will have to be made by scholars, simply on the basis of transcription errors such as those immediately above, but this is a small task compared to the greater damage that continues to accrue as long as so-called *Will to Power* books circulate in place of the entire *Nachlass*.[68]

68. I would like to acknowledge the assistance of Jeremy Murphy (civil engineering / German), summer undergraduate research intern 2014, in matters of proofreading and comparing *KSA* to the transcriptions of the handwritten *Nachlass*.

Index of Persons

Page numbers followed by n and nn indicate notes.

Subject Index

Page numbers followed by n and nn indicate notes.

The Complete Works of Friedrich Nietzsche

IN NINETEEN VOLUMES

1. The Birth of Tragedy/Unpublished Basel Writings (Winter 1869/70–Fall 1873)
2. Unfashionable Observations
3. Human, All Too Human I
4. Human, All Too Human II/Unpublished Fragments from the Period of *Human, All Too Human II* (Spring 1878–Fall 1879)
5. Dawn
6. The Joyful Science/Idylls from Messina/Unpublished Fragments from the Period of *The Joyful Science* (Spring 1881–Summer 1882)
7. Thus Spoke Zarathustra
8. Beyond Good and Evil/On the Genealogy of Morality
9. The Case of Wagner/Twilight of the Idols/The Antichrist/ Ecce Homo/Dionysus Dithyrambs/Nietzsche Contra Wagner
10. Unpublished Fragments from the Period of *The Birth of Tragedy* (Fall 1869–Spring 1872)
11. Unpublished Fragments from the Period of *Unfashionable Observations* (Summer 1872–Winter 1874/75)
12. Unpublished Fragments from the Period of *Human, All Too Human I* (Winter 1874/75–Winter 1877/78)
13. Unpublished Fragments from the Period of *Dawn* (Winter 1879/80–Spring 1881)
14. Unpublished Fragments from the Period of *Thus Spoke Zarathustra* (Summer 1882–Winter 1883/84)
15. Unpublished Fragments from the Period of *Thus Spoke Zarathustra* (Spring 1884–Winter 1884/85)
16. Unpublished Fragments (Spring 1885–Spring 1886)
17. Unpublished Fragments (Summer 1886–Fall 1887)
18. Unpublished Fragments (Fall 1887–Winter 1888/89)
19. Editors' Afterwords/Chronology of Nietzsche's Life/ General Index

Library of Congress Cataloging-in-Publication Data

Names: Nietzsche, Friedrich Wilhelm, 1844–1900, author. | Del Caro, Adrian, 1952– translator, writer of afterword. | Nietzsche, Friedrich Wilhelm, 1844–1900. Works. English. 1995 ; v. 16.
Title: Unpublished fragments (spring 1885–spring 1886) / Friedrich Nietzsche; translated, with an afterword, by Adrian Del Caro.
Description: Stanford, California : Stanford University Press, 2019. |
Series: The complete works of Friedrich Nietzsche ; volume 16 | Translated from Friedrich Nietzsche, Sämtliche Werke: Kritische Studienausgabe, ed. Giorgio Colli and Mazzino Montinari, in 15 vols.
This book corresponds to Vol. 11, pp. 423–710, and Vol. 12, pp. 9–184." |
Includes bibliographical references and indexes.
Identifiers: LCCN 2018033668| ISBN 9780804728898 (cloth : alk. paper) |
ISBN 9781503608726 (pbk. : alk. paper)
Subjects: LCSH: Nietzsche, Friedrich Wilhelm, 1844–1900—Notebooks, sketchbooks, etc.
Classification: LCC B3312.E5 D45 2019 | DDC 193—dc23
LC record available at https://lccn.loc.gov/2018033668

Typeset by Classic Typography in 10.5/12 Adobe Garamond